Closing an Era

Recent Titles in
New Directions in Information Management

Full Text Databases
Carol Tenopir and Jung Soon Ro

Automating Literacy: A Challenge for Libraries
Linda Main and Char Whitaker

Cataloging: The Professional Development Cycle
Sheila S. Intner and Janet Swan Hill, editors

Information and Information Systems
Michael Buckland

Vocabulary Control and Search Strategies in Online Searching
Alice Yanosko Chamis

Planning in the University Library
Stanton F. Biddle

The Information World of Retired Women
Elfreda A. Chatman

Insider's Guide to Library Automation: Essays of Practical Experience
John W. Head and Gerard B. McCabe, editors

Hypertext and the Technology of Conversation: Orderly Situational Choice
Susan H. Gray

Academic Libraries: The Dimensions of Their Effectiveness
Joseph A. McDonald and Lynda Basney Micikas

Recruiting, Educating, and Training Librarians for Collection Development
Peggy Johnson and Sheila S. Intner, editors

Information Seeking and Subject Representation: An Activity-Theoretical Approach to Information Science
Birger Hjørland

Closing an Era

Historical Perspectives on Modern Archives and Records Management

RICHARD J. COX

New Directions in Information Management, Number 35
MICHAEL BUCKLAND, Series Adviser

GREENWOOD PRESS
Westport, Connecticut • London

Library of Congress Cataloging-in-Publication Data

Cox, Richard J.
   Closing an era : historical perspectives on modern archives and records
management / Richard J. Cox.
     p. cm.—(New directions in information management, ISSN 0887–3844 ; no. 35)
    Includes bibliographical references and index.
    ISBN 0–313–31331–8 (alk. paper)
    1. Archives—United States—Administration—History. 2. Records—United
States—Management—History. 3. Archivists—United States—History. I. Title.
II. Series.
   CD3021.C685   2000
   025'.0068—dc21   99–089071

British Library Cataloguing in Publication Data is available.

Library of Congress Catalog Card Number: 99–089071
ISBN: 0–313–31331–8
ISSN: 0887–3844

First published in 2000

Greenwood Press, 88 Post Road West, Westport, CT 06881
An imprint of Greenwood Publishing Group, Inc.
www.greenwood.com

Printed in the United States of America

The paper used in this book complies with the
Permanent Paper Standard issued by the National
Information Standards Organization (Z39.48–1984).

10 9 8 7 6 5 4 3 2

Contents

Preface   ix

1. Mythic Modern Origins and the History of Records Management   1

2. The Birth of Records Management: The Ancients to the Dawn of
   the Industrial Age   23

3. The Birth of the Modern Records Regime and Profession   45

4. Building a National System of Records Administration   65

5. Shifting Strategies in Appraising, Scheduling, and Maintaining
   Records   91

6. Archives, Records, and Memory   127

7. Educating Records Professionals in a Hostile Age   159

8. Archives, Documentary Editing, and the Quarrel about
   Preserving Our Documentary Heritage   197

9. History's Future: American Archivists, Cyberculture, and Stasis   223

Index   243

Preface

Considering how technology and science relate to society's continuing evolution, the eminent physicist Freeman Dyson wrote these memorable words: "In every civilization, the skilled artificer has an honored place beside the scribe and the shaman."[1] Whereas Dyson was examining the role of the "artificer"— the technologist and scientist—I am considering in this book the role of the scribe—or, in this case, the modern equivalent in the archivist and records manager.

A decade of experience in teaching future archivists and records managers is at the core of this book's content. These nine chapters explore the importance of records in our modern society, a seemingly modest and mundane topic in all the glitter and glamour of the Information or Knowledge Age, by re-examining some of the historical antecedents for critical functions in the modern records profession. My motivation for writing this book comes from my conviction of the importance of records and records professionals in organizations and society, as well as the need to possess a stronger sense of the events, trends, people, debates, and controversies producing the modern records professions.

William Sullivan writes that a profession is "in business for the common good as well as for the good of its members, or it is not a profession."[2] This two-edged sword to professionalism, a concept itself much maligned in this modern era when ready access to vast quantities of information seems destined to end the expert's monopoly over certain forms of knowledge, is particularly relevant in the modern Information Age. We live in a time when so many of the new technologies seem to threaten records, government accountability, corporate memories, individual rights, and self-understanding.

The array of information technologies provides many dangers and opportunities for traditional ways of managing records. The records professionals must contend with unprecedented rates and ranges of change, and their success or lack thereof has implications for every citizen. Again, William Sullivan reminds us that a "good practitioner is indeed a specialist who has learned the rules and basic techniques of a field. . . . However, the full dimensions of expertise are only revealed when a professional must respond to new, less defined situations."[3] We are preparing future archivists and records managers to work in situations that are certainly "less defined." Many of the long-cherished ideas or concepts about records and archives were formed in societies and organizations very different from the ones in which we now operate. This book is an effort to wrestle with these ideas and to point to the future. Some of my convictions will appear conservative or traditional, as indeed they are, while others may seem too radical or theoretical, which I do not think they are. The importance of records, and the daily, unfolding challenges to the management of these records, merits new thinking and new approaches mixed with those that have stood the test of time and proven themselves.

These chapters are the result of re-writing and merging many essays written over the past decade. Where there is redundancy, and hopefully there is not so much of this that it is unnecessary or distracting to the reader, it has been left in order to stress certain key points about records and records management work in a new century. The sources of these essays were themselves disparate, ranging from commissioned essays to conference papers to essays that generated from my own preparation for teaching in the classroom. I do not consider these essays and this book to be definitive nor the last one that I write on the topic of records and archives. It represents my current best thinking about historical dimensions of the records and the records professions in the late 1990s. It has a similar purpose to what my 1990 book, *American Archival Analysis: The Recent Development of the Archival Profession in the United States*, aimed to do for archives and records management in the 1970s and 1980s. If I am still thinking, teaching, and writing about such things a decade from now, I suspect that my ideas will have shifted in other directions (and maybe I'll write another book). I honestly do not believe in definitive statements written about archives and records management, whether they are written by me; the pioneer records management thinkers Hilary Jenkinson, T. R. Schellenberg, and Margaret Cross Norton; or the new generation of leading records and archives theorists David Bearman, Terry Cook, Luciana Duranti, Margaret Hedstrom, Sue McKemmish, and Frank Upward—to name a small number of such people. The world is changing far *too* rapidly for the last word to be said or written on the subject of archives and records management.

Chapter 1 is an introduction to the general challenge of studying the history of archives and records management. Much of the first chapter comes from an essay entitled "The Failure or Future of American Archival History: A Somewhat Unorthodox View," *Libraries and Culture* 35, no. 1 (2000): 141–154.

Chapters 2 and 3 are mostly a freshly written history of the management of records. I have tried to avoid the problem of viewing past records practices only through the modern issues of records management. I am sure I am guilty of this to some extent, since I have intended these chapters as a corrective to the tendency by modern records professionals to see the origins of their work as a twentieth century development, generally concentrated in the last fifty years of this century. I have drawn portions from earlier essays, such as "The Record: Is It Evolving?" *Records and Retrieval Report* 10 (March 1994): 1–16 and "Re-Defining Electronic Records Management," *Records Management Quarterly* 30 (October 1996): 8–13, concerning the historical antecedents of contemporary archival and records management.

Chapter 4 is a re-working of a paper published in the proceedings of a 1990 conference and not widely read, it seems, in North America: "The Federal Government's Interest in Archives of the United States," in Oddo Bucci, ed., *Archival Science on the Threshold of the Year 2000* (Macerata, Italy: University of Macerata, 1993), pp. 207–241. As it turns out, the problems I wrestled with in that essay are intertwined with the history of records management in the United States and relevant for understanding the general history of records management.

Chapter 5, considering how archival appraisal and records management scheduling have developed, is drawn from a number of earlier writings, including "The Archival Documentation Strategy: A Brief Intellectual History, 1984–1994 and Practical Description," *Janus* no. 2 (1995): 76–93; "The Long-Term Maintenance of Records," *Records and Retrieval Report* 12 (April 1996): 1–16; "Records Management Scheduling and Archival Appraisal: Some Unconventional Thoughts on History, Purpose, and Process," *Records and Information Management Report* 14 (April 1998): 1–16; "Archival Anchorites: Building Public Memory in the Era of the Culture Wars," *Multicultural Review* 7 (June 1998): 52–60; and "Declarations, Independence, and Texts in the Information Age," *First Monday* (June 1999) at http://www.firstmonday.dk/issues/issue 4_6/rjcox/index.html. This chapter is longer and more complicated because this is a more critical and complex records function.

Chapter 6, considering how archives and records fit into one of the more interesting manifestations of the late twentieth century, the interest in public memory, draws on "The Concept of Public Memory and Its Impact on Archival Public Programming," *Archivaria* 36 (Autumn 1993): 122–135 and "Caught in the Web," *Records and Information Management Report* 14 (November 1998): 1–16.

Chapter 7, examining the role education has played in the historical formation of the records professions, is built around the following earlier essays: "The Masters of Archival Studies and American Education Standards: An Argument for the Continued Development of Graduate Archival Education in the United States," *Archivaria* 36 (Autumn 1993): 221–231; "The History of Primary Sources in Graduate Education: An Archival Perspective," *Special Collections* 4, no. 2 (1990): 39–78; and "Millennial Thoughts on the Education of Records

Professionals,'' *Records and Information Management Report* 15 (April 1999): 1–16. As an educator, it is difficult not to write at least one chapter on the importance of education for the history and present state of the records professions.

Chapters 8 and 9 conclude with examinations of more recent controversies in the records professions. Chapter 8, considering the relevancy of the continued publication of letterpress documentary editions, looks at this case in its broader historical contexts; this essay was originally published as ''Messrs. Washington, Jefferson, and Gates: Quarrelling about the Preservation of the Documentary Heritage of the United States,'' *First Monday* (August 1997), available at http://www.firstmonday.dk/issues/issue2_8/cox/index.html. Chapter 9 considers the future of archives in the emerging cyberculture by re-considering the historical archival culture; this essay is a revised version of a paper presented at an October 1998 conference at University College Dublin.

A word ought to be stated about the manner in which I have treated the *records professions*. I obviously write from the perspective of an archivist and an archival educator, *but* I also am convinced that archives administration or records management is useful only when brought together administratively and conceptually. Still, the historic evolution of the records professions has made this a more complicated issue than it should be. Throughout this volume, I have tried to indicate when I am writing about the records professions in a collective or unified sense and when I am writing about one branch of these disciplines. Let me state up front that I acknowledge that archivists and records managers alike have made many significant contributions to the maintenance and protection of records. I sincerely wish I could write about *the* records profession.

As usual, this book is focused on North American archives, although some of the chapters go far afield of archives and records management in one continent. It should be obvious that I have drawn on the writings of archivists and records managers from around the world, but I make no pretense that what I have stated here is relevant to *every* nation or culture. Hopefully, this book will provoke others to write on these topics from other national and cultural perspectives.

I owe, as always, many debts to colleagues and students for the contents of these essays. I have thanked these people in earlier books. Let me acknowledge two different individuals, one anonymously. First, as can be seen in this preface, a number of portions of these essays were published in the *Records and Retrieval Report*, now the *Records and Information Management Report*, a monthly technical report edited by Ann Balough and published by Greenwood. I thank Ann and Greenwood's managing editors who have supported this publication, because it has given me the opportunity to produce timely essays on professional issues. Second, I thank the anonymous reviewer of the original manuscript, who suggested there were two books here; this present volume, focusing on historical perspectives, is the first of the two volumes. Another book, focused on policy issues in archives and records management, is in preparation.

As always, I thank my wife, Lynn, and daughter, Emma, for tolerating my continuing work on issues represented in this book. Hopefully, Emma will see my music in these pages just as she sees her own elsewhere.

NOTES

1. Freeman J. Dyson, *The Sun, the Genomes, the Internet: Tools of Scientific Revolutions* (New York: The New York Public Library, Oxford University Press, 1999), p. 8.

2. William M. Sullivan, *Work and Integrity: The Crisis and Promise of Professionalism in America* (New York: HarperBusiness, 1995), p. 5.

3. Sullivan, *Work and Integrity*, pp. 174–175.

Closing an Era

1

Mythic Modern Origins and the History of Records Management

INTRODUCTION

In the intensely self-reflective and self-congratulatory writing about the modern Information Age, we find this typical statement: "Here at the end of the twentieth century, four decades into the computer age, it is increasingly obvious that the very nature of business itself is information. Many of the employees in any corporation are involved in the business of gathering, generating, or transforming information. . . . information has revised the workplace."[1] One would never know records are involved in such organizations. While it may be true that new information technologies are having a revolutionary impact on organizations, these same organizations continue to generate large amounts of records because they are required to create documentation.

MYTHIC ORIGINS

Most American records professionals believe that their profession originated about a half century ago in the midst of the federal government's efforts to control a rapidly increasing quantity of records resulting from the government's growth in size and scope, an expansion necessitated by its contending with the Depression and Second World War. In the 1940s there was a succession of legislative acts supporting such an interpretation. The Federal Reports Act of 1942, according to one standard records management textbook, was the government's "first attempt to control the paper-work burden placed on citizens and business through government paperwork requirements."[2] This was the *first* major federal policy to address records burdens in government information collection, although this act was never implemented[3] and a succession of similar efforts followed within a decade.

Government growth spurred efforts to manage records. The National Archives, founded in 1934 primarily as a cultural agency to care for the federal government's historical records, quickly found itself needing to administer current records. In 1941 it established a "records administration program" for advising about filing to facilitate eventual transfer to the National Archives. Two years later the Records Disposal Act authorized the National Archives' use of disposition schedules, although this did not stop the mounting quantity of records. Executive Order 9784, issued in 1946, required all executive branch agencies to implement records management programs and increased the records management authority of the National Archives, either evidence of progress in managing records or of the government's continuing failures to administer modern records. The records management responsibility of the National Archives was realized when the Hoover Commission on the Organization of the Executive Branch of the Government recommended in 1948 that the National Archives be incorporated into a records management bureau under a Office of General Services.[4] For the next forty years this administrative arrangement defined the role of the National Archives, although the clarity of this definition was poor as subsequent events suggest—especially regarding the relationship between archival administration and current records management and the professional identity for archivists and records managers.

Professional identity is one probable cause for the confused knowledge about the origins of records management. H. G. Jones, considering local government records, states that "because the National Archives was the main source for personnel experienced in records problems, agencies . . . enticed away archivists who proceeded to develop in those agencies experimental programs of 'records administration'—the precursor of modern records management."[5] This professional splintering is seen in the 1949 publication by the Public Administration Service, a pamphlet entitled *Public Records Administration* and written by Philip C. Brooks, a pioneering archivist in the National Archives. Twenty years later Frank Evans wrote, "in a very real sense this publication marked the close of one era and the beginning of another in the professional relations between archivists and records managers."[6] Evans's essay, written just two decades later, was an effort to heal the break between archivists and records managers, a schism that has continued until the present with poor results for both groups. In the early 1980s, for example, a debate raged in Canadian records professional circles over an article written by archivist George Bolotenko, who stated that "it seems that the archivist has to choose one of several roads: to pursue his calling as archivist-historian, or to swing ever more into the newer form of records manager as a purveyor of data, an 'information scientist'. . . . The ethos of the two are antithetical: the records manager seeks to destroy, the archivist to preserve."[7] Such perspectives were not limited to the archives side. Not too many years later a records management textbook suggested that the "distinction between archives and records centers is still based to a large extent on the type of records stored. In fact, in records management circles, archivists are sometimes unkindly referred to as pack rats, since their primary concern is the permanent preservation of all records that have or may have historical value."[8]

These attitudes seem nonsensical when considering the functions that comprise records management and archives administration. Records management encompasses forms management, files management, mail management, records surveys, and other functions—all supporting the main aim of records disposition. The Federal Records Act of 1950, coming out of the Hoover Commission, defined records management as including records creation, maintenance, and disposition and required each agency to establish an ongoing program for records management and to cooperate with the National Archives. National Archives theorists could fit all these pieces together, in effect bridging ancient and modern records practices. As Philip C. Brooks opined, "current record administration is to the archivist of today what the study of diplomatics was to the archivist of earlier times."[9] Diplomatics, the study of the form and function of records, has in a somewhat surprising fashion re-emerged in the past decade as a core knowledge for archivists, a development which will be examined at several points in this book.

The 1950 records act formalized what most modern records professionals see as critical to their origins and mandate, becoming the touchstone for subsequent developments both in federal records management and in the management of records in other organizations. Even as electronic recordkeeping technologies emerged, the National Archives explained how these new systems were encompassed by the records law. In 1985, for example, it issued a brief pamphlet describing the Federal Records Act as the "basis for the Federal Government's policies and procedures for creating, maintaining, and disposing of Federal records. The act and its related regulations define Federal records, mandate the creation and preservation of those records necessary to document Federal activities, establish Government ownership of records, and provide the exclusive legal procedures for the disposition of records."[10] Such concerns, growth in the amount of government records and the range of records responsibilities defined by the records act, led to the development of a system of regional records centers and field archives, serving as models for institutional and commercial records centers.[11] The Second Hoover Commission, in 1953–1955, focused on "paperwork management" and new programs for directives management, reports management, paperwork quality control, and clerical work measurement. This included the publication of the first *Guide to Record Retention Requirements in 1955*, thereafter published annually and still used by records managers and archivists in government and non-government organizations. Key developments in recordkeeping technologies can also be tracked, to some degree, by various amendments to the Federal Records Act. Supplements in 1976 stressed paperwork reduction and documentation of recordkeeping practices, as well as an emphasis on life cycle management.[12]

The revised Federal Records Act was reaffirmed by the Paperwork Reduction Act of 1980. The latter introduced information resources management and built on the 1977 Commission of Federal Paperwork Report, citing the mismanagement of information resources while estimating $100 billion annual expenditures on data collection, paperwork, and information handling activities. The 1980 act stated that federal managers were to have standard information policies and practices with assurance of confidentiality, and it gave the Office of Management and Budget (OMB) responsibility to set up federal information policies, principles, standards, and guidelines. The most important work of the OMB was the issuance in 1985 of Circular A-130, drafted to meet its information policy mandate. The policy circular was controversial in that it stressed economic criteria, cost avoidance, and reduction in information and information technology management, including exhorting federal managers to use commercial services and to impose user charges where appropriate.[13]

Modern records management principles, the development of essential functions like scheduling and the beginning of the evolution of records management into information resources management, materialized in the years between 1943 and 1985. But to interpret this as *all* there is to records management's origins, generally the opinion among currently practicing records managers, is to undermine *both* the importance of records and their management. Why would records managers hold to an abbreviated history of records, recordkeeping, and records management? Sociologist Maurice Halbwachs provides a clue: "Each individual who enters a profession must, when he learns to apply certain practical rules, open himself to this sensibility that may be called the corporate spirit, and which resembles the collective memory of the professional group."[14] Most records managers have bought into a kind of corporate thinking about their origins, one that has been set in place by the field's standard textbooks. There may be other reasons. The problem with the history may stem from the fact that records management has been primarily associated with business and government. Another standard records management text states that "prior to 1950, formally integrated records management programs were unknown to most business people. . . . Except for a handful of managers in the federal government . . . little effort was made to exercise control over the massive volume in offices throughout the country."[15] This pushes out of the picture earlier and some quite important efforts to manage records.

Another problem may be the generally non-historical perspective of both archivists and records managers. The records management literature is virtually devoid of historical writings, and the historical literature is very uneven in the archives field even if it is far superior to that found in records management, a topic which will be discussed later in this volume.[16] Despite many individuals entering the archives and records management field with solid educational backgrounds in history and the humanities, few seem predisposed to consider the history of records and recordkeeping, organizational recordkeeping systems, and archival repositories and the archival discipline.[17] Even some of the most influential and generally reliable archival historians and theoreticians have suffered from a kind of present-mindedness, as evident in Rosalind Thomas's critique of Ernst Posner's classic work on ancient archives.[18]

This same problem can be seen in Duranti's two-part article on the history of records management, contending the "key to an understanding of the history of records management [as being] the analysis of the function of records managers, of their contribution to societal life and to its development." Duranti argues that "perhaps our future is in our past, within the stone walls of a medieval university where scholars debated about records creation and records forms, and the study of the old science of diplomatics could constitute the foundation of the new *science* of records management."[19] While there is nothing wrong with looking for the historical origins of the present discipline, as does this book, Duranti may go too far in believing that concepts and practices developed hundreds of years before provide the *foundation*, indeed the *only* acceptable foundation, for dealing with modern records systems. Theory and methodology, in such a view, become too static. What is lost is the sense of the challenges of modern records and recordkeeping systems, the need for new solutions to these challenges, and a process that brings together older, trusted procedures with new technologies and techniques. That some records managers and archivists have taken pioneers such as Hilary Jenkinson and T. R. Schellenberg as the only reliable authorities for working with electronic records reveals how deeply engrained such a view has become for some. In careers that spanned from the First World War until the 1960s, these two records professionals wrote much that remains valuable, but it is also true that they so far predated modern recordkeeping systems as to have questionable value.[20]

The image of records and the problems with modern records and recordkeeping systems may have become a distracting issue in how records professionals view themselves and their history. The media tend to view records and paperwork management as an *evil* condition of modern society. Herbert Gans writes that " 'waste' is always an evil, whatever the amount; the mass of paperwork entailed by bureaucracy is a frequent story, and the additional paperwork generated by attempts to reduce the amount of paperwork is a humorous item that has appeared in the news with regularity over the years."[21] This has potential repercussions for records professionals since, according to Gans, the "news media's primary purpose is to inform the audience; but elected and appointed officials are, by all odds, the most intensely interested news audience. The *New York Times*, the *Washington Post*, the *Wall Street Journal*, and a handful of other print media are, among other things, intragovernmental organs of communication—professional newsletters for public officials."[22] With the media filling up their newspapers with stories suggesting the *burden* of records, the importance of properly managing records for crucial purposes such as accountability is lost or, at least, minimized.

Believing that records management is only a development of the past half century is far too simplistic. Examinations of various state records laws and records activities reveal a more checkered history. In New York, there was much

debate over establishing a records office in the early twentieth century that, even
with a serious fire in 1911 in the state capital building, led only to a central
authority for managing local government records. In New York, there was no
law for the disposition of state records until 1951 and no state archives agency
until 1978, but one cannot understand or appreciate *why* this occurred until all
the other efforts to manage public records on the state and local levels are
examined.[23] Records professionals may focus on the more recent developments
because there is some truth about the fact that records management is a *modern*
sensibility. A recent inquiry into the issues related to personal privacy in our
modern era indicates that "we have replaced watching each other at firsthand
with keeping track of each other at a distance. Federal recordkeeping is a
twentieth-century development. It was not until after 1930 that even 90 percent
of births and deaths in the United States were recorded. There was no such thing
as a passport before 1914, and in fact, it was not regularly required during
peacetime until the fifties. Only in the mid-forties did the government start using
Social Security numbers as identification numbers on government files."[24]

There are other indicators of the distinct nature of modern recordkeeping that
should encourage records professionals to consider a much larger and more
complicated historical context to their work. As the telephone became established in the early decades of the twentieth century, it began a process of significant change in personal and business communication and documentation.
This included a shift "in favor of telephone conversation, the change urged by
the relative expense of writing, copying, and filing correspondence compared to
telephoning, which is therefore cheaper and also offers the presumed advantage
of immediate dialogue." This led to problems such as making "preparation for
the business or research conversation . . . less disciplined, more relaxed and im-
provisational (often, in fact, sloppier) than the composition of a letter or memorandum. And the fact that the correspondence won't be on record makes it
easy for the conversationalists to drift toward vagary and unintentional compromise or misstatement, only to misremember and misreport their positions and
statements as much firmer and tougher after the fact than they actually were
during the call."[25] Perhaps we need to look more critically at the impact of
records and recordkeeping on every dimension of individual and organizational
life and culture, as this passage on the telephone indicates. Material culture
specialists see four forms of furniture which have long been part of homes in
Europe and America—the seat, to sit on; the table, to eat from or work on; the
box or chest, to put things in; and the bed, for sleeping.[26] The chair, table, and
chest, in one way or another, can be connected to personal recordkeeping and
efforts to administer such records. Records may be misunderstood because they
are so integrated into our everyday life.

THE FAILURE OF THE RECORDS PROFESSIONS IN
UNDERSTANDING THE PAST

Today, many lament the loss of historical perspectives in library and information science education, practice, and the information professions. Educator Donald G. Davis, Jr. asks, "Where do the values that have informed us for millennia have a place—or do they at all?"[27] It is ironic that American records professionals face a similar challenge, given the long-term tradition of history in this field and the many professionals who have such educational backgrounds.[28] But they do, perhaps the result of other priorities, an educational infrastructure only beginning to focus individuals on archives and records as important topics for study, and a weak self-image minimizing historical scholarship.

At first glance the state of American archival and records management history appears not to be a significant problem. There continues to be published a fair number of histories of archival and records programs and biographies within mainstream professional journals, suggesting all is well. What constitutes archival and records management history is too narrow. There is a lack of broader, more substantive histories of recordkeeping, archival development, and archival theory and practice. There are few in the field who seem able to connect such aspects into a more holistic view of their history. There are even fewer who cross cultures and languages to read about the development of archives worldwide.

In 1983 I noted the need for extensive state histories, institutional histories, regional histories, and a single-volume synthesis.[29] All remain needs nearly twenty years later. I discovered when I reviewed the literature in the early 1990s that very little new research had been done, creating little notice among historians.[30] The best histories of our National Archives are twenty to thirty years old,[31] and the most notable efforts to write an overview analysis of historical societies are nearly forty years old.[32] There also remains only one comprehensive history of archival development in a single state, and it is more than three decades old.[33] While there have been important new uses of primary sources for smaller studies, there have been few major monographs on archival history topics completed in recent years.[34]

The genesis of my own research and writing developed as a result of my trying to understand the evolution of archives and records programs I worked in, leading to research conducted for a master's thesis on the development of early Maryland archives. I worked on this type of research and writing with an assumption that a historical perspective helped me to understand better what I was working on and the context for why things were as they were in the organizations and profession in which I labored. I also drew on my own experience to write a rationale for the value of archival history.[35] While this essay has always been favorably commented on and cited,[36] it has not led to an upsurge of interest in the archival community for archival history. In hindsight, it may be that such a *practical* emphasis led to a very internally focused inquiry working against broader and more engaging research and scholarship.[37]

PROMISING DEVELOPMENTS FOR HISTORICAL
RESEARCH WITHIN ARCHIVY

There are promising signs within the American archival discipline, if not the records management side, regarding research on archival and records history. The expansion of graduate education has led to stronger curriculum with a more serious orientation on research, especially in attracting students with an interest in archives and records to doctoral programs. There have been little, as of yet, contributions to archival history that have had a major impact on the field or on others working in related realms. With what has been done, however, we can see a more sophisticated reliance on and interpretation of sources.[38] Moreover, some new developments, such as the creation of bibliographic standards, have led to analyses providing broader (if still applied) historical background of theory and practices.[39]

There has been a peripheral connection of education to an interest in history. With the emergence of a North American interest in the theoretical approach of diplomatics as a means for understanding records and recordkeeping systems has come a revisiting of older ideas of archival science.[40] This has led to a re-articulation of archival history. Although not directly connected to American archival history, Richard Brown's essay on a medieval recordkeeper shows the way for future work. Brown argues that archivists must not superimpose modern concepts of records on earlier concerns to manage records, especially as this has been seen in the rebirth of diplomatics as the crux of an archival science. Rather, archivists must be willing to understand the historical development of records management for what it tells us about records, not for what it suggests about the archivist's or records manager's *current* professional image.[41]

Other promising trends in research about archival and records management history exist, especially with the steady (if unspectacular in quantity) publication of articles on this topic in the primary North American journals in the field. Since 1990 every other issue of *Archivaria* and one in three issues of the *American Archivist* has an essay on archival history. This does not bode well for understanding American archival history, since many of these essays focus on Europe.[42] More important, however, has been the trend towards essays reliant on archival sources and those establishing parameters for a more complete understanding of records and archives.[43] The American archival profession is also now aging so that it is beginning to see the writing and publishing of memoirs, most notably Robert Warner's account of his effort to lead the National Archives back to an independent agency status. Memoirs have notorious problems in their veracity and utility, but Warner's story is a compelling addition to the rich and troubled history of this institution—an institution that has been intertwined with the historical evolution of the American archival profession.[44] Even with these encouraging aspects, however, it is readily obvious that American archival history is a weak link in the professional chain.

GLIMPSES FROM OUTSIDE

What is not a weak link, however, is the growing interest by those outside the archival and records profession in the historical evolution of writing, records, recordkeeping, archives, and historical sources. This interest is emerging in studies on the history of literacy, public memory, the culture wars, and the computer's societal impact.

The historical study of literacy has become a prime source of understanding how recordkeeping systems have emerged. Archivists first became aware of this area of scholarship twenty years ago when M. T. Clanchy published his work on the origins of records systems in medieval England, a far-reaching and pioneering study bridging the gap between orality and writing and implying what was occurring in contemporary society with computers.[45] While much of this scholarship may seem irrelevant to the American archivist because it concerns either ancient or medieval notions of literacy and writing, the scholarship also reaffirms more recent notions of records as transactions or challenges many of the assumptions made about the origins of archives. At the least, scholarship in this area has led to some major re-assessments about writing with more detail about how records represent writing systems.[46] Rosalind Thomas's work on Greece and Rome, for example, is a direct confrontation of long-accepted notions of centralized government archives.[47] The recreation of the medieval notion of recordkeeping because of the renewed interest in diplomatics as a core component of archival science is certainly challenged in studies by individuals such as Patrick Geary who demonstrate how unsystematic these early recordkeepers seemed to be.[48] More directly relevant are the works by David Cressy on English literacy in the era of American colonization. Cressy provides an interesting perspective on document formation, the uses of communication, and the power of records and information in Tudor, Elizabethan, and Stuart England—all supporting a fuller understanding of early American recordkeeping.[49]

The studies of historical literacy have challenged stereotypical notions of the evolution of writing and records. In essays on "alternative literacies" in Mesoamerica and the Andes, a new portrait of non-textual writing and recordkeeping emerges where "in this particular Amerindian writing tradition, a pictorial system is better suited to an environment where a multitude of often unrelated languages is spoken, allowing communication across language boundaries. By nature, alphabetic writing systems lack this flexibility."[50] Such insights help us to re-interpret the development of records and archives, discerning that it is not merely the textual information making them valuable but their role as evidence and symbol.

The larger context for the development of archives may be public memory, a strong new focus for studying the meaning of the past and enriched by interdisciplinary research.[51] Archives—both the individual records/collections and the institutional repositories—are clearly a symbolic marker on the landscape. Archives mark the past and are formed by the past, even though much of the scholarship on public memory has avoided specific or in-depth discussion of archives and historical records (see a later chapter for a discussion of this). The scholarship has become so vast and broad-reaching that it is hard not to see it as providing a more substantial framework for understanding at least the cultural significance (there are other significant non-cultural aspects as well) for the origins and subsequent development of archives. A recent study on American popular uses of the past adds much that suggests how and why archives are formed or perceived.[52]

The passing of time since the Second World War has caused many to write about how other nations are struggling to remember aspects of the horrific acts of their forebears. Some of these works have discussed the manner in which records are or have been used or neglected for such purposes.[53] While other wars have spurred on the collecting and preservation of records,[54] the aftermath of the Second World War has led to a contested context for the meaning of records. Studies about remembering painful past events have much to inform archivists about their origins and nature of their profession and its institutions.[55] Some of this has led to considerable debate about the meaning and value of archives, from the Civil War to exhibitions on the end of the Second World War.[56] Ironically, this contested past, as in the interpretation and memory of the Second World War, has also been tied to developments suggesting the importance of records in general and archives in particular. This has been most evident in the controversy surrounding the role of the Swiss banks in financing Adolf Hitler and the generations of efforts to lay claims to assets stolen from Holocaust victims.[57] The result has been a powerful new social warrant moving archives from dusty bins visited by scholars to the front pages of newspapers and on the table before public policymakers. This suggests a different kind of archival history. If studies on historic preservation can put it into broader uses by certain societal elements to fulfill a particular mandate (such as "to prompt Americans—newcomer and native alike—to accept their aesthetics, work harder, live more humbly, and appreciate Yankee traditions"[58]), we also need studies showing the factors leading to the origins and ongoing development of archives and historical records repositories.

The association of public memory and archives is even more complex. There has been an uneven reception about the importance of archives in public memory. One study about how Watergate has been perceived brings no discussion of the Presidential Records Act or of the legal wrangles and hassles over the ownership of the Nixon White House tape recordings,[59] despite a public fascination with such secret recordkeeping.[60] Another study argues how the personal accounts by journalists have become the de facto societal archives for remembering and interpreting the assassination of John F. Kennedy.[61] What has been lost is an appreciation that there is a need to study the formation of presidential records, if not the memorializing events in repeatedly establishing presidential libraries; both topics are worthy of focus by archival historians and neither has been well-treated.[62]

Even more important for a new archival history may not be the scholarship *about* public memory but the *debate* about its use in multiculturalism, textbook writing, and history standards. In these discussions and diatribes (and there are both, often side by side) we see a simultaneous rejection and elevation of the value of historical records.[63] Such debates have often proceeded with little appreciation of how archives are formed, but it is likely that continuing discussions will lead to new understanding. This is doubly important in the so-called Information Age, where the computer has become God, information *the* source of all power and prestige, and electronic networking the *only* way by which this information can be disseminated.

The exploding literature on the challenges posed and promises offered by the computer contributes to understanding the development of modern recordkeeping systems. Thomas Landauer's efforts to re-consider the claims of the computer's productivity leads him to write extensively about automated *recordkeeping* systems.[64] His work is reminiscent of earlier histories completed on office systems and work that, while examining issues such as gender and communication, provides some of the most in-depth understanding of how records and information technologies have evolved in the past century and a half.[65] In such studies is a new understanding about the importance of records and challenges confronting the maintenance of archives.

Histories of other information technologies also are useful for understanding the impact on traditional recordkeeping systems. Many archivists and records managers have lamented that the rise of telecommunications technologies such as the telephone have taken hold because of their ability to provide quicker and less costly communication than what is captured in transactional records. However, histories of the telephone suggest that its success was not certain and that its reasons for success often had little to do with its technical attributes.[66] Considering such histories should indicate to archivists the need for fuller studies of records and archives. Has the creation of archival programs been sustained by the ephemeral nature of electronic information systems? Have these new and emerging systems really affected society's ability to document itself?

The impact of computer technology on organizations and individuals has also prompted many concerns about the social, ethical, political, and other impacts of the technology.[67] From my vantage it seems that such concerns have led to a renewed interest in matters with considerable implications for understanding the history of records systems and archives, such as access and privacy, handwriting, and personal recordkeeping. Regarding privacy and access, new scholarship has emerged re-examining such complex matters as the impact of opening secret police files, the negative ramifications of government secrecy, and the problems inflicted on personal lives by preserving and opening private papers.[68] While archivists and other records professionals have written extensively on privacy and access over the past two decades, none of their work has led to significant new studies on the history of recordkeeping and archives. That this is a loss can be seen in E. Wayne Carp's recent history of secrecy in adoption practices, providing an extensive history of the evolution of adoption records systems since the mid-nineteenth century.[69]

The growing influence of electronics has also prompted a new interest in the cultural history of older recordkeeping technologies. Tamara Plakins Thornton's study of American handwriting is a prime example with a major emphasis on the evolution of scripts, the teaching of particular scribal traditions, and the emergence of autograph collecting as part of a resistance to other information technologies such as the typewriter and office equipment.[70] There has developed an intense interest in diary writing, the most intimate of personal recordkeeping approaches. The scholarship in this area stresses the history of diary writing and, in some cases, even argues that the process of personal diary writing served as a surrogate local archives and documentation process.[71] Some of the concern about the new technologies has been directed towards understanding how objects or artifacts such as records could be authentic or reliable in the new cyberculture or virtual reality, adding to our understanding of the continuing evolution of recordkeeping systems and archives. Anthony Grafton's anecdotal history of the footnote is an explanation of one form of authority.[72] An increasing interest in forgeries is another indication of such concerns, and an important one for archives, given that the origins of archival science (diplomatics) rests with the business of detecting forgeries.[73]

The development of the World Wide Web and other information technologies has also increased the sense that visualization is superseding text as writing superseded oral communication. There has been increased attention to the history of photography, and this has in some cases provided a new base for archivists to re-think the evolution of this technology as a recordkeeping system.[74] It is also no surprise that the collecting of books as well as a scholarship examining the future of the book has developed. For some it might be surprising that the writing about the collecting of books has moved into chronicling the acquisition of manuscripts and the origins of special collections.[75]

It has not only been the oncoming self-conscious onslaught of cyberculture stimulating useful scholarship with implications for archival history. While the archivist has focused on small institutional studies and biographies, more substantial studies providing probes into certain aspects of records and archives have appeared. Some historians have written detailed accounts of particular recordkeeping systems as sources, such as the census.[76] A growth in studies of non-profit management has produced some excellent studies of research institutions chronicling their fiscal management and their development as collections.[77] Textual criticism has also produced some notable work that historians of archives and records could draw on. This work ranges from the role of scribes and clerical bureaucrats in Latin America to an interpretation of the creation of the British Empire via research, classification, and documentation and critiques of individual documents.[78] The availability and value of such research is only beginning to be appreciated by archivists.

Finally, the archivist or person interested in archives might find some insights on the history of records and archives in unlikely places. A writer re-visiting his own family's past winds up waxing eloquently about his family's papers.[79] The current spate of popular writings by professionals like engineers and architects also bring surprises such as Henry Petroski's ruminations on paper clips and the pencil.[80] The continuing fascination with measure and quantification includes important references for comprehending the development of legislation for producing records, financial systems such as double-entry bookkeeping, and other kinds of records. What we are reading about in these volumes concerns the records ultimately considered for archives.[81]

CONCLUSION

If we expect to see a vibrant interest in the history of archives and records management, archivists and other records professionals need to expand their views about the topic. They need to accept the interdisciplinary nature of research in the field, but one that will enrich both those studying this within and without the disciplinary boundaries. Archivists and other records professionals have much to gain from these other fields, but it is not a one-way benefit. Archivists and records managers may have a greater sensitivity to professional issues that provides insights others might lack.

The other need is to expand archivists' and others' views beyond traditional archives—the acquiring and preserving historic manuscripts and records—to an understanding of records and recordkeeping systems. I earlier mentioned the resurgence of interest in diplomatics, but this interest has partly grown because of the challenges posed by electronic records. Archivists have been forced to rethink their cherished mission, how they define records, and whom they work for and with. Out of this comes the essence of a new power for archival history. Understanding records and recordkeeping systems naturally leads us to thinking about why they have been created, what uses they have, and issues about their maintenance. The muse of history, Clio, would be happy to help archivists and records managers in such endeavors.

A revitalized archival and records management history requires an understanding of the significance of the historical perspective for everyday, practical archival and records work. It requires the continued expansion of graduate archival education with time and opportunity to study the history of archives and recordkeeping. And, finally, it requires a scholarship with more breadth and depth than what has thus far passed for archival history. We will see a growth in the historical study of records and recordkeeping because of the modern sensibility about their importance.

Records professionals need a new and deeper appreciation of the nature and history of records and recordkeeping, not to ascribe to some sort of rigid theory or methodology nor to use history as a means to make themselves feel good about their profession and mission. Knowledge of the historical origins of records and recordkeeping systems provides the necessary context for understanding *current* records and recordkeeping systems. Such understanding is also essential for having any hope of managing these records and the systems that create them. The following chapters are an introductory effort to provide a stronger historical view about modern records management in North America.

NOTES

1. William H. Davidow and Michael S. Malone, *The Virtual Corporation: Structuring and Revitalizing the Corporation for the 21st Century* (New York: HarperBusiness, 1992), p. 65.

2. Betty R. Ricks and Kay F. Gow, *Information Resource Management* (Cincinnati: South-Western Publishing Co., 1984), p. 470.

3. There were earlier commissions and task forces charged with investigating federal records management, but these did not lead to substantial changes in practice or attitudes. For some exploration into these earlier efforts, see Bess Glenn, "The Taft Commission and the Government's Records Practices," *American Archivist* 21 (July 1958): 277–303 and Harold T. Pinkett, "Investigations of Federal Recordkeeping, 1877–1906," *American Archivist* 21 (April 1958): 163–192.

4. An overview of the history of the National Archives can be obtained from H. G. Jones, *The Records of a Nation: Their Management, Preservation, and Use* (New York: Atheneum, 1969) and Donald R. McCoy, *The National Archives: America's Ministry of Documents 1934–1968* (Chapel Hill: University of North Carolina Press, 1978), although an updated and more critical history is sorely needed.

5. H. G. Jones, *Local Government Records: An Introduction to Their Management, Preservation, and Use* (Nashville, Tenn.: American Association for State and Local History, 1980), p. 17.

6. Frank B. Evans, "Archivists and Records Managers: Variations on a Theme," *American Archivist* 30 (January 1967): 48.

7. George Bolotenko, "Archivists and Historians: Keepers of the Well," *Archivaria* no. 16 (1983): 21.

8. Terry and Carol Lundgren, *Records Management in the Computer Age* (Boston: PWS-Kent Publishing Co., 1989), p. 153.

9. Philip C. Brooks, "Current Aspects of Records Administration: The Archivist's Concern in Records Administration," *American Archivist* 6 (July 1943): 164.

10. *For the Record: Guidelines for Official Records and Personal Papers* (Washington, D.C.: National Archives and Records Administration, 1985).

11. James Gregory Bradsher, "Federal Field Archives: Past, Present, and Future," *Government Information Quarterly* 4, no. 2 (1987): 151–166.

12. For an early assessment of the importance of the Hoover Commissions for federal records management, see Robert W. Krauskopf, "The Hoover Commissions and Federal Recordkeeping," *American Archivist* 21 (October 1958): 371–399. An assessment of these commissions four decades later would be quite useful for our understanding of the *current* records challenges and issues faced by the National Archives and the federal government.

13. The circular was more controversial among librarians, primarily because it threatened the publication of free or inexpensive federal government documents, squarely counter to the library community's commitment to free access to information. See Redmond Kathleen Molz and Phyllis Dain, *Civic Space/Cyberspace: The American Public Library in the Information Age* (Cambridge, Mass.: MIT Press, 1999), pp. 118–120.

14. Maurice Halbwachs, *On Collective Memory*, ed. and trans. Lewis A. Coser (Chicago: University of Chicago Press, 1992), p. 139.

15. Mary F. Robek, Gerald F. Brown, and Wilmer O. Maedke, *Information and Records Management*, 3rd ed. (Encino, Calif.: Glencoe Publishing Co., 1987), p. 22.

16. I have written extensively about the nature of historical writing about archives and records management in a series of essays, including "American Archival History: Its Development, Needs, and Opportunities," *American Archivist* 46 (Winter 1983): 31–41; "On the Value of Archival History in the United States," *Libraries & Culture* 23 (Spring 1988): 135–151; "The History of Primary Sources in Graduate Education: An Archival Perspective," *Special Collections* 4, no. 2 (1990): 39–78; and "Other Atlantic States: Delaware, Florida, Georgia, Maryland, New Jersey, and South Carolina," in H. G. Jones, ed., *Historical Consciousness in the Early Republic: The Origins of State Historical Societies and Collections, 1791–1861* (Chapel Hill: North Carolina Society, Inc. and North Carolina Collection, 1995), pp. 102–124.

17. That an archivist would see fit to describe remedies for a phobia about the nature and use of archives held by historians and related scholars perhaps covers another aspect of the problems for the lack of a larger and longer understanding of records and recordkeeping systems; see Virginia C. Purdy, "Archivaphobia: Its Causes and Cure," *Prologue* 15 (Summer 1983): 115–119.

18. See Rosalind Thomas, *Literacy and Orality in Ancient Greece* (Cambridge: Cambridge University Press, 1992). In fact, a debate has now started on just how moderns can interpret ancient recordkeeping practices, as seen in James P. Sickinger, *Public Records and Archives in Classical Athens* (Chapel Hill: University of North Carolina Press, 1999).

19. Luciana Duranti, "The Odyssey of Records Managers," *Records Management Quarterly* 23 (July and October 1989), part 2: 9 and 10.

20. For the most extreme of such views, see Linda Henry, "Schellenberg in Cyberspace," *American Archivist* 61 (Fall 1998): 309–327.

21. Herbert J. Gans, *Deciding What's News: A Study of CBS Evening News, NBC Nightly News, Newsweek, and Time* (New York: Vintage Books, 1980), pp. 43–44.

22. Gans, *Deciding What's News*, pp. 291–292.

23. See Bruce W. Dearstyne, "Archival Politics in New York State, 1892–1915," *New York History* 66 (April 1985): 165–184.

24. Janna Malamud Smith, *Private Matters: In Defense of the Personal Life* (Reading, Mass.: Addison-Wesley Publishing Co., 1997), p. 69.

25. Don Gifford, *The Farther Shore: A Natural History of Perception, 1798–1984* (New York: Vintage Books, 1990), p. 62.

26. Craig Gilborn, *Arts of the Home in Early America: The Reliance on Tradition, 1625–1700* (Columbus, Ohio: Charles E. Merrill Publishing Co., 1969), p. 42.

27. Donald G. Davis, Jr., "Ebla to the Electronic Dream: The Role of Historical Perspectives in Professional Education," *Journal of Education for Library and Information Science* 39 (Summer 1998): 228–235 (quote p. 230).

28. This can be seen in the research they conduct, and this research has not empha-

sized historical studies. See Richard J. Cox, "An Analysis of Archival Research, 1970–92, and the Role and Function of the *American Archivist*," *American Archivist* 57 (Spring 1994): 278–288.

29. Cox, "American Archival History"; for a more comprehensive, international bibliography of the same era see Frank B. Evans, comp., *The History of Archives Administration: A Select Bibliography* (Paris: UNESCO, 1979).

30. Cox, "Other Atlantic States."

31. Jones, *The Records of a Nation* and McCoy, *The National Archives*.

32. David D. Van Tassel, *Recording America's Past: An Interpretation of the Development of Historical Societies in America 1607–1884* (Chicago: University of Chicago Press, 1960) and Walter Muir Whitehill, *Independent Historical Societies: An Enquiry Into Their Research and Publication Functions and Their Financial Future* (Boston: Boston Athenaeum, 1962).

33. H. G. Jones, *For History's Sake: The Preservation and Publication of North Carolina History 1663–1903* (Chapel Hill: University of North Carolina Press, 1966).

34. Works such as Victor Gondos, Jr., *J. Franklin Jameson and the Birth of the National Archives 1906–1926* (Philadelphia: University of Pennsylvania Press, 1981) and Burl Noggle, *Working with History: The Historical Records Survey in Louisiana and the Nation, 1936–1942* (Baton Rouge: Louisiana State University Press, 1981) remain unsurpassed. Barbra Buckner Higginbotham, *Our Past Preserved: A History of American Library Preservation 1876–1910* (Boston: G. K. Hall and Co., 1990) is closely related and examines many original sources.

35. Cox, "On the Value of Archival History in the United States."

36. Such as Barbara L. Craig, "Outward Visions, Inward Glance: Archives History and Professional Identity," *Archival Issues* 17, no. 2 (1992): 113–124.

37. This is similar to problems faced in library history: "Because a sizable percentage of all books that are read come from libraries, a broad history of the uses of literacy must eventually incorporate some history of the uses of libraries. Until now, historians of libraries have focused more on internal professional development than on readers or the circulation of books." Carl F. Kaestle, Helen Damon-Moore, Lawrence C. Stedman, Katherine Tinsley, and William Vance Trollinger, Jr., *Literacy in the United States: Readers and Reading Since 1880* (New Haven, Conn.: Yale University Press, 1991), p. 66.

38. See, for example, the theoretical contribution of Trevor Livelton, *Archival Theory, Records, and the Public* (Lanham, Md.: The Society of American Archivists and the Scarecrow Press, 1996).

39. Terry Eastwood, ed., *The Archival Fonds: From Theory to Practice* (Ottawa: Bureau of Canadian Archivists, 1992) is a good example.

40. This can be seen in the influence of the diplomatics approach at the University of British Columbia Masters in Archival Studies program and the emergence of a substantial amount of writing about the history of records systems and recordkeeping. The theoretical foundation of this approach was captured in Luciana Duranti's six-part series on diplomatics published in *Archivaria*, a series recently published as a book—Luciana Duranti, *Diplomatics: New Uses for an Old Science* (Metuchen, N.J.: Scarecrow Press for the Society of American Archivists, 1998). That diplomatics has taken on a new or reinvigorated role can be seen in the special issue of the *American Archivist* on "Diplomatics and Modern Records" (vol. 59, Fall 1996).

41. Richard Brown, "Death of a Renaissance Record-Keeper: The Murder of Tomasso da Tortona in Ferrara, 1385," *Archivaria* no. 44 (Fall 1997): 1–43.

42. In the 1990–1998 run of *Archivaria*, 20 of the 204 articles were on archival history and 11 of 17 issues had an article on this topic. In the 1990–1998 run of the *American Archivist*, 16 of the 285 articles were on archival history and 12 of the 34 issues had an article on this topic. In the *American Archivist* 6 of the 16 articles were on European archival history; in *Archivaria*, 3 of the 17 articles were on European archival history.

43. Some of these recent noteworthy essays on American archives are Alfred E. Lemmon, "The Archival Legacy of Spanish Louisiana's Colonial Records," *American Archivist* 55 (Winter 1992): 142–155; Dennis East, "The Ohio Historical Society and Establishment of the State's Archives: A Tale of Angst and Apathy," *American Archivist* 55 (Fall 1992): 562–577; Margaret O'Neill Adams, "Punch Card Records: Precursors of Electronic Records," *American Archivist* 58 (Spring 1995): 182–201; Anke Voss-Hubbard, " 'No Documents—No History': Mary Ritter Beard and the Early History of Women's Archives," *American Archivist* 58 (Winter 1995): 16–30; and Robert D. Reynolds, Jr., "The Incunabula of Archival Theory and Practice in the United States: J. C. Fitzpatrick's *Notes on the Care, Cataloguing, Calendaring and Arranging of Manuscripts* and the Public Archives Commission's Uncompleted 'Primer of Archival Economy,'" *American Archivist* 54 (Fall 1991): 466–482. A noteworthy historical analysis of theoretical matters, with implications for North American archivy, is Terry Cook, "What Is Past Is Prologue: A History of Archival Ideas Since 1898, and the Future Paradigm Shift," *Archivaria* no. 43 (Spring 1997): 17–63.

44. Robert M. Warner, *Diary of a Dream: A History of the National Archives Independence Movement, 1980–1985* (Metuchen, N.J.: Scarecrow Press, 1995).

45. A revised second edition of the original 1979 work was issued as M. T. Clanchy, *From Memory to Written Record: England 1066–1307*, 2nd ed. (Cambridge: Blackwell, 1993).

46. Of prime importance is Henri-Jean Martin, *The History and Power of Writing*, trans. Lydia G. Cochrane (Chicago: University of Chicago Press, 1994). See also the works by Jack Goody, *The Interface Between the Written and the Oral* (Cambridge: Cambridge University Press, 1987) and *The Logic of Writing and the Organization of Society* (Cambridge: Cambridge University Press, 1986), which seem to serve as points of departure for many other commentators and disciplines on writing and literacy.

47. Thomas, *Literacy and Orality in Ancient Greece*. For other interesting works on ancient literacy see William V. Harris, *Ancient Literacy* (Cambridge, Mass.: Harvard University Press, 1989) and Denise Schmandt-Besserat, *How Writing Came About* (Austin: University of Texas Press, 1996; abridged ed.). The later provides an interesting look at the origins of writing systems from tokens used to capture ancient commercial transactions.

48. Patrick J. Geary, *Phantoms of Remembrance: Memory and Oblivion at the End of the First Millennium* (Princeton, N.J.: Princeton University Press, 1994). Other interesting works on the medieval period are Brian Stock, *Listening for the Text: On the Uses of the Past* (Philadelphia: University of Pennsylvania Press, 1990) and *The Implications of Literacy: Written Language and Models of Interpretations in the Eleventh and Twelfth Centuries* (Princeton, N.J.: Princeton University Press, 1987).

49. David Cressy, *Bonfires and Bells: National Memory and the Protestant Calendar in Elizabethan and Stuart England* (Berkeley: University of California Press, 1989); *Coming Over: Migration and Communication Between England and New England in the*

Seventeenth Century (Cambridge: Cambridge University Press, 1987); and *Literacy and the Social Order: Reading and Writing in Tudor and Stuart England* (Cambridge: Cambridge University Press, 1980).

50. Peter L. van der Loo in Elizabeth Hill Boone and Walter D. Mignolo, eds., *Writing Without Words: Alternative Literacies in Mesoamerica and the Andes* (Durham, N.C.: Duke University Press, 1994), p. 84.

51. The burst of research has been well-documented in Patrick H. Hutton, *History as an Art of Memory* (Hanover: University of Vermont, 1993).

52. Roy Rosensweig and David Thelen, *The Presence of the Past: Popular Uses of History in American Life* (New York: Columbia University Press, 1998).

53. See, for example, Ian Buruma, *The Wages of Guilt: Memories of War in Germany and Japan* (New York: Meridian, 1994).

54. See, especially, the Australian experience in Alistair Thomson, *Anzac Memories: Living with the Legend* (New York: Oxford University Press, 1994).

55. An interesting study to begin with is Kenneth E. Foote, *Shadowed Ground: America's Landscapes of Violence and Tragedy* (Austin: University of Texas Press, 1997).

56. Robert Brent Toplin, ed., *Ken Burns's The Civil War: Historians Respond* (New York: Oxford University Press, 1996). The Enola Gay Exhibition debate has been particularly powerful. See, for example, Martin Harwit, *An Exhibit Denied: Lobbying the History of Enola Gay* (New York: Copernicus, 1996); Edward T. Linenthal and Tom Engelhardt, eds., *History Wars: The Enola Gay and Other Battles for the American Past* (New York: Metropolitan Books, 1996); Philip Nobile, ed., *Judgment at the Smithsonian* (New York: Marlowe and Co., 1995); and Kai Bird and Lawrence Lifschultz, eds., *Hiroshima's Shadow: Writings on the Denial of History and the Smithsonian Controversy* (Stony Creek, Conn.: The Pamphleteer's Press, 1998).

57. Tom Bower, *Nazi Gold: The Full Story of the Fifty-Year Swiss-Nazi Conspiracy to Steal Billions from Europe's Jews and Holocaust Survivors* (New York: HarperCollins Publishers, 1997); Isabel Vincent, *Hitler's Silent Partners: Swiss Banks, Nazi Gold, and the Pursuit of Justice* (New York: William Morrow and Co., 1997); and Jean Ziegler, *The Swiss, the Gold, and the Dead*, trans. John Brownjohn (New York: Harcourt Brace and Co., 1998). A similar controversy about stolen art treasures has also resulted in new studies re-exploring archives and demonstrating their importance. See Hector Feliciano, *The Lost Museum: The Nazi Conspiracy to Steal the World's Greatest Works of Art* (New York: HarperBooks, 1997); Lynn H. Nicholas, *The Rape of Europa: The Fate of Europe's Treasures in the Third Reich and the Second World War* (New York: Vintage Books, 1994); and Elizabeth Simpson, ed., *The Spoils of War: World War II and Its Aftermath; The Loss, Reappearance, and Recovery of Cultural Property* (New York: Harry N. Abrams in association with the Bard Graduate Center for Studies in the Decorative Arts, 1997).

58. James M. Lindgren, *Preserving Historic New England: Preservation, Progressivism, and the Remaking of Memory* (New York: Oxford University Press, 1995), p. 155.

59. Michael Schudson, *Watergate in American Memory: How We Remember, Forget, and Reconstruct the Past* (New York: Basic Books, 1992).

60. See, for example, Michael R. Beschloss, ed., *Taking Charge: The Johnson White House Tapes, 1963–1964* (New York: Simon and Schuster, 1997); Tom Blanton, ed., *White House E-Mail: The Top Secret Computer Messages the Reagan/Bush White House Tried to Destroy* (New York: The New Press, 1995); Stanley I. Kutler, ed., *Abuse of Power: The New Nixon Tapes* (New York: The Free Press, 1997); and Ernst R. May and

Philip D. Zelikow, eds., *The Kennedy Tapes: Inside the White House During the Cuban Missile Crisis* (Cambridge, Mass.: Belknap Press of Harvard University Press, 1997).

61. Barbie Zelizer, *Covering the Body: The Kennedy Assassination, the Media, and the Shaping of Collective Memory* (Chicago: University of Chicago Press, 1992).

62. The potential to study such records can be seen in Carol Gelderman, *All the Presidents' Words: The Bully Pulpit and the Creation of the Virtual Presidency* (New York: Walker and Company, 1997), tracking the influence of speechwriters on the modern presidency, and Harold Holzer, comp. and ed., *Dear Mr. Lincoln: Letters to the President* (Reading, Mass.: Addison-Wesley Publishing Co., 1993), including an interesting description of how the president's secretaries contributed to the creation of his records.

63. See, for example, Lynne Cheney, *Telling the Truth: Why Our Culture and Our Country Have Stopped Making Sense—and What We Can Do About It* (New York: Simon and Schuster, 1995); Todd Gitlin, *The Twilight of Common Dreams: Why America Is Wracked by Culture Wars* (New York: Metropolitan Books, Henry Holt and Co., 1995); Lawrence W. Levine, *The Opening of the American Mind: Canons, Culture and History* (Boston: Beacon Press, 1996); James W. Loewen, *Lies My Teacher Told Me: Everything Your American History Textbook Got Wrong* (New York: The New Press, 1995); Gary B. Nash, Charlotte Crabtree, and Ross E. Dunn, *History on Trial: Culture Wars and the Teaching of the Past* (New York: Alfred B. Knopf, 1997); Peter N. Stearns, *Meaning Over Memory: Recasting the Teaching of Culture and History* (Chapel Hill: University of North Carolina Press, 1993).

64. Thomas K. Landauer, *The Trouble with Computers: Usefulness, Usability, and Productivity* (Cambridge, Mass.: MIT Press, 1995).

65. The classic work of this type remains JoAnne Yates, *Control Through Communication: The Rise of System in American Management* (Baltimore: Johns Hopkins University Press, 1989). For an example of the type of study considering women in the workplace, see Margery W. Davies, *Woman's Place Is at the Typewriter: Office Work and Office Workers 1870–1920* (Philadelphia: Temple University Press, 1982).

66. Claude S. Fischer, *America Calling: A Social History of the Telephone to 1940* (Berkeley: University of California Press, 1992).

67. This is why areas of scholarship such as cyberculture and social informatics have developed. For the latter visit the Center for Social Informatics at http://www.slis.indiana.edu/CSI. For a view on cyberculture, visit The Resource Center for Cyberculture Studies at http://otal.umd.edu/~rccs.

68. Timothy Garton Ash, *The File: A Personal History* (New York: Random House, 1997); Robert Jay Lifton and Greg Mitchell, *Hiroshima in America: A Half Century of Denial* (New York: Avon Books, 1995); Angus MacKenzie, *Secrets: The CIA's War at Home* (Berkeley: University of California Press, 1997); David Rudenstine, *The Day the Presses Stopped: A History of the Pentagon Papers Case* (Berkeley: University of California Press, 1996); Janna Malamud Smith, *Private Matters: In Defense of the Personal Life* (Reading, Mass.: Addison-Wesley Publishing Co., 1997); and Mary Gordon, *The Shadow Man* (New York: Vintage Books, 1996).

69. E. Wayne Carp, *Family Matters: Secrecy and Disclosure in the History of Adoption* (Cambridge, Mass.: Harvard University Press, 1998).

70. Tamara Plakins Thornton, *Handwriting in America: A Cultural History* (New Haven, Conn.: Yale University Press, 1996).

71. See, for example, Suzanne L. Bunkers and Cynthia A. Huff, eds., *Inscribing the*

Daily: Critical Essays on Women's Diaries (Amherst: University of Massachusetts Press, 1996); Andrew Hassam, *Sailing to Australia: Shipboard Diaries by Nineteenth-Century British Emigrants* (Melbourne: Melbourne University Press, 1995); Alexandra Johnson, *The Hidden Writer: Diaries and the Creative Life* (New York: Anchor Books, Doubleday, 1997); Kenneth A. Lockridge, *The Diary, and Life, of William Byrd II of Virginia, 1674–1744* (New York: W. W. Norton and Co., 1987); Thomas Mallon, *A Book of One's Own: People and Their Diaries* (New York: Ticknor and Fields, 1984); James G. Moseley, *John Winthrop's World: History as a Story; The Story as History* (Madison: University of Wisconsin Press, 1992); Stuart Sherman, *Telling Time: Clocks, Diaries, and English Diurnal Form, 1660–1785* (Chicago: University of Chicago Press, 1996); and Laurel Thatcher Ulrich, *A Midwife's Tale: The Life of Martha Ballard, Based on Her Diary, 1785–1812* (New York: Vintage Books, 1990). The Sherman and Ulrich studies are especially useful.

72. Anthony Grafton, *The Footnote: A Curious History* (Cambridge, Mass.: Harvard University Press, 1997).

73. For interesting studies on forgeries, see Pat Bozeman, ed., *Forged Documents: Proceedings of the 1989 Houston Conference; Organized by the University of Houston Libraries* (New Castle, Del.: Oak Knoll Books, 1990); Anthony Grafton, *Forgers and Critics: Creativity and Duplicity in Western Scholarship* (Princeton, N.J.: Princeton University Press, 1990); Charles Hamilton, *The Hitler Diaries: Fakes That Fooled the World* (Lexington: University Press of Kentucky, 1991); Robert Harris, *Selling Hitler* (New York: Penguin Books, 1986); Steven Naifeh and Gregory White Smith, *The Mormom Murders: A True Story of Greed, Forgery, Deceit, and Death* (New York: New American Library, 1988).

74. Some interesting and noteworthy works include Julia Hirsch, *Family Photographs: Content, Meaning, and Effect* (New York: Oxford University Press, 1981); Marianne Hirsch, *Family Frames: Photography, Narrative and Postmemory* (Cambridge, Mass.: Harvard University Press, 1997); Celia Lury, *Prosthetic Culture: Photography, Memory, and Identity* (New York: Routledge, 1998); and John Tagg, *The Burden of Representation: Essays on Photographies and Histories* (Minneapolis: University of Minnesota Press, 1993).

75. See, for example, Nicholas A. Basbanes, *A Gentle Madness: Bibliophiles, Bibliomanes, and the Eternal Passion for Books* (New York: Henry Holt and Co., 1995).

76. Margo J. Anderson, *The American Census: A Social History* (New Haven, Conn.: Yale University Press, 1988).

77. Jed I. Bergman, in collaboration with William G. Bowen and Thomas I. Nygren, *Managing Change in the Nonprofit Sector: Lessons from the Evolution of Five Independent Research Libraries* (San Francisco: Jossey-Bass Publishers, 1996) and Kevin M. Guthrie, *The New York Historical Society: Lessons from One Nonprofit's Long Struggle for Survival* (San Francisco: Jossey-Bass Publishers, 1996).

78. Angel Rama, *The Lettered City*, trans and ed. John Charles Chasteen (Durham, N.C.: Duke University Press, 1996); Thomas Richards, *The Imperial Archive: Knowledge and the Fantasy of Empire* (London: Verso, 1993); and Jay Fliegelman, *Declaring Independence: Jefferson, Natural Language, and the Culture of Performance* (Stanford, Calif.: Stanford University Press, 1993).

79. Ian Frazier, *Family* (New York: HarperPerennial, 1994).

80. Henry Petroski, *The Evolution of Useful Things* (New York: Vintage Books, 1992)

and *The Pencil: A History of Design and Circumstance* (New York: Alfred A. Knopf, 1990).

81. Alfred W. Crosby, *The Measure of Reality: Quantification and Western Society, 1250–1600* (Cambridge: Cambridge University Press, 1997).

2

The Birth of Records Management: The Ancients to the Dawn of the Industrial Age

The emergence of complex, modern recordkeeping systems took hundreds of years, although much older systems have many complicated features. While records professionals today sometimes approach the challenges of managing records systems as if they were new challenges peculiar to the digital information era, these challenges extend back a considerable period of time. Whether what happened between the ancient era and the nineteenth century represents progress or not, it certainly represents a time when recordkeeping technologies changed, the pace of records creation grew, and the first modern problems in administering records developed. If for no other reasons, records professionals should be interested in the past.

ANCIENT RECORDKEEPING

Contemporary records professionals first must understand the modern characteristics of ancient recordkeeping. Denise Schmandt-Besserat demonstrates how early transactions were marked by token exchanges, and these tokens were eventually stored in sealed containers. The container sealing caused verification problems, leading to impressing the tokens on the containers and making the tokens unnecessary.[1] This evolved about 3500–3100 B.C. from a system of tokens that had originated at least 5,000 years before with the "development of an urban economy," the need by "merchants . . . to preserve records of their transactions," and a "complex business accountancy."[2] Another expert on writing, Henri-Jean Martin, describes the origins of Mesopotamian recordkeeping as having "three main concerns: finding appropriate ways to count or measure their goods, specifying clearly and indisputably the terms and the outcomes of increasingly complex transactions, and foreseeing the future."[3] While we must not impose modern conceptions of records on these ancient progenitors, the origins of writing, records, and recordkeeping are connected to utilitarian concerns, such as marking possessions, inscribing memorials, making lists of officials, recording laws, and documenting rules and procedures—all this while some distrust in writing remained. Records professionals who search for practical means to manage records are in good company with their ancient forebears.

Writing and recordkeeping techniques and technologies emerged over several thousand years. It is possible to trace a progression, even if not a linear one, from cuneiform to hieroglyphics around 400 years later and the alphabet nearly 2,000 years later. The uses of papyrus, parchment, paper, rolls, and the codex all mark substantial developments in writing and recordkeeping. From around 2,500 years before the time of Christ, we can see some notable developments in recordkeeping. Ebla was a society of great recordkeepers. It maintained legal, executive, administrative, military, economic, literary and other texts with all the kinds of records created today. This society also created formal systems of scribes and a school for scribes, especially needed since the Sumerian script was difficult with 2,000 symbols.[4] Recordkeeping in ancient societies had become important enough that in ancient Egypt "even the illiterate seem to have considered it prudent to include a written papyrus among their tomb furnishings, as a passport to guarantee their safe passage to the hereafter."[5] The Greek orator Lycurgus stated that "if anyone went into the Metroon [the city archives in Athens] and erased a single law, and then alleged in defense that this law meant nothing to the city, would you not have him put to death? I believe you would have been justified in doing so, if you wanted to protect the other laws."[6]

Other ancient cultures displayed a remarkable range of attitudes towards writing and records, reflecting many of the same anguished expressions directed at modern electronic information technologies. While it has become popular to ascribe modern recordkeeping and archival principles to ancient Rome and Greece, most careful research suggests that these principles were very remote from their modern counterparts. In ancient Rome, there was a preponderance of interest in recordkeeping with its government chanceries, mercantile counting houses, street vendors writing letters to order, and monument inscriptions.[7] Other scholars have demonstrated that even with the increasing interest in records, there was no central records depository, no concept of public access, an antipathy to the concept of public access, a focus on the household in which most records of importance would be kept, the public posting of selected records for maintenance, and the depositing of some records at a religious shrine as an act of worship not access.[8]

The ancient world's emerging use of writing and records was inconsistent, primarily because these were new activities. Historian Michael Grant writes that "we nowadays like our historiography to be supported by documents. . . . This did not function in the ancient world, for two reasons. First, the documents and archives, whether public or private, were hopelessly inadequate and without meaning even if relatively numerous. . . . Second, the Greek and Roman historians did not care very much about these documents and rarely quoted or even paraphrased them.''[9] Records and writing were important and prevalent enough that their management could be the brunt of jokes. Arnaldo Momigliano notes that when a Persian king could not sleep, he had the official records brought to him and read: "On that night could not the king sleep, and he commanded to bring the book of records of the chronicles; and they were read before the king.''[10]

Records were important enough in ancient society that they were seen as hallmarks of the greater civilizations. Logan, in his study of the alphabet's impact, characterized the demise of the Roman Empire as constituting the "end of an era and resulted in a dramatic discontinuity in the political and social structure of Europe." Orality re-emerged and the "civil servants who processed the paperwork in the Roman bureaucracy were suddenly unnecessary," the "major incentives to learn reading and writing suddenly disappeared," and "there was a dramatic drop in the level of literacy in the general population and scholarly activities came to a virtual standstill.''[11] While this may be an exaggeration, it nevertheless underscores that records and recordkeeping, with their management, had become critical.

Despite resisting superimposing too much of our current attitudes about records over earlier eras, viewing the notion of the record over time reveals a very different possibility—an adequate, working knowledge of a record that transcends time, place, and technology and that holds up in law and administration. In the ancient world the sense of a record emerged and evolved. Prior to any formal records, there were memory-aid devices, such as sticks with notches or cords knotted to represent transactions and to assist the creator in remembering some activity or event. Given that many of these "records" were made on very ephemeral materials in climates that were often very harsh to them, it is difficult to determine what the earliest forms of records were or how they were used. These crude "records" were created to indicate transactions between individuals and institutions and to transcend limitations that human and organizational memory possess.

The clay tablet societies of 5,000 years ago give the earliest views of ancient recordmaking and keeping. Small clay tokens were utilized as records, usually to capture transactions of counts of animals, trades, sales, and other related functions—and so our earliest documents often have the appearance roughly akin to modern grocery lists, maintained to keep track of barter, crop storage, and related activities. Such documents increased with the emergence of governments and self-conscious bureaucratic organizations (accounting for why the first archives and records centers appeared). Concerns for memory and posterity were also evident with the earliest accumulations of records, as references to rulers and chronicle-type writings indicate. These records were consciously written to mark events, to remember, and to celebrate.

In later Greece and Rome more elaborate records survive. In ancient Greece, 2,500 years ago, stone memorials were often the official record, or at least the one most often referred to by commentators, reflecting the continuing significance of oral communication. A written text was often not the most important version. In Greece and Rome documents were often lists, peppered with an increasing interest in the making of more complex government and commercial records. William Harris, in his study of ancient literacy, enumerates over forty different purposes for writing, ranging from ownership and commercial activity to legal and governmental work to commemoration and religious worship.[12] A dependence on orality and suspicion of written documents led to continuing means to identify authentic texts through seals and other forms of certification. For most inhabitants of the ancient world writing was a rare event, and the rising position of scribes indicates that records achieved a new importance. In late ancient Rome, for example, military clerks became essential to the military and government, providing the "document as a source of power."[13] This power has always resided with records and those who create, read, and manage them.

Greater reliance was being placed on documents. While it is virtually impossible to re-create what caused the transition from crude objects to more formal records, it is possible to perceive a transition from oral to written cultures and from societies that relied on more formalized symbols of facts and figures. Twenty-five hundred years ago the Greek historian Herodotus saw in writing and written records new potentials for memory, administration, and social order. He saw how writing could be used to keep track of a myriad of detailed activities in government and society. It was the beginning of the bureaucratic organization, as well as more systematically managing records produced by organizations, governments, and individuals. While documents in the ancient world might look different to us—on clay or in rolls—their functions and importance had already taken on modern characteristics. Even today, a glimpse at these early records make them recognizable as documents—there is writing, some symbols, a page-like form, and other similar characteristics transcending time and technology.

MEDIEVAL RECORDKEEPING

Records professionals who understand records management to be a peculiarly modern affair might be surprised by examining what occurred with records in the Middle Ages, roughly the time from the fifth to twelfth centuries. Historian Brian Stock states that "medieval society after the eleventh century was increasingly oriented towards the scribe, the written word, the literary text, and the document," although he argues that the "written did not supersede the oral." The major impact of writing and recordkeeping came in the "papal chancery, royal chanceries, and the lay notariate"—in other words in government and religious administration. Still, the "typical medieval and early modern state of affairs . . . is for orality to retain its functions within a system of graphic representation for language, as for instance it does in the notarial tribunal, which, in superseding oral record, nonetheless demands personal attendance and verbal testimony. What distinguished medieval from ancient literacy, it is arguable, was not the presence of such roles, but their variety and abundance." Stock understands "scribal practices almost invariably entered oral legal systems by imitating already functioning verbal institutions." By the eleventh or twelfth centuries, "men began to think of facts not as recorded by texts but as embodied in texts, a transition of major importance in the rise of systems of information retrieval and classification."[14]

The transition from orality to writing is a process that should interest modern records professionals because of the concern about a kind of orality with the electronic information networks. A study of English wills from 800–1100 shows how they represented a transition from oral to textual or scribal society. The wills contain references to writing, the functions of scribes, and the oral cere-monies marking the process of the wills. These records vary quite a bit, with little standardization.[15] Historian Clanchy has given us the most complete look at the transition from orality to writing. He notes that in medieval England "early charters tend to be rhetorical in tone and impressive in appearance, but they often lack the most elementary guarantees of their authenticity, such as the date and place of issue and the name of the scribe. These features were not felt to be necessary because the charter was seen as no more than an adjunct or afterthought to a traditional conveyancing ceremony involving living witnesses and symbolic gestures."[16] We can see these characteristics in the Domesday Book from the eleventh century. As one scholar examining this record con-cludes, these "volumes were regarded sufficiently highly to warrant the pro-duction of copies in cartularies, extracts in legal records, and at least three comprehensive abbreviations, by the thirteenth century."[17] There was a decided shift in the meaning of a record from "bearing witness" to being an actual written document—a *real* thing. The transition was neither smooth nor com-plete. While written records provided new communications devices and sources for authority, orality existed side by side for many centuries.[18]

This shift to a textual society brought other noticeable changes in record-keeping technologies. In Europe in the thirteenth and fourteenth centuries we see an increasing shift from parchment to paper for all records purposes, with an increasing number of royal decrees trying to regulate and ensure the quality of paper. King Pere, in 1352, complained that the Saracens of Jativa making paper were reducing its measurements and "they are making the said paper from a pulp so bad that shortly and spontaneously it rips and comes apart." He insisted that "good and useful pulp" be used, and he ordered careful inspection of the paper.[19] In 1231 Emperor Frederick II forbade the use of paper to compile public records of any variety; still, by the fifteenth century, paper had replaced animal skin and other recording media and had had a tremendous effect on printing, teaching, business transactions, writing, and literacy.[20] Paper was thought to be a product useful for documents not intended for preservation. Demand for paper increased because of new endeavors—teaching, business transactions, writing's impact on all levels of personal and organizational activ-ities, and the expansion of trade.

The attitude changes towards paper reflected a transformation in the nature of records and recordkeeping, with a strong growth in recordkeeping. Pope Innocent III (1198–1216) sent a few thousand letters a year, while Boniface VIII (1294–1303) sent as many as 50,000 a year. England's Royal Chancery used 3.63 pounds of wax a week (for sealing records) in the late 1220s and 31.9 pounds by the late 1260s.[21] The importance can be seen in something as mundane as double-entry bookkeeping. By the fourteenth century such bookkeeping "enabled European merchants, by means of precise and clearly arranged records kept in terms of quantity, to achieve comprehensive and, thereby, control of the moiling multitude of details of their economic lives. The mechanical clock enabled them to measure time, and double-entry bookkeeping enabled them to stop it—on paper, at least."[22]

Despite the growth in the quantity of records, their importance to changing and emerging organizations, and renewed efforts to manage records, the idea of recordkeeping was still remote from most people. Henri-Jean Martin argues that the "common people . . . accepted writing as something with magical powers that could set down the Word of God, keep the memory of the dead in funerary inscriptions, and invoke God and the celestial powers from crosses and shrines by country roads."[23] Records were tied to the middle and ruling classes. Robert Logan contends that "acquiring literacy and the other forms of specialized knowledge based upon it has been the economic strategy of the middle class throughout history." Writing was "used by merchants to keep records and organize commercial activities, and by municipal authorities to organize commercial civil affairs. Writing was also used to express, through literature, the secular and moral concerns of the middle class."[24]

Such new significance for records brought greater concern for their management. England's efforts, by the Crown, have been particularly well documented. As early as the fourteenth century, there had been attempts to establish central record offices for the Crown. Between 1320 and 1322 the records of the Exchequer were moved to the Tower of London, although by the end of that century record storage conditions were poor.[25] In England, in 1597, a general registration plan was approved by the Church and queen—requiring good records kept on parchment and the re-copying of paper records onto parchment. A reading from the previous week's records on Sunday was also required in order to sustain accurate accounts.[26]

For centuries afterward, governments, institutions, and individuals relied on oral communication, barter, rituals, ceremonies, and symbols in lieu of any general concept of the record. The lack of a literate population and the scarcity of writing materials inhibited the development of written documents as now known—textual, formalistic, and functionally specific. Monasteries maintained ecclesiastical archives, prepared detailed chronicles, and even maintained Crown records on occasion, but such activities were the exception rather than the rule 1,000 years ago. For a long time the most important aspects of documents were their symbolic features, typified by the Domesday Book in England.

Recordmaking changed slowly as trade, commerce, and government grew, and towns and businesses began to record not only financial transactions but such vital events as births, deaths, marriages, and taxes—a resurgence of the list-making and counting evident in ancient records. The origins of the modern bureaucratic state and organization brought with it a greater interest in order through the making of records. As learning and universities spread, there was growing appreciation for the use of documents as historical sources as well. Documents became more crucial as they were transformed into authorities to resolve legal and other disputes. Many of our most common types of documents (such as various government registers) came into prominence in these years, aided by the first university courses in recordkeeping practice. In England, there is the emergence of fairly standardized ways of recording charters, chirographs (two-party agreements), certificates (public statements), writs, financial records, legal records, cartularies (collections of deeds copied for protection and ease of reference), and registers (copies of outgoing documents). This standardization was inspired by a number of factors—the continuing interest in the symbolic qualities of records, authentication matters, preservation (such as the use of registers), continuing use, and legal requirements. This was part of a long struggle in the interplay between technology and culture, organizational needs, and individual responsibilities, as society had to develop a trust in the written, documentary form of the record. Jean Mabillon's *De re diplomatica* (1681), a treatise on the creation, function, and form of records, was a logical, if later, product of such interests. Brian Stock's history of literacy in this period reveals that the move from an oral to a written culture also brought with it a "reawakening of a wide range of critical methods for utilizing texts as evidence,"[27] of which the Mabillon volume is a later codification.

Medieval society's reliance on written documents dispels the idea of a recordkeeping "Dark Ages." In the twelfth and thirteenth centuries efforts were made to formalize or standardize orthography, abbreviations, nomenclature, and alphabetization in written texts. Procedures to deal with both forgeries and destroyed documents reflect a common notion of a document. There was a look to an official record, similar in appearance to our university diplomas, citations, and awards. In twelfth century Spain a destroyed record would be replaced by taking oaths about the content of the document and sending out individuals seeking information about the content of a record before it was redrafted.[28]

Records standardization came about slowly. Medieval English wills had self-conscious references to the *act* of writing and a great variety in form and content. Whatever records standardization had developed in the ancient era had been lost and had to be rediscovered. In the Americas, the concept of a record was also evolving. In the sixteenth century, the Incas developed quipus, or knotted cords, weighing up to four kilograms, with their interpretation depending on type of knot, the number of knots, the knots' position, and the color and ply of the string making up the knot. These cords were memory devices for narratives, genealogies, religious ceremonies, and may even have represented phonetics of the language used. Certainly by the time of the European colonies the prevailing notions of document were established and transplanted—letters, wills, receipts, minutes, and other forms readily recognizable today were in full use, adopted from the then current recordmaking practices of the colonizing nations.

These early efforts to manage records were fraught with problems. Keeping church registers in seventeenth century Virginia, closely modeled on the Anglican Church back home, proved a tough responsibility: "Frequently, it was as basic a problem as the illiteracy of church wardens or the shortage of ministers," according to James Cassedy. "Those preachers who did come to Virginia sometimes had little energy for recordkeeping after the physical demands of scratching out a living had been met. Then, as the population spread out along the rivers, the minister often lost close contact with the vital occurrences in his large parish. Sometimes the problem was as simple as the failure to obtain record books or other supplies from England."[29] Still, important records responsibilities emerged. The seventeenth-century Maryland courts took on the responsibility of "adjudicating the authenticity of documents," reflecting the recognition that handwritten texts could be easily altered.[30]

Many commentators have considered how the growth in records, along with their administration needs, developed because of the temptations to misuse these records. The concern for records was often tied up with a propagandist view of historical writing. Records seem to be used or misused as necessary. Thomas Burton, historian of the Cistercian abbey of Meaux in the early fifteenth century, made great use of documents, but this is what he wrote in his preface about them: "I have abridged their great length and illuminated their obscurities; I have read through the registers and added from the original documents whatever they omit; and finally I have combined the total results into this one volume with the greatest care."[31] In fact, such treatment of records was not uncommon, and the abuses (by modern standards) heaped upon them happened frequently.

Such records treatment suggests a very different concern for the emergence of diplomatics as a systematic approach and as the essence of a modern archival or records science. As recordkeepers know, this science, rooted in the seventeenth century as a result of dealing with imaginative uses of and forgeries of records in the few immediate centuries, has re-emerged.[32] But records professionals need to be careful about how they interpret the earlier efforts to manage records. As Canadian archivist Richard Brown argues persuasively in his analysis of recordkeeping in fourteenth-century Italy, it is easy to see the importance of governing bodies and rulers using records and recordkeeping to consolidate power *and* to misread some of these activities by superimposing modern records concepts.[33]

RECORDKEEPING IN THE PRE-INDUSTRIAL OFFICE

As the centuries passed, a stronger notion of the office, with a stress on records making and keeping, emerged. A good portion of the emerging office was tied to the development of bureaucracies and commercial firms with links to the marketplace. In the fifteenth and sixteenth centuries, writing played a role in the establishment of a European market, enabling people to "standardize transactions, arrange for billing and collection between places some distance apart and in places where wealth was distributed differently, and furnish capital to back enterprises that taken singly, were risky." Historian Martin notes that "from the bill of exchange to the letter of indulgence or the stock certificate, paper became a transferrable asset charged with multiple meanings." "To pass on to public writing," Martin argues, the "great administrative, judiciary, and financial files that line the shelves of public archives are eloquent proof of how states made a growing use of writing to gain an increasingly systematic grip on Western societies."[34] At about the same period, bureaucracy began to flourish in Europe. New offices had to be staffed and a demand rose for secretaries who could handle correspondence, write quickly and clearly when taking dictation, and draft documents at short notice. People had to be trained and the demand for and status of writing masters went up (positions with roles that could be compared to the role and status of computer systems analyst or programmers today).[35] In 1616 the new clerk of Parliament, Robert Bowyer, was required to take an oath designed specially for him and indicating the growing power associated with recordkeeping, requiring "making true entries and Records of the things done and past in the same," keeping "secret all such matters as shall be treated in his said parliaments and not disclose the same before they shall be published but to such as it ought to be disclosed unto."[36]

There are paradoxes in the increasing concern for records management. Despite increasing interests in records, government records in the seventeenth and eighteenth centuries were not necessarily well managed. In England there were repeated inquiries into the condition of public records and their storage and access, all producing bleak reports. In 1709, a report on the Court of Wards records discovered that they were "neglected, and in a perishing condition, in a Fishmonger's house, in Fish Yard near Westminster Hall . . . and the Fishmonger did what he thought fit with the records."[37] A 1732 report, according to Charles F. Mullett, reported on nineteen repositories and described the same conditions: "damp, dirt, and decay; leaky roofs; inadequate space and inconvenience; even totally extraneous contents such as spiritous liquors and painters' supplies."[38] There had been attempts to establish central record offices for the Crown's records as early as the 1320s. The records of the Exchequer were moved to the Tower of London, calendars and registers compiled, and recopying done. By the sixteenth century, when an interest in historical research was developing, the records of the English government had been dispersed by the proliferation of the bureaucracy. Records were stored everywhere, including the homes of officeholders. Storage and security were often the personal responsibilities, borne by private funds, of these officeholders. With the rise of private libraries and the great collectors of the English Renaissance, public records were often intermingled in these private accumulations. Even the rise of

public office oaths, specifying the exact conditions public records were expected
to be maintained in, did little to improve their maintenance. Investigations into
public recordkeeping in the early eighteenth century suggested that recordkeeping had been poor for centuries.[39]

That the English and other Europeans understood the value of records can be
seen in the fashion that they dealt with the records of native peoples and colonists in the heyday of the American colonies. The Spanish, in an effort to
stamp out Mayan idolatry, looted and burned many of their codices and manuscripts in the sixteenth century.[40] As English control over the colonies tightened
so did the specificity of its instructions about records and recordkeeping. In 1697
and afterwards, all governors who were sent from England to the colonies were
given printed copies of all acts relating to trade, with books of rates and blank
specimens of all certificates.[41] Creating and keeping records still proved to be
difficult tasks. Many governors found it hard to get vital data because of political
resistance, loss or unavailability of records, religious diversity, and disruptions
caused by frontier hostilities.[42] There were many different motivations present
in the colonial era for good recordkeeping, as there are many motivations at
work today. Cassedy writes "while Virginians collected vital data largely to
fulfill their obligations to Company, Church, and Crown in England, New Englanders did so chiefly to satisfy their own internal needs and aspirations as a
self-conscious community."[43] For New Englanders, the Old Testament showed
the value of enumerating tribes and nations: "For a people who came to regard
themselves as a chosen people it was imperative to preserve records of their
vital data in order to maintain the continuities they had perceived between earlier
chosen people and themselves."[44] As a result of such concerns, the original vital
records legislation of Massachusetts Bay was revised or renewed seven times
between 1639 and 1692: "The orderly methods implicit in the systematic collection and recording of vital data fitted in well with the concepts of thrift, hard
work, sobriety, and piety which characterized the Protestant Ethic."[45] The modern records professional would not mind seeing these attributes re-introduced
into their organizations.

Despite the increasing activity on behalf of records management, there were
contrary or countervailing forces working against such management. For these
and many other reasons, records were not completely accepted. In the seventeenth century we had *bella diplomatica* ("wars over documents"), arguments
"about which archival documents were genuine, which Catholic institutions had
a historical foundation, and which saints had actually lived."[46] These wars gave
rise to the early record sciences, such as paleography and sphragistics. Thomas
Lechford, in his 1642 *Plain Dealing: or News from New-England*, criticized
New England government, one of his complaints being that the "want of proceeding duly upon record," that is, legal proceedings were carried on orally
rather than by exchange of documents. The New England magistrates tried to
correct this with the Body of Liberties of 1641, providing that if the plaintiff
filed a written declaration, the defendant was to have "libertie and time to give

in his answer in writing, And soe in all further proceedings between partie and partie." In 1647 a law required that written declarations be filed in all civil cases in due time before court opened, so that the defendant would have time to prepare his written answer—although it took decades for written "pleadings" to become common.[47]

Conflicts over records were overshadowed by the generally poor conditions of records storage and maintenance. Such poor conditions enabled pioneer documentary editors like Ebenezer Hazard to win support for his plan to collect and publish public records and private papers.[48] If we examine the work of early historical editors, what we discover is that their work mainly consisted of gathering up records and papers scattered about and neglected, whether they were government or personal.[49] It was not until the late eighteenth century that we see much of an effort to compile and publish records.[50] Some of the same activity is evident in the quest to compile laws from the scattered colonial records, what one legal historian has termed an "orgy of code-making," even in the seventeenth century.[51] Nearly every colony passed laws regarding the better keeping of the official public records (Virginia, 1645, 1674, 1713; Maryland, 1715, 1716; North Carolina 1738; South Carolina, 1694, 1720, 1736).[52] One historian argues that Americans had to develop a new set of legal precedents because the judges there were not so well-versed in English law: "This is why the assembly compelled magistrates to purchase lawbooks and clerks of court to keep on record copies of all Virginia statutes."[53] This is also why law dictionaries, case reports, books on philosophical and procedural aspects of law, and books with advice on how to prepare and keep legal records—explaining the importance of records, the derivations of particular documents, their functions, and the conditions by which they should be used—were popular.[54]

The tendency has been to dismiss the American settlers' early interests as being only survival and as not encompassing recordkeeping, explaining the problems they had in managing their government, organizational, and personal records.[55] There is much evidence to refute this. In Connecticut, in 1644, the creation of the town meeting clerk who had to answer by the following oath, comes to mind when we want to understand the earnestness by which the colonists strove to maintain records: "Swear by the dreadfull name of the ever-living God that you will keep an entry of all grants, deeds of sale or mortgages of lands, and all marriages, births, deaths and other writings brought to you and deliver copies when required of you."[56] Even in the most severe of circumstances, there were individuals committed to recording histories—it was a part of survival. John Winthrop's history of the Massachusetts Bay colony was started as a journal primarily as information for others to join into the venture.[57]

There was a practical side. Louis B. Wright, in a classic assessment, notes that "when colonial writers sat down with a goose-quill pen and an ink pot, their minds were usually not focused upon posterity but upon some present problem. Most of them were busy and practical men who wrote, as they read, with a purpose, and that purpose was not to provide entertainment for their descendants."[58] Similar practical purposes can be seen in the Quaker "spiritual autobiographies," meant to serve as guides to others in their spiritual quests, or in the Puritans' history writing as a "tribal rite, almost a religious act."[59] Even the seemingly less religious Virginians were on a quest to start over, and their records reflected such concerns.[60] This is different from our own modern sensibilities. By using machines to write, we look back on the use of a quill pen and iron ink as a romanticized "physical act of writing."[61]

These practical interests were reflected in a renewed concern for building records repositories. In England, in the eighteenth and nineteenth centuries, records management and preservation were seen primarily as the mission to establish a central repository. The epitome of this effort was the creation of the Public Record Office in 1838, following six Royal Commissions reviewing the state of public records, but without making any real progress in the management of public records.[62] In the American colonies we see the same kinds of efforts in enacting legislation and building repositories. South Carolina passed a law in 1694 "for the better and more certain keeping and preserving of old registers and Publique Writings." Similar laws were enacted in 1698, 1719, 1739, and 1758 for the safekeeping and inspecting of public records. Maryland passed laws like this in 1692 and through the eighteenth century.[63] Nearly all of the colonies set requirements for careful recording in bound volumes, for the recording of all the activities of the government body, for careful copying of records in poor condition or for reference copies, and for compilation and printing of the laws.[64] There were other efforts to create centralized repositories. In Virginia the county court gradually moved into a central place in colonial culture and the courthouse became a more impressive structure. Courthouses were located at crossroads near the county's central area, on a green, with a tavern or ordinary nearby, and by the 1720s old wooden frame structures were being replaced by brick and stucco buildings.[65] By the early eighteenth century deliberate planning was being done, such as in Annapolis and Williamsburg, to construct cities out around prominent public buildings, many of these buildings holding official records.[66] By then the location of a courthouse could be the subject of acrimonious and protracted debate, partly because these facilities held the public records essential to not just governance but the economic and social well-being of the residents.[67]

In a few colonies separate buildings were constructed for records storage. In Maryland, after an inspection of the poor condition of the public records, Governor Benedict Leonard Calvert urged the construction of a "separate Repository for Our Old Records" as a "Security so essential to preserve the Rights of the [Marylanders] from the Injury of Common Accidents." In 1730 a brick building was constructed, sixteen feet long and twelve feet wide, with a tile or slate roof, two windows on each side, and shutters or iron bars on the windows.[68] Virginia also constructed a public record office after the 1747 fire that destroyed the capitol building in Williamsburg. From 1748 to 1780, when the state capitol was moved to Richmond, the building, still standing, was the official repository for the government records.[69] Wood buildings and wood burning fireplaces led to many problems. The capitol building of Virginia burned three times between 1698 and 1746, and this was typical of what occurred in many colonies and later states.[70] The buildings were often subject to severe climatic conditions. In 1752 a quantity of South Carolina's public records were destroyed by a hurricane. In the surveyor-general's office, records were found "floating about in four and an half feet salt water, and are thereby much injured and defaced; and some lost, notwithstanding the utmost care was then taken by the memorialist to save them, who has ever since used all possible endeavours to render them useful by sending them to ovens, sunning & airing them when weather would permit and resorting."[71] Inspections of public records were necessary because they were subject to such deteriorating conditions. A typical statement by North Carolina Governor Gabriel Johnston in 1748 was that "the Publick Records lye in a miserable condition one part of them near the Virginia Line in a place without Lock or Key; a great part of them in the Secretary's House at Cape Fear above Two Hundred Miles Distance from the other. Some few of 'em at the Clerk of the Council's house at Newbern, so that in whatever part of the Colony a man happens to be, if he wants to consult any paper or record he must send some Hundreds of Miles before he can come at it."[72] Part of this was due to the personal financial *value* (for officeholders) of the records as well, leading to the common practice of local officials maintaining public records in their own homes for convenience and protection of their lucrative fees generated from the records.

Records in the early modern era were often controversial. In the late 1680s William Penn's difficulties with governing his colony prompted the proprietor to cancel all existing laws and create new ones as part of establishing stricter control over the province. The colonials resisted in part by refusing to turn over official records.[73] A controversial change of government in South Carolina brought records into the debate as seen in the 1719 legislative act against the removal of public records: "Sundry evil-disposed and disaffected persons, in open and manifest violation and breach of the several laws of force in this Settlement, and in opposition to the now present establishment, have made away with several of the publick and private acts of Assembly, as also all the records of grants, mortgages, registries, and other titles of the several inhabitants to their respective lands, as also all the original wills, and divers other publick records of this Settlement, or concealed the same."[74] Similar contests over records happened in Maryland in 1739.[75] The greatest dangers facing official records and even personal papers resulted from the American Revolution. A daughter of a Tory official wrote that the Highlanders in Georgia "ripped open feather beds, destroyed the public papers and records, and scattered everything about the streets."[76] This may have been why records of the executive department from 1778 to 1785 were described in 1810 by Governor D. B. Mitchell as being in so "mutilated and mangled situation that they are liable to be lost and entirely destroyed unless they are transcribed into durable bound Books. . . . The frequency of applications for extracts and copies of papers having reference to proceedings of those times, renders it necessary that they should be put in some regular order by which those applications could with some facility be complied with."[77]

Fires were also a prevalent problem during this era, rivaling, at least in destruction and inconvenience, the problems caused by political disturbances. When the Georgia state house suffered a fire in 1833, it was just seventeen days later that a law passed "that the offices of the several departments of the State House be required to arrange, classify, and properly endorse such papers and documents of ancient date and little immediate use may be in their respective offices, and deposit them in some safe place in the basement story of the State House for safe keeping, and ready access, that the offices themselves may be no longer encumbered by them."[78] In 1883 the Kimball House in Atlanta burned. Because many legislators were staying there, papers of the legislature were destroyed as well, leading to the passage of a law authorizing the governor to find "some safe and suitable place in the City of Atlanta, as nearly fireproof as possible in which to store and keep such of the public records and archives as can be dispensed with by the various officers of the several departments of State."[79]

Other challenges awaited the colonists in early America. One historian describes how the effort of surviving sometimes worked against certain aspects of recordkeeping. In the seventeenth century the colonists tended to discuss death rates only in qualitative rather than quantitative terms. Why? "There was little point in keeping records of the totals, since the number of deaths was in any case beyond the control of the living and since reports of high mortality would only drive away future settlers."[80] Another historian describes how, even with some efforts to regulate the kinds of records kept, the early seventeenth-century New England colonists' recordkeeping was sporadic and the vast majority could not read anyway.[81] Mercantilism changed all that, putting greater weight on accurate figures. After 1680 the Crown expected actual trade and population figures. These figures "provided an empirical underpinning for mercantilism, an elaborate theory of politics and economics, which postulated that the number of people in a country was a component of a country's wealth and that the balance of trade as measured by import and export statistics, was the crucial sign of economic well-being."[82] The mercantile colonial policy produced increased needs for statistics, as well as greater access to official records. The construction of an elaborate administrative structure of naval officers, collectors and receivers, customs officials, and vice-admiralty courts produced new varieties of colonial records as well as a desire for better information from all the records.[83]

Mercantilism, prosperity, a sort of settling in, and a concern for English rights all contributed to a higher profile of records and their administration. By the eighteenth century in Virginia, the county court had become an important social force because of its recording role. Each year residents would bring in servants and slaves to have their ages documented for taxes and the compiled lists were placed on the church doors. The courts' importance escalated as well because of their responsibility for maintaining all land records, marriage licenses, and militia rosters.[84] Everywhere, there came stronger efforts to regulate record-keeping. The laws established for the Mississippi Territory in the late eighteenth century included provisions for recordkeeping by the judges of probate, county registers, county treasurers, and other officers. The judge in the courts of probate "shall record last wills and testaments, and make entries of the granting of letters testamentary, and letters of administration: he shall receive, put on file, and carefully preserve, all bonds, inventories, accounts and other documents, necessary to be perpetuated in his office."[85]

The desire for improved records regulation grew as the mechanical means of creating records improved and gained a stronger hold in organizations, government, and the home. Early methods of mechanical recordkeeping included press copying, where a screw-powered letter press was used with a press book, a bound volume of blank pages, and a tissue paper page. The freshly written letter was placed under a dampened page, while the other pages were protected by oilcloths, creating an impression of the letter. This device was patented by James Watt in 1780, but it only came into general use in the second half of the nineteenth century.[86] Such inventiveness in making and maintaining records suggests that we have been a recordkeeping people. Embedded in the Constitution is the aim of creating a census for purposes of determining representation and other purposes, and the census evolved into a major information and recordmaking enterprise. The 1850 census was far more extensive than earlier versions, drawing on the emerging statistical sciences. Apportionment for political representation became a minor part of the process. The connection of the census even became tied up in the early development of the computer when Herman Hollerith in 1881 began work on a new and quicker means for tabulating returns, leading to his electrical tabulating machine, first used extensively in the 1890 census. Not long after, in the early twentieth century, the federal government established a permanent census office.[87]

By the early nineteenth century a greater concern for the management of records seemed to be in evidence everywhere. In France there was founding of the Ecole des Chartes in 1821, offering the first formal education about the administration of records; the publication of the first archives manual in 1860; and publication of other major treatises on records from 1883 to 1895. In Germany a major journal on archival theory and practice was published in 1834–1836 and another started in 1860 and then 1876; handbooks and manuals appeared in 1889, 1890 and 1900. In the Netherlands the manual associated with the birth of the modern archives movement was published in 1898.[88] The increasing volume of records, recognized as a problem as early as the seventeenth century, had gained recognition as the *foremost* problem by the nineteenth century, and this led to new efforts to formulate principles for the management of the records, especially the principle of provenance. The Prussian State Archives issued in 1881 the regulations on this principle, requiring "arrangement according to source and the maintenance of the order and file designations assigned in the agency of origin." "Archival principles and theory are based on and validated by experience or practice," writes archival historian Maynard Brichford. "The principle of provenance was a response to changing conditions in the nineteenth century. These included the reorganization of postrevolutionary national governments; new types of records and new governmental functions, in part due to the secularization of religious institutions and the centralization of power; shifts between centralized and decentralized systems; systemizers who sought to cope with increasing volumes of records; scholars who created a new clientele for archives; library classification systems; and bureaucratic and professional pressures for regulations and standards."[89]

Although there was no development of an archives or records profession in nineteenth-century America, many of the concerns about records were prevalent and widely shared. Individual state governments were also trying to control the growth in the volume of records. Georgia in 1879 passed a law allowing the secretary of state to destroy certain election returns because the accumulation during the previous ten years had become very great; the law authorized the state's secretary "to destroy by burning all the election returns now on file in his office, of the elections of all officers who have served out the time for which they were elected" and authorized such destruction every four years.[90] There was also increased interest in facilities that would ensure the preservation of records of continuing value, such as constructing "fireproof" buildings wherever and whenever possible.

The real change in recordkeeping can be seen, however, in what began to occur in the typical office. After all, records laws and the construction of repositories can be traced back hundreds of years in America and in Europe,[91] but the nature of the office really had not changed during all this time. As one commentator notes, "The personal nature of the employer's control of his clerks was reinforced by the lack of common standards of office procedure: each employer developed his own." After the American Civil War the office would be reorganized into departments, new occupations (such as file and shipping clerks) would emerge, and old occupations (copyists) would finally disappear and be replaced by stenographers and typists.[92] The office of this period reflected very minor change over the previous centuries. Alfred Chandler notes that recordkeeping was the same between the Americans of the 1790s and Italians of the 1390s, a notion difficult to comprehend in our era of rapid change. In the merchant's office in the mid-nineteenth century "a business was carried on in much the same manner as it had been in fourteenth-century Venice or Florence. The staff included only a handful of male clerks. There were two or three copiers, a bookkeeper, a cash keeper, and a confidential clerk who handled the business when the partners were not in the office." Chandler contends that the "most advanced accounting methods in 1840 were still those of Italian double-entry bookkeeping—techniques which had changed little over 500 years. The major differences between the accounting practices of colonial merchants and those of the more specialized mercantile firms of the nineteenth century was that the larger number of transactions handled by the latter caused them to keep their books in more meticulous manner.''[93]

The *needs* for recordkeeping were beginning to out race the *techniques* for records creation and storage. The failure of the pigeonhole desk and the success of the vertical filing cabinet reflect what was occurring during this era. Donald Norman suggests that ''whereas the desk provides a fixed number of locations with no aids to organization, the filing cabinet provides an unlimited number of positions with few constraints on size, except that the items all have to fit within the standardized folder.'' Norman believes that the ''modern business would not have been possible without this most important cognitive artifact.''[94]

Personal efforts to cope with the need for better records creation and keeping were also evident. Thomas Jefferson kept a detailed record of all his letters from 1783 to his death in 1826, an indication of the importance he placed on the utility of his correspondence.[95] The rising interest in records can also be seen in penmanship books and handwriting manuals in the eighteenth and nineteenth centuries which impressed upon students the importance of work by having them copying ''pithy sayings'' from copybooks that ''also often included such mercantile forms as bills of exchange, bills of lading, letters of credit, receipts, invoices, and bookkeeping entries.''[96] ''Script emerged as a medium of the self,'' argues one historian.[97] Even gender issues related to the teaching of handwriting reflects who maintains records and why they need to be kept: ''Boys learned a fast and legible script, the mercantile running hand, suitable for business and public affairs, while girls advanced to the reduced-sized and painstakingly shaded ladies' epistolary, appropriate for private correspondence.''[98] Later, with the rising use of typewriters and other office automation devices, we detect a new interest in handwriting, especially in older calligraphic traditions, that probably corresponds to the late twentieth century's interest in diary keeping. All of these developments were part of the birthing pains for the modern records era.

NOTES

1. Denise Schmandt-Besserat, ''How Writing Came About,'' *Zeitschrift fur Papyrologie und Epigraphik* 47 (1982): 1–5.

2. Denise Schmandt-Besserat, ''The Earliest Precursor of Writing,'' *Scientific American* 238 (June 1978): 58.

3. Henri-Jean Martin, *The History and Power of Writing*, trans. Lydia G. Cochrane (Chicago: University of Chicago Press, 1994), p. 8.

4. James Gregory Bradsher, ''Ebla's Royal Archives,'' *Information Development* 1 (October 1985): 238–243. For a full study, refer to Jean Bottero, *Mesopotamia: Writing, Reasoning, and the Gods* (Chicago: University of Chicago Press, 1992).

5. Donald Jackson, *The Story of Writing* (New York: Taplinger Publishing Co., 1981), p. 22.

6. Quoted in Ernst Posner, *Archives in the Ancient World* (Cambridge, Mass.: Harvard University Press, 1972), p. 114.

7. Jackson, *The Story of Writing*, pp. 41, 43.

8. Anne-Marie Schwirtlich, "Archives in the Roman Republic," *Archives and Manuscripts* 9 (September 1981): 19–29.

9. Michael Grant, *Greek and Roman Historians: Information and Misinformation* (London: Routledge, 1995), p. 34.

10. Arnaldo Momigliano, *The Classical Foundations of Modern Historiography* (Berkeley: University of California Press, 1990), p. 6.

11. Robert K. Logan, *The Alphabet Effect: The Impact of the Phonetic Alphabet on the Development of Western Civilization* (New York: William Morrow and Co., 1986), p. 166.

12. William V. Harris, *Ancient Literacy* (Cambridge, Mass.: Harvard University Press, 1989), pp. 26–27.

13. Harris, *Ancient Literacy*, p. 218.

14. Brian Stock, *The Implications of Literacy: Written Language and Models of Interpretation in the Eleventh and Twelfth Centuries* (Princeton, N.J.: Princeton University Press, 1983), pp. 16, 42, 47, 62.

15. Brenda Danet and Bryna Bogoch, "From Oral Ceremony to Written Document: The Transitional Language of Anglo-Saxon Wills," *Language and Communication* 12, no. 2 (1992): 95–122.

16. M. T. Clanchy, " 'Tenacious Letters': Archives and Memory in the Middle Ages," *Archivaria* no. 11 (Winter 1980/1981): 123. See also *From Memory to Written Record: England 1066–1307*, 2nd ed. (Cambridge: Blackwell, 1993).

17. Helen Forde, *Domesday Preserved* (London: Her Majesty's Stationery Office, Public Record Office, 1986), p. 3.

18. James M. O'Toole, " 'Commendatory Letters': An Archival Reading of the Venerable Bede," *American Archivist* 61 (Fall 1998): 266–286.

19. Robert I. Burns, "The Paper Revolution in Europe: Crusader Valencia's Paper Industry—A Technological and Behavioral Breakthrough," *Pacific Historical Review* 49 (1980): 23.

20. Lucien Febvre and Henri-Jean Martin, *The Coming of the Book: The Impact of Printing 1450–1800* (London: Verso, 1984), pp. 29–40.

21. Alfred W. Crosby, *The Measure of Reality: Quantification and Western Society, 1250–1600* (Cambridge: Cambridge University Press, 1997), p. 133.

22. Crosby, *The Measure of Reality*, p. 208.

23. Martin, *The History and Power of Writing*, p. 134.

24. Robert K. Logan, *The Fifth Language: Learning a Living in the Computer Age* (Toronto: Stoddart, 1995), pp. 151, 158–159.

25. See Maurice F. Bond, "The Formation of the Archives of Parliament, 1497–1691," *Journal of the Society of Archivists* 1 (October 1957): 151–158; Edwin Green, "The Management of Exchequer Records in the 1560s," *Journal of the Society of Archivists* 5 (April 1974): 25–30; Elizabeth M. Hallam, "The Tower of London as a Record Office," *Journal of the Society of Archivists* 14 (Spring 1979): 3–10.

26. J. Charles Cox, *The Parish Registers of England* (Totowa, N.J.: EP Publishing Ltd., Rowman and Littlefield, 1974; org. pub. 1910), p. 6.

27. Stock, *The Implications of Literacy*, p. 60.

28. Lawrence J. McCrank, "Documenting Reconquest and Reform: The Growth of Archives in the Medieval Crown of Aragon," *American Archivist* 56 (Spring 1993): 256–318.

29. James H. Cassedy, *Demography in Early America: Beginnings of the Statistical Mind 1600–1800* (Cambridge, Mass.: Harvard University Press, 1969), pp. 17–18.

30. David D. Hall, *Cultures of Print: Essays in the History of the Book* (Amherst: University of Massachusetts Press, 1996), p. 103.

31. Antonia Gransden, *Historical Writing in England; II: c. 1307 to the Early Sixteenth Century* (Ithaca, N.Y.: Cornell University Press, 1982), p. 362.

32. In North America, the source for the re-birth of interest has been due to the writings and presentations of Luciana Duranti, most notably her "Diplomatics: New Uses for an Old Science," run in *Archivaria*: Part I, no. 28 (Summer 1989): 7–27; Part II, no. 29 (Winter 1989–1990), 4–17; Part III, no. 30 (Summer 1990): 4–20; Part IV, no. 31 (Winter 1990–1991): 10–25; Part V, no. 32 (Summer 1991): 6–24; and Part VI, no. 33 (Winter 1991–1992): 6–24. Duranti's work is groundbreaking in this continent (and it has now been published in one volume by Scarecrow in 1998), but it is not alone. See, for example, Olivier Guyotjeannin, "The Expansion of Diplomatics as a Discipline," *American Archivist* 59 (Fall 1996): 414–421; Bernard Barbiche, "Diplomatics of Modern Official Documents (Sixteenth-Eighteenth Centuries): Evaluation and Perspectives," ibid., 422–436; Bruno Delmas, "Manifesto for a Contemporary Diplomatics: From Institutional Documents to Organic Information," ibid., 438–452; Elizabeth Yakel, "The Way Things Work: Procedures, Processes, and Institutional Records," ibid., 454–464; Francis Blouin, "A Framework for a Consideration of Diplomatics in the Electronic Environment," ibid., 466–479; Elisabeth Parinet, "Diplomatics and Institutional Photos," ibid., 480–485; Nancy Bartlett, "Diplomatics for Photographic Images: Academic Exoticism?" ibid., 486–494.

33. Richard Brown, "Death of a Renaissance Record-Keeper: The Murder of Tomasso da Tortona in Ferrara, 1385," *Archivaria* 44 (Fall 1997): 1–43. The manner in which diplomatics has been pushed by Duranti and her followers reminds one of the recent troubles facing literary studies and the humanities, a feeling of these problems presented by John M. Ellis, *Literature Lost: Social Agendas and the Corruption of the Humanities* (New Haven, Conn.: Yale University Press, 1997). Ellis argues, among other things, that the "theory culture also has its own language, which all aspirants to membership must learn to speak and which functions to preserve an otherwise unstable situation in many ways" (p. 201). This implies a rigidity of theory that is certainly associated with the neo-Jenksonians who follow English archivist Hilary Jenkinson and who have rediscovered diplomatics as not only an essential but the only acceptable core to an archival science.

34. Martin, *The History and Power of Writing*, pp. 284, 285, 286, 287.

35. A. S. Osley, *Scribes and Sources: Handbook of the Chancery Hand in the Sixteenth Century* (Boston: David R. Godine, 1980), p. 19.

36. Quoted on p. 154 of Bond, "The Formation of the Archives of Parliament, 1497–1691."

37. Quoted on p. 221 in Elizabeth M. Hallam, "Problems with Record Keeping in Early Eighteenth Century London: Some Pictorial Representations of the State Paper Office, 1705–1706," *Journal of the Society of Archivists* 6 (October 1979): 219–226.

38. Charles F. Mullett, "The 'Better Reception, Preservation, and More Convenient Use' of Public Records in Eighteenth-Century England," *American Archivist* 27 (1964): 203–204.

39. See Green, "The Management of Exchequer Records in the 1560s"; Hallam, "The Tower of London as a Record Office"; Bond, "The Formation of the Archives of

Parliament, 1497–1691''; Hallam, "Problems with Record Keeping in Early Eighteenth Century London''; V. H. Galbraith, "The Tower as an Exchequer Record Office in the Reign of Edward II," in A. G. Little and F. M. Powicke, eds., *Essays in Medieval History Presented to Thomas Frederick Tout* (Manchester: Privately printed, 1925), pp. 231–247.

40. Brian Fagan, *Elusive Treasure: The Story of Early Archaelogists in the Americas* (New York: Charles Scribners' Sons, 1977), pp. 35–38.

41. Charles M. Andrews, *The Colonial Period of American History: England's Commercial and Colonial Policy*, vol. 4 (New Haven, Conn.: Yale University Press, 1938), p. 176.

42. Cassedy, *Demography in Early America*, p. 75.

43. Cassedy, *Demography in Early America*, p. 23.

44. Cassedy, *Demography in Early America*, p. 26.

45. Cassedy, *Demography in Early America*, p. 32.

46. Anthony Grafton, *The Footnote: A Curious History* (Cambridge, Mass.: Harvard University Press, 1997), p. 167.

47. Daniel J. Boorstin, *The Americans: The Colonial Experience* (New York: Random House, 1958), p. 26.

48. Fred Shelley, "Ebenezer Hazard: America's First Historical Editor," *William and Mary Quarterly* 12 (January 1955): 44–73.

49. See, for example, Roland M. Baumann, "Samuel Hazard: Editor and Archivist for the Keystone State," *Pennsylvania Magazine of History and Biography* 107 (April 1983): 195–215.

50. Lester J. Cappon, "American Historical Editors before Jared Sparks: 'They Will Plant a Forest . . . ,' " *William and Mary Quarterly* 30, 3rd series, (July 1973): 375–400.

51. G. B. Warden, "Law Reform in England and New England, 1620 to 1660," *William and Mary Quarterly*, 3rd series, 35 (July 1978): 668–690.

52. J. G. De Roulhac Hamilton, "Three Centuries of Southern Records, 1607–1907," *Journal of Southern History* 10 (February 1944): 3–36.

53. Warren M. Billings, "Law and Culture in the Colonial Chesapeake Area," *Southern Studies* 17 (Winter 1978): 343.

54. Warren M. Billings, "English Legal Literature as a Source of Law and Legal Practice for Seventeenth-Century Virginia," *Virginia Magazine of History and Biography* 87 (October 1979): 403–416.

55. Such as J. G. De Roulhac Hamilton, "Three Centuries of Southern Records, 1607–1907," *Journal of Southern History* 10 (February 1944): 4.

56. Quoted in Bruce C. Daniels, "The Political Structure of Local Government in Colonial Connecticut," in Bruce C. Daniels, ed., *Town and County: Essays on the Structure of Local Government in the American Colonies* (Middleton, Conn.: Wesleyan University Press, 1978), p. 65.

57. Richard S. Dunn, "John Winthrop Writes His Journal," *William and Mary Quarterly*, 3rd series, 41 (April 1984): 185–212.

58. Louis B. Wright, *The Cultural Life of the American Colonies 1607–1763*, New American Nation Series (New York: Harper and Row, 1957), pp. 154–155.

59. Peter Gay, *A Loss of Mastery: Puritan Historians in Colonial America* (Berkeley: University of California Press, 1966), pp. 54, 67, 69.

60. T. H. Breen, *Puritans and Adventurers: Change and Persistence in Early America* (New York: Oxford University Press, 1980).

61. Anne Fadiman, *Ex Libris: Confessions of a Common Reader* (New York: Farrar, Straus and Giroux, 1998), p. 90.

62. Aidan Lawes, *Chancery Lane: "The Strong Box of the Empire"* (Kew, Surrey, United Kingdom: Public Record Office Publications, 1996); see also Elizabeth M. Hallam and Michael Roper, "The Capital and the Records of the Nation: Seven Centuries of Housing the Public Records in London," *London Journal* 4 (May 1978): 73–94.

63. R. H. Woody, "The Public Records of South Carolina," *American Archivist* 2 (October 1939): 244–247; Richard J. Cox, "Public Records in Colonial Maryland," *American Archivist* 37 (April 1974): 263–275.

64. The best account of this is H. G. Jones, *For History's Sake: The Preservation and Publication of North Carolina History 1663–1903* (Chapel Hill: University of North Carolina Press, 1966).

65. A. G. Roeber, "Authority, Law, and Custom: The Rituals of Court Day in Tidewater Virginia, 1720 to 1750," *William and Mary Quarterly*, 3rd series, 37 (January 1980): 29–52. See also Warren M. Billings, "The Growth of Political Institutions in Virginia, 1634 to 1676," *William and Mary Quarterly*, 3rd series, 31 (April 1974): 225–242.

66. John W. Reps, *Tidewater Towns: City Planning in Colonial Virginia and Maryland* (Williamsburg, Va.: Colonial Williamsburg Foundation, 1972).

67. E. Lee Shephard, " 'The Ease and Convenience of the People': Courthouse Locations in Spotsylvania County, 1720–1840," *Virginia Magazine of History and Biography* 87 (July 1979): 279–299.

68. Cox, "Public Records in Colonial Maryland," p. 272.

69. Louis H. Manarin, "A Building . . . for the Preservation of the Public Records," *Virginia Cavalcade* (Summer 1974): 22–31.

70. Hamilton, "Three Centuries of Southern Records," p. 11.

71. Woody, "Public Records of South Carolina," p. 246.

72. Jones, *For History's Sake*, pp. 41, 44.

73. Louis B. Wright, *The Colonial Civilization of North America 1607–1763* (London: Eyre and Spottiswoode, 1949), p. 184.

74. Woody, "Public Records of South Carolina," p. 246.

75. Cox, "Public Records in Colonial Maryland," pp. 269–271.

76. Josephine Hart Brandon, "A History of the Official Records of the Colony and State of Georgia," Ph.D., diss., Emory University, 1974, p. 129.

77. Brandon, "A History of the Official Records," pp. 205–206

78. Brandon, "A History of the Official Records," pp. 211–212.

79. Brandon, "A History of the Official Records," p. 290.

80. Patricia Cline Cohen, *A Calculating People: The Spread of Numeracy in Early America* (Chicago: University of Chicago Press, 1982), p. 56.

81. David Cressy, *Coming Over: Migration and Communication Between England and New England in the Seventeenth Century* (Cambridge: Cambridge University Press, 1987).

82. Cohen, *A Calculating People*, p. 77.

83. Andrews, *The Colonial Period of American History*, vol. 4; Cassedy, *Democracy in Early America*.

84. Robert Wheeler, "The County Court in Colonial Virginia," in Daniels, ed., *Town and County*, pp. 120–123.

85. Historical Records Survey, *Mississippi Territorial Statutes 1799* (Birmingham, Ala.: Historical Records Survey, 1939), p. 25.

86. JoAnne Yates, *Control Through Communication: The Rise of System in American Management* (Baltimore: Johns Hopkins University Press, 1989), pp. 26–27.

87. Margo J. Anderson, *The American Census: A Social History* (New Haven, Conn.: Yale University Press, 1988).

88. Maynard Brichford, "The Origins of Modern European Archival Theory," *Midwestern Archivist* 7, no. 2 (1982): 87–101.

89. Maynard Brichford, "The Provenance of Provenance in Germanic Areas," *Provenance* 7, no. 2 (Fall 1989): 54–70 (quotations from pp. 63 and 69).

90. Brandon, "A History of the Official Records," pp. 283–284.

91. We need to be careful in differentiating between *interest* in recordkeeping and records with *actual* care given them and their management. Consider New York state government. While there were many instances of interest in records from the mid-seventeenth century onward, it was not until 1971 that a state archives law passed and until the end of that decade that a state archives was staffed in a serious manner; see Bruce W. Dearstyne, "Development of the New York State Archives Program," *The Bookmark* 39 (Winter 1981): 67–71.

92. Margery W. Davies, *Woman's Place Is at the Typewriter: Office Work and Office Workers 1870–1920* (Philadelphia: Temple University Press, 1982), p. 20.

93. Alfred D.Chandler, Jr., *The Visible Hand: The Managerial Revolution in American Business* (Cambridge, Mass.: Belknap Press of Harvard University Press, 1977), pp. 16, 37, 37–38.

94. Donald A. Norman, *Things That Make Us Smart: Defending Human Attributes in the Age of the Machine* (Reading, Mass.: Addison-Wesley Publishing Co., 1993), pp. 160, 161.

95. See Andrew Burstein, "Jefferson and the Familiar Letter," *Journal of the Early Republic* 14 (Summer 1994): 195–220.

96. Tamara Plakins Thornton, *Handwriting in America: A Cultural History* (New Haven, Conn.: Yale University Press, 1996), p. 9.

97. Thornton, *Handwriting in America*, p. xiii.

98. Thornton, *Handwriting in America*, p. 56.

3

The Birth of the Modern
Records Regime and Profession

In the space of a few decades in the midst of the Industrial Revolution, the means for producing a record moved from pen and hand to nearly complete mechanization. Economic, organizational, and societal implications followed, some foreseen, some completely unanticipated. Out of this emerged the semblance of a records profession, part of the professionalization of society and its organizations. Whether the source of this profession was the file clerks, librarians, historians, or some combination depends upon one's perception of modern records management. Nevertheless, as the modern records profession developed, the focus of its labors, the record, seemed to get lost briefly amidst information concerns. Technology, with its propensity to generate chaos, also worked against the orderly managing of records.

MECHANIZATION OF THE OFFICE

The mechanization of the office and the organization's records began much earlier than many modern records professionals, used to the rapid changes of office automation, assume. Engineer James Watt patented in 1780 the letter book, where a press and damp tissue were used to make copies, and not long after Ralph Wedgwood patented an early type of carbon paper. By the end of the nineteenth century, David Gestetner introduced stencil copying.[1] With these changes came a new concern for system and order. Well into the nineteenth century papers were stuck on spikes or tied in bundles, creating more than a few challenges for even the smallest organization, requiring everything to be moved to locate a single document and minimizing the use of records. The vertical file, as one solution, was introduced in 1892[2] and had a great impact assisting business "organize and make accessible the growing amount of written correspondence and documentation''[3] by bringing together incoming, outgoing, and internal correspondence, and other documents.[4] More subtle improvements, such as carbon paper, also became significant tools in office records management. Carbon paper had been introduced in the United States as early as 1823, but it was only in tandem with the typewriter that it began to be used. By the early twentieth century it was the prevalent form of copying, primarily because carbon paper was more economical, adaptable, and well-suited to newly developing internal communications (along with the increasing use of circular letters, general orders, manuals, notes, forms, and in-house magazines).[5]

The dramatic changes in mid-nineteenth-century American business, such as with the emergence of the railroads, pushed the use of a system of daily reports and other kinds of records and information systems. As business historian, Chandler characterizes one of these railroad leaders, Daniel McCallum: "no earlier American businessman had ever had the need to develop ways to use internally generated data as instruments of management."[6] Records systems were being used to control information creation and use, as James Beniger argues, inspiring a "stream of innovations in information processing, bureaucratic control, and communications."[7] The ultimate change in records and information systems was dramatic, even if not as dramatic as the last quarter of the twentieth century. Beniger contends that "in 1780 a modern American office might contain printed business forms and file cabinets, communicate via mail, parcel post and courier, subscribe to various types of news publications, and hire financial and other professional information sources. . . . A century later, the modern American office had added a dozen major information technologies and services: telegraph and telephone, international record carriers and other local delivery services, newsletter, loose-leaf and directory subscriptions, news and advertising services, and different security services."[8] The impact of even simple records devices was tremendous. As another historian remarks, "With the humble manila folder—portable, resortable, expandable—and its four-drawer file cabinet the chronological tyranny of the press-book archive was broken. All the information on an account, a transaction, or an employee was enveloped in one thin, easily accessible file."[9] It is difficult to sort out what came first, changes in the technology or management philosophies. Historian JoAnne Yates, for example, thinks "it was not growth per se that required the development of the internal communication system, but the managerial philosophy that evolved in response to growth. Formal internal communication [including new, systematic records systems] became a managerial tool for coordination and control."[10]

Efforts to automate records and information became more sophisticated as technologies improved. Herman Hollerith, searching to prove the value of his punch-card machine, widely regarded as the precursor of the computer, offered to help Baltimore organize its health department records.[11] These punch cards became familiar by the 1950s when they were associated with bureaucracy and represented an era's social ills as a "symbol of alienation." The cards "stood for abstraction, oversimplification and dehumanization . . . people abstracted into numbers that machines could use [and] where people had to change their ways to suit the machines.''[12] Many records professionals would agree with this assessment, acknowledging their own struggles with technology.

The strange career of the punch card, from salvation for government and business needing to process rapidly large quantities of data to symbol of impersonal technologies, provides continuing lessons for records professionals working with the escalating uses of office records and information technology. Records professionals, throughout the twentieth century, have been subjected to America's love affair with technology. ''From the 1820s onward, with the development of new or improved machines, modes of production, communication, and transportation, and particularly after the introduction of the railroad,'' writes historian John Kasson, ''Americans increasingly identified the progress of the nation with the progress of technology, and native inventors became the objects of a national cult.''[13] A recent history of computing suggests that ''America was gadget-happy and was caught up by the glamour of the mechanical office.''[14] This fascination, or obsession, with technology brought other changes to the culture of organizations and the office that are still in process. Office mechanization in the late nineteenth century brought many women into the workplace, and the current increasing use of electronic communications and word-processing equipment is also bringing immense changes to the modern office, including the elimination of many clerical positions.[15]

Early office machines—such as calculators for basic arithmetical functions, bookkeeping machines for ledgers, and tabulating systems for stored data—were established by the 1930s, paving the way for the reception of computers in the 1940s and 1950s as well as being a harbinger of the impact of mechanization on managing records. The telephone posed new challenges in the socialization of the office and for records creation and maintenance, leading to a ''radical change in personal communication,'' but for businesses ''voice transmission, scratchy and often indistinct, could be an adjunct [to written records] at best.''[16] The array of new devices was both varied and great, supplementing the traditional means of managing records. Zuboff, in her *In the Age of the Smart Machine*, describes how the period of the 1870s through the 1930s was one of increasing introduction of information technologies, from the typewriter to many other devices such as mechanical messengers, envelope machines, statistical machines, bookkeeping machines, and copiers—making clerks able to do a much wider range of tasks. New books on office management appeared, such as William Henry Leffingwell's 1925 *Office Management: Principles and Practice*, introducing Taylorism into the office, with the aim to simplify all office tasks, including records management, via filing cabinets, forms, and office supplies, with a specific control device for every task.[17]

The emergence of office technology impacted those who identified themselves as records professionals. The origins of archives and records management operations alike occurred during the same time that the new office automation methods were taking hold. There were, of course, other motivations for the origins of these programs that had little to do with the desire to mechanize. The origins of the state government archives in the American South, the progenitors of the modern American archives *and* records management movement, were tied up with a mixture of Progressivism, belief in objective truth and scientific history, pride in region, and the ability to work with old-line politicians.[18] Others have seen more in these new records and information technologies than merely a desire for more efficient office routine. Angel Rama, considering the change from colonies to nations in Latin America from 1880 to about 1920, sees first the power associated with writing and the changing nature of who possessed power. First it was the administrators, legal advisors, and politicians, but then there was a shift to those in education, diplomacy, and journalism.[19]

We can perceive the impact of the new technologies on archives and records management in different ways. Researchers into office routine have discovered that records are ordered by office workers to provide accountability.[20] Concerns with orderliness and accountability may have as much to do with the supposed efficiency and economy brought by the new office technologies. Through much of the nineteenth century, for example, medical care was individualistic and not very well regulated and, as a result, recordkeeping was sporadic, poor, and reliant on the personal memory of physicians. There were exceptions. Massachusetts General adopted in 1837 an amendment to the hospital by-laws requiring each physician to "keep a daily record of every important fact in the history of patients and as soon as possible to enter it in a handsome manner in the case book of the department."[21] But medical recordkeeping at this and other hospitals did not become systematic until much later, probably as a result of the increasing records, the new office technologies, and the professionalization and regulation of medicine itself. In 1897 the hospital appointed its first custodian of records, followed in 1904 with a separate centralized room for the records with a card index.[22] As medical education emerged at the end of the nineteenth century, teaching needs suggested a new importance for the records. In 1900 Walter Cannon, a student at the Harvard Medical School, recommended that printed versions of cases be used in teaching, and within two decades cases were prominent in education and medical journals publishing them. This use "drew attention to the value of accurate and complete medical records,"[23] suggesting the continuing sense we have of how the use of media technology ties in with records and recordkeeping. Several generations later medical professionals were worried about whether the immense dependence on the computer for medical records was not, in fact, undermining the veracity and utility of the medical record as a diagnostic tool.

THE REVOLT AGAINST THE PAPER RECORD

The greatest challenge records professionals now face is the development of a mentality that equates the paper record with bureaucracy and, hence, as an obstacle to organizational efficiency and competitiveness. The government commissions, appearing nearly every decade or so from 1888 to the recent efforts by Vice President Al Gore to "re-invent" government, were all charged with determining new and better ways to manage records and suggest a source for supporting government consultants as well as fueling the worst stereotypes of records as a problem of bureaucratic inefficiency. Such attitudes have long been a staple in fiction. A recent popular novel had this passage: "The rest of us have a drawer, a notebook, a file folder. Juliane has seven grubby envelopes for the safekeeping of the printed testimony of her existence. For many Greenlanders, the most difficult thing about Denmark is the paperwork. The state bureaucracy's front line of paper: application forms, documents, and official correspondence with the proper public authorities. There is a certain elegant and delicate irony in the fact that even a practically illiterate life like Juliane's has sloughed off this mountain of paper."[24] These attitudes have also fueled an industry of management tomes. Hammer and Champy, in their popular book on organizational management, *Reengineering the Corporation*, state that "if people in different parts of the organization have to telephone one another frequently or send a lot of memos or E-mail messages, that probably means a natural process has been inappropriately broken apart."[25] Other popular books on organizational management have pushed similar notions. Osborne and Gaebler, in their *Reinventing Government*, write that "in attempting to control virtually everything, we became so obsessed with dictating *how* things should be done—regulating the process, controlling the inputs—that we ignored the outcomes, the *results*."[26]

That these processes are tied up with records and recordkeeping can be seen in more cautious suggestions. Kearns, in his treatise on accountability (a key concept for records management), argues that the "bureaucratic structures and red tape, which Osborne and Gaebler denounce, do indeed inhibit the flexibility and entrepreneurship of government agencies. But, for better or worse, they are also the primary instruments of public accountability designed to prevent abuse of power and to limit the autonomy of public officials."[27] Such concerns have been heightened by the use of the computer by every office worker or individual at home. A writer in a major business journal chronicles the still continuing tension between the digitization of records with the increasing use of paper. Making many predictions about the decline of paper, the article featured photographs of offices *buried* in paper and described a "paper paradox: As an explosion of information flows in bits across electronic networks, the Internet and on-line services, the ability to create low-cost, high-quality, personalized paper-based documents on demand ramps up paper usage to unprecedented levels."[28]

Some commentators have wisely pointed out that the rush to adopt every new technology for mundane recordkeeping processes can become both self-destructive and silly. In one of the recent evaluations about the ramifications of society's dependence on computers, Edward Tenner states that "when anything seems to be getting cheaper, a recomplicating effect is around the corner. Voice annotations of spreadsheets and other documents are a perfect example. Just when software was finally making it possible to share documents across computer systems and business programs, the multimedia document raises its head. It hogs disk space, remains partly unreproducible on most of the world's computers, erects new (if no doubt temporary) obstacles to file sharing, and above all makes it impossible for anybody to get full information from a printout, no matter how many colors it may have. All this for what footnotes or an explanatory paragraph could accomplish at a fraction of the cost."[29] What should be most interesting to records professionals is that the use of computers for records and information resources management has led to the recognition by many outside the field that society and its organizations cannot manage all information without diminishing it from time to time in an orderly fashion. "For the first time in human history," write two information scientists, "a strategy of information exclusion has become urgent. The new strategy relies on excluding the greater portion of the messages transmitted, so as to focus on a manageable few."[30]

RECORDS, INFORMATION, OR KNOWLEDGE MANAGEMENT

The negative connotations of paperwork, the new technologies used in records creation, and the necessary changing skills and knowledge needed by archivists and records managers have led to new forms of records management in the last two decades of the twentieth century. This is not something anyone should be surprised about, since as one sociologist of professions notes, a "dominant position confers short-run power, not long-run imperium. No profession can stand forever."[31] This must especially be the case with professions built about the use of rapidly changing information technologies. If one needs affirmation of this, then one needs only check Bruce Sterling's "Dead Media Project." This project has amassed a list of numerous media, many used for records and recordkeeping systems, that have long since ceased to be used actively. Interestingly, the quantity of media accelerates in the post-computer age.[32] For one aspect of the records professions, that of archivists, these rapid media changes have given it a bad connotation. In a reference to refereed journals, one commentator writes that "these journals are effective as archives, but ineffective as a means of timely communication among scientists—it can easily take years from the submission of a manuscript to its publication, and by that time the field has moved on."[33] Archives, for many, have assumed the role of an *antiquated* response to how to manage records and information. On the other hand, records management has become associated with paper, a medium often associated with inefficiency. As a result, information or knowledge has gained the primary focus of records professionals, rather than the record with its importance for evidence and accountability.

Yet, the revolt *against* the record has failed in some substantial ways. The angst caused by changing technologies far pre-dates the computer. Michael Buckland, an information scientist who has examined how records, books, and artifacts relate to each other, describes the ever shifting notion of the definition of a document in the late nineteenth century from printed texts to encompass museum objects and archival materials. Buckland argues that documentalists—like Otlet and Briet—"increasingly emphasized whatever functioned as a document rather than traditional physical forms of documents."[34] These new efforts on information systems led to the desire to recapture the importance of records. As one recent commentary suggests, "For several years, members of the archival, records management, and information technology communities have been conducting research and attempting to design solutions for these long-term problems [about the need to manage records in electronic information systems]. . . . The key goal has been to define what is required to transform an information system into a record-keeping system."[35] Even the International Council on Archives, an association which has to work through complex cultural and national issues to reach consensus, has agreed to a much stronger definition of records: "A record is recorded information produced or received in the initiation, conduct or completion of an institutional or individual activity and that comprises content, context and structure sufficient to provide evidence of the activity."[36]

A nearly universal interest in defining and understanding records and their importance is present. In one of the background papers used for preparing the ICA report, Alf Erlandsson notes that "reports indicate that document management systems, designed to manage textual electronic information that may not necessarily qualify as records have been marketed as recordkeeping systems, and accepted by records managers as such, causing loss of context and evidential value in records 'managed' by such systems."[37] Such recognition has not been limited to the records community. From these concerns, debates, and discussions about the challenges posed by modern information technologies, the form and function of records have re-appeared. Computer scientists, such as Jeff Rothenberg, have re-affirmed some of the basic characteristics of a record: "Ideally, bit streams should be sealed in virtual envelopes: the contents would be preserved verbatim, and contextual information associated with each envelope would describe those contents and their transformation history."[38] Such efforts are crucial, since nearly everywhere one can look, it is possible to find concern about the continuing value of records. Historian Donald Ritchie notes the "declining qualitative value" of modern records: "As the records of government agencies, corporations, and other institutions have multiplied, their worth has decreased. Mass mailings tell less about their authors than did the handwritten correspondence of the past. Memoranda often disguise what actually happened or try to shift responsibility. Telephones, fax machines, electronic mail, and other modern means of communication have reduced the reliance of traditional written documentation. As researchers gain access to modern records, they often discover them to be unrevealing and uninformative."[39]

In the 2,000 years before the twentieth century, changes in the record's physical manifestation pale in comparison to changes brought about by electronic information technology, from the birth of the telegraph in the mid-nineteenth century to the computer and innovative software. The accelerating use of information technology has also caused problems, first and foremost with control, and this marks the origins of our modern information age and the distress about the record. James Beniger sees this in many aspects of the modern world, such as in the transition from family-sized to large-scale businesses, contrasting the "traditional means of control—family partnerships, the southern 'gentleman's code,' the community relations that bound farmer and storekeeper" with what has resulted from later "technologies of information processing, transportation, and communication."[40] This is the essence of the Control Revolution, the "development of technologies far beyond the capability of any individual, whether in the form of the massive bureaucracies of the late nineteenth century or of the microprocessors of the late twentieth century. In all cases it was not the novelty of the commodities processed . . . that proved decisive . . . but rather the transcendence of the information-processing capabilities of the individual organism by a much greater technological system."[41] Beniger's longer historical view provides the opportunity to see the modern Information Age, and records, in a very different light.

There are other views. Neil Postman has been a recent critic, discerning a "technopoly" with "beliefs that the primary, if not the only, goal of human labor and thought is efficiency; that technical calculation is in all respects superior to human judgment."[42] Here, we have some sense of the recent problems defining a record. Postman suggests that the "milieu in which Technopoly flourishes is one in which the tie between information and human purpose has been severed, i.e., information appears indiscriminately, directed at no one in particular, in enormous volume and at high speeds, and disconnected from theory, meaning, or purpose."[43] Such views suggest that the traditional notion of a record has *no* place in the modern information society, and why we often see the amazing diversity of definitions for something as essential as a record.

The rapid development of powerful personal computers brought chaos to organizations' ability to manage records, despite the motivation for computerization as a control mechanism. A study of the use of electronic information technology at United Nations organizations identifies the symptoms of this chaos as disorganization in managing electronic and paper records, control of documents to users, new communication systems, loss of access to official organization records, and lack of expertise to handle these problems.[44] In a particular organization an individual manages his or her personal files, collaborating electronically with others on the production of particular documents and groups of records. When and how a record appears and is used is a matter of concern in an environment where texts readily appear and disappear. "As society becomes more dependent on computers, we also become more and more vulnerable to computer malfunctions and to computer misuse—that is, to malfunctioning hardware and software and to misuse by human beings."[45]

The new information technologies have had a significant impact on the view of the record. David Bearman, an astute commentator on the nature of the record, charts the transition from records as "physical things" to records (in electronic form) which are "virtual things."[46] Technologists, such as Ronald Weissman, have corroborated such notions: "Paper records are tangible *things*. Electronic documents are evolving *processes*."[47] The advent of the electronic document has made it tempting to ignore some traditional aspects of records. A study on the breadth of use in the federal government of electronic databases reflects this with a definition of databases not focusing on the record but on the "collection of data."[48] The problems that can occur have become fairly obvious. One records management consultant argues that the evolution to the oft-predicted "paperless" office failed because the hardware and software engineers have not paid sufficient heed to the most basic of documents—the "form" and the manner in which such forms are used, relied upon, and stored. And as this critic notes, the form is a very old notion of the record that has maintained its most basic characteristics despite numerous advances in information technology.[49]

RE-DEFINING ELECTRONIC RECORDS MANAGEMENT

In the January 1996 *Records Management Quarterly*, Belden Menkus characterizes what he terms the "re-discovery" of electronic records management.[50] It is seriously flawed in interpretation but somewhat typical in its particulars. The disruption between archivists and records managers provides a confusing front to the technologists at an extremely critical juncture in the transition to electronic age offices and organizations. Now is when the information managers and systems designers are increasingly asking questions about how to manage masses of information, including what information should be maintained for how long. While some technologists (anyone who is relying on information technology as a solution to the management of information and records), such as Negroponte and Rheingold, do not consider how information maintenance will be resolved (do they assume everything will be saved?), others, such as Buckland, design into information systems a preservation function.[51]

Menkus's view is that after a quarter of a century of neglect, what he terms a period of "inaction," electronic records management has been re-discovered. This re-discovery has primarily occurred within the government sector, driven by the *Armstrong v. Executive Office of the President* court case (the PROFS case) and the rising use of electronic messaging systems. The substance of the re-discovery of the electronic records management issues is a focus on the "completeness of a record's content." Menkus also argues that while there has been a renewed emphasis on electronic records management, the issues are not new and were in fact being discussed by federal government records professionals like Everett Alldredge in the 1960s. But Alldredge, and others like him, were ignored because they were not followed "by a comparable leader and innovator." Meanwhile, the technology has changed rapidly and left behind records managers who will now "have to work exceptionally hard to catch up with what has taken place in the world of information handling." Menkus then suggests that records managers need to have new roles within the organization.

The author also comments on electronic records management's nature, defining both records and management. He provides a brief history of records management, with a fairly traditional view of its origins in the United States National Archives as a means to control the proliferation of records. His definition builds on the "cradle-to-grave control of the processes" related to the records life cycle as the crux of electronic records management. Menkus sees little change with records creation, partly because it is here "where records management had its first major impact" in the influence of better quality records, or with any other aspect of the records life cycle. According to him, the "only difference is that those who need to be taught are using surprisingly powerful laptop microcomputers instead of Number 2 pencils and lined paper pads." Forms, directives, mail, and vital records continue to be the focus of records managers.

The argument by this author is that records management, except for the need for records managers to prepare themselves to work with new technologies, does not need to change. Menkus states that "in approaching an involvement in records management one should recognize that it involves more changes in form than in substance." Data warehouses, databases, and other such matters are little more than old records concepts translated into electronic systems and new jargon. Records managers will now simply be responsible for electronic records. Menkus argues that one fundamental truth—"people will create those records that they want to create and will retain those records that they want to retain and will destroy almost any records that they feel like destroying"—cuts across the paper-based office to that of the new electronic, networked organization. He advocates scheduling and related traditional records management concerns as relevant in electronic records management.

Menkus provides an extremely re-assuring description of electronic records management *for* records managers currently working. He ends by stressing the opportunities for better success in managing records and a venue that will enable records managers to provide real services to organizations needing assistance with the increasing complexities of the new information technologies. The substance of the message seems to be that the traditional records manager can make the transition to administering electronic records easily enough. The real questions and issues are not, however, addressed in this article.

The simplest point to counter concerns the historical interpretation by Menkus about the lapse of interest in and then rediscovery of electronic records management. He essentially argues that there had been no activity in this realm from about 1970 until the mid-1990s. While this interpretation might fit with the records management profession, it does not square with what had occurred in the North American archival profession during the same time. Within the archival profession there has been tremendous activity regarding the management of electronic records, including that carried out by the National Archives. In the late 1960s there were the initial efforts to manage what were then termed machine-readable records. During the 1970s and 1980s there were debates and discussions about the application (their validity) of archival principles to the electronic systems, the first manuals of codified practice, the initial efforts to establish electronic archives programs, and sustained continuing education workshops and institutes designed to re-tool working archivists. There was no Dark Ages of electronic records management, although the degree of success (measured by the establishment of viable electronic records programs) in working with the increasingly sophisticated electronic recordkeeping systems was uneven.[52] What Menkus may have done is to misinterpret the earlier era in the light of the more recent vigorous activity of the first half of the 1990s. It is, to borrow a phrase from Todd Gitlin's book on the culture wars, as if Menkus "worships at the shrine of history but is innocent of facts."[53] Menkus may be more guilty of just providing a fairly terse commentary, but the interpretation is faulty enough as to be meaningless in the light of current records management concerns.

What Menkus does capture is the sense of a rediscovery, although he has the specifics a bit confused. Returning to the archival profession, it is true that new concepts for managing electronic records have come to the fore in the early 1990s. Due to a number of factors, including the PROFS case, a re-commitment to managing electronic records developed with a stress on defining the record, articulating the characteristics of records through particular tools long used by systems and software designers, and through a dependence on the social and other warrants (law, best practices, professional standards) defining records and their management. The recordkeeping functional requirements project at the University of Pittsburgh has been one effort, although there have been others stressing the specifics of records, such as the project being carried out at the University of British Columbia.

Here we have to re-visit the particulars of the historical account drawn by Menkus. One of the results of the PROFS case that this author missed is that the National Archives was on a side of the fence different from what one might have expected (although this fits with his view of the loss of this organization's leadership). While Menkus provides a pivotal historical role for this federal institution in leadership in both records management and electronic records management, something must have happened for it to be lectured to by a United States district court judge about the fact that printing out electronic mail messages was not a satisfactory tactic because it distorted the particular elements that made the electronic mail messages records. Or, to put it another way, the National Archives was reminded that its way of dealing with the PROFS messages from the Reagan-Bush White House was a violation, in principle at least, of the Federal Records Act. Tom Blanton, on the other side in the case, suggests that "we need a reinvented National Archives, a vigorous information watchdog. Otherwise, NARA will be relegated to the role of the nation's attic; and there, among the cobwebs, will roam the ghost of government accountability."[54] Fortunately, the case has been well documented by legal scholars, archivists, and public activists and does not need to be described in detail.[55] However, it is important to turn to the definition of record provided by Menkus in his article.

Menkus interprets the court case as being a legal precedent for a long-held records management principle, that of the "completeness of a record's content." The ruling of the court was in favor of a definition of a record with structure, content, and context. Printing out the electronic mail distorted structure and tossed off context, making its content meaningless, or at least open to question. The problems with the author's view of records are revealed when he defines records management by records *and* then management. Menkus describes records as "organized units of information that are comprehensive, authentic, accurate, reliable, and contemporaneous with the events and decisions that they purported to reflect." Records are "not necessarily physical entities" but they do have "both a structure and inherent unity." The potential problem with this definition is that Menkus does not identify records as transactions, nor does he adequately reflect that they have structure, content, and context or that the weakening of any aspect of one of these weakens the others. Within the past five years a group of leading archivists and records managers have developed a precise definition of the record as a transaction created for evidence purposes.[56] The problem with Menkus's view is a problem shared by other records managers and archivists, the stress on information and the emphasis on the data processing concept of document as a substitute for records. The emphasis on information probably has as much to do with the records managers' efforts to connect to the information professions, not unlike the opinions shared by related professionals such as archivists and librarians. As long as records are understood to be valuable for purposes beyond information, such as accountability and evidence (to use the recent terms) or administrative, legal, and fiscal (to use the traditional terms), this is not a serious matter. The more serious concern is the adoption of the data processing notion of document.

The notion of document has proved to be the crux of the problem. Too many records managers adhere to the data processing notion of a document as a transaction set or message, a pile of stuff held together for a particular purpose, from a report to the transmission of miscellaneous data to another party. This is similar to the documentalist's notion of document as a "generic term to denote any physical information resource."[57] While the current development of electronic document management systems can be used to manage records,[58] we need to realize that records, a transaction with a structure, content, and context to satisfy the evidence requirements of an organization, are at best a subset of these entities. There are differences stemming from creation, nature, and value. The distinction is closely related to the comments by Menkus about the records manager not being intimidated by the data processor. Records managers and archivists need to understand that data processors are there to design systems meeting users' needs (meaning records professionals need to communicate to them the elements of records and the importance of the records being managed in the electronic systems).[59]

One of the other problems with the Menkus essay is that the author makes current records management concepts, those that developed in the old industrial office and with paper files, compatible with the post-industrial office and its electronic recordkeeping systems. Because Menkus contends that there was a void in new records management developments after 1970, perhaps because he was looking for these developments in the wrong place, he does not see the new ideas being proposed as viable means to manage electronic records. What are some of these new approaches?

A number of proposals for archivists and records managers to drop the custodial solution in favor of non-custodial approaches in which they manage records via procedures, policies, partnerships, and planning have been made.[60] While the records manager may be comfortable with this notion because of his or her usual reliance on policies, there is a fundamental difference with the stress on the possible lack of custodianship. Many records managers are still connected to a warehousing approach, as are archivists. Archival theorists Luciana Duranti and Terry Eastwood, educators at the University of British Columbia, have argued forcibly that the kind of control needed to protect the integrity of records cannot occur without physical custody in order to make sure that those who might want to distort the records or who have the greatest reason to tamper with the records will not be able to do this.[61] They argue for custodianship. At present, the archival profession remains divided about this matter, but the nature of recordkeeping systems probably may dictate a post-custodial approach *and* ensure the integrity of records.

Other archivists, with greater experience with electronic records and just as strong a commitment to the nature of records as the focus of the archivist and records manager, such as David Bearman and Margaret Hedstrom, argue that electronic records cannot be managed in a custodial fashion. As Bearman suggests, ''any approach to managing electronic information will need to be sufficiently flexible to accommodate substantial change.''[62] A post-custodial approach seems to be the best idea for enabling records managers to deal with electronic recordkeeping systems because it puts a responsibility on *both* records creators and records managers. Still, the unifying point between the post-custodialists and custodialists is that they must preserve the fundamental nature of the records; the mechanisms and details for determining how this might happen can be worked out later.

Another difference in recent thinking about records is the shift from focusing on records as physical artifacts to considering records as evidence needed to be managed for a variety of purposes. Both archivists and records managers, for very different reasons (cultural versus administrative, research versus fiscal and legal), have stressed the administration of the physical, paper record as the priority of their programs rather than reflecting on the continuing value of records for evidence, accountability, and memory purposes. This stress on the record as artifact has both hindered records professionals from seeing their larger responsibilities as well as relegated these professionals in their organizations to clerical positions and functions. Instead, they need to stress what a record is, why it is important, and its particular characteristics. At the heart of this activity is the role of both archivists and records managers in understanding records and recordkeeping systems in order to support both the organization in which they work and to benefit society. Doing otherwise has had the records manager focused on matters such as efficiency and economy (hence the continuing stress on trying to schedule all records for destruction?) and the archivist on cultural and research values. This diminishes these records professionals from being able to stress the role of records in capturing the essential evidence of an organization's activities and in providing the crucial foundation for accountability and institutional memory.

Archivists and records managers need to develop a coherent approach to electronic records management because they need to assume that the majority of recordkeeping systems will be electronic and because institutional managers and technical professionals are beginning to understand better the challenges of managing information in electronic form. The declining costs, the greater array of software, and the increasingly hospitable legal environment are providing a means by which recordkeeping systems will be transferred to electronic systems and used in electronic means.

The technology also can be used to ensure organizational memory, something archivists and records managers should have been conveying as part of their message. As one recent proposal states, "organizational memory provides information from the past that reduces transaction costs, contributes to effective and efficient decision making, and is a basis for power within organizations." The same essay notes that the "need to recognize and develop the information-systems aspect of organizational memory is growing ever stronger with the increasing weight of knowledge work, as a consequence of environmental demands imposed on organizations, and because of the capabilities offered by advanced information technologies, which are increasingly used by organizations."[63] The reason for more serious work by archivists and records managers is that this particular proposal rests on the "core competence of an organization ... rooted in the experiential knowledge of its members."[64] Records professionals know that the core for organizational memory is records and the ability to access these records. It is another reason why archives and records management programs need to be combined and the artificial distinctions made between archivists and records managers should be eliminated.

Menkus describes a scenario where the records management profession ignored electronic recordkeeping and information systems, but where their basic concepts and approaches remained relevant. There is a different version, a continued period of great activity leading to recent breakthroughs in the concept of records and, hence, in the business of archivists and records managers. Whereas Menkus argues that all the records manager need do is to become better versed in the rapidly changing information technology, my argument is different. The records manager and archivist needs to stress records, understand recordkeeping systems, and communicate these concerns to the institutional managers and information technologists. While searching for "win-win relations" and working "constructively" is good advice, the more important matter is having a firm concept of *records* as the key to all *records* work.

CONCLUSION

Challenges to and obstacles for the management of records are not new. Hall, in his history of English public archives, contends that "as long as the Records were regarded as part and parcel of the contents of the treasure of the Crown they were guarded with the same jealous care as the other contents of the royal treasuries, but the growth of the departmental system gave opportunities for abuses which could not be easily checked."[65] Different "abuses" have emerged in more recent centuries, as competing media have been developed, public scrutiny of government officials waxed and waned, and new systems with vastly different technical requirements shifted the responsibility for records to professionals and technicians who do not understand the importance of records. What we have been left with, even in highly industrialized nations such as the United States, has been a breakdown of any sort of national system for the management of records and the information and evidence they contain.

NOTES

1. Alan Delgado, *The Enormous File: A Social History of the Office* (London: John Murray, 1979), pp. 80, 83.

2. Delgado, *The Enormous File*, p. 68.

3. JoAnne Yates, *Control Through Communication: The Rise of System in American Management* (Baltimore: Johns Hopkins University Press, 1989), p. 56.

4. Yates, *Control Through Communication*, pp. 61–63.

5. Yates, *Control Through Communication*, pp. 46–50.

6. Alfred D. Chandler, Jr., *The Visible Hand: The Managerial Revolution in American Business* (Cambridge, Mass.: Belknap Press of Harvard University Press, 1977), p. 104.

7. James R. Beniger, *The Control Revolution: Technological and Economic Origins of the Information Society* (Cambridge, Mass.: Harvard University Press, 1986), p. 220.

8. Beniger, *The Control Revolution*, pp. 279–280.

9. Thomas J. Schlereth, *Cultural History and Material Culture: Everyday Life, Landscapes, Museums* (Ann Arbor, Mich.: UMI Research Press, 1990), p. 165.

10. Yates, *Control Through Communication*, p. 2. Archivist Barbara Craig provides an insight when she argues that "procedures affect the context of records, while materials affect their physical quality." Craig, "Copying Devices," in Barbara L. Craig, ed., *The Archival Imagination: Essays in Honour of Hugh A. Taylor* (Ottawa: Association of

Canadian Archivists, 1992), p. 107. Craig notes that the physical forms became more varied, along with the increase in records.

11. Joel Shurkin, *Engines of the Mind: The Evolution of the Computer from Mainframes to Microprocessors* (New York: W. W. Norton and Co., 1996), pp. 73–74.

12. Steven Lubar, " 'Do Not Fold, Spindle or Mutilate': A Cultural History of the Punch Card," *Journal of American Culture* 15 (Winter 1992): 44. See also Arthur L. Norberg, "High-Technology Calculation in the Early 20th Century: Punched Card Machinery in Business and Government." *Technology and Culture* 31 (October 1990): 753–779.

13. John F. Kasson, *Civilizing the Machine: Technology and Republican Values in America 1776–1900* (New York: Grossman Publishers, 1976), p. 41.

14. Martin Campbell-Kelly and William Aspray, *Computer: A History of the Information Machine* (New York: Basic Books, 1996), p. 27. They also surmise that "American office's late start compared with Europe" made America more susceptible to automation because "it did not carry the albatross of being a first mover with old-fashioned offices and entrenched, archaic working methods" (pp. 26–27).

15. Anita Rapone, "Women's Work: Offices and Opportunity," AHA *Perspectives* 21 (January 1983): 13–15.

16. Claude S. Fischer, *America Calling: A Social History of the Telephone to 1940* (Berkeley: University of California Press, 1992), p. 35.

17. Shoshana Zuboff, *In the Age of the Smart Machine: The Future of Work and Power* (New York: Basic Books, 1988), pp. 115–119.

18. William S. Price, Jr., "Plowing Virgin Fields: State Support for Southern Archives, Particularly North Carolina," *Carolina Comments* 29 (March 1981): 41–47.

19. Angel Rama, *The Lettered City*, trans and ed. John Charles Chasteen (Durham, N.C.: Duke University Press, 1996).

20. Lucy A. Suchman, "Office Procedure as Practical Action: Models of Work and Design," *ACM Transactions on Office Information Systems* 1 (October 1983): 326–327.

21. Stanley Joel Reiser, "Creating Form Out of Mass: The Development of the Medical Record," in Everett Mendelsohn, ed., *Transformation and Tradition in the Sciences: Essays in Honor of I. Bernard Cohen* (Cambridge: Cambridge University Press, 1984), pp. 303–304.

22. Reiser, "Creating Form Out of Mass," p. 304.

23. Reiser, "Creating Form Out of Mass," pp. 307–309.

24. Peter Hoeg, *Miss Smilla's Feeling for Snow*, trans. F. David (London: Flamingo, 1994), p. 21.

25. Michael Hammer and James Champy, *Reengineering the Corporation: A Manifesto for Business Revolution* (New York: HarperBusiness, 1994), p. 123.

26. David Osborne and Ted Gaebler, *Reinventing Government: How the Entrepreneurial Spirit Is Transforming the Public Sector* (New York: Plume, 1993), p. 14.

27. Kevin P. Kearns, *Managing for Accountability: Preserving the Public Trust in Public and Nonprofit Organizations* (San Francisco: Jossey-Bass Publishers, 1996), p. 24.

28. Glenn Rifkin, "The Future of the Document," *Forbes ASAP* (October 9, 1995): 42–60 (quotation from pp. 46–47).

29. Edward Tenner, *Why Things Bite Back: Technology and the Revenge of Unintended Consequences* (New York: Alfred A. Knopf, 1996), p. 203.

30. Jorge Reina Schement and Terry Curtis, *Tendencies and Tensions of the Infor-*

mation Age: The Production and Distribution of Information in the United States (New Brunswick, N.J.: Transaction Publishers, 1995), p. 125.

31. Andrew Abbott, *The System of Professions: An Essay on the Division of Expert Labor* (Chicago: University of Chicago Press, 1988), p. 141.

32. See http://www.mediahistory.com/dead/archive.html.

33. John Shore, *The Sachertorte Algorithm and Other Antidotes to Computer Anxiety* (New York: Penguin Books, 1986), p. 19.

34. Michael K. Buckland, "What Is a 'Document'?" *Journal of the American Society for Information Science* 48, no. 9 (1997): 808.

35. Timothy J. McGovern and Helen W. Samuels, "Our Institutional Memory at Risk: Collaborators to the Rescue," *Cause/Effect* 20 (Fall 1997): 19–21, 49–50 at http://cause-www.colorado.edu/cause-effect/cem97/cem973table.html.

36. Committee on Electronic Records, *Guide for Managing Electronic Records from an Archival Perspective*, ICA Studies CIA 8 (n.p.: ICA, February 1997), 2.1 at http://www.archives.ca/ica/p-er/guide_0.html#top.

37. See Section 5.2 at http://www.archives.ca/ica/p-er.

38. Jeff Rothenberg, "Ensuring the Longevity of Digital Documents," *Scientific American* 272 (January 1995): 47.

39. Donald A. Ritchie, *Doing Oral History* (New York: Twayne Publishers, 1995), p. 132.

40. James R. Beniger, *The Control Revolution*, pp. 166–167.

41. Beniger, *The Control Revolution*, p. 185.

42. Neil Postman, *Technopoly: The Surrender of Culture to Technology* (New York: Knopf, 1992), pp. 51–52.

43. Postman, *Technopoly*, p. 70.

44. Richard E. Barry, "Managing Organizations in a Runaway Electronic Age," in Angelika Menne-Haritz, ed., *Information Handling in Offices and Archives* (New York: K. G. Saur, 1993), pp. 27–55.

45. Tom Forester and Perry Morrison, *Computer Ethics: Cautionary Tales and Ethical Dilemmas in Computing* (Cambridge, Mass.: MIT Press, 1990), p. 1.

46. David Bearman, "New Models for Management of Electronic Records by Archives," *Cadernos Bad* 2 (1992): 65.

47. Ronald Weissman, "Virtual Documents on an Electronic Desktop: Hypermedia, Emerging Computing Environments and the Future of Information Management," in Cynthia J. Durance, comp., *Management of Recorded Information: Converging Disciplines; Proceedings of the International Council on Archives' Symposium on Current Records* (New York: K. G. Saur, 1990), p. 54.

48. National Academy of Public Administration, *The Archives of the Future: Archival Strategies for the Treatment of Electronic Databases* (Washington, D.C.: NAPA, 1991), pp. 12, 21–22. See also the U.S. House Committee on Government Operations, *Taking a Byte Out of History: The Archival Preservation of Federal Computer Records* (Washington, D.C.: U.S. Government Printing Office, 1990).

49. Robert Barnett, *Why the Paperless Office Miscarried* (Belconnen, Australia: Robert Barnett and Associates, June 1993).

50. Belden Menkus, "Defining Electronic Records Management," *Records Management Quarterly* 30 (January 1996): 38–42.

51. Nicholas Negroponte, *Being Digital* (New York: Alfred A. Knopf, 1995); Howard Rheingold, *The Virtual Community: Homesteading on the Electronic Frontier* (New

York: HarperPerennial, 1994); and Michael Buckland, *Information and Information Systems* (New York: Praeger, 1991). In fact, it is the records life cycle with the need to appraise records that is identified by Buckland as one of the reasons that records management and archives is a "complex" business; "On the Nature of Records Management Theory," *Proceedings of the ARMA International 35th Annual Conference, 1990* (Prairie Village, Kans.: ARMA, 1990), pp. 801–813.

52. See Richard Cox, *The First Generation of Electronic Records Archivists in the United States: A Study in Professionalization* (New York: Haworth Press, 1994) for my views on this period. This study includes extensive references to the essays, reports, and other studies from and about this period, roughly 1960 to 1990.

53. Todd Gitlin, *The Twilight of Common Dreams: Why America Is Wracked by Culture Wars* (New York: Metropolitan Books, Henry Holt and Co., 1995), p. 175.

54. Tom Blanton, ed., *White House E-Mail: The Top Secret Computer Messages the Reagan/Bush White House Tried to Destroy* (New York: The New Press, 1995), p. 11. For a description of the case, see David Bearman, "The Implications of *Armstrong v. Executive Office of the President* for the Archival Management of Electronic Records," in his *Electronic Evidence: Strategies for Managing Records in Contemporary Organizations* (Pittsburgh: Archives and Museum Informatics, 1994), pp. 118–144. To add to this, we can see that the National Archives has often been forced to deal with important records issues. Historian Anna K. Nelson recently wrote in the case about the Richard Nixon records that the "National Archives have rarely exhibited the courage needed to stand up to these challenges, acquiescing in the claims of Nixon and his associates that many documents were purely personal communications" instead of federal records; see her "Open the Nixon Papers," *Chronicle of Higher Education* 42 (February 2, 1996), p. A48. The most thorough discussion of this case is David A. Wallace, "The Public's Use of Federal Recordkeeping Statutes to Shape Federal Information Policy: A Study of the PROFS Case," Ph.D. diss., University of Pittsburgh, 1997.

55. In addition to the Bearman essay, see Catherine F. Sheehan, "Opening the Government's Electronic Mail: Public Access to National Security Council Records," *Boston College Law Review* 35 (September 1994): 1145–1201; James D. Lewis, "White House Electronic Mail and Federal Recordkeeping Law: Press 'D' to Delete History," *Michigan Law Review* 93 (February 1995): 794–849; and Philip G. Schrag, "Working Papers as Federal Records: The Need for New Legislation to Preserve the History of National Policy," *Administrative Law Review* 46 (Spring 1994): 95–140.

56. David Roberts, "Defining Electronic Records, Documents and Data," *Archives and Manuscripts* 22 (May 1994): 14–26 is a good example of this approach. The most complete reflection on this matter resides in David Bearman's *Electronic Evidence*.

57. Michael Buckland, *Information and Information Systems* (New York: Praeger, 1991), p. 47.

58. Richard E. Barry, "Electronic Document and Records Management Systems: Towards a Methodology for Requirements Definitions," *Information Management and Technology* 27 (November 1994): 251–256.

59. This is, admittedly, not an easy task, as Nathaniel S. Borenstein's *Programming As If People Mattered: Friendly Programs, Software Engineering, and Other Noble Delusions* (Princeton, N.J.: Princeton University Press, 1991) suggests. Still, the first hurdle to be jumped is for archivists and records managers to know what their message to data processors and allied professionals must be.

60. David Bearman and Margaret Hedstrom, "Reinventing Archives for Electronic Records: Alternative Service Delivery Options," in Margaret Hedstrom, ed., *Electronic Records Management Program Strategies* (Pittsburgh: Archives and Museum Informatics, 1993), pp. 82–98 and Frank Upward and Sue McKemmish, "Somewhere Beyond Custody," *Archives and Manuscripts* 22 (May 1994): 136–149 are examples of this argument.

61. See, for example, Luciana Duranti, "Archives as a Place," *Archives & Manuscripts* 22, no. 2 (1994): 242–255 and Terry Eastwood, "Should Creating Agencies Keep Electronic Records Indefinitely," ibid., pp. 256–267.

62. Bearman, *Electronic Evidence*, pp. 75–76.

63. Eric W. Stein and Vladimir Zwass, "Actualizing Organizational Memory with Information Systems," *Information Systems Research* 6, no. 2 (1995): 86.

64. Stein and Zwass, "Actualizing Organizational Memory," p. 112.

65. Hubert Hall, *Studies in English Official Historical Documents* (Cambridge: Cambridge University Press, 1908), p. 24.

4

Building a National System of Records Administration

The irony in considering the history of modern records management, with the predilection to see its origins concentrated in the federal government, is the lack of a national records system. For many decades the American federal government expressed an interest in the preservation and management of archival records, including establishing a National Archives, endorsing documentary publications, funding a variety of archival causes and projects, and legislating to protect archival records and guarantee their continuing use. But what does this interest really mean? Is there a coherence to it? We can ask a deceptively simple question: Is there a system of archives and records management in the United States? The answer is no.

Americans are pragmatic. The lack of a system of archives has contributed to a barrier to the successful protection of the nation's documentary heritage and the schism between archivists and records managers and between records and other information professionals. There remain many opportunities for archivists and other records professionals to influence the public and the government in the preservation and management of records. American archivists and records managers must be more adamant in demanding a change of vision and greater accountability. Whereas in the past the National Archives was looked upon as the professional leader and the logical influencing agency for archival matters on Capitol Hill, this institution no longer completely fulfills that role. As this role of the National Archives waned, a void opened which no other professional association or institution has filled. The records professions require a new form of leadership and perhaps a new message about the importance of records.

Although there have been many studies regarding the federal government's support for archives and records, they provide an incomplete sense of the nature and parameters of such activities. The reason for this is quite simple. The majority of articles and books written on this topic have approached it from an institutional (or, sometimes, biographical) perspective. These writings analyze various aspects of the origins and development of the National Archives—the national government's primary institutional manifestation of its archival interest.[1] There have been few efforts to place the National Archives in the broader context of the national government's records and information policies, activities, and support or in the changing American records professions. What we have is a detailed, almost microscopic, view of the national government's interest in its own records as evident in the programs, successes, and failures of the National Archives. What one misses is a satisfactory accounting of the federal government's broader concerns, or lack thereof, for *all* the records of the nation, whether they be state and local government, corporate, or private. Given the prevalence of many records professionals to draw on policies, procedures, and practices of the National Archives, the incomplete understanding of where this institution fits into the broader system of records management philosophies and perspectives has serious implications. This institution's embroilment in litigation in the past decade is an indication of important problems requiring explanation and understanding.

This skewed analysis of the records management and archival activities in the United States may be due to the fact that the records professions and their institutions are relatively recent phenomena in this country, especially when compared to European counterparts. The archival community emerged in the early twentieth century, while the National Archives and the Society of American Archivists (the primary professional archival association) were founded in the mid-1930s. Other important aspects of the American archival profession, such as a professionally staffed SAA headquarters and the creation of other important archival institutions—such as in local governments and corporations—have emerged even more recently. Only during the past two decades has a self-consciousness among archivists developed encouraging investigation.[2] Records managers emerged from the formation of the archives discipline and, hence, they are an even more recent development. This youthfulness may also account for the unevenness of interest by the national government in archives and records administration, or it may be the result of the struggles of proceeding beyond the *value* of records to implementing *solutions* in their management (a challenge we can detect from the ancient world all the way through the complex modern electronic information devices).

What are the fuller dimensions of the national government's interest in archives and records? While the origins and development of the National Archives are part of this, we also need to consider legislation that protects (or sometimes harms) the documentary heritage, public funding to support the preservation and management of archival materials, nationally funded efforts to study and plan for the improvement of archival administration, and the national government's occasional endorsement of the interests of professional archival and records associations and programs in their efforts to strengthen the preservation of the nation's records.

There are rich lodes of documentation regarding the origins, nature, and changing spectrum of initiatives to preserve America's documentary heritage.[3] What follows is only a *framework* for new analysis needing to be done by archivists, records managers, and other researchers interested in archives and records issues in the United States. It is a preliminary *interpretation* of the national government's support of archives and records, based upon my reading of the extant and relevant studies, work in private and local and state government archives, participation in archival professional associations on state, regional, and national levels, and discussions with archivists and other records professionals over the past three decades. While I am convinced that the framework or interpretation presented here is an accurate one, I also believe that it is important that others recognize that it is mainly a preliminary effort to deal with a very complex topic.

What follows also considers the larger political and professional context of American archives and records work, something often left out of histories focusing on specific movements, individuals, or institutions. There is a description of the present federal government's degree of interest in records and the institutions and profession that care for these materials—a highly speculative assessment, since there is a wide range of opinion about what the national government's role should be and what it actually is. An effort to reveal how this present scenario has developed, by examining the historical evolution of the national government's participation in the management of the nation's documentary heritage, is the next part of this discussion. Finally, there is consideration of the needs for the national government's activities on behalf of the preservation of the country's archives and other records management, trying to answer the question, what should be the national government's role in the continuing maintenance of this (or any) country's documentary heritage?

To understand the American national government's role in archives, it is essential to understand that there is no real national archival or records system, first pointed out by then New York state archivist Larry Hackman in the mid-1980s.[4] I define a system as a group of elements working together for a common objective and held together by some legal, regulatory, or administrative structure. Although the American archival profession has a mission and at one point invested considerable resources in compiling a detailed plan to meet it,[5] archival cooperation and the mechanisms and justifications for supporting such cooperation are generally weak. Archival institutions tend to work in isolation, and the profession has not developed a coherent, sustained advocacy role on behalf of the preservation of archives. This has not nurtured an environment in which the national government's support of archives can be more firmly established. The informal and confusing connection with records management is part of this general problem.

Although there is a National Archives and it has been a dominant institution in preserving America's documentary heritage and managing generally records since its founding over sixty years ago, the National Archives exists apart from any unified or structured archival or records system, *except* its own. The National Archives has a group of field branches that preserve and make available federal archival records in various regions of the country. These branches were added to the federal records centers more than thirty years ago partly, in the words of then Archivist of the United States James B. Rhoads, to create a "decentralized, truly national, archival system to bring as many sources as possible to the researcher who may not find it convenient to spend days, weeks, or even months doing research in Washington."[6] Rhoads's concept of a system was notable, but the reality is that the branches were an afterthought to the National Archives' efforts to manage the many records of the national government created outside of Washington, D.C., where they could be most readily used and stored in an economical manner.[7]

Likewise, the presidential libraries represent another effort by the National Archives to construct a country-wide archival system. These libraries started in the late 1930s and were officially established in the mid-1950s primarily to resolve the problem of the records of the presidency, considered as private papers prior to the Presidential Records Act of 1978 and often falling prey to destruction, auction, and dispersal in unsatisfactory ways. Although the libraries have been criticized for many reasons, most often for allowing the construction of monuments to individuals or perpetuating the notion of an "imperial" presidency, the presidential libraries have been managed and viewed as part of the *internal* National Archives system. Their only major differences with other parts of this system have been the efforts by the various libraries to acquire the private papers of prominent individuals and organizations associated with specific presidential administrations and the museum functions that have become an attraction for popular audiences. As one commentary on these libraries suggests, the individual presidency works against the libraries sustaining a broader national archival or records system: the "presidential library will remain a monument to the individual president—a necessary monument to provide for the preservation of the historical record and to insure that presidential papers are available to scholars."[8] In this sense, the libraries are evidence of the lack of an American archival and records system. Before the Watergate scandal in the Nixon administration, the libraries represented the pinnacle of a compromise for the safety of the presidential records *without* resolving the issue of whether they were private papers or public records.[9] Still, the presidential libraries have often been lauded by researchers for consolidating vast quantities of archival records and manuscripts in generally convenient locations, much as the federal records centers have been applauded.

While there are national laws affecting recordkeeping in state and local governments, these governments have been pretty much left to fend for themselves. There is no comprehensive federal law or set of policies relating to this nation's archival records. One proposal has been made for a national historical records policy because the United States has "not yet spoken clearly as a nation about why such records have enduring value to a prosperous and democratic society, about what the public interest dictates regarding minimum acceptable conditions for such records, and about the appropriate role of the Federal government and others in meeting these conditions."[10] Although this proposal was an articulate call for such a policy, there is little evidence that any national association or institution is using it, or another alternative, in promoting a comprehensive policy.[11]

The same conditions hold true for the relationship between state and local governments. The ramifications of this lack of a systematic approach to archives are clearly seen in the management of local government records. While most states have local government records programs located in their state archival agencies, the nature of these programs represent a potpourri of efforts. Some have full-staffed programs that provide both records management and archival assistance, some have strong laws to back up their work with the political subdivisions, while others are virtually unstaffed and offer no more than advice when that advice is sought.

Local government archival records are found everywhere, defying any effort to see a systematic treatment of them. A 1988 national directory of archives and manuscript repositories revealed the existence of only twenty-six local government archives in the entire country, with the remainder of what local government archival records have been preserved found in public libraries, colleges and universities, historical societies, museums, and state archives. While the total of such programs has increased over the past decade, the proportion of local governments possessing full programs remains very small. Many of these local public records found their way into such repositories because there was *no* provision by their governments for their maintenance, prompting nineteenth and early twentieth century researchers to rescue these records from potential destruction and to deposit them in safer institutions.[12] It is also why one statement of principles for local government records, issued by the National Association of State (now Government) Archives and Records Administrators, noted that the "principles are general and must be interpreted and applied in light of state and local laws and traditions."[13] While such laws and traditions will always be important, they should not be the primary driving force behind what occurs with local government archival records.[14]

The lack of collaboration between archivists and records managers working in governmental institutions is also evident in their efforts to perform certain basic functions, such as appraisal. Government records professionals have long recognized that there are strong connections in origin, purpose, and form between federal, state, and local government records. The records of a local agency are most greatly shaped by federal and state regulations and funding. The precise kinds of information and the character of the records are often dictated by what other governmental entities require through law or via the pressure of funding availability. Despite the interrelatedness of these records, records professionals have not until recently begun to consider means by which to develop and support cooperative appraisal and descriptive approaches. Now archivists are exploring whether automated bibliographic systems can be used for this purpose, but this was a short-lived initiative and one without clear conclusions. State government records administrators discovered that their notion of appraisal and the manner in which they document it are vastly different even for similar kinds of agencies and records and require some additional systematization before effective cooperative appraisal is undertaken. The lack of national policy and strong leadership, from archivists and elsewhere, have worked against the development of such records cooperative ventures.

This absence of a national records system can also be seen in how business corporations care for their records. The federal, state, and local governments are primarily interested in corporations' records for acquiring revenue from taxation, protecting employees in their wages, health and safety, and from discrimination, and in protecting the citizens from unfair or dangerous corporate activities such as inferior products and environmental protection. As a result there are several thousand sections of federal laws with recordkeeping requirements, some sections having nearly 400 different rules regarding recordkeeping. None of these have any serious implications for the archival management of corporate information systems.[15] As a result there is a relatively small number of corporate archives programs in the United States. For example, in the early 1980s it was estimated that there were no more than 200 corporate archives in the United States, with nearly half of these programs concentrated in five of fifty states.[16] "It is common knowledge," one corporate archivist wrote, "that corporate archives are not at the top of the priority list of goals in most American businesses."[17] The archives that exist do so because of some peculiar interests held by the managers and owners of those businesses, generally for corporate image and public relations, rather than any external archival requirements or incentives. At the same time, these corporations have made immense investments in records and information resources management programs—especially in technology intended to bring greater efficiency to information administration.

Adding to this problem with corporate archives has been the archival profession's own uneasiness and uncertainty about how to document these institutions and the splintering of the records professions. Many archivists and private and public archival institutions remain wedded to the concept of collecting the records of corporations even in the face of huge quantities of documentation.[18] What results is the acquisition of only bits and pieces of the archival records that ought to be saved and the possible loss of considerable quantities of other important archival records. Other archivists have recently argued that carefully formulated archival documentation strategies need to be developed that determine what corporations should be documented and that encourage corporations to establish effective archival programs. One business historian expressed in frustration that it would be better to save all the records from a small number of businesses than to face making sense of the remnants that archivists have collected through other means; some archivists have agreed and have made efforts to develop new appraisal strategies.[19] What is missing are national government incentives encouraging the preservation of and access to the records of these corporations, similar to what has occurred with other valuable cultural resources, such as historic sites and buildings. Also missing is the participation of records managers. This has become especially important in an age in which vast quantities of information are automated and controlled by commercial vendors that provide access for fees, often at exorbitant rates.[20] What complicates making progress with the corporate records is that so many businesses have established records and information resources management programs with only an emphasis on *current* records, reflecting one of the negative results from a records community long ago split between archivists and records managers.

Some confusion may result from my allusions to private and public or government archives. In the United States, national, state, and local government records programs exist only to administer records created by those governments. There are other archival repositories (such as colleges and universities and historical societies) that acquire the personal papers of prominent individuals and families and the archival records of institutions or that serve to manage the archival records of their own institutions (such as businesses, religious organizations, and professional associations). To make matters more complicated, some of the latter repositories are completely or partially supported by government funds and also acquire the archival records of local government. This is the result of many factors, including the late development of government archives, an indomitable collecting spirit, practical needs to preserve certain neglected archival records, and archival legislation that is restricted to government records. This is partly why American archivists clearly distinguish between government archives ("the noncurrent records of an organization or institution preserved because of their continuing value") and private manuscripts ("bodies or groups of personal papers with organic unity, artificial collections of documents acquired from various sources usually according to a plan but without regard to provenance, and individual documents acquired by a manuscript repository because of their special importance").[21]

Another indication of the lack of a national records system is that many records do not find repositories in the existing archival institutions and are subject to widely divergent practices and policies. This is another characteristic of the public-private nature of archives in the United States. The personal papers of members of the U.S. House and the Senate are only typical examples of such problems. There are no guidelines, at least partly because there are "variations in the political environment in which state legislators function, the diversity of legislative styles and traditions among the states, differing established modes of conduct and patterns of activity between state assemblies and senates, and individual differences among the numerous incumbents elected to legislative office."[22]

Surveys of various state archives practices for certain kinds of records created by all or most of the state governments are also revealing. Although public welfare case records have definite archival value, state archives and records programs treat these records in a variety of manners according to different perceptions of confidentiality requirements, the informational value of the records relative to their bulk and space requirements, and legal authority by the state archives to manage such records.[23] This leads to fundamental questions some archivists have asked—what do the records in all the archival and records repositories in the United States constitute? Do they represent a thorough documentation of the nation, or a chance rag-bag of important, but uneven accumulation of, historical records? Do they provide a sufficient base for understanding the historical development of the nation, its institutions, and its citizens? Do they provide adequate provision for concerns such as accountability, memory, and evidence (themes treated throughout this volume as essential for managing records)? Is there need for a more systematic approach to the identification of *what* records should be preserved?[24]

The national government's funding sources for archival activities have been divided administratively, emphasizing different concerns and issues with generally only ad hoc cooperative efforts. We have no solid knowledge of the actual financial support for archival programs and their records because the funding is scattered about in a myriad of public funding agencies. Archival-related activities have been funded by the National Endowment for the Humanities, National Historical Publications and Records Commission (an arm of the National Archives), the Library Services and Construction Act (primarily for academic archives and special collections), the Institute of Library and Museum Services (for archives of museums and manuscripts held by these institutions), and a variety of other funding programs. These are *all* national government–funded programs that provide financial aid to various cultural organizations, usually through competitive grants for projects with specific aims. With the exception of the NHPRC support, most of these funding initiatives have only included archives as part of the larger bulk of cultural resources, primarily those held in the library and museum repositories, and they have often missed the important reality that in order to preserve the records of continuing value there must be a comprehensive records management program in place. Although this funding has had a significant impact on archives in certain areas, the total amount of funding has been extremely limited, and there seems to have been no consistent or long-term guiding principles or commitment to national government funding. Statements on the national funding of arts and humanities show that many are still grappling with questions such as how much should be spent by the federal government in light of continuing budget deficits and in comparison to other government programs and even what are the priorities within arts and humanities programs.[25]

Legislation, political administration, and governmental funding all have failed to create or sustain a coherent national records system in the United States.

What are the reasons for this absence of a national records system? How does the absence of this system affect the condition of America's documentary resources? How should it be addressed, or should it be addressed at all? Is this lack of a national system a major obstacle to ascertaining and winning the appropriate support from the national government for archives? Are such problems and challenges a legacy of the centuries of efforts to deal with managing records and archives?

Some of the reasons are clearly the result of the general historical development of the United States itself. From the end of its colonial existence and the beginning of its national identity, the United States has had a federal form of government, although the nature and opinion of federalism has changed through the years. A federal system of government provides that a national government and governments of member units of the nation will rule over the same land and people, each operating in differing authorities and making certain decisions independent of each other. There is both centralization and decentralization simultaneously, originally developed because of mistrust of centralized authority tempered by recognition of the need for such authority in certain instances and areas.[26]

Archival institutions and other records programs developed in this historical federal context. This is why state governments developed archival programs *before* the federal government, why some states established archival programs eighty years before others, why state archives reflect such great diversity, why the care of local governments' archives is so uneven, and why other unsystematic features characterize American archives and records programs. The federal government form has also contributed to the proliferation, complexity, and sometimes confused state of documentation. One leading archival commentator recently made the following observation: "A redistribution of responsibility for many basic societal functions and changes in organizational structure also make the documentation landscape more complex. In the government arena, the *new federalism* means that programs which once were the exclusive domain of a federal, state, or local government agency are now shared among the various levels of government. Agencies at all levels of government subcontract with providers in the private sector for direct services. In universities, research projects with joint government and corporate sponsorship are carried out by teams whose members reside on many campuses and who communicate at conferences and through electronic mail."[27] The comment on "new federalism" by this archivist refers, of course, to former President Reagan's efforts to reduce the regulatory roles of the national government, along with its budget, through the termination or significant reduction of many national operations and reformulation into large, loosely structured block grants. State and local governments now possess greater responsibility in both funding and policy.[28] Despite such shifts, the essential nature of federalism remains the same.[29]

The lack of a national records system is also partly perpetuated by the schismatic nature of the archival, records management, and information professions in the United States. These schisms testify to the wisdom of America's founders that self-interest and ambition dominate human nature, requiring a constant diligence through checks and balances or, at the least, that the system of professions continues to reflect one of its most important aspects, the competition between professions for control and authority.[30] Although the debate has subsided somewhat, archivists argued among themselves and with other disciplines for over a half-century about whether they were part of the historical or information professions.[31] Archivists grew out of the historical profession by the 1930s, records managers split from the archivists in the 1950s, government archivists and records managers formed their own association in the 1970s because of concern about the dominance in the Society of American Archivists of manuscript curators, and regional, state, and municipal archival associations emerged in the 1970s as an alternative to the national associations. The result is a potpourri of activities that often work against each other or that fail to take advantage of mutual interests and concerns. This proliferation of professional archival and records associations has also worked against the development of a national archival system. Whatever the reasons, the existence of these organizations have given the American records profession a distinct characteristic that sometimes makes it difficult for archivists and records managers to work together and to speak as a profession.[32] What voices, then, should the national government and its citizens listen to about better support for the archival records in the United States? Can these voices unite in order to advocate for a systematic national archival policy?

This lack of a professional hegemony is why certain other elements of a national archival and records system have failed to take hold. There is no truly integrated comprehensive national inventory of archival records.[33] There is also, and perhaps most importantly, less agreement about a systematic body of knowledge supporting the archives and records management professions in this country, producing a continuing discussion about whether what archivists know is primarily based on what they do or on theoretical principles.[34] There is also uncertainty about the archivist's precise relationship to the other historical and information professions. While records managers generally view archives as a function of a comprehensive records management program, their basic textbooks either ignore the topic or provide misleading and inaccurate information about the administration of archival materials. Yet, archivists remain somewhat unsure about how to incorporate records management into their work, especially in light of the increasing uses of electronic records.[35] To the outsider, the American records professions must seem to be an incomprehensible maze.

Despite such challenges, there are many ways that the present American national government reflects its interest in the preservation and management of archives and records. The highest profiled interest is through the institutions that have significant responsibility for the documentary heritage. The National Archives sits at the top of these institutions with its main buildings, federal records centers, and presidential libraries staffed by hundreds of professional archivists.

This institution's recent opening of a state-of-the-art archival facility has given it, and the archival mission, a higher profile in the 1990s. Throughout its history, the National Archives staff has provided national, as well as international, leadership to the archival community, contributing to the profession's theory and practice.[36] The National Archives' funding branch, the National Historical Publications and Records Commission, has also provided support for the American archival profession's work by underwriting research, publication of archival administration texts, conferences, and similar efforts.

Other institutions also reflect the national government's interest in archives and records in general. The Library of Congress has not only a large national manuscripts collection but has provided the superstructure for the development of the US MARC Archives and Manuscripts Control format and investigated preservation issues of importance to the archival community.[37] This institution demonstrates that in United States libraries also serve as archival repositories, acquiring and preserving the archival records of their local communities or concerned with defined topics. The Smithsonian Institution also supports an immense number of manuscript and archival collections and has provided leadership in the development of archival automation and other areas.[38] The Smithsonian is indicative of the fact that in the United States museums and other cultural organizations often provide archival services. There are other federal agencies employing historians and archivists to ensure that their archival records are preserved and their agencies documented as thoroughly as can be. The United States Senate has a Senate Historical Office ensuring that the records of that body are well cared for and that the papers of individual senators are placed in appropriate archival repositories.[39] The United States Corps of Engineers has sponsored the writing of an impressive series of histories, heavily based on its own and other records, that has drawn attention to the importance of an historical understanding of the Corps' work and the value of such historical research in general.[40]

It is difficult to determine the national government's commitment to the country's documentary heritage by merely identifying the many federal agencies involved with archival activities and then analyzing their contribution to the records profession's mission. Many of the activities and contributions of these programs occur despite hardships resulting from the national government's tentative commitment to preserving archives and managing all records. Funding levels for archival programs and legislation guarding the documentary heritage help to round out a fuller picture of the national government's interest in archives. Both show the results of the unsystematic nature of American archives and the influence of the federal form of government that characterizes the United States.

The national government's dollar amount for archival institutions and records projects seems impressive, but it falls far short of what it might be. The funding limitations are obvious in a report by researchers of the National Archives comparing expenditures for this institution: "In a democratic society, citizens expect the government to preserve the records of enduring value and to make them available to the public. The amount of money allocated to archives frequently reflects the degree to which citizens and lawmakers appreciate the valuable functions that archives perform. The expenditure for the National Archives of Canada is approximately $2.14 (Canadian dollars) per capita. In the United States some of the states allocate over $1 per capital for their state archives. Yet the current budget for the National Archives is only 50 cents per capita."[41] SAA's then President John Fleckner testified in April 1990 before a congressional subcommittee that the national government's financial support of archives constituted "neglect." The annual allocation of the NHPRC has vacillated between only $4 million and $5 million, with roughly half of that money designated for documentary editing projects that can preserve only a minuscule portion of this nation's historical records[42] and the remainder divided up among arrangement and description projects, support of consulting and institutional self-study, cooperative initiatives, educational programs, and national projects in research and publication. Altogether, the commission provided about $18 million for archival records projects from 1977 through 1987, slightly less than $2 million a year for a decade; this amount has remained basically the same since then. When it is considered that there are roughly 10,000 archivists working in the United States in well over 5,000 repositories and that there are countless thousands of other institutions that need but don't have archival and records programs,[43] the level of funding for archives provided by the commission looks paltry indeed. The much higher national government funding levels for libraries, to nearly $1 billion in recent years, attests to the library profession's larger size, higher visibility, and more aggressive political advocacy.[44]

This funding does not look much better when combined with all the other national funding of archival projects and programs and compared to the total national government budget. If all the funds of the NEH, IMLS, National Archives, and Library of Congress, along with other arts and humanities and library programs, were added together, they would constitute less than 1 percent of the national government's budget.[45] Only a small portion of all this programmatic funding is devoted to the preservation and management of archival records and manuscript collections. Over the 1980s, the NHPRC and NEH only provided about $70 million for archival projects. This came at a time when federal support for state and local government exceeded a quarter of their annual budgets on the average, leading to the federal government's more pervasive influence on all governmental levels and citizens (despite the "new federalism") than the nation's founders ever foresaw.[46]

Current national government legislation also provides an uneven or unsteady concept of the national government's interest in America's documentary heritage and records. On the one hand, there is a labrinyth of legislation affecting and guiding the maintenance of national government records,[47] while on the other hand, there have been definite problems in ensuring that the legislation is effectively carried out. The National Archives itself has concluded that while its authority to appraise and accession government records has been hindered by the removal of direct records management responsibilities to the General Services Administration in 1985 (when the National Archives regained administrative independence), its own ability to meet these responsibilities even before then had been mixed.[48] To this day, however, the cornerstone of national government records legislation remains the Federal Records Act of 1950, which established records management operations in the national government and placed the National Archives under the General Services Administration until the more recent independence legislation.

While the National Archives has operated reasonably well under a variety of records laws, the changing political administrations seem intent on challenging the integrity of archival records. Some of the primary historical landmarks in records legislation have occurred as the result of the presidency's efforts to ignore existing regulations and procedures. The lawsuit about the White House's automated mail system that was used by some of the individuals involved in the controversial Iran-Contra affair is an example. The Reagan-Bush administrations contended that this system did not fall under any legal definition of records, was backed by the National Archives in this, and both were sued by a group of professional associations, researchers, journalists, and interested citizens. Just two days before President Reagan left office he signed an executive order that gave him lifelong authority to prevent disclosure of privileged papers created by or for him during his presidency, an act in direct contradiction of the Presidential Records Act of 1978, which made these records public and required them to be transferred to the National Archives.[49] Such actions have operated contrary to an array of laws and authorities providing solid written protection of the archival integrity of such records.[50] Complicating these problems and challenges have been problems with mission identification and leadership at the National Archives. While some lament that the records professions do not give enough credit to the National Archives for the good it has done,[51] others argue that the Archives has failed to be as strong and energetic as it could be, citing inadequate priorities and mismanagement.[52]

Such problems reflect the difficulty of a national government information policy in which records professionals and their records ought to play a significant role and have an important stake. But national information is not a tranquil stream that is easy to float along; it is more like a treacherous river after heavy rains. There is no consistent national information policy, and there are a huge number of constituencies (archivists among them, but often weakly heard) clamoring for what they think the national information policy should be or, and more confusing, how the array of national information policies should relate to one another.[53] Privacy, freedom of access, copyright, the effect of technology, costs of access, information as a resource and its reuse for commercial gain, foreign access and competition, and national government dissemination of information are all aspects of information about which the national government is expected to maintain a coherent policy. Some want added to this the archival mission to identify, preserve, and make accessible the records of archival value. Thus far, the national government's policy toward archival records and records management has been expressed through its prime institution, the National Archives, its limited funding support for archival projects and initiatives, and legislation often enacted during crises concerning public ownership of certain records. The present lack of clarity is the result of the national government's traditional interest in archival records, tied back to the federal government form and other practices that emerged in the breech to preserve America's documentary heritage.

How has the national government's interest in archives and records, both those of the national government itself and those created by other governmental agencies and private entities, evolved? The national government expressed concern for managing records from its establishment in 1789, one of its first statutes making provision for government agencies to establish filing systems and keep records. This was not unique to the American national government, since the American colonial governments had all enacted similar legislation and such legislation was a reflection of European tradition. But this act was not a conscious effort to provide for archival records, nor did it exist as part of a broader commitment to preserve the archival records of the nation. The pattern of care for the nation's documentary heritage in the late eighteenth and early nineteenth centuries was one of an antiquarian interest in preserving old manuscripts and records for research and enjoyment wherever and however they could be preserved. Privately funded and run historical societies began to emerge as repositories for manuscripts and archives in this time, but the acquisition for preservation of such materials was equally shared by private autograph collectors, researchers who gathered whatever materials they could for their writings, and publishers who prepared documentary editions. Individuals like Ebenezer Hazard, Lyman Draper, Jeremy Belknap, Jared Sparks, and George Bancroft made the main efforts to preserve America's historical treasures, and without them and their initiatives many more valuable private and public records would have been lost.[54] In none of this was there any visible or invisible hand of the national government directing that the historical records of the country be preserved, perhaps because during these early years the quantity of records that the government itself created and managed was small.[55]

The first interest in the nation's archival records had to wait until the mid-nineteenth century. During these years the national government from time to time authorized the purchase of records for deposit in a national institution, underwrote the publication of a documentary edition, funded the copying of archival records abroad, and made certain limited provisions for the national government's own records.[56] Before then, prominent public officials like Thomas Jefferson expressed concern for the loss of historical records, but their concerns did not lead them to seek official government intervention in their preservation. The government's range of interests was limited, since during this time individuals (except historians and antiquarians) had very specific notions about documents, public and private. As one historian notes, "documents were for use, and when they ceased to have use they were destroyed. When they were retained by the person or institution that had generated them, it was either because they continued to have use or because no one had gotten around to disposing of them."[57] As this historian suggests, the vast array of historical societies, libraries, and museums formed to collect and publish archival records were really after documents that most of society had relegated to not having any real utility. It should not be surprising, then, that the national government was not devoting much attention to such matters. Several generations of work by the directors and curators of these institutions would transform these views, but this was at best a gradual process.

By the late nineteenth century the national government was directing some attention at least to its own records. The aftermath of the American Civil War and the 1876 centennial of the Declaration of Independence inspired a more national self-consciousness about its past, leading to a proliferation of publications and the establishment of historical societies and museums that would serve as repositories for public and private archives. The national government was not immune to the new interests. The Department of State issued a published set of calendars to their historical archives in 1893, but this seemed to be at best an example only of isolated interest, since the government did not embark on a campaign to work with the full panorama of the nation's archives. This was, instead, left to the American Historical Association's Historical Manuscripts Commission (1895) and Public Archives Commission (1899). The association, led by dynamic and persuasive leaders like J. Franklin Jameson, succeeded in finally getting the national government to found and support an archives in 1934 (after numerous attempts since the 1880s), but other work by this time was still extremely limited. Victor Gondos, in the fullest chronicle of the movement for the National Archives, concludes that the reason for the incredibly long gestation period for this institution was "legislative sloth": "The national legislators had too many other and more material interests than the archival problem to occupy and grip their attention. Here and there, some were willing to pay lip service to the problem, at least to the extent of recognizing its existence. But by and large, congressional ignorance of the values at stake, compounded by suspicion of the motives of the proponents, and congressional insistence on the time-honored pork barrel, hamstrung all efforts at archival progress."[58] The Historical Records Survey (1936–1942) must be seen first as an effort to employ the unemployed rather than the launching of an ambitious new national government program on behalf of America's documentary heritage. Its short life, and even the destruction of many of the valuable finding aids and research of the survey in the years shortly after its termination, indicates that no new national agenda for archives had suddenly been christened.[59]

The National Archives became *the* national government's interest in archives for two generations at least. The Depression and the Second World War became the main issues for Americans and their government for the decade following the establishment of the National Archives. Aside from some involvement of archives staff (and archivists from elsewhere) in ensuring the protection of the vital national records in case of the war reaching American shores, the National Archives' establishment was the primary archival attention by the government. Determining who should be appointed archivist of the United States, where the agency's first staff should come from, how the institution should be structured, what principles should govern its work, what records should be brought into the repository, and other matters were the essential focus of the national government during the first two decades of the National Archives. These were all internal affairs for the institution. Facing this challenge, the National Archives responded by becoming a national (and international) archival leader, contributing to the archival profession's basic theories and providing leadership in critical matters through the years. Indeed, the National Archives and its staff was an important building block in the foundation of both the American archival and records management professions.

If there has been a catalyst for the development of a national archival pro-fession leading toward a national system, it has been the funding program of the National Historical Publications and Records Commission. Organized as part of the legislation creating the National Archives in the 1930s, the National Historical Publications Commission (as it was originally named) was dormant until 1950. In that year it was revived to provide guidance to the preparation of documentary editions, reflecting its original name, that were being done by his-torians and university and commercial presses. In the 1970s, due to external pressure from the archival community, the commission's role was expanded to provide funding for archival records projects and its name was changed.

The NHPRC has provided millions of dollars for published editions of his-torical documents and for the appraisal, arrangement, description, and preser-vation of historical and archival records.[60] Perhaps more important, the commission has supported the publication of many basic archival texts, educa-tional initiatives, and national standards projects that have fundamentally changed the character of the American archival community. So significant has been NHPRC's effect on the archival profession, that the possible 1981 demise of an appropriation for the records and editing programs led to funding of state assessment and reporting projects that had a tremendous impact on the depth of knowledge that archivists possess about their repositories and the holdings in these institutions. These reports have been repeatedly drawn upon by archivists in subsequent state and national archival activities.[61] However, while there has been increasing attention to records management issues, these issues remain peripheral, with no counterpart funding for records management.

It is not coincidental that the emergence of the NHPRC in the mid-1970s marked a period of intense new activity within the archival community. Al-though the NHPRC, armed with its federal funding, was an important catalytic agent, the National Archives was not faring as well, evidence that the greater professional activity was resulting from factors other than any increased national interest in archival matters. Starting at least by the mid-1970s, the national government seemed intent on expressing its concern for archival records in ways that hindered the National Archives. This institution lost many of its former records management responsibilities, was plagued by poor leadership from its parent agency (the General Services Administration), and was put into a stagnant financial situation with no major increases, a process that lessened the National Archives' ability to meet its mandate.[62] From 1982 through 1984, the National Archives galvanized professional archival activity via the movement of archivists and related professionals to win its administrative independence, only one indication that professional archivists *and* users of archival sources were not at all pleased with the national government's interest in and support of the country's documentary heritage.[63] Just after the National Archives became independent, the release of the *Report of the Committee on the Records of Government*, a study funded by several private foundations, revealed that this premier federal archival program had fallen considerably behind in many essential areas. The *Report* noted that the National Archives lacked capability and authority to manage the records of the national government, especially those records being created in electronic formats.[64] In one of the best characterizations of this period, Larry Hackman noted the following about this report: "The National Archives has not yet achieved visibility and support, either within the federal establishment or with the general public, commensurate with its functions and comparable to other major cultural agencies. Nor has the National Archives provided leadership to the broader archival community, particularly to state and local government records and archives programs where, according to the report, federal conditions are by and large replicated."[65] Later assessments have suggested that the report has not had the effect intended.[66]

One important fact to keep in mind is that throughout the commission's life, it has had to fight annually for every cent from the administration and its existence has been sometimes seen as tenuous. The amount of funding for this organization has been extremely marginal. This is, perhaps, a more accurate expression of the national government's interest in the archival records of the United States. It can also be seen in other ways as well.

Legislation has been a preoccupation for archivists and records managers for a long time, sometimes the result of their initiative, sometimes in reaction to actions taken externally that threaten dire consequences to the nation's records. The 1974 passage of a presidential records act was the result of Richard Nixon's resignation as chief executive of the United States. Archivists' and records managers' concerns intensified later with the 1976 copyright law (threatening the scholarly community's ability to copy archival records for their use), legislation on privacy and access (complicating archival practices), and the Federal Paperwork Commission's examination of the overall management of the national government's records (with little attention to archival concerns). Acts on government records and information policy continued through the 1980s and the 1990s, up to and including government information locator services promising greater access to records and other information sources. The more recent efforts have had at best indirect influence on such legislation and policies, partly because it is difficult to determine how to have such a role and because the national government bureaucrats, Congress, and the various presidential administrations still do not normally think of archivists, records managers, or their records when considering such matters.

The federal system is one contributing factor to the mixed qualities of federal government support, but it is not the place to look to for solutions or to lay the blame. Federalism can be shaped to incorporate desires by the citizenry, interest groups, and government to carry out changing agendas, such as in how the national government has shifted and remolded its attention to public education due to differing political agendas and historical events.[67] Consider the lack of a suitable historical records or information policy and the potential alternatives. Robert Mckeever, a political scientist, comments that "good public policy consists of much more than merely a smooth policy system." Continuing along this line, he states that "if efficiency of policy delivery were the sole aim, then centralization and even authoritarianism might well be best suited to achieving it: the fewer institutions and individuals playing a role in the making of public policy, the greater is the chance for agreement and efficient policy making. However, this ignores the vital fact that most Americans want not only efficient policy making, but also democratic, or at least open, policy making. And open policy making is not simply a good thing in itself, it is a precondition of effective policy making. . . . Seen in the light of this conflict between openness and efficiency, the best policy-making process is not that which sacrifices the one for the other, but rather that which balances the two in the manner most appropriate to serving the particular values and policy needs of any given society."[68] Waldo Leland, instrumental in bringing together the first groups of archivists and other records professionals, was attuned to this problem ninety years ago. In a paper at the first meeting of the Conference of Archivists in 1909, he stressed that archivists had to "secure the legislation which will insure the proper preservation and administration of all of our public records." But this is a difficult task because the American form of government, he noted, is decentralized among state and national governments.[69]

Getting the national government to clarify and to increase its support in national archival and records management activities through the creation of a national archives or records policy is a monumental task. Individuals who have worked for clarification of federal policy in other areas, such as in the arts, have struggled in this both because of the energy and resources needed for political advocacy and the worry about the impact, through restrictions or imposition of viewpoints, of government officials, Congress, and presidencies on the freedom of artistic expression. Archivists have also worried about such things, expressing concerns about the manner in and degree to which the national government should be involved in preserving the nation's documentary heritage. Maynard Brichford, a past president of the Society of American Archivists, stated that the "concept that federal funds should be used to create a unitary national archival system or to identify and preserve state, local, and nongovernmental records of long-term value is not self-evident. A large part of documented America is, and should remain, unrelated to federal and state government support, coordination, and planning."[70] Brichford offered no real alternate vision for what the national government's responsibility for America's archival records ought to be.

Such views, which I would characterize as ambivalent—interest in financial support but no interest in anything that might be construed as restrictive or critical—are not unique to archives or records management. Does this mean that in an open, democratic society with a federal form of government that archivists and records managers should not seek a national records policy or to influence other information and records policies affecting the integrity of the archival record or of records and their management in general? Certainly not. The concepts that Larry Hackman spelled out in his ideas for such a policy are admirable and should be pursued, since they seek to get the national government to affirm that archival and other records are essential to the well-being of our society. Seeking a national policy on any issue is an effort to get the government and citizens to express the importance of that issue.

Here we can turn to what has been stated about such a policy for the arts: "To most Americans who might give it any thought, it would not appear a good idea to have a public policy in the arts that was official. And the United States has none. If there indeed exists public policy about the arts, which even many in the field are not clear about, it is the product of plural influences, and government is only a most recent, if vivid, example." Additionally, "No policy in any field is truly coherent or consensual, and a policy is not inherently a manifesto. What we may really be digging for are clues to the values placed on the arts by society."[71] Records professionals must seek to communicate more effectively to the national government the value of archives and records to society. Archivists have penned some very persuasive and articulate expressions of these values,[72] but it is uncertain who has listened to and understood these sentiments. Archivists and records managers ought to be in a position to influence any policies, legislation, and other activities that the national government engages in to ensure that they don't endanger but support the documentary heritage. And archivists and records managers should work to educate the government officials and various administrations so that they are aware of the basic values of the documentary heritage. This will not be easy, of course, since the interest of elected officials and government bureaucrats is often more in a mythological interpretation of the past that requires the preservation of hardly more than an handful of documents to serve as sacred texts or symbols for the democratic society.[73] Nevertheless, the quest to develop a greater awareness by the national government of the importance of records certainly states what ought to be one of the highest components of the records professions' agenda in the United States. While we can't expect the national government to fund fully every aspect

of every archival institution or every organization's records management operation in this country, we should expect that it will support a premier national
archives for its own records, not take any action that will harm the documentary
heritage, enact or endorse measures that will encourage archival records to be
preserved and accessible, and provide a level of financial support that is in
proportion to the importance of archival and other records to the well-being of
the nation and its citizens. Defining these needs better is the task that American
archivists and records managers now have before them.

This portrait of the national government's interest in archives and records
reflects the condition of a young nation and even younger archives and records
management professions. This youth provides the American archivist or records
manager an attitude in keeping with the pioneering spirit of this nation. In seeking to acquire the greater support of the government, the American archivist and
records manager will be able to, in fact must, build on traditional principles
without being handcuffed by them. Older principles must be re-evaluated and,
if necessary, revised. There is still a need for newer principles, especially in
working with new information technologies and in capturing the attention of the
national government in caring for its archival and other records. Archivists and
records managers in the United States are making great strides in doing this,
and they face the challenges of the modern information age with anticipation
and excitement.

NOTES

1. The major studies completed on the National Archives include H. G. Jones, *The
Records of a Nation: Their Management, Preservation and Use* (New York: Atheneum,
1969); Donald McCoy, *The National Archives: America's Ministry of Documents 1934–
1968* (Chapel Hill: University of North Carolina Press, 1978); Victor Gondos, Jr., *J.
Franklin Jameson and the Birth of the National Archives 1906–1926* (Philadelphia: University of Pennsylvania Press, 1981); and Timothy Walch, ed., *Guardian of Heritage:
Essays on the History of the National Archives* (Washington, D.C.: National Archives
and Records Administration, 1985).

2. The period from the late 1970s through the 1980s was a particularly volatile period
in American archival and records management history. Among other things, there was a
major effort to assess the condition of historical records in all the states, production of
a major professional agenda and plan, implementation of an individual certification program, re-evaluation of and expansion in graduate archival education, and a spirited effort
to gain independence for the National Archives. For a description of this period and these
events, refer to Richard Cox, *American Archival Analysis: The Recent Development of
the Archival Profession in the United States* (Metuchen, N.J.: Scarecrow Press, 1990).

3. For the possibilities of such needed study, see Frederick J. Stielow with James
Gregory Bradsher, "Archival Enterprise," in Donald G. Davis, Jr., and John Mark
Tucker, *American Library History: A Comprehensive Guide to the Literature* (Santa
Barbara, Calif.: ABC-CLIO, 1989), pp. 215–225, as well as citations in earlier chapters.

4. Larry J. Hackman, "A Perspective on American Archives," *Public Historian* 8
(Summer 1986): 25–27.

5. *Planning for the Archival Profession: A Report of the SAA Task Force on Goals and Priorities* (Chicago: Society of American Archivists, 1986).

6. Quoted in James Gregory Bradsher, "Federal Field Archives: Past, Present, and Future," *Government Information Quarterly* 4, no. 2 (1987): 156.

7. Refer to Bradsher, "Federal Field Archives: Past, Present, and Future."

8. Cynthia J. Wolff, "Necessary Monuments: The Making of the Presidential Library System," *Government Publications Review* 16, no. 1 (1989): 58.

9. J. Frank Cook, "'Private Papers' of Public Officials," *American Archivist* 38 (July 1975): 299–324; Pamela R. McKay, "Presidential Papers: A Property Issue," *Library Quarterly* 52 (1982): 21–40; and Raymond Geselbracht, "The Four Eras in the History of Presidential Papers," *Prologue* 15 (Spring 1983): 37–42 all provide a useful perspective on these institutions.

10. Larry J. Hackman, "The United States Needs a National Historical Records Policy!" *History News* 43 (March/April 1988): 32.

11. For an explanation of some of the reasons for these problems, refer to Edie Hedlin, "*Chinatown* Revisited: The Status and Prospects for Government Records in America," *Public Historian* 8 (Summer 1986): 46–59.

12. For a case study of the location of public records in such institutions, see Christopher P. Bickford, "Public Records and the Private Historical Society: A Connecticut Example," *Government Publications Review* 8A (1981): 311–320.

13. Bruce W. Dearstyne, "Principles for Local Government Records: A Statement of the National Association of State Archives and Records Administrators," *American Archivist* 46 (Fall 1983): 454.

14. The principles and assumptions for local government records stated in the New York plan for managing local government records are, for example, not unique to this state but generally universal in this nation. This report noted, among other things, that state government had a "legitimate role" in the administration of local government records because of legal relationships, obligations by the state to promote effective and efficient government, the documentation of state government often found in local public records, and the origins of some local records because of state programs. See *The Quiet Revolution: Managing New York's Local Government Records in the Information Age* (Albany: New York Local Government Records Advisory Council, December 1, 1987), pp. 5–6.

15. See Donald S. Skupsky, *Recordkeeping Requirements: The First Practical Guide to Help You Control Your Records . . . What You Need to Keep and What You Can Safely Destroy!* 2nd ed. (Denver: Information Requirements Clearinghouse, 1989). During the past decade, it is likely that the number of requirements has increased.

16. An excellent review of the development of North American corporate archives, clearly revealing that efforts to preserve such records have operated outside of the national government, is Christopher Hives, "History, Business Records, and Corporate Archives in North America," *Archivaria* 22 (Summer 1986): 40–57. An up-to-date directory, compiled by the Society of American Archivists Business Archives Section, is available at http://www.hunterinformation.com/corporat.htm. It suggests a larger number of corporate archives, but there is no summary data suggesting relative health or strength of these programs.

17. Douglas A. Bakken, "Corporate Archives Today," *American Archivist* 45 (Summer 1982): 280. For the continuing challenges to American business archives and records programs, see Elizabeth W. Adkins, "The Development of Business Archives in the

United States: An Overview and a Personal Perspective," *American Archivist* 60 (Winter 1997): 8–33.

18. For insights into the various problems and challenges caused by such approaches, refer to James M. O'Toole, ed., *The Records of American Business* (Chicago: Society of American Archivists, 1997). The various essays in this volume suggest both more sophisticated methods for acquiring the records of businesses and the dangers involved in remaining committed to such acquisition agendas.

19. JoAnne Yates, "Internal Communications Systems in American Business Structure: A Framework to Aid Appraisal," *American Archivist* 48 (Spring 1985): 141–158. For an effort by archivists to respond to this problem, see Philip N. Alexander and Helen W. Samuels, "The Roots of 128: A Hypothetical Documentation Strategy," *American Archivist* 50 (Fall 1987): 518–531 (Route 128 is the location of a group of high-technology companies ringing Boston, Massachusetts, that have developed since the Second World War).

20. See, for example, James A. Nelson, ed., *Gateways to Comprehensive State Information Policy* (Lexington, Ky.: Chief Officers of State Library Agencies through the Council of State Governments, 1990).

21. Frank B. Evans et al., "A Basic Glossary for Archivists, Manuscript Curators, and Records Managers," *American Archivist* 37 (July 1974): 417, 426. The current directory has revised the definition for archives—"the documents created or received and accumulated by a person or organization in the course of the conduct of affairs, and preserved because of their continuing value," but it has left the definition for manuscripts generally unchanged; Lewis J. and Lynn Lady Bellardo, comps., *A Glossary for Archivists, Manuscript Curators, and Records Managers* (Chicago: Society of American Archivists, 1992), pp. 3, 22.

22. Paul I. Chestnut, "Appraising the Papers of State Legislators," *American Archivist* 48 (Spring 1985): 160. For an illuminating view of why these records have been less than uniformly dealt with, see Patricia Aronsson, "Appraisal of Twentieth-Century Congressional Collections," in Nancy E. Peace, ed., *Archival Choices: Managing the Historical Record in an Age of Abundance* (Lexington, Mass.: Lexington Books, 1984), pp. 81–101.

23. R. Joseph Anderson, "Public Welfare Case Records: A Study of Archival Practices," *American Archivist* 43 (Spring 1980): 169–179.

24. See Helen Willa Samuels, "Who Controls the Past," *American Archivist* 49 (Spring 1986): 109–124 for an early posing of such questions.

25. Robert F. Lyke, *Arts and Humanities: FY88–FY89 Funding Issues*, IB82026 ([Washington, D.C.: Congressional Research Service, Library of Congress], February 23, 1988). The debates about such funding have become more protracted, intense, and divisive as these endowments have been attacked for political, cultural, and administrative reasons. For a very personal and insightful glimpse of such recent debates, see John Frohnmayer, *Leaving Town Alive: Confessions of an Arts Warrior* (Boston: Houghton Mifflin Co., 1993).

26. For some useful studies of American federalism, refer to William H. Riker, *The Development of American Federalism* (Boston: Kluwer Academic Publishers, 1987) and William K. Hall, *The New Institutions of Federalism: The Politics of Intergovernmental Relations 1960–1985* (New York: Peter Lang, 1989).

27. Margaret Hedstrom, "New Appraisal Techniques: The Effect of Theory on Practice," *Provenance* 8, no. 2 (Fall 1989): 5.

28. For a concise description of the recent massive changes in the federal structure, refer to David B. Walker, "American Federalism: Past, Present and Future," *Journal of State Government* 62 (January/February 1989): 3–11 and Timothy J. Conlan, "Federalism at the Crossroads: Conflicting Trends, Competing Futures," ibid., 50–55.

29. Martha Derthick, "The Enduring Features of American Federalism," *Brookings Review* 7 (Summer 1989): 34–38.

30. See, for example, Andrew Abbott, *The System of Professions* and, for comments on the Abbott book and its implications for the archival profession, Richard J. Cox, "Professionalism and Archivists Revisited: A Review Essay," *Midwestern Archivist* 15, no. 2 (1990): 5–15.

31. For some of the strongest arguments, see George Bolotenko, "Archivists and Historians," *Archivaria*, and the responses in issues 17 through 20: no. 17 (Winter 1983–1984): 286–308; no. 18 (Summer 1984): 241–247; no. 19 (Winter 1984–1985): 185–195; no. 20 (Summer 1985): 142–147; and Mattie U. Russell, "The Influence of Historians on the Archival Profession in the United States," *American Archivist* 46 (Summer 1983): 277–285.

32. Patrick M. Quinn, "Regional Archival Organizations and the Society of American Archivists," *American Archivist* 46 (Fall 1983): 433–440.

33. See Avra Michelson, "Description and Reference in the Age of Automation," *American Archivist* 50 (Spring 1987): 192–208, and Nancy Sahli, "National Information Systems and Strategies for Research Use," *Midwestern Archivist* 9, no. 1 (1984): 5–13. An older essay on this effort is Francis L. Berkeley, Jr., "History and Problems of the Control of Manuscripts in the United States," *Proceedings of the American Philosophical Society* 98 (June 1954): 171–178.

34. Frank G. Burke, "The Future Course of Archival Theory in the United States," *American Archivist* 44 (Winter 1981): 40–46; Lester J. Cappon, "What, Then, Is There to Theorize About?" *American Archivist* 45 (Winter 1982): 19–25; Gregg D. Kimball, "The Burke-Cappon Debate: Some Further Criticisms and Considerations for Archival Theory," *American Archivist* 48 (Fall 1985): 369–376; and John W. Roberts, "Archival Theory: Much Ado About Shelving," *American Archivist* 50 (Winter 1987): 66–74.

35. William Benedon's classic text, *Records Management* (Los Angeles: Trident Shop, 1969), devoted only four pages to company archives, mostly consisting of a list of relevant or potential archival records. Things have not improved very much over the past two decades, however. Irene Place and David J. Hyslop in their *Records Management: Controlling Business Information* (Reston, Va.: Reston Publishing Co., 1982) provide only a page on business archives with advice like "local professional librarians are usually knowledgeable about archival procedures, but for special problems, consult the state archivist at the state capitol" (p. 269). Even records management textbooks that devote at least a chapter to archival work provide at best scanty coverage of archival principles and practices; see, for example, Ira A. Penn, Anne Morddel, Gail Pennix, and Kelvin Smith, *Records Management Handbook* (Brookfield, Vt.: Gower Publishing Co., 1989). Archivists have not done much better in the manner in which they present records management in their writings, viewing it often only as a tool to achieve their ends or misrepresenting it as a profession interested in only the destruction of records.

36. T. R. Schellenberg has been the best known of the archivists who have worked in the National Archives; for assessments of his influence see Jane F. Smith, "Theodore Schellenberg," *American Archivist* 44 (1981): 313–326 and Richard C. Berner, *Archival Theory and Practice in the United States: A Historical Analysis* (Seattle: University of

Washington Press, 1983). See also Trudy Huskamp Peterson, "The National Archives and the Archival Theorist Revisited, 1954–1984," *American Archivist* 49 (1986): 125–133 and J. Frank Cook, "The Blessings of Providence on An Association of Archivists," ibid., 46 (1983): 31–41.

37. The early history of the development of the important manuscripts collection in the Library of Congress can be seen in Fred Shelley, "Manuscripts in the Library of Congress: 1800–1900," *American Archivist* 11 (January 1948): 3–19. The development of the US MARC Archives and Manuscripts Control format is chronicled through an already voluminous body of literature, too cumbersome to review thoroughly here, in archival and library journals.

38. See, for example, Avra Michelson, ed., *Archives and Authority Control: Proceedings of a Seminar*, Archival Informatics Technical Report 2 (Summer 1988), which reprints the papers of a conference sponsored by the Smithsonian.

39. Richard A. Baker, "The Records of Congress: Opportunities and Obstacles in the Senate," *Public Historian* 2 (Summer 1980): 62–72.

40. See the review essay by Jeffrey Stine in the *Public Historian* 2 (Spring 1980): 91–96 for a description of a representative group of these histories. For some indication of the scope of the national government's interest in historical publishing, see Joseph P. Harahan and David M. Pemberton, "United States Federal History: A Bibliography," *Government Publications Review* 16 (1989): 463–488.

41. Page Putnam Miller, *Developing a Premier National Institution: A Report from the User Community to the National Archives* ([Washington, D.C.]: National Coordinating Committee for the Promotion of History, 1989), p. 36.

42. Documentary editing has had a long and interesting history in the United States, but it has largely functioned outside of the archival profession. Documentary editors generally more closely ally with the historical profession, possess their own professional association, and work under their own standards and principles. For a fuller explication of my views, see Chapter 8 in this book.

43. The figures for the numbers of archivists and archival repositories is a very rough estimate on my part, based on the number of programs listed in various museums, archives, and historical societies and the various memberships of the national and regional professional archival associations.

44. For some interesting insights into the matter of national government library support, see Redmond Kathleen Molz, *Federal Policy and Library Support* (Cambridge, Mass.: MIT Press, 1976) and David Shavit, *Federal Aid and State Library Agencies: Federal Policy Implementation*, Contributions in Librarianship and Information Science, no. 52 (Westport, Conn.: Greenwood Press, 1985).

45. These figures are derived from Susan Boren, *Arts and Humanities: Funding Issues in the 101st Congress*, IB90050 ([Washington, D.C.: Congressional Research Service, Library of Congress], April 17, 1990) and Wayne C. Riddle, *Federal Assistance to Libraries: Current Programs and Issues*, 89–197 EPW ([Washington, D.C.: Congressional Research Service, Library of Congress], March 22, 1989). The percentage of funding has declined, of course, in the past decade as the arts programs have come under attack by an array of politicians, citizens groups, and others.

46. Richard Hodder-Williams, "Redefining Federalism: The Primacy of Politics Over the Constitution," in Richard Maidment and John Zvesper, eds., *Reflections on the Constitution: The American Constitution After Two Hundred Years* (Manchester, England: Manchester University Press, 1989), pp. 29–37.

47. *Basic Laws and Authorities of the National Archives and Records Administration* ([Washington, D.C.: National Archives], October 1985).

48. *NARA and the Disposition of Federal Records: Laws and Authorities and Their Implementation: A Report of the Committee on Authorities and Program Alternatives* ([Washington, D.C.: National Archives and Records Administration], July 1989).

49. M. B. Schnapper, "How Reagan Put Wraps on His Records," *Legal Times*, July 17, 1989.

50. *NARA and Presidential Records: Laws and Authorities and Their Implementation: A Report of the Task Force on NARA Responsibilities for Federal Records and Related Documentation* ([Washington, D.C.: National Archives and Records Administration], March 1988).

51. See especially McCoy, *The National Archives*, for this point of view.

52. See especially United States House Committee on Government Operations, *Taking a Byte Out of History* (Washington, D.C.: Government Printing Office, 1990) and United States Senate Committee on Government Affairs, *Serious Mismanagement Problems at the National Archives* (Washington, D.C.: Government Printing Office, 1992).

53. For a fuller description of national information policy and the role of the archival profession, see Cox, *American Archival Analysis*, ch. 14.

54. Cappon, "American Historical Editors before Jared Sparks": 'They Will Plant a Forest . . . ,' " *William and Mary Quarterly*, 3rd series, 30 (July 1973): 375–400; Leslie W. Dunlap, *American Historical Societies 1790–1860* (Madison, Wis.: Privately printed, 1944); and David D. Van Tassel, *Recording America's Past: An Interpretation of the Development of Historical Studies in America 1607–1884* (Chicago: University of Chicago Press, 1960).

55. James Gregory Bradsher, "A Brief History of the Growth of Federal Government Records, Archives, and Information 1789–1985," *Government Publications Review* 13 (1986): 491–505.

56. See Van Tassel, *Recording America's Past*, for the best general background on these activities. Some early documentary editors, like Peter Force, managed to lobby for and gain modest amounts of money from the national government to provide partial support for the publication of historical documents; Norman F. McGirr, "The Activities of Peter Force," *Columbia Historical Society Records* 42 (1942): 35–82.

57. Henry D. Shapiro, "Putting the Past under Glass: Preservation and the Idea of History in the Mid-Nineteenth Century," *Prospects* 10 (1985): 244.

58. Gondos, *J. Franklin Jameson and the Birth of the National Archives 1906–1926*, pp. 175–76.

59. For an interpretation of the Historical Records Survey that suggests this, see Burl Noggle, *Working with History: The Historical Records Survey in Louisiana and the Nation, 1936–1942* (Baton Rouge: Louisiana State University Press, 1981). For the destruction of many of the HRS records themselves, see Leonard Rapport, "Dumped from a Wharf into Casco Bay: The Historical Records Survey Revisited," *American Archivist* 37 (April 1974): 201–210.

60. Sandra P. Anderson, Larry J. Hackman, and Timothy Walch, "The Distribution and Pattern of NHPRC Records Program Funding in the States, 1976–1980," *American Archivist* 44 (Summer 1981): 240–242; Larry J. Hackman, "The Historical Records Program: The States and the Nation," *American Archivist* 43 (Winter 1980): 17–31.

61. Nicholas C. Burckel, "National Historical Publications and Records Commission State Assessment Reports in Historical Perspective," *Midwestern Archivist* 14, no. 2

(1989): 71–82, and F. Gerald Ham, "Documenting America: Observations on Implementation," *Midwestern Archivist* 14, no. 2 (1989): 83–92.

62. Hedlin, *"Chinatown* Revisited," pp. 52–53.

63. Page Putnam Miller, "Archival Issues and Problems: The Central Role of Advocacy," *Public Historian* 8 (Summer 1986): 60–73 recounts in detail these efforts during this period. See also Robert M. Warner, *Diary of a Dream: A History of the National Archives Independence Movement, 1980–1985* (Metuchen, N.J.: Scarecrow Press, 1995).

64. *Committee on the Records of Government: Report* (Washington, D.C.: The Committee, 1985).

65. Larry J. Hackman, "A Perspective on American Archives," *Public Historian* 8 (Summer 1986): 19.

66. Anna Kasten Nelson, "The 1985 Report of the Committee on the Records of Government: An Assessment," *Government Information Quarterly* 4, no. 2 (1987): 143–150.

67. Early government funding was intended to develop a public school system, since education was deemed fundamental to democracy. Later efforts were directed to specific geographical areas or social groups that were determined to possess certain educational needs. Equality in education emerged as an essential aspect of a democratic society and to redress social ills. More recently, the presidential administrations have gone to block grants that reduce the emphasis on equality and access to educational opportunity. The increasing national government debt has also led to the first major declines in national support of education and the possibility of a reversal of national educational policy. All of this has occurred within the federal system. See Deborah A. Verstegen, "Two Hundred Years of Federalism: A Perspective on National Fiscal Policy in Education," *Journal of Education Finance* 12 (Spring 1987): 516–548.

68. "Obituary for the 'Living' Constitution? Policy Making and the Constitutional Framework Two Hundred Years On," in Maidment and Zvesper, eds., *Reflections on the Constitution*, pp. 200–201.

69. Waldo G. Leland, "American Archival Problems," *American Historical Association Annual Report 1909* (Washington, D.C., 1911), pp. 342–43.

70. *American Archivist* 47 (Fall 1984): 435.

71. W. McNeil Lowry, "Introduction," in *The Arts and Public Policy in the United States* (Englewood Cliffs, N.J.: Prentice-Hall, 1984), p. 1.

72. Consider, for example, Wilfred I. Smith, "Archives and Culture: An Essay," *Modern Archives Administration and Records Management: A RAMP Reader*, PGI-85/WS/32 (Paris: UNESCO, December 1985), pp. 427–441, and Hugh Taylor, "The Collective Memory: Archives and Libraries As Heritage," *Archivaria* 15 (Winter 1982–1983): 118–130.

73. A good view of this can be obtained from Richard E. Neustadt and Ernest R. May, *Thinking in Time: The Uses of History for Decision Makers* (New York: Free Press, 1986).

5

Shifting Strategies in Appraising, Scheduling, and Maintaining Records

Until the twentieth century, the emphasis on records was in their creation and storage. The rapid escalation of records creation brought a decided shift to considering new ways to maintain and selectively destroy records, representing a historic shift in the management of records and archives. Nothing like these functions had developed earlier, and these innovative approaches brought continuing debate and discussion.

THE MEANING OF RECORDS MAINTENANCE

Records managers and archivists struggle with what it means to maintain records. Archivists used to think in terms of "permanent" or "enduring," but the expression more likely to be used now is "continuing."[1] The terminological implications should be obvious. Issues of financial resources, ideal and nearly unattainable environmental standards, and electronic recordkeeping systems have all conspired to raise significant doubts about preservation. For records managers, the concerns are quite different. Legal liabilities, short-term administrative and fiscal priorities, electronic recordkeeping systems, and misunderstanding of archival objectives cast doubts about organizational records being maintained for very long. Records managers get so caught up in reducing the volume of records that they sometimes bring risk to their organizations through the destruction of records essential for ensuring corporate memory. Despite these challenges, both archivists and records managers need to devise ways to maintain records for decades, for as long as the records creator exists, and longer. The archivist needs to understand that preservation is not a value-neutral concept. The records manager needs to comprehend that long-term records maintenance is not only for scholarly purposes.

"Preserve" comes from the French *preserver* meaning to save from an evil that might happen. It is a word formed from the prefix *prae* meaning "before" and *servare* meaning "to keep or to protect." There is a sense of the word meaning to keep something in existence or to make something last. The word also implies preserving by keeping something in one's possession, but this is not an assumption that can be made any longer—a result of the changing nature of the records media.

Preservation is a vital component of records professionals' work. For archivists, preservation is the central tenet of their mission, connected with the selection of what records should be saved as well as their acquisition and use. As a result of the life cycle notion of records, preservation is also part of the records managers' mission. The ultimate end of preservation is use, the continuing utility of records for their creators and the larger society. Archivists break preservation into segments, ranging from conservation treatment of specific documents to preservation management of repository holdings. For archivists the main endeavor has been in mass treatments, control of environment and storage, and phased treatment.[2]

Preservation is core to the records professionals' mission, although it is changing because of the transforming of disciplinary knowledge and evolving recording media. There have been five major preservation approaches in the American archival profession, similar to what other countries and cultures have experienced. *Housing and publication* emerged in the late eighteenth century as the initial venues for preservation. By the 1930s publication was being rapidly replaced by *reformatting*, with new technologies enabling the reproduction of documents. At about the same time *treatment* emerged as a preservation strategy. *Preservation administration* was dominant in the archival community by the early 1980s. Finally, a new emphasis on *production standards* has now come to the fore, setting off debate and new and complicated issues regarding the nature of these standards, how quickly standards can be developed, and whether standards will support records formats. All this progress has been vastly overwhelmed by the *immensity* of the preservation problems. Education is insufficient, funding has not kept pace, the majority of records repositories have insufficient programs, and as a community records professionals sometimes seem unable to develop new and better strategies. At risk is the loss of millions of archival records, and society and institutional memory.[3]

The historical society typifies early preservation concepts. Starting with the Massachusetts Historical Society in 1791, within a century it was the rare town, city, or state that lacked such an organization with a mandate to "collect" historical and archival records. Most were so preoccupied with collecting that they also tended to acquire rare, interesting, and even bizarre documents and artifacts related to American and world history (Egyptian mummies, ancient coinage, religious artifacts, and natural history curiosities sat on the shelf next to family manuscripts and institutional archives). Preservation meant relocating materials into the historical society's headquarters for their protection and the convenient use of researchers (even if the facilities, hours of operations, and membership issues made accessibility a complicated matter). Historical societies also believed in publication as a major preservation activity and sought to publish selections from their archives; hundreds of volumes of personal, family, political, and business records poured from their presses.

Preservation as housing and publishing has affected the work of all records professionals. When the first state government archives were established in the early twentieth century, they gathered the records for the researchers, and their only real perception of preservation was in removing records from offices to the new facilities. This method has not been abandoned, despite the advent of new electronic records systems. The debate of centralization versus decentralization of such systems may be testimony to a paradigm shift, but it is also evidence of a long-lasting concern to place archival records in structures where they can be controlled, managed, and consulted.

Facility construction has taught us much about caring for records. The first archival facilities lacked climate controls and other preventive care measures, while the new National Archives facility, opened in 1995, includes moveable shelving with optimum environmental controls, special facilities for electronic, photographic and other such records, and other improvements learned from previous generations of building construction and design. As one of the most expensive federal buildings in history, this may be a model archival facility, but it was built in the modern electronic information age, a strange time to emphasize facilities. One might well question the wisdom of the National Archives. It lost considerable credibility with Congress and the Executive Office, perhaps at least partly due to the resource-consuming activities involved in building a new facility. It lost track of a mission, continuing to operate on the old paradigm of centralization of archival records, even those in electronic form. As the recent case about the deletion of electronic mail concerning the Iran-Contra affair suggests, the National Archives—despite having the largest concentration of electronic records archivists in the world—struggled with defining a record. The new building reflects the National Archives as a cultural program, not as the archives for the federal government.

Delineating a mission for records programs can be a contentious process, mixing collecting, protecting society's culture, attending to the needs and interests of organizations, meeting legal and fiscal concerns, and symbolic purposes, although affording facilities appropriate for the long-term maintenance of records remains a great challenge. A study in the mid-1980s revealed that most state government archives lacked proper facilities and faced immense challenges to preserve their holdings effectively.[4] The shift to electronic systems for recordkeeping and communication has further complicated this by raising expectations of individuals hooking up remotely to stores of information, moving from the historical to a living record or virtual, not physical, documents. Equating the maintenance of records with facilities needs to be re-thought by archivists and records managers. Records programs will serve as locators of records rather than the site in which researchers come, as there is a blurring of function between record creator, disseminating source of the record, and the record's custodian or manager.

Many records professionals think of reformatting (microfilming or digitizing) as the preferred preservation methodology. This confuses means with ends, but there are historical reasons for this continuing orientation. The genesis of reformatting stems from the older interests in the publication of historical records, a preservation mechanism even older than that of housing, when antiquarians, historians, and other scholars transcribed and published records. Throughout the eighteenth and nineteenth centuries, governments sought to improve the condition of public records by recopying, rebinding, and publishing. Nearly every historian of this time saw the responsibility to publish lengthy extracts of original records, not just for interpretation but in order to *preserve* as many of the records as possible—believing that they might be the last individuals to examine an original record.

Documentary publishing supported the age of "documania," when there was tremendous popular interest in history and its sources.[5] Autograph collecting emerged as a national pastime. Decorative arts reflected documentary themes, such as with the mid-nineteenth-century album quilt mimicking autograph books. Massive copying projects in European archives continued through the middle of the nineteenth century, unrivaled until later in the twentieth century. The nineteenth-century scientific historians, stressing archives as their laboratory, supported documentary editions, typified by the American Historical Association's Historical Manuscripts Commission (1895) producing edited versions of the documents of great Americans. The later Public Archives Commission (1899) resulted in a miscellany of published and unpublished records surveys, but the writings of this period suggest that historians preferred the texts of the actual documents multiplied in published form rather than archival finding aids. It is often argued that such documentary projects exist today to increase public awareness of such records, but the rationale is that it provides the best means for preservation and access. This latter argument ignores the high costs, as well as the political and scholarly problems in determining what records to publish and the slow process involved in producing documentary editions. The current considerations of digitizing paper records may involve the same challenges.

There are precedents for the current fascination with digitization. Microfilming became commercially and technically viable by the 1920s. By the 1930s government and corporate records programs utilized it, and by the 1960s microfilming was evident in virtually every records operation. Better technical standards for archival microfilm, micrographics technology stability, and the ease of training microfilm technicians made it difficult to not use the technology. However, whether what is filmed represents the priority preservation problems or not is a completely different matter. Combination records management and archives programs probably face the greatest challenges in this regard, where there is always pressure to microfilm in order to reduce storage space or to ensure security. Microfilm programs tend to take on a life of their own.

Microfilming is a much more cost-efficient preservation approach than nearly any other preservation option, although it requires labor-intensive processing before filming and environmentally sound storage facilities for film maintenance. While it is often more expensive than is assumed, it is a reliable approach with plenty of sources for solving problems.[6] Microfilming may be the most straight-forward preservation option other than adopting the use of non-alkaline storage materials, and records programs may adopt it because progress is easily tracked, even with problems. How does it affect the use of records? What should be microfilmed? What are the selection criteria for determining what records should be filmed? What about control over the records when they are more widely available on microfilm? What is lost by the reproduction of original records via microfilm? These, and many other questions, have not been analyzed. Records professionals do not know the effectiveness of a half-century of use of micro-filming as a preservation mechanism.

Despite such questions, the development of electronic networking, especially the Internet, has given new life to preservation reformatting. While the archival profession's use of the Internet has archivists posting archival finding aids on it and answering reference queries, some are also providing full-text retrieval of their archival records in electronic form. Explorations into the use of scanners for creating electronic images of documents, as well as employing CD-ROM, have led archivists into new notions of the traditional reformatting paradigm.

These challenges also point out how limited thinking has been about records preservation approaches. What will the electronic capture of a record mean for its integrity and authenticity? What will happen to the necessary aspects of a record's context and provenance if reformatted into an electronic form? Is it worth reformatting older records in traditional formats, such as paper textual records and photographs, when records professionals have not kept pace with the management of records *originally* created as electronic records? Large-scale investments in micrographics technology were often little more than a means to miniaturizing the voluminous paper records, and poor decisions about what should be filmed were often made. Commitment to micrographics programs sometimes became a consumer of resources needed for other priority records and information concerns. Microfilming can often become *the* rationale for the records management program, rather than part of an arsenal of tools to be used in the effective administration of records.

While reformatting is a preservation management approach, treatment of in-dividual records has long been a preoccupation of records professionals. In the 1930s William Barrow set up shop at the Virginia State Library in Richmond and began work for that state's library and archives, providing treatment facil-ities for other archival and historical records repositories and conducting re-search into conservation treatments. Barrow's contribution was deacidification and lamination, similar to microfilming in enabling employees to be "trained" to operate the equipment. The lamination process offered an assembly-line operation for strengthening old and weakened historical records, and while expensive enough to be out of the reach of most archival programs, it was simple enough in design and application to become *the* archival treatment option for nearly half a century.

The Barrow technique was widely adopted because it was oriented to individual documents, a legacy of the older antiquarian interest in the uniqueness of records. When Barrow started, conservation treatment was primitive and unscientific. There was a considerable lack of understanding of the chemical and physical properties of records. Conservation treatment was often little more than rebinding or minimal stabilization, and restricted to a minor portion of documents. The lack of scientific research and professional conservators and the mechanical aspects of the lamination process led to its abuse. Significant strides have been made in conservation treatment. Regional conservation centers provide expertise at reasonable prices, obtaining significant grants to lower prices for treatment and supplies, offering basic continuing education, and focusing preservation leadership. The conservator corps has grown over the last three decades, and the more important problem now is the insufficient financial resources available to archival and records programs to employ such professionals.

There is more awareness how conservation relates to broader preservation objectives and activities. Twenty years ago, archivists generally equated conservation treatment with preservation, stressing the individual document rather than holdings management. Part of this is a better understanding of conservation needs,[7] including awareness that these needs are greater than existing financial and human resources or that conservation techniques stretch understanding records values. Conservation treatment requires devotion to records with intrinsic value, but intrinsic value is poorly defined. Archivists think they know a good record requiring attention when they see one, when the prioritization of selection for conservation has out paced selection criteria. Archival appraisal requires better-defined criteria, more rigorous methodology, and improved understanding of the application of appraisal strategies. There is too much guesswork and haphazard effort in appraisal, and it is perhaps out of the realization of such problems that archival preservation management developed.

Determining records' value is further complicated by what conservators really understand about records. Conservators and preservation administrators focus on archival holdings sometimes without understanding how those holdings had been formed or relate to other documentation; after all, these professionals are experts in the technical composition of recording materials not in the nature of records and recordkeeping systems or basic archival principles. Since preservation and conservation is a form of re-appraisal (because many current archival holdings will deteriorate and be lost before any resources are available to save them), it seems problematic that these specialists can participate in decision making about preservation, especially conservation treatment. Who makes the conservation treatment decisions? Are there two very different cultures (three, if we add to these some of the distinct qualities of the records management culture) operating within archival and other institutions holding historical records?

By the end of the 1970s the American archival community faced a preservation crisis, the gulf between financial and human resources expended on preservation and the declining physical shape of the holdings increasing exponentially. As a result, archivists began to develop a more realistic sense of preservation. There was a renewed emphasis on continuing education workshops, spawning a variety of practical efforts to provide a storage environment. The common language that seems to pervade the present archival profession's preservation sense stems from such efforts. Special conferences were held throughout the 1980s and the reports, professional articles, working groups, and other results of these meetings permeated the archival profession.

In the mid-1980s a number of states, led by New York and supported by the National Endowment for the Humanities, assessed the preservation condition of archives and libraries and proposed strategies. Additional individuals entered the preservation discussions, gained public attention to the scope of the preservation dilemma, and strengthened the concept of preservation management. The 1983 Ritzenthaler manual (revised and re-issued a decade later) on archival preservation was both a summary of this approach as well as a stimulant bringing together the conservation, preservation, and restoration functions with adept, practical advice on all aspects of archival administration.[8] Preservation management also brings into its realm records managers. Preservation management is a broad, practical approach to complex concerns and challenges. Records managers can use preservation management, with little change, in their records programs, for the design and administration of facilities, training records staff, and communicating to records creators about why and how records with long-term maintenance needs can be managed.

THE STRANGE, INTERTWINED HISTORIES OF ARCHIVAL APPRAISAL AND RECORDS MANAGEMENT SCHEDULING

Preservation, encompassing conservation, is a form of re-appraisal, since it involves value judgments for allocating resources for additional care of records. There is a synergy here, perhaps unrecognized by many records professionals because they have segmented the records management scheduling and archival appraisal functions, even though the origins of their basic principles and methodologies are closely connected. The long-standing notion of the records and recordkeeping systems life cycle, logically connecting scheduling and appraising for disposition decisions, reveals their mutual origins. In the United States, the primary sources of *both* appraisal and scheduling have been the pioneering government records professionals working with massive records quantities and recordkeeping systems in complex political environments, providing the impetus to reduce *and* control records. Even the increasing weaknesses evident in scheduling and appraising have become apparent in government's use of new recordkeeping technologies, increasing records quantities and complexities and need for control and reduction (a contested matter because of the claims by some that the massive memory capacities of the technologies themselves provide *the* solution to the growing quantities of records and information).

The modern records schedule—with its list of series titles, retention periods, and disposition instructions—is a product of the Federal Records Disposal Act of 1943. This legislation attempted to rectify a half-century of failed efforts to manage the disposition of federal records, contending with what already seemed like a massive records clogging. Starting in 1889, executive department administrators could recommend, for congressional approval, records for destruction. Even in the days long before a large modern government bureaucracy, this was not a tenable solution. One of the earliest requests for records destruction was submitted by the Treasury Department in January 1890, and it was 188 printed pages in length. Greater than the problem of cumbersome procedures for records destruction was that, until 1912, the federal government had no provision for determining records as having permanent or continuing value; most agencies, unless moving offices or undergoing some administrative changes, hardly bothered to manage records. To resolve the problem of the loss of archival records, President Taft issued in 1912 an executive order requiring the agency lists to be sent to the librarian of Congress for review before being sent to Congress. Without specified criteria for determining what records should be destroyed or any mechanisms or qualified records professionals for records analysis, however, there was no safeguard or incentive for agencies to be concerned about records.[9]

There was an increasing sense of what records could be disposed. Between 1894 and 1930 some federal agencies were allowed to destroy routine records such as vouchers, invoices, and checks without submitting lengthy lists either to Congress or the librarian,[10] recognition about what was not working as government grew and the quantity and quality of government records increased and changed. The General Disposal Act of 1939 provided for a disposition operation for all agencies, whereby they sent disposal lists to the National Archives for approval and then the Archives sent the list on to Congress for final authorization.[11] This shifted the process into the hands of records professionals (although then novices in appraising or scheduling), but it remained an unwieldy process. The Federal Records Disposal Act of 1943 rectified the procedural problems by allowing for continuing schedules with administrative, legal, and research values as guides. Two years later Congress modified the act to allow certain common series of records to be scheduled more readily, leading to the concept of general records retention schedules. By 1949 six such general schedules were in use, and the Federal Records Act of 1950 pulled the records management program within the National Archives and its new administrative home, the General Services Administration.[12] From this point on, there would be more general schedules leading up to electronic records, the latter perhaps representing the intellectual and practical collapse of scheduling.

There has not been enough analysis of the history of scheduling and appraising to determine with precision the origins and subsequent development of the records schedule. From our modern vantage the schedule—described and duplicated in *every* records management textbook—looks like something that has been always there, a methodology not to be questioned or challenged as the cornerstone of records management work. So ingrained is the function of scheduling in the records manager's practical and philosophical toolkit that David Stephens calls the lack of usable schedules for electronic recordkeeping systems "one of the profession's greatest failures."[13] A failure it is, but maybe for reasons different than what Stephens identifies—the "great majority of electronic recordkeeping systems are designed without a pre-defined methodology for eliminating data, text, and image files at a point in their life cycle at which they have no further value."[14]

This failure with electronic recordkeeping systems is surprising since scheduling is very practical. It is possible that the idea for scheduling was generated from outside of what had become the biggest records management factory in the world—the United States federal government—and the greatest agency responsible for administering records—the National Archives. In a 1941 National Archives publication, Edna B. Poeppel noted that in business records administration "every well-organized filing department is guided by a manual of operations, which describes the general filing procedure, the flow of work, the type of papers in each file, the methods of indexing and filing, and the use of guides, folders, and labels. The manual indicates whether material is of permanent or temporary value and notes the period after which temporary material may be destroyed."[15] Later Poeppel mentions that "in recent years committees have been appointed by some organizations, such as banks, department stores, and public utilities, to study files and records and to determine their value and period of retention."[16] Thus, general records schedules were known before their subsequent development by the National Archives. Scheduling records was developing out of the same necessities of office management as filing and routing memoranda. Posner attributes the concept to discussions at the 1942 and 1943 Society of American Archivists meetings, also noting that the State of Illinois adopted the use of general schedules in 1943.[17]

As general records schedules and the scheduling process emerged in the early 1940s, it was evident that *how* records would be identified as permanent was in an extreme state of flux. In 1940 Philip Brooks of the National Archives presented his ideas about what records should be preserved primarily by providing a long description about how to reduce their volume—including transferring records to historical societies and libraries, microfilming, and representative sampling techniques.[18] Six years later, even as the first use of general records retention schedules emerged, G. Philip Bauer provided a long discourse on the inadequacies of the appraisal work of the National Archives without a single reference to records scheduling as part of the process.[19] Bauer's omission was evidence of the decided shift in early appraisal theory and practice in the National Archives away from the records management concept of scheduling. It was indicative of the ultimate schism between records managers and archivists a decade later. Many archivists saw scheduling as a housekeeping technique to clear out routine records so that they could get to the records of interest to scholarly researchers. Early writings on this topic allude to the tensions between those advocating records management and those stressing archival values for historical researchers.[20]

Led by their theorist in residence, T. R. Schellenberg, the National Archives adopted as guiding principles the ideas of primary and secondary values, the latter divided into evidential and informational values and both essential to documenting government and for determining what records would be useful for researchers. Given the demands on the early government archivists, the preponderance of their academic backgrounds in history and the humanities, and the think-tank environment of the early National Archives, it was inevitable that more self-reflection would be devoted to appraisal. As Terry Cook suggests, Schellenberg was rejecting the idea of his English counterpart, Hilary Jenkinson, that records creators determine what records would be maintained. Cook argues that the ''Schellenbergian distinction between 'records' and 'archives' has tended to emphasize the differences between records managers and archivists, and between records and archives, rather than their similarities and interconnections.''[21] That some archivists and records managers discuss schedules within the context of Schellenberg's primary and secondary values is besides the point, given the breakdown of both the use of scheduling and the assignation of values in the electronic recordkeeping regime. That Jenkinsonian concepts have re-emerged, with an emphasis on impartiality and objectivity and leading to some new debates about archival theory and methodology[22] (debates missing the point that neither the Jenkinsonian or Schellenbergian mindsets are infallible with the new recordkeeping approaches) is the result of the struggle that all records professionals feel when confronted with the need to make choices about what records to maintain.

These problems were evident even in the early formation of scheduling and appraisal approaches. Recent arguments about appraisal are reminiscent of the debates of a half-century ago forming the initial concepts of evidence and information, with these recent discussions presaged in the writings of the archival pioneers of the 1930s through the 1950s. Schellenberg argued in 1956, not long after the formation of the predominate appraisal concepts *and* scheduling mechanisms, that ''ascertaining values in records cannot be reduced to exact standards'' and can be ''little more than general principles.''[23] Margaret Cross Norton thought each appraisal decision to be ''borderline.'' Archivists have continued to wrangle over these principles and the degree of exactitude. Yet, if archivists carefully view the entire body of their writings on appraisal they will see that there is a small set of guiding principles ranging from the challenging notion that all recorded information has some continuing value to the need to reduce the massive quantity of information to make it usable to being involved with the records creator as far up the life cycle of records as possible.

Developing appraisal principles has involved debate, experimentation, and continued soul-searching, all in the face of increasing practical problems in managing modern records. It is the same as what the archival and records management pioneers originally faced. Hilary Jenkinson stated that the bulk of records, caused by easier duplication and other uses of modern technology, is a "new and serious matter" requiring the archivist's attention.[24] Margaret Cross Norton, writing at about the same time, stated that the growing quantity of government records meant that the "emphasis of archives work has shifted from preservation of records to selection of records for preservation." She advocated a process whereby the archivist worked as a records manager, so that the quantity of records could be reduced by selection *and* through the application of photographic processes and the prevention of unnecessary records accumulation.[25]

Even the pioneers argued among themselves or erred. Most archivists point to the classic statements on evidential and informational values as the criteria to be followed and, indeed in the United States at least no archivist or records manager seems capable of considering appraisal or scheduling *without* mentioning Schellenberg's values models (whether they know that they came from Schellenberg or not). There have also been detractors, such as Norton, who argued that "records are created for one purpose and for one purpose only, namely, to fulfill an administrative need; and if the records fulfill that need, the archivist considers them adequate. . . . If, as often happens in the case of government records, the documents tend to take on value for purposes of historical or other research, that is so much 'velvet.' "[26] Everywhere the stresses in older appraisal and scheduling concepts can be detected. The need to reproduce records in other than their original formats led to new concepts such as intrinsic value.[27] The orderly process of records creation, best enunciated in the century-old Dutch manual, has long been in need of careful re-working.[28] A sanguine belief that a records pioneer like Jenkinson could have foreseen records systems we now are contending with should easily die when we also note that he believed records "destruction is an operation which can only be practiced with undoubted safety in one case—that of word-for-word duplicates."[29] It is why Boles and Greene reacted to the neo-Jenkinsonianism of Duranti by contending that archives is an applied discipline where "archivists must ply their trade on a daily basis using methodologies that work rather than employing methodologies that are theoretically correct."[30] But this may go too far still. Terry Cook states it better when he notes archival appraisal ought to be seen as a "work of careful analysis and of archival scholarship, not a mere procedure."[31]

Archival appraisal's status as analysis, scholarship, or procedure constitutes the recent history of the macro-appraisal concept. In 1984 the archival documentation strategy was introduced, although its origins include twenty years of archival, library and information science, and history approaches. The influence of the documentation strategy as a catalyst for discussion about archival theory, methodology, and practice was rapid. By 1991 and the Association of Canadian

Archivists meeting in Banff, the documentation strategy had become one of the primary means for commentary on appraisal theory. At present, it has become a component of a suite of methodologies associated with archival "macro-appraisal," a major source for recent books on archival appraisal approaches, and a stimulant for a reconsideration of the main purposes of the appraisal responsibility.

The seminal essays published on the archival documentation strategy testify that it was formulated because of the increasing quantity of records, the rapidly developing complexity of their form, and the challenges associated with the interrelatedness of records creators[32]—all indicative of an uneasiness many archivists felt when conducting appraisal. American archivists had become deeply aware of the chaotic manner in which appraisal was being carried out and the seemingly confused purposes served by appraisal, and their attention shifted to cooperation and coordination as a way of bringing order to a vast universe of documentation. Much of this problem stressed the traditional values ideas. Ann Pederson states that this was the strategy whereby you "wait until the activity has abated, then look at the documentary residue and salvage the most representative remains." She argues that archivists knew from the beginning the trouble with this approach. It was assumed that the archivists would have access to the "representative records creators," the "whole body of records from creating agencies," "persons knowledgeable about the functions and activities that created and used the material" and "accurate information about the research community"—it would also require an "army of archivists."[33]

The archival documentation strategy generated discussion about appraisal theory and methodology. It prompted some re-assertions of classical archival theory, stressing not the "attribution of values," as Luciana Duranti describes it, "but the nature of records and the role of the archivist as mediators and facilitators, custodians and preservers of societal evidence, not documenters and interpreters, or even judges, of societal deeds."[34] Such views remain reactions to the early expressions of the strategy stressing collecting and ignore the facts that creators of records are not often the best judges of what records have continuing value to them, that they want advice on what records should be maintained (from lawyers, administrators, and archivists), and that any approach requiring archivists to examine *all* records is doomed because of the magnitude of the records universe.

The documentation strategy's value is seen in the evolution to functional analysis and acquisition strategies. Terry Cook contends that archivists must move appraisal from the usual taxonomy of records values and characteristics to the "most important societal functions, records creators and records-creating processes." He sees the documentation strategy as a "secondary, supplementary step to be used *after* corporate and institutional records have been appraised on the basis of provenance, a provenance rooted *conceptually* in the records-creators' mandated functions—not artificial functions—and by using a structural-functional matrix."[35] The similarity of documentation and acquisitions strategies is not just evolutionary but the matter of a pragmatic approach to the growing universe of records with which archivists and other records professionals must contend. Documentation strategies, functional analysis, and appraisal strategies all share a similar origin as new approaches to the significant challenges represented by the rapidly evolving modern recordkeeping systems. Archivists and records managers cannot approach the documentary universe without some strategic or methodological frameworks for cutting it to a manageable size.

As archivists struggle with the increasing quantity of records, electronic records management, and appraisal methodologies, many have strengthened their view of evidence over information. The weaknesses of the values approach have become more evident. The American Institute of Physics Center for the History of Physics in documenting modern physics and allied sciences,[36] proposals for documenting New England,[37] efforts to redefine collecting approaches using the documentation strategy,[38] reflections on how to contend with fringe and other religious organizations,[39] and pioneering efforts to apply the documentation strategy to geographic regions[40] all pinpointed continuing problems posed by values and moved toward more analytical and team-oriented approaches instead. We have innovative recommendations for appraising the records of hospitals,[41] science and technology,[42] higher education,[43] business,[44] and geographic regions.[45] The documentation strategy, whatever its limitations, has helped the North American archivist to re-think archival appraisal, and for some it has been part of a return to the record, stressing continuing evidence as the linchpin of the archival record and accountability and corporate memory.

The move by Canadian and other archivists to a functional appraisal approach, whereby records creators' ''functions, programs, activities, and transactions'' are understood first, has capped off a decade of new archival appraisal work.[46] The functional approach is a thorough rejection of the values concept as a serendipitous search for the good stuff for researchers, mainly historians—in favor of a more systematic effort. It also returns appraisal, and by implication records management scheduling in the organizational environment, to an analytical process rather than the utilization of a formula or template, especially as it builds on business process or transaction analysis already being used in organizational settings.[47] Catherine Bailey, reflecting on the use of functional macro-appraisal approaches at the National Archives of Canada since 1991, summarizes the importance of the latest appraisal developments: ''My own early experience with appraisal has shown that the assignment of values to records (evidential, informational, etc.) is very easy to accomplish, as every record is evidence of some action, and every document contains information of value to someone other than the creator. Thus, this traditional, taxonomic method of appraisal makes it much easier to recommend the preservation of material rather than its destruction, and can lead to the acquisition of many records of little or no value. The macro-appraisal model's clear definitions of the three factors of the citizen-state interaction (program, agency, and client), allows a sharper focus to be obtained more quickly in the appraisal of any government or institutional record."[48]

Bailey's assessment suggests an important point concerning how archival appraisal relates to records management scheduling and vice versa. Unless the records manager is *only* interested in clearing out records, it is unwise to determine only audit, legal, regulatory and other requirements for records maintenance in developing schedules. Like the archival values of evidential and informational, these can be easily associated only with destruction, not helping to identify the records essential for important matters such as corporate memory. Any process relying too heavily on formulaic approaches will run into difficulties with modern records systems.

While the twentieth century was a time for the modern records profession to develop and for new records techniques to be formulated, tested, and refined, by the dawn of the twenty-first century more uncertainties about these methods have emerged. First, how can records selection be effectively done in an era of culture wars, ethnic conflicts, and other troubling issues? Second, how can the preservation of paper records, even crucial ones like the Declaration of Independence, be maintained in the light of immense challenges posed by electronic records?

ARCHIVAL ANCHORITES: BUILDING PUBLIC MEMORY IN THE ERA OF THE CULTURE WARS

The American landscape is covered by cultural institutions, the result of what historian Mike Wallace terms an "heritage binge."[49] Art and history museums are a sign of stability and culture, providing an organized interpretation to the chaos of the past. Science, industry, and technology museums reflect progress as the result of technical innovation and comment on the future. Libraries provide a sort of town reading hall or, in the new century, a gateway to the Internet, desperately clinging (according to some observers) to a concept of free and wide access to information. Historical societies provide both understanding and enjoyment of the past, surrogate attics for storing the miscellaneous debris of human activity. College and university special collections of rare books, printed ephemera, and manuscripts serve scholars.

Together, these cultural institutions build public memory. By this, I do not mean that these organizations somehow magically provide a consensus about our nation's history. It is clear that they do not, either in interpretation or in how they make use of the artifacts from the past. The same photograph, handled by different cultural institutions, can be seen as work of art and creativity, as evidence of a societal or organizational function, as a text to be read and interpreted, as a visual representation to evoke nostalgia, or as decoration for the museum restaurant. Seeing such differences in mission, we can also understand that these cultural institutions create a dialogue about past and present.

What such differences suggest is a complexity not always appreciated. While many Americans may view them as little more than Sunday afternoon diversions or alternatives to attending movies or wandering about shopping malls, these cultural repositories reflect all the complexities of the society they inhabit. It is not possible to view an exhibit without wondering how the items on display were obtained or how they were selected. But do most people think about such issues? Or do they simply take for granted the authority of the institution, accept its taxonomies, and buy into its interpretations? And in our technocratic society, providing many outlets for many voices claiming authority or equal authority, can such questions be ignored without undermining one's ability to evaluate information and evidence?

Archival repositories typically reflect the issues and challenges faced by American cultural institutions. These repositories began in the late eighteenth century in the form of historical societies and rapidly expanded a century later with the establishment of government, corporate, and university archives. Although archivists constitute a small profession, their importance in preserving evidence of the past and determining the nature of society's memory is substantial, even with only 5,000 to 10,000 institutions and probably not more than 10,000 to 20,000. Individuals who are members of professional archival associations, from the national to the regional and local, total around 5,000 archivists (many repositories are not professionally staffed).

Despite the archival community's size, there is a public perception of archives and historical manuscripts. The Civil War and baseball documentaries by Ken Burns, aired on public television and marketed on video, helped create a sense of archives. The popularity of Civil War diaries and letters supported this. The end of the Cold War and the opening, and in some cases selling, of the archives of the former Soviet Union stimulated interest in the nature of archival records. The newspapers have regularly featured revelations in formerly closed archives. Stories about wars and civil strife around the world have included reports about the destruction of cultural repositories, including archives, because of their symbolic importance for national or ethnic identity. Even the political controversies from campaign financing to congressional ethics include records, as do important public debates about matters such as the involvement of Swiss banks in supporting the Third Reich or the tighter regulation of the tobacco industry. While the public understanding of archives is certainly less than it should be, these institutions and their holdings have certainly been in the public view often enough.

The issue that should galvanize public attention is why certain records are deemed to be worthy of long-term maintenance or preservation. Given the obvious symbolic importance of archives, one should wonder about the nature of their accumulation or assemblage. Sadly, little has been written for a general audience about the nature of archival appraisal, or even to the importance of archives to society. And given the current period of multiculturalism and culture wars, the process by which ordinary records are elevated to the status of archives is important to understand. Minorities and ethnic groups understand that records documenting their past must be preserved and available for use.

Archivists in the United States have traditionally conceptualized appraisal as not being particularly complicated, using ideas about the values of evidence and information as guides for identifying records meriting preservation or destruction. All records are evidence of transactions, but it is the importance of the function the transaction reflects that determines the evidence's importance. All records also are information sources, generally possessing importance for purposes beyond those dictating their creation. This kind of value extends both from interests of particular social groups and researchers and the fact that any record or recordkeeping system is the product of a complex array of social, economic, political, organizational, and other forces. While this value is often nebulous, and while it has certainly played havoc with the conduct of archival appraisal because it can be so subjective, it can have a valuable role in identifying records possessing particular societal or research uses.

The emerging multicultural society puts the work of records professionals in another light. The original and most influential articulation of the records value for appraisal purposes occurred during a very different time. The primary theorists on appraisal of records in North America and Europe wrote during the 1920s through the 1950s, and most of the subsequent writing on this topic has been a commentary on these pioneers. People in the United States held a stronger degree of consensus about what it meant to be an American, as well as a more settled notion of truth and evidence. While historians adhered to a variety of schools of thought about this issue, it was basically a moot point for the average American (and archivist as well). Now, society seems to be splitting apart or, at least, becoming more complex, and a task like appraisal is also more complicated.

How do records professionals cope with the emerging American multicultural society? Is multiculturalism a social reality, or is it another ideological or political "ism" that needs to be considered critically? Are our feelings about this new state of affairs more the result of regrets about the former mythology of the melting pot story than about what might be another manifestation of a changing society? Should multiculturalism be a guiding force for determining the value of records? The culture wars and the advent of the multicultural perspective suggest that at least some portions of society are challenging archival repositories to be more representative or inclusive.

Trying to direct the archival enterprise in a period of social unrest is nothing new; the pioneering Southern state archives were part of an effort to re-establish a Southern white hegemony, requiring the re-invention of the past among other things. In earlier times, records professionals were often supporting a particular view of society (whether it was for particular social and economic elites in collecting programs like historical societies or a positivist idea of evidence created by particular organizations such as corporations and governments). The current societal discord seems far more problematic because it is ever changing, complex, and extremely divisive. Minimally, it seems that the multicultural aspects of our society deserve to be documented in a meaningful and explicit fashion.

It should not be difficult to understand the challenges that multiculturalism presents, the latest concept arguing that the various cultural and ethnic backgrounds making up the American populace should be treated equally as viable and legitimate aspects of our society. It is, in part, a recognition that our country has always been a nation of immigrants, as well as the fact that we have had a more varied, non-European immigration in the past few decades. It is also the outcome of two generations of civil rights movements, first by African Americans, then by American women, then by Native Americans, and finally by nearly every other part of the populace with some stake in a special status or identity.

The recognition of a varied American population is not a peculiar archival challenge. However, some militant multiculturalists argue that their cultures should be treated as equal or superior influences on society, even when historically that might not be the case. Multiculturalism is, then, the antithesis of the "melting pot," a blending of the various national, cultural, and ethnic ingredients. Archivists must wrestle with all these forces, and it is not a purely academic exercise facing them as they appraise records in a multicultural society. The emotions and often equally persuasive but opposing arguments can lead to confusion and frustration. The debates and harangues about the proposed national history standards for elementary and secondary school students reveal that trying to find the common is not so easy anymore, and this might appear to be the most telling for archivists who often see themselves as historians or working for historical scholarship. Funded by the National Endowment for the Humanities under the Bush administration, the proposed standards were produced by the National Center for History in the Schools housed at UCLA and quickly raised the hackles of many different groups. Typical of the many efforts of the past decade to define basic literacy levels, these standards sought to set what all students should know about American history. The debate led to the appointment of new panels to review the standards (in this case, the Council for Basic Education, a non-profit organization promoting school reform), and the new panels suggested that the problem was less the method advocated than the examples used. Conservative politicians and scholars attacked the standards, convinced that they ignored historical figures such as George Washington and Thomas Jefferson and seminal documents such as the Bill of Rights and the Constitution, distorting the picture of American society. The new panels suggested that these examples and the accompanying questions led students to make one-sided conclusions, for example, slighting the religious beliefs of the European settlers in favor of discussion about the religion of Native Americans and blacks.[50]

If the tense discussions about the national history standards were unusual then the decisions needing to be made by archivists might not seem so complicated. However, these debates have emerged everywhere, pitting politicians, community activists, commentators and the media, and scholars against each other in troubling ways for professionals like archivists who make decisions about documenting society. Debates about federal funding for the arts have often become absorbed with the rare outrageous example of artistic endeavor, hardly casting any real light on the role and importance of art in modern society. What are the implications for archivists working in art museums and organizations? The debate about Afro-centrism reveals even more the dilemma faced by modern archivists, since it shows that multiculturalism often settles on debates about the nature of evidence. Mary Lefkowitz argues for the supremacy of evidence, the ability to critique evidence, and against fiction, fable, and indoctrination—lamenting that "evidently we have reached a point in historical study where motive, however perceived, is more important than evidence."[51] If we reject the basic evidence found in records, why should there be archives or why should archivists worry about appraisal? How can archivists rise above these heavily contested debates in order to preserve the records needing to be preserved?

Nathan Glazer has given us the most positive view about a multicultural society. In supporting the affirmative statement that is his book title, Glazer states that what he means is that "we all now accept a greater degree of attention to minorities and women and their role in American history."[52] Acknowledging that this does not mean that social ills, such as racism or economic inequities, have been solved, Glazer has documented a sea change in our perception of American society. If this is an accurate assessment, and I suspect it is, one should then anticipate that the American archival community has devoted greater attention to such matters. What we find, however, is a more complicated story, and the complications reflect the problems endemic to our current opposing views of multiculturalism.

Given the importance of appraisal to the archival mission, in that this function determines what an archives holds as well as what records society may possess to understand its past, why is it that we have had such little discussion about the challenges of appraising in our contested, fragmented, disharmonious society? Archivists do not lack appraisal knowledge or methodology, so the problem may be archivists' view of their work as an intellectually inferior form of professionalism, what Edward Said called thinking of "as something you do for a living, between the hours of nine and five with one eye on the clock, and another cocked at what is considered to be proper, professional behavior—not rocking the boat, not straying outside the accepted paradigms or limits, making yourself marketable and above all presentable, hence uncontroversial and unpolitical and 'objective.' "[53] Since nearly every major political and other controversy surfacing these days somehow involves records, it is difficult for the records professional to be non-controversial. Given that it is the archivist who often makes the final determination that something will be saved or not, and that any decision may provoke outrage from some group in our factious society, how can the archivist avoid controversy?

There are many different avenues archivists could follow. Archivists could pursue meaning in the evidence found in records, trying to stay out of the factious debates. Neil Postman seeks a unifying theme for education, "to make meaning through the creation of narratives that give point to our labors, exalt our history, elucidate the present, and give direction to our future."[54] He worries that providing equal footing only serves to devalue everything as well, and the archivist could end up by acquiring lots of interesting stuff without some grander scheme in mind. Others have echoed such concerns. Todd Gitlin asks how can multiculturalism serve as a focal point when it tears apart and often does not allow for commonalities? Gitlin points out that a "map colored strictly by gender (or race, or religion) does not account for the complexity of the world, does not allow anyone to navigate a society that is, by any definition, multiple, replete with perspectives."[55]

Archivists could also seek to gather records that document all sorts of representative social groups and viewpoints. Historian Mike Wallace concludes that "at long last, the American past [in museums and repositories] is as crowded, diverse, contentious, and fascinating as is the American present."[56] It is what Nathan Glazer thought made us all multiculturalists. Does this hold true for archives? Archival programs can be fairly passive recipients of records from any group wanting to place its records in the repositories, returning to the symbolic value that archives can hold for any social entity. Such actions would create another problem. Social critic Wendell Berry states that avoiding a direct grappling with the past's complexities "cannot tell me where I am."[57] Arthur Schlesinger, Jr. contends that the "purpose of history" is "not group self-esteem, but understanding of the world and the past, dispassionate analysis, judgment, and perspective, respect for divergent cultures and traditions, and unflinching protection for those unifying ideas of tolerance, democracy, and human rights that make free historical inquiry possible."[58] Passive approaches certainly bypass the "analysis, judgment, and perspective" wanted by Schlesinger. Many archives have thrown open their doors to collect the records and artifacts of any group, partly to counterbalance the older biases of previous acquisition. The results are often unsatisfactory, as one might expect, with materials of dubious value finding their way into these repositories.

Archivists might also focus on society's crucial aspects, although how one identifies these aspects might be difficult. Since anyone should know that the appraisal and preservation of records, such as those related to the Holocaust atrocities, is not about fulfilling an agenda to make people feel good but about preserving essential (and discomforting) evidence crucial to the records creators and society, this use of history could be an important guide for archivists. We know that the Nazis were meticulous recordkeepers, although they designed their records systems to hide their deeds. Archivists have found that the extent and context of such documentation provides crucial evidence, transforming the routine (like the bank accounts of Holocaust victims in Swiss banks) into the extraordinary.

There is yet another manner in which archivists can contend with the complicated modern society. Crucial to the identity of many social groups is having some of its documentation in archival and historical manuscript repositories. These groups, some once shunned by established repositories, have worked to create places where their archival memory—essential to their status—can be protected; in other words, many have set up their own repositories, hired their own archivists, or had members of their group trained to work competently as archivists.

All of these appraisal approaches are evident today. The American archival community supports repositories with mandates for documenting the varied population groups of this nation. In this respect, multiculturalism would seem to pose few problems. Some of these programs are quite old and stem from the activities of private collectors (such as the Schomburg Center for Research in Black Culture at the New York Public Library), the work of scholars (such as represented with the women's history collections at the Schlesinger Library at Radcliffe College), the historic identity and roles of colleges and universities (such as the Sophia Smith Collection at Smith College), or follow the older patterns of historical societies (such as the American Jewish Historical Society). The influx into archives of individuals trained as social historians in the 1960s and 1970s renewed sensitivity to documenting ethnic groups, minorities, and women, and repositories such as the Balch Institute for Ethnic Studies and the University of Minnesota Immigration History Research Center became important programs. The thematic or subject orientation to the acquisition of personal, family, and institutional records aimed on filling in documentary gaps has been a major orientation in the North American archival profession since at least the 1960s. This approach emerged from the New Social History (both reflecting archivists trained as social historians and responding to the new research initiatives by historical scholars and other researchers), and it quickly led to the creation of new archival programs, especially at universities. More recently other types of special theme collecting programs have been established, such as the Gay, Lesbian, Bisexual, and Transgendered Library/Archives located in Philadelphia. There may be a better way to deal with a multicultural society, but this array of archives with ethnic and minority records seems to make multicultural archives a great success story.

It is a success story if looking for archivists to be sensitive to multicultural issues and concerns, but upon closer examination we do not know whether the archival profession has progressed in adequately documenting the multicultural society. A lot of stuff has been collected, but what does this represent? Archivists and manuscripts curators have collected willingly, but they have not necessarily described in any detail the criteria for what is preserved. Archives and archivists need to create a dialogue with the public about the past, its complexities, and the challenges of documenting society and any portion of it. Archivists need to document the political and other dimensions of the formation of a documentary heritage that is multicultural in nature. Robert O'Meally and Genevieve Fabre note that "in our modern pluralistic societies, the idea of a total history supported by a global memory has given way to decentered microhistories and to a multiplicity of memories.''[59] This may well be, but if archives and historical societies are to serve as repositories for the records and artifacts of these memories than there must be more discussion about how they are selected, acquired, and preserved. This ought to be the new mandate for archival appraisal in the current multicultural society.

Archivists can cope with such challenges by refining their appraisal approaches. While archivists have long acknowledged the need to be more sensitive to the complexities of society in their acquisition and appraisal, they stressed acquiring or collecting instead of more systematic appraisal. This implies the need for a calculated effort to engage the public in understanding what needs to be preserved. While such collecting has been valuable for its diversity of archival records preserved, it has not always been dealt with forthrightly or in a fashion that provides substantive objectives. The 1990s are not the 1960s. Multiculturalism has led to disputes about the veracity of sources, as well as created the unenviable situation of needing to balance records about one group with those of another since all sources and all viewpoints seem equal. Archivists, who honestly dealt with matters of social injustice via the acquisition of source materials, are liable to the same complaints and muddles that pioneer social historians have run into working on history standards and other causes. The role of the archivist is not to reform society but to identify and preserve the evidence created by its institutions and inhabitants. This is not an easy road to follow. The Smithsonian thought it was providing a balanced approach, based on new evidence, when it scripted an exhibition celebrating the fiftieth anniversary of the end of the Second World War, and it was attacked by veterans groups, politicians, columnists, and social commentators. Some historical society directors and archivists who, trying to interpret the past realistically, have been forced to retreat and some have even lost their jobs.

It is the role of archivists to argue for the preservation of evidence necessary for understanding the past. This may seem like the proverbial exercise of splitting hairs, since it suggests a high degree of objectivity that is not attainable. Without belaboring the point of objectivity, let me argue that archivists need to focus on documentary goals that strive to preserve essential evidence of how individuals, institutions, and social groups operate. The stress by many archivists on gathering information either to serve the needs of particular research clienteles or to assist in the identity and social position of particular persons or groups is prone to distortion within an era beset by culture wars.

Archivists can rethink their functions as protecting evidence found in records serving the creators of the records while also ensuring that the records' creators can be held accountable to society. Archivists need to help organizations creating records to manage records essential for administrative, fiscal, and legal purposes, adding other records that build a foundation for the memory of the organization. Organizational memory is not a cultural objective (it is not intended to satisfy either academic or arcane interests of internal and external researchers), but an objective that works toward the organization having the information from the evidence of past activities and decisions for future activities and decisions. This does not mean, of course, supporting an organization wanting to destroy deliberately records holding it accountable to regulatory bodies and society. A clearer appraisal goal on evidence can better resist this. Archives and archivists collecting information to ensure that particular societal groups and institutions are represented do not necessarily do any better than accumulating an interesting assortment of records.

Archival documentation strategies (ensuring the participation of records creators, custodians, and users) and macro-appraisal approaches (emphasizing what should be documented and evaluating the records *after* the determination of what should be documented) both have promise. What these concepts offer in selecting which records are archival in the multicultural era is a focus on the evidence of transactions, identifying those most essential to concerns like accountability and corporate or societal memory. Instead of an open-ended saving all or any information of potential use, an impossible task at best, the new appraisal principles return us to key concerns and strategic approaches. Certainly one strategic approach is seeking to document the debates about multiculturalism.

Some will argue that this opens archivists to relying on certain kinds of organizations (like governments and corporations) with biases toward many societal elements, ending with a documentary heritage screwed up and neglecting the richness and complexity of our social fabric. There are many problems with such criticisms. Many of these organizations provide deep levels of data about a wide array of social groups and, in some cases, they provide the best evidence we could have in documenting the many cultural and other groups in our society. One of the lessons of the New Social History, perhaps overlooked a bit in light of the archivists' aggressive acquisition of the records and other stuff related to underdocumented groups, is that normal governmental, organizational, and personal papers could be employed in new and creative ways to understanding these groups.

There are certain logical steps to follow. The most obvious is becoming more energetic in acquiring records documenting all sides of the multicultural realm. Ensuring that the records of both Afro-centrists and their critics are acquired and preserved by reputable archival repositories is one way of achieving this. We can go even farther to achieve this objective. The archival community needs to ensure that the records of the media, government, and all other organizations somehow playing a crucial role in the debates about multiculturalism are also protected and available for scrutiny.

Doing this will not be easy. Lawrence W. Levine reminds us that these current struggles are not new in the university and society. Levine suggests that the very problems that the university and historians have been accused of, the critics have been guilty of violating themselves (misusing sources, lacking authorities, presentism) in leveling their charges. He notes that the "complexity of knowledge, the complexity of culture, the complexity of the world, and the complexity of the United States itself became more difficult and more dangerous to deny and more imperative to confront and comprehend.''[60] Archivists, seeking to document multiculturalism, will be confronting an area that is contentious and controversial. Moreover, this will bring archivists into the quirky realm of memory and history. Pierre Nora contrasts the structured rationalistic approaches to history and its sources with the more free-form and constantly evolving ideas about memory.[61] This brings up matters such as the fabrication of sources, misrepresentations and misinterpretations of what we can derive from historical sources, and just plain making sense of all available sources providing a glimpse into the past.

Archivists can navigate in these dangerous waters. Documenting their own appraisal decisions will help provide a clue to future generations, and the creation of a paper trail will provide justifications about how the records saved relate to other records not protected. Archivists, as they describe their holdings, need to be more direct in providing information about the origins of the acquisition, describing why a group of records was then thought to be worth preserving. Researchers will understand the original perceived values, and archivists can reinterpret as well as reappraise the records as needed. If a group of individuals representing a particular ethnic community approaches a local historical society or college and university special collections with the request that records are important to this group's historic identity, the repository should explicitly describe why and how these records were accepted.

Doing this serves prospective researchers, but it also is an extension of the archival community's sensitivity to working with such groups. Terry Cook, a leader in formulating the macro-appraisal approach, provides the most relevant clue to where we need to be going in the documentation of a multicultural society. In a sensible argument about how archivists should approach the voluminous records of government and other organizations, Cook suggests that archivists need to be sensitive to the interests of societal groups believing themselves underdocumented or somehow threatened by what they perceive to be the power structures.[62] This sensitivity must follow the use of strategic approaches to identifying the most essential evidence needed by society and, perhaps more importantly, engage publicly in discussions about records and evidence. Archivists should work with these groups, fully disclosing that they are also documenting the debates about multiculturalism itself. This might be the most important activity that archivists and their allies could undertake in documenting this significant aspect of society. When other high-profile debates emerge about records and evidence (such as the controversy about the Enola Gay exhibition at the Smithsonian), archivists and their professional associations need to take stands—however unpopular—about the importance of records and the evidence they contain.

If archivists contribute to the building of public memory by collecting interesting stuff with little consideration of the nature of contemporary culture, what they acquire may be of questionable value for future researchers. If our society moves toward a post-ethnic or post-multicultural society,[63] then it is important for archivists to document the process. Otherwise, it is possible that what future researchers will be studying are the anchorites, the people who withdrew from the world, to work in archives. Archivists, instead, need to work with all the contentious factions in the culture wars, and they need to engage in broader public discussion of how public memory is constructed. There is a sense that ordinary records can become extraordinary symbols when they are moved to archives. In reality, only a small portion of these records, such as the Declaration of Independence, should be deemed as having such symbolic value. What should be deemed to be important is the evidence these archives provide for understanding past and present.

DECLARATIONS, INDEPENDENCE, AND TEXT IN THE INFORMATION AGE

If the World Wide Web existed in 1776, there is no question that the Continental Congress would have placed its Declaration of Independence on it to make the document freely accessible to as many as possible. The Declaration was to be publicly read—it was after all a *declaration*. This is why the Declaration is often used as an example of a great rhetorical document.[64] The Declaration's meticulous structure, a legal indictment making a moral argument and intended to be both read and heard, is not accidental. The first printings carried with it, mistakenly, diacritics made by Jefferson to indicate *how* the Declaration was to be publicly read, reflecting its multiple purposes. This was not the *sacred* document we have made it, but an *action* document justifying a bold political move of possibly short-lived importance and requesting help.

Records, when they are created, are usually deemed to be valuable, utilitarian and temporary, or infused with symbolic value. The Declaration is certainly one of those documents with ''symbolic'' value, although this has not always been the manner in which this document has been viewed. Half of its history has been one of neglect, the other half a time of making amends for this neglect.

The Declaration's story is not unique in the annals of government or recordkeeping. Alexander Stille's recent essay in *The New Yorker* about the National Archives' efforts to contend with obsolete recordkeeping technology and its advice to federal agencies to print out on paper many electronic records reveals such perplexities about our era. ''One of the great ironies of the information age,'' Stille writes, ''is that while the late twentieth century will undoubtedly record more data than have been recorded at any other time in history, it will almost certainly lose more information than has been lost in any previous era.'' Stille worries about the fact that half of the National Archives' budget goes to storage, that it seems unable to get a handle on the management of electronic records, and that the growing ''vast accumulation of records makes it nearly impossible to distinguish the essential from the ephemeral.''[65] Another irony might be that the National Archives is devoting an extraordinary amount of attention to the Declaration when it is secure and the text well known (if often contested), while many millions of other records seem endangered. *Our* reaction to the Declaration may confuse how records are perceived by our society and in our government.

Considering the Declaration of Independence in the modern information age provides revelations about electronic documents, records and accountability, permanence, relics, democratic governance, public memory, and the future. Lawrence Wroth, considering colonial printing, writes: "There is no greater degree of interest inherent in an old printing press than in a spinning wheel of the same period; it is the difference in the spiritual implications of the two machines which keeps the one alive in men's minds while the other stands cold and stark in the museum or gathers dust in the attic."[66] But today, it is the original manuscript Declaration that sits in the Rotunda of the old National Archives building, not gathering dust but preservationists and foundation funds to preserve and display a symbol of our nation's origins. Does this document possess "spiritual implications"? Does its words still have significance? Are our views of this document changing as we seem to drift away from its most powerful and eloquent words and ideas? Do we lavish attention on it out of some sort of national guilt?

It is as symbol that the document raises so many questions. It is not hard to surmise that printing gave to government the ability to make public its acts. "Printed matter announced a new age," Daniel Boorstin writes, "not of 'engrossing' but of diffusing." Boorstin continues that "in the new age of typography it was not the uniqueness of an 'engrossed' copy sequestered in some archive but the publicity of print that gave authenticity and authority to acts of government." Now here is where we see the potential the eighteenth-century republicans might have had for the World Wide Web. Boorstin argues that "in a free American society the printing press made it possible for citizens to have access to the most significant public acts in privacy and at their convenience. . . . The multiplying copies of the *printed* proposed Constitution were symbols of an opening society in which eventually all would have a right to know and judge the public business."[67] We can see the Web as a massive printing press, as some already have.[68] This fact would not have escaped the attention of the authors of the Declaration, especially Jefferson who argued for the editing and publishing of documents more than two centuries ago as the best means for preserving such records.

Wroth and Boorstin suggest a pejorative meaning for archives. "Dusty" and "sequestration" are not positive terms for any institution, *especially* archives. Thinking about the Declaration makes one wonder about what element of the document we should focus on—the intent of the Founders, the words' current interpretation, or the original manuscript and its story as an object first of abuse than of reverence. Why is it that we would worry about this ancient document when the text is so readily available? Should we lavish so much attention on this single document when there are millions of records risking loss because of the fragile electronic recording media? That the Declaration has been featured in both espionage novels and comic books as the object of affection and the target of terrorists suggests the symbolic importance of the document, but these are *fictional* accounts.[69] Terrorists might be more content to allow the nation's documents to disappear naturally in that mysterious land known as cyberspace.

That Americans have had ambivalent feelings about their historic records can be seen in a brief history of the Declaration as document.[70] Historian John Bodnar reminds us that the "Declaration of Independence was not generally considered a sacred document at all before 1800," and its reputation only began to change as it became immersed in the testy political debates in the early nineteenth century.[71] The document's history suggests this to be an understatement. On July 19 Congress decided that the Declaration should be inscribed on parchment and engrossed by every member. A parchment version was ready by August 2 and signed by John Hancock, and as other members became available, the document was unrolled and signed.

During the Revolutionary War the Declaration was moved numerous times, along with other records of the young government. As the British threatened, the Declaration was moved, first to Baltimore at the end of 1776, then to a county courthouse in 1777, and back to Philadelphia in the summer of 1778. Even after the war, the Declaration did not find a permanent home. In June 1783, when several hundred American soldiers demanding back pay marched into the city, the Declaration was sent with Congress to Princeton, New Jersey. From then until the mid-nineteenth century, the Declaration was transported repeatedly between the capitols (Annapolis, Trenton, Philadelphia, and, finally, Washington, D.C.).

At the new Capitol, the Declaration moved from building to building. When the British threatened Washington in 1814, the Declaration was transported to a Virginia gristmill, then moved to Leesburg in that state, where it was stored in a linen bag with other documents. As the fiftieth anniversary of the Declaration approached, President John Quincy Adams had it printed using a "wet-pressing" to produce a facsimile, hastening the original's deterioration. Adams's act marked a turning point. By the mid-nineteenth century, the Declaration's fate seemed to be improving. In June 1841 Secretary of State Daniel Webster declared that the document should be displayed, moving it to the State Department's Patent Office Building. At this building, the Declaration remained for thirty-five years, hanging on a wall opposite a tall window where it faded amid extreme temperature fluctuations. With the Centennial, a new phase of the Declaration's history commenced. When it was put on display in 1876 in Philadelphia, the Declaration's physical appearance raised concern, and Congress established a committee to consider its preservation. This congressional committee asked the National Academy of Sciences to study the Declaration's condition, concluding that the document could not be restored and that it should be kept out of the light.

Despite the committee's recommendations, the Declaration was displayed for eighteen years in the new State, War, and Navy Building, when in 1894 it was finally taken off of display because of its faded condition and stored in a steel case. From then the story of the Declaration involves careful physical monitoring and the move to its permanent exhibition shrine at the National Archives building. The National Academy of Sciences in 1903 recommended that the Declaration be kept out of the light, but there was such a demand to see the document that the State Department began to make plans for having it displayed somewhere else. Preservation expert Clapp relates that "by 1919, the State Department began to feel that possession of this document was a nuisance. People insisted on seeing it, and if they couldn't see it informally, they would get letters from important people addressed to the secretary of state to assure a private exhibition. The secretary of state therefore decided to entrust it to somebody whose business it was to handle documents—the librarian of Congress."[72] The Declaration was displayed at the Library of Congress in 1924, where it remained for the next thirty years except for a few years storage at Fort Knox during the Second World War.

By the Second World War the Declaration was an object of study and a sacred American text. In 1940 one of the guards noted a crack in the upper right-hand corner of the document, leading to yet another long report on the document's condition and a new position, keeper of the collections. Alvin W. Kremer, filling that position, began a series of regular photographic records, adding to the growing archives *about* the Declaration. Armed with all these studies, the Declaration was moved in 1952 to the new exhibit space at the National Archives, its permanent home, and sealed in a Thermopane glass case with inert helium gas and a measured amount of water vapor. Surrounded by archivists and preservation specialists at the National Archives, the Declaration became an object of regular detailed analysis. There was a major physical examination in 1981. In 1987 a $3.3 million computerized imaging system designed by NASA's Jet Propulsion Laboratory was installed, leading to another physical examination the following year.

Preservation pioneer Verner Clapp started a 1971 essay on the Declaration with this sentence: "The Declaration of Independence is one of the most abused documents in the history of preservation of documents."[73] Something seems wrong with such an assessment. Rather, it seems that the Declaration, during the past 100 years, has been the most fawned over document in our history. This is certainly the case in the past decade. In the mid-1990s the Declaration was examined with a fiber-optic device. As one of the conservators noted, "We are really the first to definitively document all of the features of the Charter documents. . . . It's painstaking work but this information will be invaluable."[74] This was only a warm-up. In 1998 it was announced that the Pew Charitable Trusts was granting the National Archives $800,000 to supplement federal funds for reencasing the Declaration, Constitution, and Bill of Rights on display. In 2001 the documents will be taken off display for eighteen months for the reencasing.[75] A long article in the *New York Times* revealed that the funds were being partly used to re-install all of the documents (including the Constitution and the Bill of Rights) in a more modern exhibition.[76]

During the time the National Archives has been monitoring the deterioration of the Declaration, it has also been contending with the growing use of ever more sophisticated electronic information technology to create and maintain records. In an article meant to raise concerns about this, a journalist stated, "The parchment has yellowed and the ink is badly faded, but with a bit of effort one can still make out the words of the Declaration of Independence and the Constitution, penned more than two centuries ago. Both are painstakingly preserved by the National Archives in Washington, D.C., not merely as historic curiosities but, in the words of an official sign, as testimony 'to the accountability of a government that lays itself open, through its records, to the scrutiny of present and future generations.' "[77] The intent was to show that the older recordkeeping systems, despite whatever challenges they provided, were at least *more likely* to be around for the next century.

There is no reason, of course, to castigate archivists for clinging to older forms of records because of symbolic or other values. The multiplication of the Declaration's text does not mean the original should rot. After all, we know that for many records the text is intimately tied to its form. Roger Chartier writes that "any comprehension of a text is necessarily dependent on a knowledge of the material forms it has taken."[78] There are complications revisiting the Declaration in the Information Age. Chartier's statement equally well applies to those records created in electronic form, and it is not hard to imagine that the next writers of a new Declaration (something of equal importance in the twenty-first century as the Declaration was to the eighteenth) would be using Hyper Text Markup Language (HTML) for placing the document on the World Wide Web. Given the mixed results by archivists managing electronic records, could they preserve such a document for two centuries? There are questions beyond the effectiveness of managing electronic records. Is the symbolism of the founding documents like the Declaration and their display in the Rotunda of the National Archives a symbolism for *all* Americans?

The concern about the display of a symbolic Declaration is complex and compelling. Pauline Maier argues that the monument at the National Archives is completely wrong because it suggests a "glorious but dead past." In her estimation a *vital* document does not belong among the "mummified paper curiosities lying in state at the Archives."[79] Others have had similar thoughts about this. Some see such focus on these older documents as problematic, as a form of civic religion gone astray in which we have lost sight of the historic context and circumstances of the creation of the documents and simply paralyzed our ability to govern ourselves.[80] Even these criticisms capture the abiding interest in these fundamental records and the utility of their information and evidence.

For some commentators, such symbolism is tied up with more intricate historical events. James Atlas wonders if the "rhetoric of our primary documents affirms a vision of America to which most of us assent,'' since ''those documents were framed by a dissenting elite for a nation that consisted of a few thousand souls. How are we to address the vastly different constituency that has emerged since the white, male Founding Fathers sat down with their quill pens to compose their decrees?''[81] How far do we go with enshrining the original manuscripts in a federal building?

Determining the symbolic significance of a small group of essential American texts is only part of the story. The real issues relate to the uses intended for texts like the Declaration and the future of new significant American documents. Historian David Thelen notes how the ''printing press and subsequent mass media turned opinion from a face-to-face interaction into an artificial assembly of invisible individuals.'' Thelen comments on the Declaration: ''In justifying their declaration of independence by appealing to 'a decent respect to the opinions of mankind,' the founders of a new American nation in 1776 addressed a faceless audience that would encounter their declaration in the new mass media.''[82] Looked at in another way, these same American colonists transformed into revolutionaries, transported to a later time and place, would certainly have made use of the Web. The issues of moving the document for protection would never have materialized, although perhaps other equally weighty issues about the *permanence* of the text would have caused more consternation. However, can something on the World Wide Web even possess symbolic importance as an original manuscript like the Declaration can?

Using media like the Web has other implications. For one, it does not necessarily help anyone write better. Theodore Roszak writes that the ''computer contributes nothing essential to the life of the mind'' and notes that ''information [such as that found on the Web or in other electronic form] is worthless if it is not informed by ideas, values and judgment.'' Roszak believes the Web to be the ''product of a predatory entrepreneurial sensibility.''[83] A predatory sensibility it is indeed, and one with no responsibility for long-term maintenance of what is placed on it. Who or whatever places something on the Web assumes responsibility for it, and few have figured out what this means. Printing out a Web site seems ridiculous when one tries to deal with the multiple links, critical to the hypertext documents residing on the Web. But how does one effectively maintain an electronic version of such a site? If electronic mail has proved to be so difficult, maintaining Web sites poses a greater challenge. I doubt that one would be visiting an electronic Declaration in the National Archives rotunda in the future, but maybe we shouldn't be worrying so much about the parchment version that sits there now.

The Declaration's symbolism changes as the Information Age morphs into a Knowledge Age dependent on electronic technology. We know that as Americans tried to overcome the lack of a long history, patriots believed that Divine Providence had given America a special mission. By the early nineteenth century, the Fourth of July ''became literally the holy day of obligation for American patriots'' and the status of the Declaration began to move from forgotten document to sacred text.[84] By the late nineteenth century acquiring complete sets of signatures of the Declaration signers had become the epitome of autograph collecting.[85] Now, at least for older eras, such as the time of the American Revolution, we can study fragments of early printings and manuscripts, discovering new facts about the production of such records and the dissemination of public texts. But will we have such fragments in the developing Information Age?[86] Electronic fragments tend to be gibberish.

What would remain of the Declaration and its historical context two hundred years from now if these records were electronic? One might assume that *more* could be saved. Joshua Meyrowitz writes that "through electronic 'documents', future generations will experience a new sort of past. 'History' was once a discursive script written and acted by the rich, the powerful, and the educated. Because of their discursiveness, historical sources were also filled with arguments, propositions, ideas, and ideals. The growing archives of audio and videotape, however, thrust the common person into history; simultaneously, they reveal what is common even about our leaders. And the 'language' of these records is the experience-presentational-analogic form of gesture, feeling, and experience."[87] I am not quite so positive about this. And given that Meyrowitz wrote this over a decade ago, in a more innocent age (technology speaking), others should be skeptical as well. For the past thirty plus years archivists and others have labored to create mechanisms for dealing with electronic records and other digital media. Much has been saved, more has been lost, and more seems doomed.

Perhaps we have already been given a real test, as well as opportunity, about this challenge. We know well that there remains a great amount of tentativeness about just what might possibly be saved; should everything be printed out on paper or maintained in electronic form? Can we really handle more paper? If we attempt to save records created in electronic form in some electronic state, how do we account for rapidly changing hardware and software? And while we ruminate on how to do this, there have already been *other* declarations posted on the World Wide Web.

After the passing of the Telecommunications Reform Bill in 1996, Internet activist John Perry Barlow drafted a "A Declaration of the Independence of Cyberspace." Reacting to efforts by Congress to govern what could be said on the Internet, Barlow argues in his declaration that "this bill was enacted upon us by people who haven't the slightest idea who we are or where our conversation is being conducted." Borrowing from the spirit of the older Declaration, Barlow writes, "Governments derive their just powers from the consent of the governed. You have neither solicited nor received ours. We did not invite you. You do not know us, nor do you know our world. Cyberspace does not lie within your borders. Do not think that you can build it, as though it were a public construction project. You cannot. It is an act of nature and it grows itself through our collective actions." More specifically, his declaration asserts that "in the United States, you have today created a law, the Telecommunications Reform Act, which repudiates your own Constitution and insults the dreams of Jefferson, Washington, Mill, Madison, DeToqueville, and Brandeis. These dreams must now be born anew in us."[88] Renewing the spirit of the Declaration (the first one) is what should be the aim of refurbishing the exhibition at the National Archives.

Think about the issues raised by Barlow's declaration for free speech, censorship, access, and government regulation. Barlow's immediate posting of his text on the Web certainly underscores that this is the *new* printing press for revolutionary proclamations. But does this new declaration possess some symbolic or spiritual value in its electronic form? Is there a need to preserve the Barlow declaration in its *electronic* state rather than a more traditional printed version? Is something lost in paper versions, given that this is a declaration about cyberspace? If we deem it essential to retain Barlow's text as an electronic document, what assurances do we have that it won't be lost as the Web shifts and changes?

The Declaration on display should not be allowed to become an ancient symbol, an artifact entombed in a sarcophagus, mostly preserved as a curiosity. What should be displayed there is the story of the Declaration's own plight, its near misses, its transformation into an important national symbol, and the problems with its physical deterioration. But more importantly, the document should be the centerpiece of an exhibition focusing on the *greater* dangers facing records created as part of newer electronic systems and government itself.

The Declaration should become a reminder that without the documents representing the quest for freedom, and not just a few like the Declaration and the Constitution, that our very freedom might be in jeopardy. Sitting next to the wonderfully preserved Declaration ought to be examples of records lost because of technological obsolescence and examples of records nearly destroyed by government efforts to cover up the stories of abuse of powers. Then the Declaration and its costs of maintenance might mean more to more Americans. After all, in the Declaration itself, one of the complaints arrayed against King George is that he "has called together Legislative Bodies at Places unusual, uncomfortable, and distant from the Depository of their public Records, for the sole Purpose of fatiguing them into Compliance with his Measures." Certainly the loss of so much of our documentary heritage due to the technical problems of modern recordkeeping will do more to make our records inaccessible for the purposes of accountability, memory, and evidence they were intended to provide. In fact, perhaps Barlow's declaration should be displayed on a computer monitor *next* to the original Declaration where people can look at it *and* the World Wide Web. This reflects that Jefferson and his committee's original Declaration is still vital as inspiration for *other* declarations. The exhibition in the National Archives Rounda becomes vital, then, and not the viewing at a funeral.

NOTES

1. James O'Toole, "On the Idea of Permanence," *American Archivist* 52 (Winter 1989): 10–25.

2. The starting point for reading about preservation of records is Mary Lynn Ritzenthaler, *Archives and Manuscripts: Conservation*, Basic Manual Series (Chicago: Society of American Archivists, 1983; rev. ed., 1994), with sections on definitions and philosophy, the nature of archival materials, causes of deterioration, the proper environment and storage, and preservation procedures.

3. See Paul Conway, "Archival Preservation Practice in a Nationwide Context," *American Archivist* 53 (Spring 1990): 204–222, which provides the most in-depth and best critical assessment of the resources supporting the preservation of archival records; the Conway study is the benchmark for future research on this topic.

4. Howard Lowell, *Preservation Needs in State Archives* (Albany, N.Y.: National Association of Government Archives and Records Administrators, February 1986); a summary of the report is Howard P. Lowell, "The Quiet Crisis in State Archives," *Records Management Quarterly* (April 1988): 23–24, 26, 36.

5. David D.Van Tassel, *Recording America's Past: An Interpretation of the Development of Historical Societies in America 1607–1884* (Chicago: University of Chicago Press, 1960).

6. See Nancy E. Gwinn, ed., *Preservation Microfilming: A Guide for Librarians and Archivists* (Chicago: American Library Association, 1987) and Nancy E. Elkington, ed., *Digital Imaging Technology for Preservation* (Mountain View, Calif.: Research Libraries Group, Inc., 1994).

7. Many states have completed statewide preservation assessments. New York Document Conservation Advisory Council, *Our Memory At Risk: Preserving New York's Unique Research Resources* (Albany, N.Y.: The Council, 1988) is the first statewide analysis of the preservation needs of research materials.

8. See note 2 for a full citation to this important publication.

9. James Gregory Bradsher, "An Administrative History of the Disposal of Federal Records, 1789–1949," *Provenance* 3 (Fall 1985): 5. See also his "A Brief History of the Growth of Federal Government Records, Archives, and Information 1789–1985," *Government Publications Review* 13 (1986): 491–505.

10. Bradsher, "An Administrative History," p. 6.

11. Bradsher, "An Administrative History," p. 7.

12. Bradsher, "An Administrative History," pp. 11–12, 15.

13. David O. Stephens, "Megatrends in Records Management," *Records Management Quarterly* 32 (January 1998): p. 6.

14. Stephens, "Megatrends," p. 6.

15. Ernst Posner, Helen Chatfield, and Edna B. Poeppel, *The Role of Records in Administration*, Staff Information Paper 11 (Washington, D.C.: National Archives and Records Service, 1975, org. pub. 1941), p. 17.

16. Posner, Chatfield, and Poeppel, *Role of Records*, p. 17.

17. Ernst Posner, *American State Archives* (Chicago: University of Chicago Press, 1964), p. 324.

18. Philip C. Brooks, *What Records Shall We Preserve?*, Staff Information Paper 9 (Washington, D.C.: National Archives and Records Service, 1975, org. pub. 1940).

19. G. Philip Bauer, *The Appraisal of Current and Recent Records*, Staff Information Circular 13 (Washington, D.C.: National Archives and Records Service, 1976, org. pub. 1946).

20. Robert Bahmer, "Scheduling the Disposition of Records," *American Archivist* 6 (July 1943): 169–175; Philip C. Brooks, "Archival Procedures for Planned Records Retirement," *American Archivist* 11 (October 1948): 308–315; and Isadore Perlman, "General Schedules and Federal Records," *American Archivist* 15 (January 1952): 27–38.

21. Terry Cook, "What Is Past Is Prologue: A History of Archival Ideas Since 1898, and the Future Paradigm Shift," *Archivaria* 43 (Spring 1997): 28.

22. Luciana Duranti, "The Concept of Appraisal and Archival Theory," *American Archivist* 57 (Spring 1994): 328–344; Frank Boles and Mark A. Greene, "Et Tu Schellenberg? Thoughts on the Dagger of American Appraisal Theory," *American Archivist* 59 (Summer 1996): 298–310.

23. T. R. Schellenberg, "The Appraisal of Modern Public Records," *National Archives Bulletin* 8 (Washington, D.C.: National Archives and Records Service, 1956), p. 44.

24. Hilary Jenkinson, *A Manual of Archive Administration*, rev. 2nd ed. (London: Percy Lund, Humphries and Co., 1966), pp. 137–138, 148–149.

25. Thornton W. Mitchell, ed., *Norton on Archives: The Writings of Margaret Cross Norton on Archival & Records Management* (Carbondale: Southern Illinois University Press, 1975), pp. 232–233, 239.

26. Mitchell, ed., *Norton on Archives*, pp. 250–251.

27. National Archives and Records Service, *Intrinsic Value in Archival Material*, Staff Information Paper 21 (Washington, D.C.: National Archives and Records Service, 1982); Kimberly J. Barata, "Questioning Aesthetics: Are Archivists Qualified to Make Appraisal or Reappraisal Based on Aesthetic Judgments?" *Provenance* 12, nos. 1 and 2 (1994): 63–82.

28. Samuel Muller, J. A. Feith, and R. Fruin, *Manual for the Arrangement and Description of Archives* (New York: H. W. Wilson, 1968; org. pub. 1898).

29. Jenkinson, *Manual of Archive Administration*, p. 147.

30. Boles and Greene, "Et Tu Schellenberg?" p. 309.

31. Terry Cook, "Mind Over Matter: Towards a New Theory of Archival Appraisal," in Barbara L. Craig, ed., *The Archival Imagination: Essays in Honour of Hugh A. Taylor* (Ottawa: Association of Canadian Archivists, 1992), p. 47.

32. Helen W. Samuels, "Who Controls the Past," *American Archivist* 49 (Spring 1986): 109–124; Larry J. Hackman and Joan Warnow-Blewett, "The Documentation Strategy Process: A Model and a Case Study," *American Archivist* 50 (Winter 1987): 12–47.

33. Ann Pederson, "Dr Frankenstein Revisited: Creative Experiments in Archival Selection and Appraisal," *New Zealand Archivist* 4 (Spring/September 1993): 3.

34. Duranti, "Concept of Appraisal and Archival Theory," p. 343.

35. Terry Cook, "Documentation Strategy," *Archivaria* 34 (Summer 1992): 182, 184, and 188.

36. Joan Warnow-Blewett, "Documenting Recent Science: Progress and Needs," *OSIRIS*, 2nd series, 7 (1992): 267–298.

37. Philip N. Alexander and Helen W. Samuels, "The Roots of 128: A Hypothetical Documentation Strategy," *American Archivist* 50 (Fall 1987): 518–531.

38. Ellen Garrison, "The Very Model of a Modern Major-General: Documentation Strategy and the Center for Popular Music," *Provenance* 7, no. 2 (1989): 22–32.

39. Richard J. Cox, "Evangelical Religious Institutions Consider Their Archival Needs: A Review of the 1988 Evangelical Archives Conference Proceedings," *Provenance* 7 (Spring 1989): 66–79 and Teresa Thompson, "Ecumenical Records and Documentation Strategy: Applying 'Total Archives,'" *Archivaria* 30 (Summer 1990): 104–109.

40. Richard J. Cox, "A Documentation Strategy Case Study: Western New York," *American Archivist* 52 (Spring 1989): 192–200.

41. Joan D. Krizack, ed., *Documentation Planning for the U. S. Health Care System* (Baltimore: Johns Hopkins University Press, 1994).

42. Joan K. Haas, Helen W. Samuels, and Barbara T. Simmons, *Appraising the Records of Modern Science and Technology: A Guide* (Cambridge, Mass.: MIT Press, 1985).

43. Helen W. Samuels, *Varsity Letters: Documenting Modern Colleges and Universities* (Metuchen, N.J.: Scarecrow Press, 1992).

44. James M. O'Toole, ed., *The Records of American Business* (Chicago: Society of American Archivists, 1997).

45. Richard J. Cox, *Documenting Localities: A Practical Model for American Archivists and Manuscripts Curators* (Metuchen, N.J.: Scarecrow Press and Society of American Archivists, 1996).

46. Cook, "What Is Past Is Prologue," p. 31.

47. Harold E. Thiele, Jr., "Appraisal, Provenance, and the Computer Revolution: An Examination of Organizational Records in the Electronic Age," *Katherine Sharp Review*, no. 6 (Winter 1998), at http://edfu.lis.uiuc.edu/review/6/.

48. Catherine Bailey, "From the Top Down: The Practice of Macro-Appraisal," *Archivaria* 43 (Spring 1997): 113–114.

49. Mike Wallace, *Mickey Mouse History and Other Essays on American Memory* (Philadelphia: Temple University Press, 1996).

50. For some sense of the various arguments about these standards refer to Lynne Cheney, *Telling the Truth: Why Our Culture and Our Country Have Stopped Making Sense—and What We Can Do about It* (New York: Simon and Schuster, 1995); Lawrence W. Levine, *The Opening of the American Mind: Canons, Culture and History* (Boston: Beacon Press, 1996); and Gary B. Nash, Charlotte Crabtree, and Ross E. Dunn, *History on Trial: Culture Wars and the Teaching of the Past* (New York: Alfred B. Knopf, 1997).

51. Mary Lefkowitz, *Not Out of Africa: How Afrocentrism Became An Excuse to Teach Myth as History* (New York: Basic Books, 1996), p. 52.

52. Nathan Glazer, *We Are All Multiculturalists Now* (Cambridge, Mass.: Harvard University Press, 1997), p. 14.

53. Edward W. Said, *Representations of the Intellectual: The 1993 Reith Lectures* (New York: Vintage Books, 1994), p. 74.

54. Neil Postman, *The End of Education: Redefining the Value of School* (New York: Alfred A. Knopf, 1995), p. 7.

55. Todd Gitlin, *The Twilight of Common Dreams: Why America Is Wracked by Culture Wars* (New York: Metropolitan Books, Henry Holt and Co., 1995), p. 208.

56. Wallace, *Mickey Mouse History*, p. 302.

57. Wendell Berry, *Sex, Economy, Freedom and Community: Eight Essays* (New York: Pantheon Books, 1993), p. 172.

58. Arthur M. Schlesinger, Jr., *The Disuniting of America: Reflections on a Multicultural Society* (New York: W. W. Norton and Co., 1992), p. 99.

59. Genevieve Fabre and Robert O'Meally, eds., *History and Memory in African-American Culture* (New York: Oxford University Press, 1994), p. 7.

60. Levine, *The Opening of the American Mind*, pp. 64–65.

61. See Pierre Nora, "Between Memory and History: Les Lieux de Memoire," in Fabre and O'Meally, *History and Memory in African-American Culture*, pp. 284–300.

62. Terry Cook, "Many Are Called but Few Are Chosen: Appraisal Guidelines for Sampling and Selecting Case Files," *Archivaria* 32 (Summer 1991): 25–50.

63. See David A. Hollinger, *Postethnic America: Beyond Multiculturalism* (New York: Basic Books, 1995).

64. Stephen E. Lucas, "The Stylistic Artistry of the Declaration of Independence," *Prologue* 22 (Spring 1990): 25–43.

65. Alexander Stille, "Overload," *The New Yorker* (March 8, 1999): 38, 43, 44.

66. Lawrence C. Wroth, *The Colonial Printer*, 2nd ed. (Charlottesville: The University Press of Virginia, 1938), p. 3.

67. Daniel J. Boorstin, *Cleopatra's Nose: Essays on the Unexpected* (New York: Random House, 1994), pp. 66, 70, 72.

68. Jonathan Wallace and Mark Mangan, *Sex, Laws, and Cyberspace: Freedom and Censorship on the Frontiers of the Online Revolution* (New York: Henry Holt and Co., 1997), p. 228.

69. Jeffrey Archer, *Honor Among Thieves* (New York: HarperPaperbacks, 1993) and *The Amazing Spiderman* 1, no. 325 (Late November 1989).

70. A popular history of the original Declaration is Patricia E. Carr, "The Document That Traveled," *American History Illustrated* 9, no. 4 (1974): 26–33.

71. John Bodnar, *Remaking America: Public Memory, Commemoration, and Patriotism in the Twentieth Century* (Princeton, N.J.: Princeton University Press, 1992), p. 23.

72. Verner Clapp, "The Declaration of Independence: A Case Study in Preservation," *Special Libraries* 62 (December 1971): 504.

73. Clapp, "The Declaration of Independence," p. 503.

74. Quoted in Warren E. Leary, "Nation's Vital Documents Get Checkups," *New York Times*, February 14, 1995.

75. "Preserving the Charters of Freedom," *The Record: News From the National Archives and Records Administration* 4 (March 1998): 5.

76. Warren E. Leary, "New Framers of the Nation's Constitution Work to Preserve a Heritage," *New York Times*, February 7, 1999.

77. Laura Tingley, "Whoops, There Goes Another CD-ROM," *U.S. News and World Report*, February 16, 1998 (no page numbers—published in the electronic version).

78. Roger Chartier, *Forms and Meanings: Texts, Performances, and Audiences from Codex to Computer* (Philadelphia: University of Pennsylvania Press, 1995), p. 5.

79. Pauline Maier, *American Scripture: Making the Declaration of Independence* (New York: Alfred A. Knopf, 1997), p. 215.

80. Such as Daniel Lazare, *The Frozen Republic: How the Constitution Is Paralyzing Democracy* (New York: Harcourt Brace and Co., 1996).

81. James Atlas, *Battle of the Books: The Curriculum Debate in America* (New York: W. W. Norton and Co., 1990), p. 119.

82. David Thelen, *Becoming Citizens in the Age of Television: How Americans Chal-

lenged the Media and Seized Political Initiative During the Iran-Contra Debate (Chicago: University of Chicago Press, 1996), pp. 161–162.

83. Theodore Roszak, "Shakespeare Never Lost a Manuscript to a Computer Crash," *New York Times*, March 11, 1999, p. D8.

84. John F. Berens, *Providence and Patriotism in Early America 1640–1815* (Charlottesville: University Press of Virginia, 1978), pp. 114–115.

85. Moncure D. Conway, "The Story of the Declaration of Independence," *The Open Court* 5 (July 2, 1891): 2859–2861.

86. One study examines a fragment of an early printing and determines that it was an early reading version printed for the use of Congress, made before the final printing known as the Dunlap Broadside. Wilfred J. Ritz, "From the Here of Jefferson's Rough Draft of the Declaration of Independence to the There of the Printed Dunlap Broadside," *Pennsylvania Magazine of History and Biography* 116 (October 1992): 499–512.

87. Joshua Meyrowitz, *No Sense of Place: The Impact of Electronic Media on Social Behavior* (New York: Oxford University Press, 1985), p. 109.

88. This Declaration was posted all over the Web, and it can be found, among other places, at http://www.webtc.com/. For more about Barlow see his homepage at http://www.eff.org/~barlow/ and the chapter on Barlow in John Brockman, *Digerati: Encounters with the Cyber Elite* (San Francisco: Hardwired, 1996).

6

Archives, Records, and Memory

Records are valuable for their evidence, accountability, *and* memory—linking the critical functions of appraisal to description and access. Every researcher writing about the importance of records attributes such value to the ability of these documents to provide a glimpse into the memory of individuals, organizations, and society. We view memory differently. A half-century ago records were the raw materials of history. Now, records are part of a vast accumulation of materials weaving the fabric of the past. Society, rushing head on with its many technologies in the front, struggles to hold onto any semblance of a past. There is a fear that records and archives will be lost.

THE CONCEPT OF PUBLIC MEMORY AND ITS IMPACT
ON RECORDS MANAGEMENT

American archivists have been debating the place of public programs for a quarter of a century. Some records professionals believe that if they work harder to create a more prominent profile for themselves and their programs, then there will be direct and measurable dividends for any such investment. The upsurge of publication on public memory in the United States adds a richness of texture to records professionals' potential understanding of their (and their records') importance in society. Two books, one on the John F. Kennedy assassination and the other on the Watergate scandal, are good examples, reflecting the nature of archives and records in American memory.[1] Zelizer's book on JFK reveals a distinctive shift of authority for understanding the past from the record to the news media. Schudson's Watergate study avoids discussion of the Presidential Records Act of 1974, for records professionals the most tangible impact of the

Nixon Watergate scandal, and reflects the lack of visibility of records in this aspect of American public memory.

Why do scholars from many disciplines seem prone to ignore the value of records in the formulation of public memory? The paucity of archival history research is one reason, providing a weak reference for public memory scholars and making it easy to neglect records and professional records communities. For decades in the United States, archivists debated their relationship to professional historians, ruminating on their professional identity and purpose.[2] What archivists should be concerned about is how well they communicate their mission to others than just scholarly researchers. During the same period, records managers struggled with the focus of their professional mission—whether it is records, information, or knowledge—and all the typical dimensions of a discipline, from education to credentials.[3] Records managers should expand their calling to a constituency wider than only records creators, holding true to the importance of records.

Public memory (the public—government and citizens—perceptions and uses of the past) has become a topic of great interest for historians and cultural critics. Collaboration between more traditional intellectual, political and institutional history, and social history drawing on other disciplines, research in American public memory has produced major studies.[4] They have much to say to records professionals, especially about the archival community's public programming and records managers' need to formulate a public mission.

It is assumed public memory has influenced archives significantly, or that the related idea of organizational memory has transformed records managers' thinking about their responsibilities. Archivists know that "archives are sometimes said to be society's collective memory."[5] Archivists use the notion of memory, believing records are "set aside consciously as memorial of the action or actions giving it existence" and that "archives provide material for the extension of human memory."[6] Transactional records are crucial to organizational memory. The increasing attention in the past twenty years by archivists about public programming and advocacy relates to what historians of public memory are examining, even though their references to archives or the general importance of records are spotty.

Archivists have considered public programs since the 1970s, when they had their consciousness raised about their relationship to the public, most notably by Elsie Freeman. Freeman called for greater attention to the public, including the adoption of a client-centered approach.[7] While records managers can empathize with this objective, they seem unsure about its meaning—moving from an emphasis on economy and efficiency to broader information and knowledge management concepts valued by their employing organizations. One would be hard-pressed to find similar arguments in the records management literature, where utility and legal concerns seem to predominate.

The year 1982 was a watershed for archivists and public programming. Along with Freeman's spirited rationale for public service came a basic manual on the subject and immersion in a campaign to regain the administrative independence of the National Archives. The public programming manual is the starting point for reading about this topic.[8] Prior to it, most American archivists perceived public service as an element or benefit of reference services. As this manual was published, Society of American Archivists President David Gracy made "Archives and Society" his theme, and his speeches, articles, and task force and committee assignments pushed public programming and advocacy into the mainstream.[9] Gracy raised the consciousness of archivists about the public, although his focus was more introspective (concentrated on archival image). No basic archival text now ignores the topic,[10] although some archivists lament how it is perceived by their colleagues.[11] Other than references to a service mentality, there is no counterpart to the public programming emphasis in the records management literature.

Public programming is crucial to archival theory and methodology. James O'Toole, among many, ties the act of recording to memory with his observation that "in its more or less insatiable desire to gather, comprehend, and utilize data, humanity has long sought means to fix knowledge in such a way that it can be called back to mind when necessary or desirable."[12] The writings by historians on public memory provide another means for records professionals to consider the origins of their institutions, explain their subsequent development, and realize ways they should view the public's perception of records.

John Bodnar's study of public memory and patriotism demonstrates the conflicting tensions within the United States about its past and the idea that "public memory emerges from the intersection of official and vernacular cultural expressions."[13] Bodnar contests the general assumption that public memory emerges from political discussion concentrated upon economic or moral problems and sees it emerging from "fundamental issues about the entire existence of a society: its organization, structure of power, and the very meaning of its past and present."[14] Current problems only stimulate discussions regarding the uses of the past. Bodnar traces ideas about public memory from the nineteenth-century developing nation-state where the modern national government and nation concept came to be dominant influences on public memory. Bodnar discourses on communal forums (ethnic celebrations and urban commemorations), regional forums (the Midwest before and after the Second World War), and national forums (the work of the National Park Service and the Civil War centennial and the American Revolution bicentennial).

What are the main aspects of recent American public memory? Bodnar sees a shift in the ethic-oriented forums to a "collective performance for profit and boosterism," with an increasing emphasis on the "inevitable and painless transformation of diverse folk cultures into a unified American culture."[15] In the communal and regional forums, Bodnar similarly notes how local interests became subsumed by national and other political factors and, furthermore, how the celebrations changed from group identity and pride to recreation and leisure activities.[16] This public memory transformation was facilitated by the "expanding power of government,''[17] responsible for an unprecedented growth in records and the emergence of modern archives and records management—topics not discussed by this historian. Local, state, and federal government entities increasingly sought to orchestrate commemorations and activities to ensure that the nation's interests were paramount; for example, the government-supported mural programs "provided local populations with a view of the past that was reassuring."[18] The National Park Service and the national celebrations of the Civil War and American Revolution demonstrate the increasing influence of the national government on public memory, Bodnar suggesting that "they stood as massive cultural bookends that attempted to contain volumes of dissent and indifference to the civic messages of leaders."[19] Bodnar concludes that public memory moved to a fundamental conflict between national (or official) and vernacular memory.[20]

Bodnar has few references regarding archives and historical records repositories. He briefly mentions the changing image of the Declaration of Independence to a "sacred document." In a pageant, there is reference to a college professor's call to create a repository for housing books, pamphlets, and newspapers published by Norwegian-Americans. The activities of the American-Irish Historical Society are mentioned. The State Historical Society of Wisconsin's involvement in that state's centennial celebrations is chronicled. There is a brief reference to the Civil War centennial supporting records microfilming. And, finally, there is a reference to an archival and oral history project in Alabama as part of the American Revolution celebration.[21]

Considering the origin and nature of many archival programs as public memory activities, so little discussion should be surprising. The founding of the state government archives in Maryland was directly tied to the tercentenary celebration of this state's colonial founding.[22] The National Archives was the result of a long, hard-fought campaign that drew upon the strengths and energies of many patriotic groups and was marketed as a war memorial.[23] Even the establishment of college and university archives is most typically the result of anniversaries and other commemorative events.[24] A large portion of our archival and historical manuscript repositories is an artifact of public memory.

David Glassberg provides another view of public memory by examining historical pageantry's imagery in the early twentieth century, seeing such imagery as "both a reflection of the larger culture, and its prevailing ways of looking at the world, and a major element in the shaping of that culture."[25] Glassberg considers the rise of the "historical oration," explaining the "sacred as well as the worldly significance of past events" and supporting a common view of progress.[26] These orations displayed tributes to the nation, but they were equally as important as a means to stimulate local community development, corresponding to and supporting the burgeoning popular interest in local history. Relics displays, monuments, publication of colorful souvenir books, parades, and reunions were used in these activities. "Civic officials piled historical artifact, narrative, and image upon image in antiquarian detail to bring the full weight of tradition to bear upon their neighbors, discharging what they felt was their sacred duty to teach their beliefs and values to the public and to explain the present residents' unique place in a succession of past and future residents who together constituted the historical community."[27] Like Bodnar, Glassberg perceives that these celebrations, despite the diversity of participants and observers, supported a "broadly conceived but loosely defined civic ideal."[28] Glassberg also detects the growing effort by government to control these pageants for an overt civic ideal.

Glassberg provides detailed descriptions of urban pageantry in the early twentieth century, considering tensions about whether the pageants should be patriotic and civic in origin or primarily recreational. The shift to deliberate uses of the pageants was fairly rapid, becoming "not only a new medium for patriotic, moral, and aesthetic education envisioned by genteel intellectuals, but also an instrument for the reconstruction of American society and culture using progressive ideals." During the First World War "pageantry . . . submerged the dramatic expression of local and regional identity in mass demonstrations of national loyalty."[29]

Glassberg chronicles how local communities perceived the pageants' value, putting "the spirit of unanimity around a unique local identity."[30] Community development, along with a mix of patriotic and nationalistic themes, became their focus: "As a result of exposure through the national media and popular expectations raised by that media, historical pageants in different regions of the nation, places with apparently different local histories, displayed similar images of their past, present, and future. But this similarity of historical images and ritual action embedded in the pageant form also reflected concerns and desires . . . for promoting pious beliefs and virtuous behaviors, wholesome expressive recreation, local community cohesion, and a deep faith in orderly progress."[31] Tying all this together was the notion of progress.[32]

Glassberg considers the development of patriotic and hereditary societies in the late nineteenth century, many of which eventually became archival repositories. Many pageant leaders sought local manuscripts and historical materials. The pageant directors urged new local history research, "foreshadowing many ideas of social historians later in the century."[33] Eventually the patriotic and hereditary societies turned to historic preservation and history museums and the pageant masters worked elsewhere, such as convincing American Telephone and Telegraph Company of the importance of establishing an archives and historical library.[34] Given the nature of these organizations, one would suspect that Glassberg's interest in archives and records would be strong and play a larger role in his story, but this is not the case.

With the National Archives and the Historical Records Survey, and numerous other historical manuscript and archival records repositories, originating at this time, there may be a connection with the historical pageantry movement. It is also possible that before the Second World War there was a strong public historical interest that the fledgling records profession could have utilized more extensively than it did. The National Archives used the Freedom Train just after the Second World War to harness the public's strong patriotism in support of the preservation of historical manuscripts and archives.[35] None of these issues are considered by Glassberg. Like Bodnar's study, Glassberg's work pays little attention to the founding of archival and historical records programs or the development of an archival profession, diminishing an opportunity for records professionals to understand more fully how their own work fits into the public's interest in the past. Since many of the institutions founded as the result of such festivities eventually assumed responsibility for the management of current records, such as happened with the Southern state archives as the century progressed, records managers also lost something of their history as well.

Michael Kammen's book is another ambitious study on American public memory, intended to answer the question "when and how did the United States become a land of the past, a culture with a discernible memory (or with a configuration of recognized pasts)?"[36] The result is an encyclopedic chronicle of how Americans have viewed their past. As he describes his study, "I am fascinated by the phenomenon of a society becoming its own historian—for better and for worse."[37] Part of his interest also derives from his recognition that despite history's professionalization, it is popular or public memory that is most relevant to most Americans. Clearly, then, records professionals ought to be concerned with how this societal self-made history views archives.

Kammen divides his work into a quartet of long discourses on chronological segments of the American past. He examines the idea of tradition in America before 1870, a period when there was innovation but no notable interest in the public perception of the past by government at any level. As Kammen suggests, during most of the nineteenth century Americans did not pay much attention to anything approaching a public memory. Kammen also examines the periods 1870–1915, 1915–1945, and 1945–1990. Although Kammen's encyclopedic detail overwhelms precise answers to the questions he poses at the outset of his book, his attention to archives, manuscript collecting, and related activities is much more comprehensive than that of Bodnar and Glassberg.

Kammen's *Mystic Chords* has many references to the development of historical records and archival repositories. Before 1870, Kammen notes the founding of the Massachusetts Historical Society, Philadelphia collector John Fanning Watson, the American neglect of government records, the burgeoning development of state and local historical societies, early efforts by the federal government to care for its records, and the work of collector and editor Peter Force.[38] Kammen interweaves the interest in the preservation of historical sources throughout his text in a manner that will please most records professionals, although this has been better documented in other studies. His comment about "tradition-oriented organizations [including historical societies] that arose to promote the remembrance of national and local roots in a physically mobile society"[39] is certainly astute, but it is an observation made by others such as David D. Van Tassel and George Callcott.[40]

Kammen's many references to archives and historical manuscripts are uneven and disappointing. The period 1870–1915 was the era of the rise of state government archives and the origins of the modern American archival profession (closely associated with both history and librarianship). But the reader discovers only a miscellany of references to such events, the creation of some specialized archives (such as the Schomburg research center at the New York Public Library and the Burton Library in Detroit), the proliferation of patriotic and historical societies, and an increased government interest in history.[41] The neglect is more obvious for the years from 1915 until the present. Despite the state archives movement and the quest for a National Archives, Kammen makes incidental references to the establishment of archival programs and the work of individual collectors,[42] despite the close relationship of these programs and people to commemoration and celebration of the past. Kammen notes the varied nature, such as "collecting . . . was generally not the sort of rational, orderly, and prudent activity that we tend to assume it always must have been," or the "decentralization of resources played a significant part in the democratization of tradition in the United States during the 1930s and '40s."[43] The National Archives movement, already documented as a significant public memory feature, is only discussed in a few pages.[44] He refers to a miscellany of archival and historical manuscripts programs, the work of collectors, the role of national parks as repositories, the establishment of presidential libraries, and the impact of significant events, such as Watergate and Alex Haley's *Roots*, on records management.[45] Kammen's most comprehensive comments are reserved for the Freedom Train, providing a rather straightforward narrative and noting that this event made " 'Our American Heritage' a hackneyed phrase that appeared relentlessly from orations to upbeat cartoons—a legacy that has endured for more than four decades."[46]

Kammen's study reveals how such perceptions shift from generation to generation. The impact of public memory on archives and records management is not seriously considered. Nevertheless, Kammen, Bodnar, and Glassberg produced studies records professionals will find useful in understanding their efforts to secure support for the documentary holdings. Archivists and records managers may debate the degree of importance public programs and advocacy for their other functions, but few seem prone to argue that such activities are inappropriate. These studies have much to offer records professionals in understanding public programming, but their omissions are an indication of how far archivists and records managers have to go to build a profile of their historic place in the development of North American society. Careful scholarship by records professionals on the history of their discipline and their institutions is needed so that they cannot be ignored by historians.[47] Not only is such scholarship a legitimate and valuable exercise for what can be learned about records programs and practices, but it can be seen as a form of public outreach in clarifying the nature and purpose of records. Furthermore, records professionals need to write about archives and records issues in the journals of other disciplines and in more public-oriented or popular outlets, including the many new electronic journals. Issues such as long-term maintenance, access, and selection are all topics already being addressed by other disciplines, and there is no reason why these disciplines would not welcome the views of archivists and records managers.

There is another lesson from these public memory studies. Archivist Kent Haworth argues that his profession has been misguided in promoting itself, suggesting that archivists need to return to basic principles. He correctly argues that "our purpose requires no justification; it requires, instead, understanding, belief, and articulate assertion."[48] The histories demonstrate that the public interest in the past can be fickle and vacillating. Haworth says records professionals must demonstrate the continuing importance of the evidence of archives, while many others who have written on public programming suggest a continuing barrage of activities such as exhibitions, speeches, and press releases. Archivist Tim Ericson's statement that "everyone is interested in archival records—in history" but "most people do not realize it yet"[49] is probably true, but the nature of such interests (as these public memory studies reveal) is constantly changing. Archival outreach activities will be susceptible to swinging moods by the public unless archivists and records managers build a solid foundation, understanding that the "purpose of the archivist is to hold in trust for society the evidence of the truth, the evidence of justice and injustice in the society our archives document."[50] Likewise, Terry Cook writes that for archivists "idealism and a sense of holistic vision rather than utilitarianism and a sense of market imperatives must prevail."[51] This makes more sense than to gain an interest for archives and other records in a society in which the "heightened appetite for the past reveals not so much engagement with history as either nostalgia and/or a means of celebrating the present."[52]

Records professionals need to be students of society, as well as of their organizations, to do effective public programming. Sociologist Edward Shils notes that "a society which is strewn with pieces of its own past does not necessarily love them."[53] What reason is there for archivists and records managers to believe that they have done more than gather up some pieces, given some of the challenges posed by appraisal and scheduling (discussed in the previous chapter)? Bodnar, Glassberg, and Kammen provide maps which records professionals can use in understanding this, but there is another perspective. Image, awareness, education, and use operate within the context of how society views its past. In a review of these histories, John Gillis sees them as marking the end of the "era of national memory."[54] But these works can suggest something more profound—the natural ebb and flow of the public interest in history. Historian Gillis senses this, writing that the "best strategy seems to be to stay alert to the shifting shapes in which memory now presents itself. Memory has a way of escaping our grasp just when we think we have captured it on paper, in the archive, or on exhibit. It is not that the public is fickle, but rather that any attempt to fix the past automatically unsettles it. Memory is not a thing, but an interactive, interpretive process."[55] This suggests that records managers and archivists should remain focused on their primary responsibilities. They should not abandon public programming, but they also should not be caught in the changing interests in the past—the weathervane one archivist described a generation ago and that is reflected in the images of records and records professionals.[56] The World Wide Web has created some powerful new winds that records professionals must contend with.

CAUGHT IN A WEB: THE INTERNET, MEMORY, AND RECORDS

Archivists and records managers are busily creating World Wide Web sites, digitizing holdings and holdings guides for the Web, refining standards to enable them to maximize use of the Web, writing grants to support these activities, and seeking or re-educating staff for these endeavors.

It is a heady time, as many records and information professionals have eagerly embraced the most optimistic notions about the World Wide Web, particularly its promises to provide near universal access and to eliminate traditional gatekeepers such as editors, publishers, and governments. Sherry Turkle contends that "much of the conversation" about such things is "steeped in a language of liberation and utopian possibility."[57] Other scholars have seen such view points as part of a technological culture where the "main ideology . . . is that virtually all of our problems—ethical, economic, political—are subject to technical solutions."[58] The Internet has been especially prone to such views.[59] Influential news managers have featured articles declaring the end of the personal computer era as "pervasive computing" (the use of devices building on networking) takes over.[60] Putting up a Web site is essential if an institution is really committed to access to and use of their records, although archivists and records managers, descended from the ancient recordkeeper, clearly serve gatekeeping functions that can seem counter in spirit to the proponents of a free electronic network (the long recognized connection of the records custodian to the priest and privileged access to sacred texts).[61] Archivists and records managers can, they surmise, using the technology, enhance the public and policymaker's understanding of the importance of records and archives, increase use, target new researcher constituencies, and raise financial resources. They can bring the importance of records to the public, and, perhaps, eliminate those jokes and common misunderstandings about records and records professionals.

Or, one wonders, records professionals can increase the confusion about records and archives to an unprecedented degree. Creative and, perhaps, plainly routine uses of electronic networking can build a new kind of community that transcends those able to visit the repository physically. Management guru Peter Drucker wrote thirty years ago that "old wisdom—old long before the Greeks—held that a community was limited to the area through which news could easily travel from sunrise to sunset."[62] Records, also playing an important role in building communities, were likewise limited to use in a repository. The direct, connective power of the World Wide Web promises to build new communities, producing a kind of communal act formerly tied to print newspaper and its descendants like television.[63] Perhaps records professionals can argue that every time an individual uses a record or visits an archives that he or she becomes part of a communal act, but what this act represents may well have to do with how carefully records professionals consider the Web's implications and the content of their posted messages.

The use of the World Wide Web, or any electronic means of communication, has implications for changing information-seeking behavior, culture, individual identity and group cohesion, and other aspects of our individual, organizational, and social contexts and lives. The Web has been likened to a "knowledge repository," replacing traditional repositories like archives and libraries or at least blurring such distinctions.[64] Some believe the Web and other means of electronic dissemination are collapsing or breaking down traditional disciplinary boundaries. Gary Stix writes about how in the scientific community the increasing reliance on electronic journals is speeding up reporting on research, leading to a "live record of how thinking on a research problem evolves," and how the "electronic network blurs boundaries between experimentalist, author, publisher, reviewer, and archivist." [65] Print, manuscript, record, and book may all become blurred beyond recognition.

This does not imply that archivists and other records professionals should shun the Internet and Web. What it suggests, however, is that records professionals need to understand more about the nature and dynamics of modern cyberculture, just as their predecessors have worked to comprehend oral and print cultures. They need to see how information creation, use, and maintenance may bring profound affects on cherished aspects of archival and records management principles and practices, especially comprehension of for the record. Records professionals must ask are: Can archivists and records managers fully embrace the emerging cyberculture? If the computer screen has become the metaphor for our age,[66] where does this leave the record that archivists and other records professionals care for and manage?

Or, to ask these questions in another way, is the record *on*, *behind*, or *replaced* by the computer screen? This is a post-modern question, something we can detect by seeing how other disciplines concerned with evidence are also struggling. Kevin Walsh, musing over historic preservation, argues that "a sense of place is reliant on that place possessing characteristics which reveal temporal 'depth.' " Records have such depth. He continues, however, that the "combination of certain forms of conservation and post-modern architecture work together to undermine a sense of place. . . . [T]he selective conservation of certain buildings is akin to removing one's favorite quotes from a wide and varied selection of books and imposing them in a new and artificial context."[67] Placing a miscellaneous or highly selective array of records on the Web can have a similar result, minimizing the full value of records.

It is the rare archivist or records manager who does not have some knowledge of and experience with the Internet and the Web. Technically, the Internet is a "global information system"[68] with high-speed local loop to residential users, very high-speed backbone digital transport network, network of information users, and an integrated choice of services to the subscriber.[69] What is better known about the Web is its speed of growth, once estimated as increasing at over 300,000 percent annually.[70]

The point of departure for records professionals considering *how* to utilize the World Wide Web is what a record represents. Records professionals know (in fact nearly everyone—records creator, user, and custodian—knows this) that a record has a particular connection to time and place, as well as a physicality (whether it be on paper or in bits and bytes). While archivists and records managers do not want to emphasize records as artifacts, becoming slavishly curatorial in the managing items valuable for evidence and information, they must admit that records do have a similarity to artifacts with their location in time, space, and the physical world. In a classic essay in material culture, the authors suggest that "all archaeological data . . . can be said to possess three inherent dimensions . . . a location in space . . . [a] fix in time . . . and . . . certain physical attributes of form."[71] Can't the same be stated about records? Records professionals can look to rare book colleagues who have struggled with these issues. Peter S. Graham demonstrates the problem, arguing that "special collections . . . are collections of artifacts, whereas the network and its nodes are repositories of volatile electronic information. . . . Artifacts (we used to call them books) come under the classical definition of mass, for they have weight and occupy space. Information on the net does not."[72] What happens, then, when records are put on the Web?

While records were not at first dated (before about 2,500 years ago), since then they have been conspicuously dated and tied to events and, hence, to time. Historian Rosalind Thomas notes the "almost total absence of dates on any written texts . . . before 500 B.C. and many thereafter." She suggests that the "officials of each year were themselves . . . mnemonics for the year." "Our own obsession with dating is partly the product of an antiquarian and record-conscious society which thinks it may possibly need the date one day."[73]

The Western notion of time was refined by the emergence of writing into formal recordkeeping. Scholars perceive a "new kind of time" occurring in the eleventh to the fourteenth centuries. Earlier, time was marked by relating the "events significant enough to stick in the memory of witnesses to the proceedings described"—such as on the "Feast of St. Severinus, on a market day," and so on. By the thirteenth century specific dates were given, and "time through the text became something new: no more the subjective experience of a relative distance in the course of the world or the pilgrimage of the writer, but an axis for absolute reference on which charters could be nailed like labels. By the end of the fourteenth century, the date on a charter could even be tied to the mechanical tower-clock."[74] The notion of time as portrayed by records became more precise with the emergence of better timekeeping instruments in the seventeenth and eighteenth centuries. The narratives of records and related information sources were calibrated according to these instruments.[75]

The essence of records is their connection not just to time but to precipitating functions and events, both a warrant for and context of the records. Records professionals might not worry, *at first*, about the impact of the World Wide Web on a "record." After all, the Web is nothing more than a communications tool to be used creatively, and writing and recordkeeping have always been tied to media. If that is what written language and recordkeeping have evolved from, could not the Web, with its reliance on design, visuals, and communication also spell the transition to a new kind of records creation and maintenance?

Since many earlier communications systems have existed side by side with their predecessors, the Web will exist along with other paper and electronic systems, such as the traditional book and record. This has happened before, as the "evidence for Greece shows *both* a sophisticated and extensive use of writing in some spheres and what is to us an amazing dominance of the spoken word."[76] And "perhaps writing can exaggerate or strengthen tendencies already present, rather than transform them, but what is fundamental are the pre-existing features. Writing does not descend onto a blank slate."[77]

We can consider more recent developments. Some scholars contend that "television no more 'replaced' radio in the 1950s than radio had 'replaced' newspapers or magazines in the 1930s—or to continue the parallels, no more than television will be supplanted by specialized on-demand cable channels and on-line computer networks in the 1990s. After the hyperventilating about 'revolutionary media' subsides, Gutenberg still will coexist with the Internet."[78] This leads to a speculation that "although new media are seen . . . as transforming culture and modes of consciousness, they do so by *adding* to the spectrum of communication forms, rather than by destroying old means of communicating."[79]

Unfortunately, many archivists and other records professionals ignore the Web's implications—that it may challenge records maintenance. Charles McClure and J. Timothy Sprehe examined whether web postings are official government records or not in order to develop better records management and preservation strategies. The analysis is fascinating and disturbing, demonstrating how most state governments and selected federal government agencies are not even thinking about Web sites' implications at all. One of the most interesting points is archivists' clinging to the notion that all government publications have permanent value, meaning they need to save all Web sites as publications. This idea of all government publications being permanently valuable has been a poor idea ever since it was conceived.[80] Most of the discussion about the archivists' Web sites has questioned their purpose, design, accessibility, and content.[81]

Does the World Wide Web bring different elements to communication not present before? Or does the Web enhance or exaggerate certain behaviors that work against a more conservative interpretation of its potential impact on long-established activities such as recordkeeping? One of the essential roles of records has been tracking time. Our sense of time has always been tied up with various media, as Sven Birkerts reminds us: "The depth of field that is our sense of the past is not only a linguistic construct, but is in some essential way represented by the book and the physical accumulation of books in library spaces. In the contemplation of the single volume, or mass of volumes, we form a picture of time past as a growing deposit of sediment; we capture a sense of its depth and dimensionality."[82]

Can the Web serve this function as well? One of the attractive aspects of using the computer is its ability to enable us to change, quickly and at will, documents we create and store on it. The attractiveness of the computer is its malleability. "The ability to alter the content of a document—experimenting with different phrasings, rearranging things, cutting and pasting—this may be the defining characteristic of the digital computer.... The power of manipulation is the sine qua non of the modern computer, its core competency."[83]

This speed of change is so much a part of our reliance on devices like the World Wide Web that there is wide recognition that the Web itself may be short-lived (and what does this mean for all those libraries and archives investing resources into it?). More important, however, may be the way records professionals use the Web. We tend to browse rather than to read, to look for relevant material to resolve information needs quickly rather to investigate evidence. An effort to describe "digital literacy" evaluates the differences wrought by the Internet. "We read books, but we browse the Web," partly because the "hypertext page is similar in many ways to precodex documents; as with a papyrus roll, what you see on-screen must be read by 'scrolling' through the document."[84]

The Web fosters immersion in trivia, hardly an interest that sustains archives—unless we value records for trivial information. One historian considers that "we have become a nation of trivia experts: state capitals, batting averages, the Academy Awards, Civil War battles and battlefields, TV reruns and quiz-show hosts, the height of our presidents, ad nauseum." He goes on to say that "each fact exists as a discrete entity; there is no context, no larger picture that descrambles the dots. History, in this light, resembles the evening news: a downtown fire, chemical spills on the interstate, falling interest rates, a riot in South Korea, and the local basketball team loses a game. Is the news too fragmented? Do we lack perspective? No matter: Tomorrow it will be history."[85]

The Web might be more like one large textbook, and modern textbooks have been likened to little more than travel brochures by Jacques Barzun. "Its principle is: bits and pieces. It reminds one of the TV commercial, the preview of the film, the broken-up talk show, the scatter-shot news report."[86] Such issues require us to consider carefully the Web, and its impact on our concepts of time, place, and memory.

TIME, THE WEB, AND RECORDS

Time is an integral part of life. We all face death, but in the meantime, we live reasonably ordered lives by measuring our activities against time's movement. While time is an idea, it is also tied into natural processes; our use of clocks and writing are efforts to capture time. We can see time's importance because of how it is connected with all aspects of life. "Time is, first of all, an *idea*—the idea that an ordered sequence can be recognized in our states of conscious." Our calendar draws on "not only nature's rhythms but also religion, politics, and human intrigue." In each society's calendar, time is seen as a "dimension of life that ultimately can be submitted to cultural control. The material embodiment of time evident in the book, the codex, the carved door lintel, the ceremonial stela, as well as the grandfather clock—all have the effect of making past and future concrete and official."[87]

Our perception of time is different from other cultures and past societies, or as Robert Levine argues, "one needs to understand the fundamental values of a culture before coming to terms with its time sense." Time is *not* a neutral element. The notions of time existing now are quite different from the concepts predating the rise of industrialism and the advent of mechanical timekeeping. The development of better timekeeping devices, and reliable ones did not emerge until well into the nineteenth century, brought a new "regimentation and co-ordination."[88] When the telegraph was invented, the notion of time was radically transformed by the new communications system, eliminating time and space as standard barriers to human communication. Neil Postman argues that the "electric telegraph was the first communication medium to allow the speed of a message to exceed the speed of the human body. It broke the historic connection between transportation and communication. . . . The telegraph eliminated in one stroke both time and space as dimensions of human communication, and therefore disembodied information to an extent that far surpassed both the written and printed word."[89]

Technology forced time's standardization. "Rapid communications by telegraph, faster travel by railroad, stage, and steamboat, interstate and interregional commerce all demanded a uniform standard of time. By 1860 astronomical time, telegraphical time signals, and regional standard time had risen to fill the void. In the process, these innovations established new authorities for time, and new models for self-government and social regulation."[90] The push for standard time was significant to modern time. "Away from the world of telegraphs and railroad trains, there was no reason to care. Only the railroads, the ultimate symbol of commercial expansion, progress, and the conquest of space, had the motive and the power to reform public timekeeping."[91] The idea of standardizing time "epitomized new ideas about time's nature, ideas that in turn contributed to a major reorganization of work, leisure, and the individual's relation to society."[92]

Is the World Wide Web another time-breaking technology like the telegraph, telephone, and telefax? Or, is it something with new and different expectations and possibilities? It is essential that records professionals know that with improving communications has come a new expectation for how fast we will know about something (some things are not worth knowing about unless we can learn about them quickly). News was once measured by information conveyed over months, then weeks, days, and now real time. Jon Katz writes that "Americans now take for granted—though it's unprecedented in the history of information—that when a story . . . erupts, we will see pictures of it unfolding in real time."[93]

Time has collapsed, with serious implications for archivists and records managers, especially in the manner in which time has been transformed in the last decade as a result of electronic networking. Change is constant, and the notion of the past or any value assigned to the past has been swept aside. We now seem to measure time and value, relevancy and utility by the remarkably brief time assigned to computer hardware and software. Cultural critic Kirkpatrick Sale writes that a "high-tech society is ever-changing and unsettled, always caught in that rush of improvement and innovation that generally goes by the name of 'progress'. . . . [I]t is obvious that such a society will find the idea of the past . . . either irrelevant or, worse, impedimental. . . . The past is by definition imperfect, inadequate, impoverished."[94] Technologist turned critic Clifford Stoll adds that "within two years, the value of a computer drops in half. Within five years, it's pretty much been superseded. . . . Yet nobody figures on this short lifetime of communications lines when talking about the free information on the Internet."[95]

There is a falseness to electronic time, akin to prisoners who concoct a new kind of time in their unfortunate circumstances "by remembering past experience. They temporarily forget their unavoidable confinement by focusing their attention on memories. Remembered time substitutes for real time."[96] What happens to the individual who withdraws to the Web? A loss of a sense of the past will undermine any interest in worrying beyond more than the near future, and if that is the case, who will worry about using the older records making up archives or being stored in records centers? What good will it do for archivists and records managers to expend resources in building Web sites or even making full texts available over the Web? The Web suggests it does not make much difference if there is a long-term possibility for maintenance (and, perhaps, records professionals in their rush to use the Web have contributed to this problem as well, not considering how and why they will preserve Web sites of their own and their organization). A lack of seriousness in purpose results from this kind of focus.

If a record is an object captured in both time and space, which it is, then records professionals must be worried about using the World Wide Web as a communications *and recordkeeping* device. A record, to be valuable as evidence of a transaction, *freezes* time. Increased reliance on the Web for information may lead to data with no context, connection to a warrant and function, or place in time. Authenticity and reliability of records found on the Web are suspect. Since anyone with access to a computer and an account on an online service can post a Web site, how do we know what is genuine or trustworthy? And if the browsing or searching done on the Web, akin to aimless wandering in a bookstore or library, is liable to elevate any information found to useful source, how will factors such as time (a crucial part of the evidence of any record) be accounted for?

PLACE, THE WEB, AND ARCHIVES

Records mark time, creating a place for evidence about the past. Place is essential to understanding *both* time and memory. Place, whether we characterize it as real or virtual, is connected in intimate ways with time and memory. A geographer notes that "places are fusions of experience, landscape, and location, they are necessarily bound up with time and memory as well."[97] An historian considers landscape to be the "work of the mind. Its scenery is built up as much from strata of memory as from layers of rock."[98]

Place is essential to self-identity, providing the means by which we interact with other people, and it is now recognized as a crucial factor in human development, like genetics and history. Many commentators cite the importance of place. One writes that "our ordinary surroundings, built and natural alike, have an immediate and a continuing effect on the way we feel and act, and on our health and intelligence. These places have an impact on our sense of self, our sense of safety, the kind of work we get done, the ways we interact with other people, even our ability to function as citizens in a democracy. In short, the places where we spend our time affect the people we are and can become."[99] Another suggests that "throughout history, people of all cultures have assumed that environment influences behavior. Now modern science is confirming that our actions, thoughts, and feelings are indeed shaped not just by our genes and neurochemistry, history and relationships, but also by our surroundings."[100] Such perspectives have emerged partly in reaction to the dangers to place posed by electronic telecommunications forming a new *virtual* place. Real places are memory storehouses, much the same as archives, museums, and libraries. One historian writes that "identity is intimately tied to memory. . . . Urban landscapes are storehouses for these social memories, because natural features such as hills or harbors, as well as streets, buildings, and patterns of settlement, frame the lives of many people and often outlast many lifetimes."[101]

What happens to place on the Web, a world bounded and defined by electronic networking and communications technologies? Technologies, from the telephone to the automobile (even the communal experience of quilting), as a social *and* mechanical function, influence place and how we view it.[102] Technology and place have always been connected, as one technologist recognizes when he writes, "cities have . . . become the domains of bureaucracy and technology rather than places to live. Houses, streets, roads have undergone their twentieth-century redesigns simply to facilitate commercial and technological possibilities and the forms of government they appear to require."[103]

Can the Internet replace or substantially enhance memory, especially since the nature of the Web's permanence is an important question? Some argue about how scholars need to enter the real (physical and interpersonally defined) community from their cloisters, and the Web seems ideal for supporting this.[104] Is something lost in such dependence on the Web? Many, lauding the Web's wonders celebrate it for its "placelessness" "that will allow everything—people, goods, resources, knowledge—to be available anywhere, often instantaneously, with little regard for distance or place."[105]

Others—more cautious, critical or cynical—view the new cyberplaces as "fragmented" or "decentered." Examining the changing views of the modern city, one notes, "We can no longer read the city as a totality: it is heterogeneous, fragmented, dismembered, decentered." It represents a "new metrospace that defies any imageable form," and it has partly become this because of cyberspace. "Cyberspace is a new electronic, invisible space that allows the computer or television screen to substitute for urban space and urban experience."[106] We have had other warnings about this. Stephen Doheny-Farina notes we need a "geophysical" not an "electronic" view of society. He writes that the "revolution that must be joined is not one that removes us from place but one that somehow reintegrates the elements of our dissolving placed communities."[107]

Many consider the Web in terms formerly associated with the physical world, or respond to software and computer games because of the qualities of visual appeal they bring. Amidst all the hype about technology and the Web, there may be a *new* longing for place. Sherry Turkle states that the "lessons of computing today have little to do with calculation and rules; instead they concern simulation, navigation, and interaction." Computers have become "psychological objects." She sees that "we are learning to see ourselves as plugged-in technobodies."[108] This can be seen in video games: "Myst did not go platinum because it was an intriguing puzzle adventure. The people who bought it were not scratching a heretofore undiscovered itch for phase state logic brain teasers. Many of them never made it past riddle number one.... They paid for the scenery. Myst was gorgeous."[109]

The language describing cyberspace is not accidental. A writer, describing his building a structure, argues that "the culture of information is ultimately hostile to architecture, as it is to anything that can't be readily translated into its terms—to the whole of the undigitizable world, everything that the promoters of cyberspace like to refer to as RL (for 'real life'). And yet notice how even these people are drawn to architectural and spatial metaphors, as if to acknowledge that, even now, architecture holds an enviable, inextinguishable claim on our sense of reality. Such terms as 'cyberspace,' 'the electronic town hall,' 'cybershacks,' 'homepages,' and 'the information highway' belong to the great tradition of raiding architecture for its real-world palpableness—its *presence*—whenever someone's got something more ephemeral to sell. ... But architecture would do well to distrust this sort of flattery, because the cyberculture's interest in place is cynical and ultimately very slight."[110] This longing is evident even in legal circles where cyberspace is beginning to be treated as a place in order to apply existing laws or to mold new laws for its governance.[111]

Creating records secures order to the an organization's or a person's activities. While circumstances surrounding records creation may be chaotic, recordmaking is orderly, following conventions or responding to warrants (laws, regulations, and best practices). Such rules are intended to impose order, but the Web's attraction seems to be that it offers no particular order, while enhancing access speed and multiplying linkages in ways never imagined. A linguist notes that "in order to prevent Babel breaking out in committees or lecture halls, we have to impose very strict social rules on how people behave in these situations." Contrast this with the Net: "For one thing, the impersonality of the electronic highway seems to make people less discrete in their interactions with others than when they communicate face to face."[112]

"Cyberspace" is a "place" needing *new* road maps. A mathematician states that "as business reports and scientific research papers, newspapers and other periodicals, databases and electronic mail, textbooks and other books all increase rapidly, the number of interdependencies among them rises exponentially. New ways to link, classify, and order the traffic on the information highways of the future are necessary if we're to thread our way through the mounds of raw data strewn among them."[113] The impact of cyberspace on text and records may be more extensive than any previous media technology. "Our current revolution is obviously more extensive than Gutenberg's," writes one book historian. "It modifies not only the technology for reproduction of the text, but even the materiality of the object that communicates the text to readers. . . . The substitution of screen for codex is a far more radical transformation because it changes methods of organization, structure, consultation, even the appearance of the written word."[114]

The current emphasis of cyberspace is satisfying information needs and creating a new mechanism, independent of time and place, for working and cooperating. One proponent for networking technologies argues that the "Internet is as much a collection of communities as a collection of technologies, and its success is largely attributable to both satisfying basic community needs as well as utilizing the community in an effective way to push the infrastructure forward."[115] Another proponent suggests that the Internet provides the opportunity for an "enhanced 'context of work' " because it brings together people, knowledge types, and knowledge formats in a way that is unprecedented. It "creates a context of work in which ideas and facts flow so widely, with such little resistance, and with such high resolution that productivity will rise to much higher levels and knowledge accumulate at a much faster rate than ever before attained or even imagined."[116] Hundreds, if not thousands, of such predictions have been made about the Web.[117]

Such claims do not account for the fact that records need to be connected to particular functions and activities to serve as legitimate records. The graphic interface on the computer screen provides a kind of false security that you are some*where*. There can be a false sensation of place in the electronic environment, which bitmapping enables: "Data, for the first time, would have a physical location—or rather, a physical location *and* a virtual location: the electrons shuttling through the processor and their mirrored image on the screen."[118] Data are tied together with the "graphic interface"—which gives the impression "as though you were doing something directly with your data, rather than telling the computer to do it for you."[119] "This digital age belongs to the graphic interface," is the most telling assessment; "Information-space is the great symbolic accomplishment of our era."[120] It is important in other ways. "Beneath all the browbeating and messianism, there is this one guiding principle: zeros and ones lead inexorably toward a more fragmented experience of the world, or at least the world that comes to us over the modem and the cathode-ray tube." "And yet against all that dislocation and overload and multiplicity, there is the interface. . . . [T]he interface serves largely as a *corrective* to the forces unleashed by the information age."[121]

The degree to which the World Wide Web may create havoc because of new use of text and graphics has to be considered cautiously. Early printing apparently worried some for what it might do to community and the individual. Postman believes that "typography fostered the modern idea of individuality, but it destroyed the medieval sense of community and integration."[122] With the Web, the emphasis on access has overridden everything else, and the risks of decontextualizing everything should not seem be a desirable objective for records professionals. Sven Birkerts thinks we have been "transformed by the pure possibility of access. . . . Every place, once unique, itself, is strangely shot through with radiations from every other place."[123] Some critics have even placed cyberculture into a post-modern perspective.[124]

Words like isolation and distraction are commonly used by cyberspace critics as a new reality, and with a little extrapolation, it is easy to see a threat to records and archives. Stoll argues that computer networks "isolate us from one another and cheapen the meaning of actual experience. They work against literacy and creativity. They undercut our schools and libraries."[125] An earlier philosophical assessment suggests that "by bringing many different types of people to the same 'place,' electronic media have fostered a blurring of many formerly distinct social roles. Electronic media affect us, then, not primarily through their content, but by changing the 'situational geography' of social life." More importantly, "many Americans may no longer seem to 'know their place' because the traditionally interlocking components of 'place' have been split apart by electronic media. Wherever one is now—at home, at work, or in a car—one may be in touch and tuned-in."[126] This can be disturbing for records professional, since archives and records centers have always been viewed as *places*.

If we shuffle off into "social cubicles," then we may turn away from real records in archives, libraries, and museums for substitute experiences. David Shenk uses this phrase, even as he considers many of the Web's positive attributes. Shenk argues that we do have a sense of connection on the Internet. "The blossoming of the World Wide Web, functioning as a global electronic library equally accessible by all who are connected only enhances the sensation" of a "shrunken electronic world." "Web pages are as varied as humanity itself and yet they are all connected to one another," but we are not in a new kind of town square, but in "social cubicles." Put into such cubicles, "humankind begins to lose the most valuable thing it has ever had: common information and shared understanding."[127]

Place is not considered by cyberculturists as buildings and furniture—the stuff we normally associate with place—but by telecommunications systems and software. MIT Professor William J. Mitchell suggests that "being online may soon become a more important mark of community membership than being in residence." He continues that "we are entering the era of the temporary, recombinant, virtual organization—of business arrangements that demand good computing and telecommunications environments rather than large, permanent home offices."[128]

An increasing number of economic studies on information technology suggest we need to look at such claims more critically. The *New York Times* report on downsizing provides a context for this, noting that "America is deep in midpassage between two economic eras: the old era of making things and of job security, and the new one of service and technology, takeovers, layoffs, and job insecurity."[129] The new automated office fits into this work transformation by making "the irony of computerization . . . apparent. The pastel-walled, air-conditioned, computerized office turns out to be a far more complex, possibly dangerous place than even the most hardbitten Luddites of the 1960s had dared to predict."[130] "Despite industry calls for usability, then, the computing world of the 1990s turns out to be a patchwork of stand-alone machines and networks, professionals and amateurs, always in a state of tension between the productivity benefits greater power brings and the learning and support costs that it requires."[131] The economic impact on place by the technology is worth pondering, as some sociologists argue that "high technology will destroy more jobs than it creates. The new technology has fewer parts and fewer workers and produces more product."[132] Such studies contend that "after a quarter of a century during which computers displaced . . . major office machines—especially typewriters, adding machines, and mechanical calculators," they "all but eliminated the job category of file clerk, [and] by the 1980s many major corporations took advantage of the information 'revolution' to decentralize their facilities away from cities to suburbs and exurbs."[133]

MEMORY, THE WEB, AND ARCHIVES

Memory may be the most endangered in considering the Web as a critical element in society. Real place is being replaced by cyberplace—but place and memory are intertwined. Landscape, for example, is important. "Societies and cultures have many other ways to sustain collective values and beliefs, including ritual and oral tradition, but landscape stands apart from these—like writing—as a durable, visual representation."[134] This geographer also suggests that "Landscape is more than a passive reflection of a nation's civil religion and symbolic totems. Landscape is the expressive medium, a forum for debate within which those social values can be discussed actively and realized symbolically."[135] The importance of place for memory goes back a long way, as a classic study notes that the first step in memorization "was to imprint on the memory a series of *loci* or places."[136] Hasn't the Internet and the Web removed a sense of place? What does this do to memory?

The present interest in the study of public memory may be one outcome of the changes that technologies such as networked communications systems have brought to society. Australian historian Paula Hamilton argues that the debate about memory is "characterized by a profound pessimism about contemporary society and this is reflected in the language of loss or mourning: words like rupture, fissure, fracture, underline assumptions about the loss of continuity that the existence of a previously coherent somehow organic memory presumes."[137] Another scholar argues that historians today in the media culture have become more aware of memory, "more readily disposed to analyze the images through which the past is remembered. They contend that history is no more than an official memory, one among many possible ways in which to imagine the past."[138] "The distinguishing feature of Western culture in our postmodern age is its syncretism. Today there is no consensus about the value of topics, fields, or methods of approaching the past. . . . We might say that in our postmodern culture we no longer have a strong sense of the places of our memory. To some extent, this state of affairs reflects the waning appeal of particular traditions. In another, it reflects the nature of memory in an electronic age in which elements of tradition are continually broken up and reused in a kaleidoscope of reconfigurations by television and other electronic media."[139]

Given that archives and records are a crucial source of societal memory, this may be the most potentially damaging to the role and realm of the archivist and records manager. Archives are popularly associated with memory, propelling many to use them. Mary Gordon speculates that "all of us in the archives are acknowledging the insufficiency of memory. The falseness of the myth of continuity. The loss of living speech. Our own inability to live with the blanks. To live in the enveloping whiteness of imagination and of love."[140] And records are closely connected with memory, as when Matt Matsuda distinguishes the "Latin roots which distinguish 'monument' from 'document.' *Momumentum* is linked to *monere*, to 'make remember,' while *documentum* is tied to *docere*, to teach or instruct. Though both monument and text locate and preserve the past through visual practices (seeing, reading), words have an explicit pedagogical function which is only implied by the veneration or celebration of commemorative imagery. Monuments guard the past, but words instruct the present and teach the future."[141]

A characteristic of the Web, and the Information Age in general, is the rapidly falling cost of memory storage and the increased technical capability of hardware and software. However, the speed of hardware and software obsolescence creates a situation where the more we put in digital form, the more we risk losing. The technical problems are exacerbated by technologists being interested peripherally in memory. What do the technologists leave behind? Van Kornegay writes of visiting the office of a recently deceased colleague at the University of South Carolina, lamenting that an interesting life could be compressed "onto a half-dozen small plastic squares." He continues: "The computer is a great reservoir of memory for keeping track of our daily lives, but it levels all of life's milestones—from the momentous to the mundane—into an unremarkable string of zeros and ones. An indispensable tool for living, it also makes us easy to bury when we die."[142] There is a tension in technological solutions to records creating and memory.

Some newer records technologies, like photography, brought new perspectives or positive approaches outweighing the challenges of the technologies themselves. Because of photography, it seems that the "past is always at our fingertips, always available on paper or plastic for instant replay. The moment as we experience it is a little less important than it used to be: it can always be 'taken' and stored for later review. We now weep a little less for our losses, our relentless changes, because the evidence of photography prevents our nostalgia from embellishing too much the actual features of our past. . . . Photography has transformed our memories from narrative, from diaries and letters, to pictures and sound."[143] Will we be able to say this about the Web ten or twenty years from now?

The greater risk in using the Web may not be a technical matter but may result from how it feeds society's thirst for trivia and quick results, or its postmodernist flavor. The Web can enhance the interest in nostalgia rather than evidence. As one historian notes, "nostalgia tends to be history without guilt, while this elusive thing called 'heritage' is the past with two scoops of pride and no bitter aftertaste."[144] He states that the "unfortunate thing about this heritage boom is that it can lead, and has lead, to commercialization, vulgarization, oversimplification, and tendentiously selective memories—which means both warping and whitewashing a fenced-off past."[145] What about the Web boom?

The Web supports the post-modernist tendency to see value in *everything* (or *nothing*). One critic of post-modernism argues that "in the end the problem with post-modern social science is that you can say anything you want, but so can everyone else. Some of what is said will be interesting and fascinating, but some will also be ridiculous and absurd. Post-modernism provides no means to distinguish between the two."[146] The possibility of records and information on the Web being separated from their context raises the likelihood of real damage to personal and societal memory. A psychologist notes, "it is now clear that we do not store judgment-free snapshots of our past experiences but rather hold on to the meaning, sense, and emotions these experiences provided us." He states that "memories are records of how we have experienced events, not replicas of the events themselves." "In order to be experienced as a memory, the retrieved information must be recollected in the context of a particular time and place and with some reference to oneself as a participant in the episode."[147]

The Web may be the latest in a long-line of technologies creating problems for personal memory. "Beginning in the nineteenth century and exacerbated dramatically by the recent ascendance of electronic media, the crisis of memory involves a progressive sense of disconnection from the past and traditional forms of remembering. Society's most important memories now reside in the electronic archives of the mass media, not in the heads of individual rememberers and storytellers. With such immense amounts of information electronically coded and readily available, the memory-preserving role of elders with stories to tell and knowledge to impart has been diminished considerably."[148]

We can see technologies as part of a massive move in favor of relentless change and business rather than cultural memory and continuity. A historian of popular culture contends that machines have always threatened memory, such as the telegraph, which push change and commerce, not the "preservation of cultural memory."[149] Arguments for a return to diplomatics as the essence of an archival science seem like a reasonable target given that the new technologies bring a greater possibility of manipulating records. Will we have a return to the problems of the Renaissance, when there was a "flood of new texts and information" about the ancient world and the study of the past "was heavily polluted by streams of fraudulent matter . . . aimed above all at recreating a past even more to the taste of modern readers and scholars than was the real antiquity uncovered by technical scholarship. Many of the early recorders of monuments and inscriptions filled in missing texts in their notebooks just as they would the missing limbs and heads of statues, moved by the exuberant desire to see the ruined past made whole again; others, still less scrupulous, supplied whole new texts."[150] There is evidence of this in contemporary documentary filmmaking.[151]

SO WHAT DO ARCHIVISTS AND RECORDS MANAGERS DO?

Archivists and records managers are noticing the problems, challenges, and opportunities posed by the communications technologies and their post-modernist-like embracing. They see the destruction of traditional elements making up records and changing uses of information, killing any reliance on records. Archivists' concerns have been weakly expressed, especially in light of their interests in being information pacesetters.[152] Part of this is the mythology of the open road, a mythology appropriated for the Internet and World Wide Web. Archivists and other records professionals want to travel that road, to be significant players in the Information Age, rather than becoming road kill—and as a result, they can be reluctant to criticize the era's promises.

Records professionals need to question Information Age promises and work to bring together the electronic era and the traditional record. They need to understand who has established the parameters for creating and disseminating information and evidence. Others are taking a similar stance with the printed book, and the record is no less important. Taking up such issues is critical, given the importance of records for society. John Seely Brown and Paul Duguid discuss "documents" as the "means to make and maintain social groups, not just the means to deliver information." They argue that it helps us to understand the "evolution of Web as a social and commercial phenomenon," bringing the changes to these documents into a new light: "some claim that written documents are moving from the permanence of old forms to the performance of new ones. Certainly, notions of 'real-time response,' 'collaborative work,' 'multi-authored hypertexts,' 'shared documents,' 'relational databases,' 'on-line editing,' 'continuous up-dates,' 'interlinked data,' 'live video links,' and other properties suggest that their malleability makes new documents significantly different from old ones. Those who struggled for years with stencils and White Out undoubtedly appreciate the shift from fixed to a different sense of fluid." They note that "the fixed, immutable 'document' is best understood not as an inferior and outdated alternative to conversation or other types of unmediated and immediate communication, but, in appropriate places, as an object that plays valuable social roles because it mediates and temporizes, records traces and fixes spaces, and demands institutions as well as technologies of distribution. Attempts to introduce time stamps, hash marks, and other forms of electronic version identification stress how important to social and particularly legal institutions the idea of a fixed state of a document is."[153]

Archivists and records managers must not become technological determinists, instead seeing that networks like the Web are as much political, cultural, and economic factors as they are technical advances. Engineer Henry Petroski reminds us that the "form, nature, and use of all artifacts are as influenced by politics, manners, and personal preferences as by that nebulous entity, technology."[154] All records and information professionals need to be cautious about just how much they assume might change. As one commentator writes, "The claims being made for the digital highway, I recalled, had been made for the automobile, the telephone, and the television, too."[155] We want to use the World Wide Web to support a rational and realistic archival and records management mission, not to have the Web become confused as being *the* mission.

Records professionals must develop new and improved roles in the cybernetic age. Talat S. Halman, a professor of Near Eastern Languages and Literatures, writes about the library disappearing into the computer screen, becoming virtual; he sees librarians not disappearing but becoming "highwaymen" directing traffic on the information superhighway. Small local libraries will disappear but the major national or central libraries "will be converted into museums where you will serve as custodians and curators."[156] Archivists and records managers as Information Age highwaymen is certainly an improved role over that of passive records custodians or clerks. Archivists and records managers understand that change will occur, but the issue is managing the change to benefit their mission. Bookstores are becoming libraries, other media are challenging archives, and buildings of books are being pushed aside by digital books.

Archivists and records managers have to be concerned with what might happen to the record, especially for accountability and evidence. They need to take the message of the importance of records to the public. The lack of response to this challenge has potential dire circumstances. Lynne Sharon Schwartz states that "if those of us who live by language become superfluous in years to come, it will not be because of the advance of technology, but the loss of coherent discourse."[157] Archivists and records managers need to defend the value of evidence and records. This means pushing harder for the reality of evidence, its essential truthfulness even if it is open to interpretation or misuse. They cannot abandon the value of records and recordkeeping systems in favor of the notion of information.

The World Wide Web ought to be viewed by records professionals as just another tool to be used in their records mission, not a reason for a new mission or even its foundation. The construction by archivists and records managers of Web sites ought to convey this mission, to enhance access to records, and to provide a new means to advocate records. And records professionals need to be mindful to convey such a mission knowing what the Web may mean for perceptions about time, place, and memory. As such notions become more blurred or confused, records take on a more crucial role.

NOTES

1. Barbie Zelizer, *Covering the Body: The Kennedy Assassination, the Media, and the Shaping of Collective Memory* (Chicago: University of Chicago Press, 1992) and Michael Schudson, *Watergate in American Memory: How We Remember, Forget, and Reconstruct the Past* (New York: Basic Books, 1992).

2. This self-absorption can be seen in the nature of debates in the American archival profession in the 1970s and 1980s, described in Richard Cox, *American Archival Analysis: The Recent Development of the Archival Profession in the United States* (Metuchen, N.J.: Scarecrow Press, 1990).

3. These interests are best reflected in the quarterly journal of the Association of Records Managers and Administrators, the *Records Management Quarterly*. The journal itself has been the focus of much of this concern, with some stressing that the journal needs to become more scholarly and research-oriented rather than devoted to only practical articles and product profiles. The transformation in 1999 to the *Information Management Quarterly* heralds just such changes.

4. The works in question are John Bodnar, *Remaking America: Public Memory, Commemoration, and Patriotism in the Twentieth Century* (Princeton, N.J.: Princeton University Press, 1992); David Glassberg, *American Historical Pageantry: The Uses of Tradition in the Early Twentieth Century* (Chapel Hill: University of North Carolina Press, 1990); and Michael Kammen, *Mystic Chords of Memory: The Transformation of Tradition in American Culture* (New York: Alfred A. Knopf, 1991). There are other

studies which could have been included in this chapter, but the volumes under discussion here provide a more than adequate sampling of the recent research and writing on this topic. A good summary of the extensive nature of this literature can be found in Patrick H. Hutton, *History as an Art of Memory* (Hanover: University of Vermont, 1993).

5. Kenneth E. Foote, "To Remember and Forget: Archives, Memory, and Culture," *American Archivist* 53 (Summer 1990): 379.

6. Terry Eastwood, "Towards a Social Theory of Appraisal," in Barbara L. Craig, ed., *The Archival Imagination: Essays in Honour of Hugh A. Taylor* (Ottawa: Association of Canadian Archivists, 1992), p. 74.

7. Elsie T. Freeman, "In the Eye of the Beholder: Archives Administration from the User's Point of View," *American Archivist* 47 (Spring 1984): 111–123.

8. Ann Pederson, *Archives and Manuscripts: Public Programs* (Chicago: Society of American Archivists, 1982).

9. See, for example, David B. Gracy II, "Our Future Is Now," *American Archivist* 48 (Winter 1985): 12–21; "What's Your Totem? Archival Images in the Public Mind," *Midwestern Archivist* 10, no. 1 (1985): 17–23; and "Is There a Future in the Use of Archives?" *Archivaria* 24 (Summer 1986): 3–9.

10. Ann Pederson, ed., *Keeping Archives* (Sydney: Australian Society of Archivists, Inc., 1987), ch. 11; James Gregory Bradsher, ed., *Managing Archives and Archival Institutions* (Chicago: University of Chicago Press, 1989), ch. 16; William J. Maher, *The Management of College and University Archives* (Metuchen, N.J.: Society of American Archivists, 1992), pp. 315–331; and Richard Cox, *Managing Institutional Archives: Foundational Principles and Practices* (Westport, Conn.: Greenwood Press, 1992), ch. 6.

11. Such as Timothy L. Ericson, " 'Preoccupied with Our Own Gardens': Outreach and Archivists," *Archivaria* 31 (Winter 1990–1991): 114–122.

12. James O'Toole, *Understanding Archives and Manuscripts*, Archival Fundamentals Series (Chicago: Society of American Archivists, 1990), p. 7.

13. Bodnar, *Remaking America*, p. 13.

14. Bodnar, *Remaking America*, p. 14.

15. Bodnar, *Remaking America*, pp. 55, 71, 73.

16. Bodnar, *Remaking America*, p. 113.

17. Bodnar, *Remaking America*, p. 114.

18. Bodnar, *Remaking America*, p. 128.

19. Bodnar, *Remaking America*, p. 206.

20. Bodnar, *Remaking America*, p. 251.

21. Bodnar, *Remaking America*, pp. 23, 61, 69, 140, 208, 238.

22. See Richard Cox, "A Century of Frustration: The Movement for a State Archives in Maryland, 1811–1935," *Maryland Historical Magazine* 78 (Summer 1983): 106–117.

23. Victor Gondos, Jr., *J. Franklin Jameson and the Birth of the National Archives 1906–1926* (Philadelphia: University of Pennsylvania Press, 1981) is the fullest study on the movement to establish this institution.

24. Maher, *The Management of College and University Archives*, p. 8. For a specific case study, refer to Michael F. Kohl, "It Only Happens Once Every Hundred Years: Making the Most of the Centennial Opportunity," *American Archivist* 54 (Summer 1991): 390–397.

25. Glassberg, *American Historical Pageantry*, pp. 1, 2.

26. Glassberg, *American Historical Pageantry*, p. 9.

27. Glassberg, *American Historical Pageantry*, p. 19.

28. Glassberg, *American Historical Pageantry*, p. 23.

29. Glassberg, *American Historical Pageantry*, pp. 67, 225.

30. Glassberg, *American Historical Pageantry*, p. 225.

31. Glassberg, *American Historical Pageantry*, p. 123.

32. Glassberg, *American Historical Pageantry*, p. 139.

33. Glassberg, *American Historical Pageantry*, p. 117.

34. Glassberg, *American Historical Pageantry*, pp. 245, 247.

35. James Gregory Bradsher, ''Taking America's Heritage to the People: The Freedom Train Story,'' *Prologue* 17 (Winter 1985): 229–245.

36. Kammen, *Mystic Chords*, p. 7.

37. Kammen, *Mystic Chords*, p. 17.

38. Kammen, *Mystic Chords*, pp. 48, 52–53, 55–57, 64, 72, 74–78.

39. Kammen, *Mystic Chords*, p. 74.

40. George H. Callcott, *History in the United States: Its Practice and Purpose* (Baltimore: Johns Hopkins Press, 1970) and David D. Van Tassel, *Recording America's Past: An Interpretation of Historical Studies in America 1607–1884* (Chicago: University of Chicago Press, 1960).

41. Kammen, *Mystic Chords*, pp. 96, 125, 148, 156, 183–185, 233, 247, 249, 272, and 277.

42. Kammen, *Mystic Chords*, pp. 343, 439, 440, and 461.

43. Kammen, *Mystic Chords*, pp. 315, 317.

44. Kammen, *Mystic Chords*, pp. 446–447, 477–478.

45. Kammen, *Mystic Chords*, pp. 555, 566, 612–613, 632, 641, 643, 661, and 680.

46. Kammen, *Mystic Chords*, p. 581.

47. See Richard Cox, *American Archival Analysis*, ch. 8.

48. Kent Haworth, The Principles Speak for Themselves: Articulating a Language of Purpose for Archives,'' in *The Archival Imagination*, p. 94.

49. Ericson, ''Preoccupied,'' p. 118.

50. Haworth ''The Principles Speak for Themselves,'' p. 94.

51. Cook, ''Viewing the World Upside Down: Reflections on the Theoretical Underpinning of Archival Public Programming,'' *Archivaria* 31 (Winter 1990–1991): 130.

52. Harvey J. Kaye, *The Powers of the Past: Reflections on the Crisis and the Promise of History* (Minneapolis: University of Minnesota Press, 1991), p. 20.

53. Edward Shils, *Tradition* (Chicago: University of Chicago Press, 1981), p. 52.

54. John Gillis, ''Remembering Memory: A Challenge for Public Historians in a Post-National Era,'' *Public Historian* 14 (Fall 1992): 93.

55. Gillis, ''Remembering Memory,'' p. 99.

56. F. Gerald Ham, ''The Archival Edge,'' *American Archivist* 38 (January 1975): 5–13.

57. Sherry Turkle, *Life on the Screen: Identity in the Age of the Internet* (New York: Simon and Schuster, 1995), p. 246.

58. Stanley Aronowitz, ''Technology and the Future of the Work,'' in Gretchen Bender and Timothy Druckrey, eds., *Culture on the Brink: Ideologies of Technology* (Seattle: Bay Press, 1994), p. 15.

59. James Burke and Robert Ornstein, *The Axemaker's Gift: Technology's Capture and Control of Our Minds and Culture* (New York: G. P. Putnam's Sons, 1997), pp. 286–287.

60. See "Onward to Pervasive Computing," p. 18, and "The Future of Computing: After the PC," pp. 79–81, in the September 12, 1998 issue of *The Economist*.

61. Jack Goody, *The Logic of Writing and the Organization of Society* (Cambridge: Cambridge University Press, 1986), pp. 16–17.

62. Peter F. Drucker, *Technology, Management and Society* (New York: Harper and Row, 1967), p. 87.

63. Leah Hager Cohen, *Glass, Paper, Beans: Revelations on the Nature and Value of Ordinary Things* (New York: Doubleday/Currency, 1997), p. 11.

64. Ellen Ullman, *Close to the Machine: Technophilia and Its Discontents* (San Francisco: City Lights Books, 1997), p. 78.

65. Gary Stix, "The Speed of Write," *Scientific American* 244 (December 1994): 107, 111.

66. Ivan Illich, *In the Vineyard of the Text: A Commentary to Hugh's Didascalion* (Chicago: University of Chicago Press, 1993), p. 3; Neil Postman, *Teaching as a Conserving Activity* (New York: Dell Publishing Co., 1979), p. 39.

67. Kevin Walsh, *The Representation of the Past: Museums and Heritage in the Post-Modern World* (New York: Routledge, 1992), p. 84.

68. This is at http://www.fnc.gov/Internet_res.html.

69. Francois Fluckiger, "From World-Wide Web to Information Superhighway," *Computer Networks and ISDN Systems* 28 (1996): 525–534.

70. Robert Hobbes Zakon, "Hobbes Internet Timeline v2.5," at http://info.isoc.org/guest/zakon/Internet/History/NIT.html.

71. J. Deetz and E. S. Dethlefsen, "Death's Head, Cherub, Urn and Willow," in Susan M. Pearce, ed., *Interpreting Objects and Collections* (London: Routledge, 1994), p. 31.

72. Peter S. Graham, "New Roles for Special Collections on the Network," at http://aultnis.rutgers.edu/texts/spclnet.html.

73. Rosalind Thomas, *Literacy and Orality in Ancient Greece* (Cambridge: Cambridge University Press, 1992), p. 90.

74. Ivan Illich and Barry Sanders, *ABC: The Alphabetization of the Popular Mind* (San Francisco: North Point Press, 1988), pp. 41–42.

75. Stuart Sherman, *Telling Time: Clocks, Diaries, and English Diurnal Form, 1660–1785* (Chicago: University of Chicago Press, 1996).

76. Thomas, *Literacy and Orality*, p. 4.

77. Thomas, *Orality and Literacy*, p. 24.

78. Edwin Diamond and Robert A. Silverman, *White House to Your House: Media and Politics in Virtual America* (Cambridge, Mass.: MIT Press, 1995), pp. 20–21.

79. Joshua Meyrowitz, *No Sense of Place: The Impact of Electronic Media on Social Behavior* (New York: Oxford University Press, 1985), p. 19.

80. Charles R. McClure and J. Timothy Sprehe, *Analysis and Development of Model Quality Guidelines for Electronic Records Management on State and Federal Websites; Final Report January 1998*, at http://istweb.syr.edu/~mcclure/nhprc.

81. Jenni Davidson and Donna McRostie, "Webbed Feet: Navigating the Net," *Archives and Manuscripts* 24 (November 1996): 330–351; William Landis, "Archival Outreach on the World Wide Web," *Archival Issues* 20, no. 2 (1995): 129–147; David Wallace, "Archival Repositories on the World Wide Web: A Preliminary Survey and Analysis," *Archives and Museum Informatics* 9, no. 2 (1995): 150–168.

82. Sven Birkerts, *The Gutenberg Elegies: The Fate of Reading in an Electronic Age* (Boston: Faber and Faber, 1994), p. 129.

83. Steven Johnson, *Interface Culture: How New Technology Transforms the Way We Create and Communicate* (New York: HarperEdge, 1997), p. 211.

84. Paul Gilster, *Digital Literacy* (New York: John Wiley and Sons, 1997), pp. 135, 137.

85. Peter Carroll, *Keeping Time: Memory, Nostalgia, and the Art of History* (Athens: University of Georgia Press, 1990), p. 205.

86. Jacques Barzun, *Begin Here: The Forgotten Conditions of Teaching and Learning* (Chicago: University of Chicago Press, 1991), p. 42.

87. Anthony F. Aveni, *Empires of Time: Calendars, Clocks, and Cultures* (New York: Basic Books, 1989), pp. 5, 87, 336.

88. Robert Levine, *A Geography of Time: The Temporal Misadventures of a Social Psychologist, or How Every Culture Keeps Time Just a Little Bit Differently* (New York: Basic Books, 1997), pp. 63, 65, 188.

89. Neil Postman, *The Disappearance of Childhood* (New York: Vintage Books, 1994, org. pub. 1982), p. 70.

90. Michael O'Malley, *Keeping Watch: A History of American Time* (New York: Viking, 1990), p. 54.

91. O'Malley, *Keeping Watch*, p. 100.

92. O'Malley, *Keeping Watch*, p. 146.

93. Jon Katz, *Virtuous Reality: How America Surrendered Discussions of Moral Values to Opportunists, Nitwits and Blockheads like William Bennet* (New York: Random House, 1997), p. 67.

94. Kirkpatrick Sale, *Rebels Against the Future: The Luddites and Their War on the Industrial Revolution; Lessons for the Computer Age* (Reading, Mass.: Addison-Wesley Publishing Co., 1995), pp. 213–214.

95. Clifford Stoll, *Silicon Snake Oil: Second Thoughts on the Information Highway* (New York: Anchor Books, 1995), pp. 70–71.

96. Daniel Alkon, *Memory's Voice: Deciphering the Mind-Brain Code* (New York: HarperPerennial, 1992), p. 11.

97. Kent C. Ryden, *Mapping the Invisible Landscape: Folklore, Writing, and the Sense of Place* (Iowa City: University of Iowa Press, 1993), p. 39.

98. Simon Schama, *Landscape and Memory* (New York: Alfred A. Knopf, 1995), pp. 6–7.

99. Tony Hiss, *The Experience of Place* (New York: Vintage Books, 1990), p. xi.

100. Winifred Gallagher, *The Power of Place: How Our Surroundings Shape Our Thoughts, Emotions, and Actions* (New York: Poseidon Press, 1993), p. 12.

101. Dolores Hayden, *The Power of Place: Urban Landscapes as Public History* (Cambridge, Mass.: MIT Press, 1995), p. 9.

102. Philip Abbott, *Seeking Many Inventions: The Idea of Community in America* (Knoxville: University of Tennessee Press, 1987).

103. Anthony Smith, *Software for the Self: Culture and Technology* (New York: Oxford University Press, 1996), p. 53.

104. Hayden, *The Power of Place*, p. 76.

105. William Knoke, *Bold New World: The Essential Road Map to the Twenty-First Century* (New York: Kodansha International, 1996), pp. 20–21.

106. M. Christine Boyer, *Cybercities: Visual Perception in the Age of Electronic Communication* (Princeton, N.J.: Princeton Architectural Press, 1996), pp. 119, 139, 242.

107. Stephen Doheny-Farina, *The Wired Neighborhood* (New Haven, Conn.: Yale University Press, 1996), p. xi.

108. Turkle, *Life on the Screen*, pp. 19, 25, 177.

109. J. C. Herz, *Joystick Nation: How Videogames Ate Our Quarters, Won Our Heads, and Rewired Our Minds* (Boston: Little, Brown and Co., 1997), pp. 150–151.

110. Michael Pollan, *A Place of My Own: The Education of an Amateur Builder* (New York: Random House, 1997), pp. 218–219.

111. Jonathan Wallace and Mark Mangan, *Sex, Laws, and Cyberspace: Freedom and Censorship on the Frontiers of the Online Revolution* (New York: Henry Holt and Co., 1997).

112. Robin Dunbar, *Grooming, Gossip, and the Evolution of Language* (London: Faber and Faber, 1996), pp. 195, 204, 205.

113. John Allen Paulos, *A Mathematician Reads the Newspaper* (New York: Basic Books, 1995), p. 128.

114. Roger Chartier, *Forms and Meanings: Texts, Performances, and Audiences from Codex to Computer* (Philadelphia: University of Pennsylvania Press, 1995), p. 15.

115. Barry M. Leiner et al., "A Brief History of the Internet," at http://www.isoc.org/internet-history/.

116. Paul Evan Peters, "Is the Library a 'Place' in the Age of Networks," at http://educom.edu/web/pubs/review/review/Articles/2916 2.html.

117. Howard Rheingold, *The Virtual Community: Homesteading on the Electronic Frontier* (New York: HarperPerennial, 1993) and Douglas Rushkoff, *Cyberia: Life in the Trenches of Hyperspace* (New York: Harper San Francisco, 1994).

118. Johnson, *Interface Culture*, p. 20.

119. Johnson, *Interface Culture*, p. 21

120. Johnson, *Interface Culture*, p. 215.

121. Johnson, *Interface Culture*, pp. 236–237.

122. Neil Postman, *Amusing Ourselves to Death: Public Discourse in the Age of Show Business* (New York: Penguin Books, 1986), p. 29.

123. Birkerts, *Gutenberg Elegies*, p. 120.

124. Charlene Spretnak, *The Resurgence of the Real: Body, Nature, and Place in a Hypermodern World* (Reading, Mass.: Addison-Wesley Publishing Co., 1997).

125. Stoll, *Silicon Snake Oil*, p. 3.

126. Meyrowitz, *No Sense of Place*, pp. 6, 308.

127. David Shenk, *Data Smog: Surviving the Information Glut* (New York: HarperEdge, 1997), pp. 110, 111, 121.

128. William J. Mitchell, *City of Bits: Space, Place, and the Infobahn* (Cambridge, Mass.: MIT Press, 1995), pp. 68, 97.

129. New York Times, *The Downsizing of America* (New York: Times Books, 1996), pp. 112.

130. Edward Tenner, *Why Things Bite Back: Technology and the Revenge of Unintended Consequences* (New York: Alfred A. Knopf, 1996), p. 182.

131. Tenner, *Why Things Bite Back*, p. 199.

132. Stanley Aronowitz and William DiFazio, *The Jobless Future: Sci-Tech and the Dogma of Work* (Minneapolis: University of Minnesota Press, 1994), p. 3.

133. Aronowitz and DiFazio, *The Jobless Future*, pp. 48–49.

134. Kenneth E. Foote, *Shadowed Ground: America's Landscapes of Violence and Tragedy* (Austin: University of Texas Press, 1997), p. 33.

135. Foote, *Shadowed Ground*, p. 292.

136. Frances A. Yates, *The Art of Memory* (Chicago: University of Chicago Press, 1966), p. 3.

137. Paula Hamilton, "The Knife Edge: Debates About Memory and History," in Kate Darian-Smith and Paula Hamilton, eds., *Memory and History in Twentieth-Century Australia* (New York: Oxford University Press, 1994), p. 11.

138. Patrick H. Hutton, *History as an Art of Memory* (Hanover: University of Vermont, 1993), p. 2.

139. Hutton, *History as an Art of Memory*, p. 166.

140. Mary Gordon, *The Shadow Man* (New York: Vintage Books, 1996), p. 164.

141. Matt K. Matsuda, *The Memory of the Modern* (New York: Oxford University Press, 1996), p. 62.

142. Van Kornegay, "Short-Term Memories: A Death in the Information Age," *The Information Science* 12 (October/December 1996): 439–440 (quotation p. 440).

143. Julia Hirsch, *Family Photographs: Content, Meaning, and Effect* (New York: Oxford University Press, 1981), p. 45.

144. Michael Kammen, *In the Past Lane: Historical Perspectives on American Culture* (New York: Oxford University Press, 1997), p. 157.

145. Kammen, *In the Past Lane*, p. 221.

146. Pauline Marie Rosenau, *Post-Modernism and the Social Sciences: Insights, Inroads, and Intrusions* (Princeton, N.J.: Princeton University Press, 1992), p. 137.

147. Daniel L. Schacter, *Searching for Memory: The Brain, the Mind, and the Past* (New York: Basic Books, 1996), pp. 5, 6, 17.

148. Schacter, *Searching for Memory*, p. 305.

149. George Lipsitz, *Time Passages: Collective Memory and American Popular Culture* (Minneapolis: University of Minnesota Press, 1990), p. 6.

150. Anthony Grafton, *The Footnote: A Curious History* (Cambridge, Mass.: Harvard University Press, 1997), p. 26.

151. Robert Brent Toplin, ed., *Ken Burns's The Civil War: Historians Respond* (New York: Oxford University Press, 1996).

152. Bernadine Dodge, "Places Apart: Archivists in Dissolving Space and Time," *Archivaria* 44 (Fall 1997): 122.

153. John Seely Brown and Paul Duguid, "The Social Life of Documents," at http://www.firstmonday.dk/issues/issue1/documents/index.html.

154. Henry Petroski, *The Evolution of Useful Things* (New York: Vintage Books, 1992), p. 20.

155. Mark Slouka, *War of the Worlds: Cyberspace and the High-Tech Assault on Reality* (New York: Basic Books, 1995), p. 91.

156. Talat S. Halman, "From Babylon to Librespace," *IFLA Journal* 21 (November 1995): 257–260 (quote p. 258).

157. Lynne Sharon Schwartz, *Ruined by Reading: A Life in Books* (Boston: Beacon Press, 1996), p. 24.

7

Educating Records Professionals in a Hostile Age

Knowing that records are important to society and that records professionals face complicated and troublesome issues ought to indicate the nature of their education. In this chapter, education is examined historically. The focus is on the education of archivists, for two reasons. Archival education is the older and more comprehensive of the instructional systems for records professionals, dating back sixty years and always at the graduate level. Records managers continue to rely on undergraduate offerings, with less well-defined standards and reliance on apprenticeship. The more important reason is that archival education, especially with its interdisciplinary orientation, provides the strongest platform for the education of *all* records professionals. While there are problems with this, the development of more comprehensive educational programs, a stronger professional literature, and a greater research tradition all suggest that graduate archival education programs are evolving into the primary gateway to the records professions.

THE HISTORY OF NORTH AMERICAN ARCHIVAL EDUCATION

Over the past twenty years, the Society of American Archivists (SAA) and its counterpart, the Association of Canadian Archivists (ACA), developed guidelines for a Master's of Archival Studies degree (MAS). In the United States, the SAA moved from a largely apprentice-based three-course program in 1977, reaffirmed in 1988, to a fuller description for a master's degree. The SAA MAS guidelines are heavily influenced by the 1988 ACA education guidelines. They describe the work and mission of the archivist, affirming that the most appropriate setting for professional formation is "an institution of higher learning that

provides a unique forum for disciplined study, research, and experimentation"
and that the MAS degree should "constitute the only recognized preappointment professional education for archivists." This statement counters the
belief that education can occur in short-term institutes or workshops. James M.
O'Toole calls this a "workshop mentality" which, first, "accustoms both educators and students to thinking about their discipline in summary, overview
fashion," second, "trains us to break archival subject matter into discreet
blocks," and, third, "leaves us with an irresistible disposition toward practical-
ity."[1] As a result, some foreign commentators consider the United States to be
mired in a primitive age of archival development.[2] Only comprehensive graduate
education, such as represented by the MAS or its equivalent, can move the
records profession to "education" rather than mere "training," where " 'education' is a process of systematic instruction designed to develop one's intellectual powers and to acquire a body of knowledge."[3]

SAA's guidelines describe "conceptual foundations"—the role of archives
in society, the work of an archivist, the education of an archivist, and a flexibility
to respond to changing needs and conditions. The roles of archives in society
are providing administrative, legal, and cultural services to their parent organizations and society. This defines archives, archival document, archival science,
archival studies, and archival education. These foundations support an "intellectual framework" for archival education that is interdisciplinary and the basis
for "life-long" learning. Most telling in this part of the guidelines is the statement that "archival studies is in a dynamic and evolutionary state," prompting
a call for educational "innovation and educational specialization," understanding that university administrators will be less prone to react positively to pre-
scriptive standards imposed by professional associations and more likely to
respond to a general, flexible curriculum. Given the nature of archival theory
and practice, educational programs will develop along similar curricular lines
anyway.[4]

Another part of the guidelines is devoted to "knowledge areas," identified
as core and shared knowledge. The core, meaning what *all* archival students
should be taught, includes the context of information, archival history and the
character of the profession, archival theory, archival methods, the application of
archival theory and methods, and records management. This knowledge, a topic
drawing heated debate in the United States, is the axis upon which the MAS
degree rotates. The fundamental reason for the MAS degree is that this level of
knowledge and theory requires a graduate education. After graduation, the working archivist spends a career applying this theory and knowledge, as well as
identifying areas where additional education is needed. This is education, rather
than training; or as Canadian archival educator Tom Nesmith states, the "primary aim of graduate archival studies is to educate students to learn about
archives rather than to teach them as much of existing knowledge and practice
as can be covered."[5] The shared knowledge areas include the management sciences, information and library science, preservation, and historical and other

research methods. It is important that "archival" knowledge and theory takes the forefront in the curricular construction of this program, perhaps marking the end of the sixty-year-old American debate about the placement of archival education by adhering to a separate MAS degree. These guidelines support this view with statements such as archivists' "professional competence must be guaranteed by a strong archival education" and archivists "need to be firmly grounded in the principles and methods of archival science, and to have a broad knowledge of the field of archival studies."

A final part of the guidelines describes "infrastructures," containing three crucial statements. First, "a graduate archival studies program should be formally recognized" by its host institution, by having "department status," or an "autonomous status within the department(s) or school to which it is attached." Second, "at least one full-time, tenure track position is required to establish and maintain an archival studies program." Third, "two-thirds of the students work should be dedicated to the archival knowledge area, while one-third should be related to the contextual and the complementary knowledge areas." Furthermore, "students should routinely undertake major research activities producing scholarly papers . . . , and should conclude their studies with a thesis or a comparable original project."

Why did the SAA propose an MAS degree as a minimal guideline for graduate archival education? Some argued that the reasons may be because of an inferiority complex regarding what foreign colleagues have accomplished in archival education, misguided notions of the extent of archival knowledge and theory, and misinformed steps to specialize. History suggests why stronger, more explicit guidelines were necessary, replacing similar guidelines adopted only six years before.[6] In 1985 SAA's education committee determined that the 1977 guidelines needed revision and a task force of three was appointed for this task. At that point the committee had been relatively inactive, mostly reacting to tasks assigned by the SAA governing council or by SAA presidents. The subcommittee discussed its assignment, reviewed the lengthy literature on archival education,[7] and prepared a draft that was ultimately revised and approved in early 1988.

Several important points need to be stated about the nature and purpose of the 1988 graduate education guidelines. They were primarily a *revision* of the 1977 guidelines, an effort to flesh out a bare bones document. They were a *foundation* document for other work by the education committee. The subcommittee deliberately avoided the practicum issue, for example, because it was perceived that the knowledge base for archival work had to be defined first and practical applications could be considered later. That the 1988 guidelines did not result in companion practicum and continuing education guidelines is evidence that they were not adequate at the time to advance the profession. The subcommittee also strongly believed that the three-course sequence was inadequate, but it also believed that the American archival profession in 1986 was not ready to support an MAS degree. It opted to draft guidelines as a stepping

stone to more comprehensive programs, by articulating a curriculum content
that could not possibly be handled effectively in three courses. The subcommittee also hoped that its work would inspire the profession to better graduate
programs, paving the way for the employment of more full-time regular archival
educators.

These efforts were misguided. Most education "programs" have offered only
a few courses and, as Tim Ericson has shown,[8] assumed that they could cover
the curriculum content in these few courses or lectures. SAA also did not use
the guidelines as a basis for developing a coherent philosophy of continuing
education or even for the construction of its education directory. Schools continued to report a potpourri of offerings with little discernible evidence of any
relationship to the guidelines, and these schools are listed with other programs
which have a stronger focused archival and records core curriculum. Despite an
individual certification effort in the past decade, archivists then comprised a
profession willing to let anyone define their discipline and work.

There is considerable evidence supporting the need for graduate programs
modeled on something like the MAS degree. Alan D. Gabehart studied employers' qualifications for entry-level archivists. Surveying 636 archival institutions, Gabehart found that "while almost half of the respondents said that the
establishment of a graduate degree program in archival science in the United
States would probably be beneficial in some positions but would not be essential
for the profession, one quarter claimed that the establishment of such a program
is essential for the advancement of the profession." Gabehart concludes that
"since the Society of American Archivists has already developed guidelines for
graduate archival education programs, a graduate degree program in archival
science be scrutinized as a possible alternative to its certification program."[9]
Gabehart also concludes that "more than 500 new full-time positions for archivists in the United States can be expected within five years."[10] This suggested
the viability for MAS degree programs; if each graduated ten to twenty archivists
with the MAS annually, these positions could be filled with such individuals
and support the further development of such programs.

There is more evidence. The responsibilities faced by records professionals
such as archivists suggest the need for a comprehensive and coherent curriculum.
Even a cluster of a half-dozen courses can be uneven in covering the full range
of archival work and the knowledge base when one needs to consider diverse
matters such as management, appraisal, new descriptive standards, reference
with more complicated privacy and access issues, preservation and the new
recordkeeping technologies, and the specialized needs of scientific and technological and other such archives. Teaching archival appraisal, for example, in
fourteen weeks of reading, discussion, research, lecturing, visiting, and testing
can still seem cursory for such a complicated topic. Frederick J. Stielow argues
that "archival graduate students have so much to debate, learn, research, and
enjoy. The student experience should be designed with such Aristolean 'leisure'
in mind and the hope that coming generations will push the archival knowledge

base well beyond current comprehension."[11] James O'Toole more succinctly notes that "a real course, whether in archives or any other professional discipline, is one that explores in some detail and at some leisure a defined and significant topic."[12]

Other studies support how important the MAS degree could be to the education of future archivists. Donald L. DeWitt examined the steady appearance of the MARC AMC format in job advertisements, contrasted with how little the format was being taught in graduate programs.[13] It is difficult to squeeze more into a few courses. Likewise, Elsie Freeman argues that public programs and service have been ignored, laying the blame on the archivist's outlook on "organizational rationality and not client needs."[14] Public service aspect is not taught because there are *few* courses available to most educators, many archival educators are adjuncts as concerned with fostering student employees for their own programs, and the perceived greatest need is reducing processing backlogs (hence the overemphasis on arrangement and description).

It is only in comprehensive programs that adequate grounding in archival studies can be provided. This is obvious when considering the full dimensions of archival knowledge. Luciana Duranti argues that this knowledge constitutes a "science" with a "theory" and a "methodology,"[15] although she is far more dogmatic than most. The idea of a firm knowledge base is not a new idea (Frank Burke stated it clearly in 1981),[16] but it has been mixed up with the continuing reliance on workshops and institutes creating the illusion of being able to create instant archivists and individual certification. This has not worked because, as Terry Eastwood states, "it is difficult to see certification strengthening competence in the absence of strong and uniform standards of education."[17]

FOCUSING ON RECORDS AND RECORDKEEPING SYSTEMS

Although the American archival profession has more clearly defined guidelines outlining the range of topics that should be covered in graduate archival education, archival educators still face the challenge of *how* to educate individuals. That challenge is particularly clear when considering a 1988 survey of graduate archival education undertaken by the Society of American Archivists' former education officer, Timothy Ericson. As Ericson points out, the traditional configuration of three courses is "hard pressed to cover adequately even all the fundamentals of archival work" described by the SAA guidelines. The staple of graduate archival education, the introductory survey course, spends so little time on any given topic as to be virtually meaningless except as an "archives appreciation" course. According to Ericson, "an [average] total of 19 and 1/2 minutes" is spent in these courses on the "nature, origins, and development of communication, data manipulation, and record-keeping systems." Only another hour and a half on the "origin and development of archival principles and methods" can be added to this.[18]

The neglect of these topics contrasts with the recent emergence of increased interest by the archival profession in the history of recordkeeping and its own development. A survey of literature on archival history in 1983 revealed at best an uneven coverage and quality of research.[19] Three years later, however, the Society of American Archivists formed an Archival History Round Table, and research in this area has continued to be of *some* interest to the profession. The 1988 and 1994 SAA guidelines included historical study on recordkeeping and the archival profession as part of an ideal knowledge needing to be conveyed to prospective archivists.[20] Despite this reputed value, there are few graduate courses that devote serious attention to the history of recordkeeping and archival administration.

The development of recordkeeping—encompassing records systems' origins, uses, technologies, and their social contexts and impacts—and the history of archival administration and records management are closely related. Record-keeping includes the origin of record systems and efforts to manage already created records. Archival history covers the development of institutions that collect and care for records possessing continuing value, as well as the origin of archival principles and practices and the development of the profession. The management of records has been a consistent theme or issue in the various disciplines involved in developing records or information systems. It is difficult to think about such systems apart from the efforts to manage them, just as it is hard to imagine understanding the history of archival and records administration separately from the ever changing communications and information technologies and policies. Basic archival principles were often developed because of chal-lenges faced in appraising, preserving, and managing recorded information.[21] Many of the persistent concerns of the archival profession have been shaped by contemporary records, most notably the increasing use of electronic information technology. The recent emergence of a field of communications history speaks to such concerns, building on the notion that "to understand the nature of the information age we live in we must have some sense of how it came to be. The present has to be seen as part of a long sequence of developments that cannot be regarded as mere historical curiosities. Those who fail to understand the past will be ill equipped to comprehend a contemporary world where major cultural-technological shifts often occur in less than a generation. Also, few modern technological innovations have no precedent in some past development.''[22] Such sentiments should not be difficult for archivists, many of whom are trained as historians, to understand.

There is also value to the archival profession in the study of its own devel-opment,[23] from addressing the contemporary concerns and issues of the profes-sion to assisting institutional self-evaluation and planning. The study of archival history builds a valuable set of case studies helping archivists to understand the life cycle of cultural institutions like archival repositories. It could be instructive to determine why similar institutions, such as state archives, vary so greatly in size, functions, and quality. These case studies could be used in the assessing and planning of archival institutions, as well as the education of prospective archivists. The study of archival history advances understanding about how archival principles and practices have developed in response to changing recordkeeping systems and what the shortcomings of these principles and practices may be in light of modern records characteristics.

The potential use of archival history, including record and information systems, in graduate archival education is great. There may be no better introduction to the archival profession for students than to study current archival concerns or recordkeeping systems historically, providing a better understanding of the present profession and its literature.[24] Students who come to the study of archival administration from other related fields, as many do, could also use this as a way of comparing the development of their own fields to archival practice while enriching archivists' understanding of how their vocation fits into the broader historical and information professions.[25] International comparisons, something rarely undertaken in the archival profession, are other possibilities.[26]

Studying the historical development of recordkeeping likewise has many values for the education of archivists. This topic serves as a "gateway" through which students and the profession can examine fundamental questions about the nature of records and information. The rapidly changing nature of electronic information technology not only raises issues about how archivists can identify, preserve, and make available for use electronic records with archival value but poses questions about how society has adapted to other earlier far-reaching changes in information technology and the implications of these adaptations. Elizabeth Eisenstein's statement that the "shift from script to print affected methods of record-keeping and the flow of information"[27] not only makes us want to know what these effects were but what they might tell us about the present shift from print to electronic form. Such understanding is absolutely crucial for work in many basic archival functions, most notably appraisal, arrangement and description, and reference. Appraisal, as just one example, is considerably enriched as well as made more efficient by an understanding of varying historical uses of communications within institutions.[28] Hugh Taylor noted the importance to archivists of understanding the changing nature of records, writing that the "significance of speech changed when writing became widespread, and likewise the significance of writing changed when print dominated the scene. Now automation has changed the individual's *relationship* with writing and print." As a consequence, the "meaning [of records] is no longer seen as being limited to content within the context or provenance and fonds, but must be sought also in the technology of the medium which has, since earliest times, had a profound effect on society as a whole."[29]

A decade ago, the history of recordkeeping and archival administration was given brief attention in graduate archival education. Most archival educators gave one or two lectures, even while thinking that these subjects were vital to introducing students to archival practice, the profession, and the nature of records and information. Many archival educators held fairly low opinions regarding the expansion of their programs to include the history of recordkeeping and archival administration, believing that these topics should be taught as part of a course on historiography and historical methods. At the time archival educators thought that they would always be restricted to a few courses, with insufficient material to use in teaching such a course.

There is a distinct connection between how the histories of recordkeeping and archival administration and books, printing, libraries, and librarianship have been taught. Despite what appears to be a substantial amount of research in the history of libraries, books, and printing, these topics have been ignored in graduate library education—leading to laments about the demise of a "strong historical flavor" in graduate library science education. The rising interest in modern information technology has been partly the culprit, although the manner in which these historical topics has been traditionally taught, an emphasis on more practical or marketable skills, and increasing preoccupation with library professionalism have also been identified as problems working against teaching about historical subjects.[30]

Although the history of archives and recordkeeping seems to have barely a toehold in graduate archival education programs because of their small size, it appears these topics are also neglected because of lack of understanding of their value. Since the larger (in numbers of courses) graduate archival education programs are generally located in the library and information science programs or joint library-history programs, such views obviously work against the teaching of these topics. The history of recordkeeping and archives are viewed as rather esoteric topics rather than as meaningful knowledge essential to the ongoing work of the practicing archivist.

Recordkeeping can be traced from its oral antecedents through the development of writing through various phases or periods of record and information systems. Although it is highly unlikely that practicing archivists will ever be responsible for every type of record system, this study would help archivists appraising, describing, preserving, and providing reference with insights into records creation, nature, and continuing use. The history of archival administration can be connected to the evolution of recordkeeping. Both developments have been heavily influenced by their societal contexts, evident easily in cataclysmic events such as the French Revolution and in more evolutionary changes reflected by historical writing.[31]

Students should study the development of recordkeeping, information systems, and the archival profession, assisting them to understand the symbiotic relationship between recordkeeping and archival administration. Students need to understand that *both* record and information systems and archival administration reflect broader social environments. Historian J. R. Pole comments that the destruction and survival of records happen for reasons more complicated than pure accident or simple neglect—"the records that survive are themselves the direct *consequences* of past social and political decisions. . . . They present the present mind with a choice that is vast and variable but never merely random.''[32] There are now writings commenting on the archival implications of contemporary record and information systems, such as Hugh Taylor's essays,[33] suggesting why archivists need to have a thorough understanding of record-keeping and information systems. The changing nature of the professions managing information (the emergence of information science—a combination of library science, computer science, abstracting, indexing, communications science, behavioral science, and other disciplines) after the Second World War is especially important for students to understand.[34] Students should understand that society's concept of information is being constantly transformed, and how records are maintained, or not maintained, can be partly seen by what these changing perspectives have been in the past and what they may become.[35] Not only are archival and records management principles and practices changing, but the records professions' place and purpose in the information professions and society are also being transformed, even if these changes are imperceptible to the participants.

Oral tradition and the transition to writing makes sense as a prologue to recordkeeping systems and archival administration, sharply focusing on the written records that archivists and records managers administer. The recent discovery of orality, driven by anthropological studies and modernity's mass communications, reveal writing and its connection to oral tradition to be among the first major changes in communications technologies challenging records professionals. As Jan Vansina notes, the importance of oral communications methods are essential to humanity: "The mind through memory carries culture from generation to generation. . . . Oral tradition should be central to students of culture, of ideology, of society, of psychology, of art, and, finally, of history." Add records professionals to this list. As Vansina later writes, "oral traditions are documents *of the present*, because they are told in the present. Yet they also embody a message from the past, so they are expressions *of the past* at the same time."[36]

The origins of writing systems, as communications and recordkeeping systems, will be of obvious interest to the records student. Students should possess some knowledge about early writing systems and formats—clay tablets, cuneiform, hieroglyphics, and phonetic alphabets—and how they are reflections of specific cultures and epochs.[37] Such knowledge is not intended to help students manage such records but rather to provide broad understanding of where the records forms come from; such knowledge should increase the effectiveness of records management by helping records professionals understand more about the form and function of recorded information.

A review of ancient, medieval, and early modern (up through the late Renaissance) recordkeeping systems and archives sets the scene for later comprehension of the development of "modern" archives and the rapid and problematical challenges of information systems over the past several hundred years. Posner's text on ancient archives remains the standard on this topic (although it has been challenged) and is quite useful for understanding ancient recordkeeping practices and archives. His work provides detailed descriptions of early records and reveals some very modern features of early archival operations. Viewing the elevated status of ancient scribes and records custodians is especially illuminating in light of the more recent laments over the poor public image of the archivist, archival institutions, and the archival mission. Of course, in these years archives were close to rulers, wealthy families, and the literate elite.[38]

The medieval period contrasts to earlier periods in recordkeeping and archival administration. There was a re-emergence in the importance of records for governance and administration, evident by the creation of the Domesday Book in eleventh-century England. These years witnessed increasing literacy, moving from reliance on orality to writing. The record shifted from having symbolic importance to recognition of its content as the primary value, similar to the way that the modern person views records. M. T. Clanchy charts this transition from where the medieval person would "listen to an utterance rather than to scrutinize a document visually as a modern literate would" to where written documents were trusted.[39] The importance of this historical shift is seen in the research and writings of social anthropologists like Jack Goody. Goody finds that "the religious word acquires a physical embodiment of its own and shifts from being a more or less integral part of the culture into having a more or less distinct, sometimes determining, later diminishing, role with a larger measure of structural autonomy." Goody also notes that the "relationship of law to society becomes formalized with the advent of writing. . . . the written law achieves a kind of autonomy of its own, as do its organs."[40] What kinds of related changes are evident in the shift from text and print to electronic representations should engage students preparing to be records professionals.

Recordkeeping in early modern Europe on the eve of American colonization and in early America itself gives a glimpse of increasing uses of early information technology, such as the printing press, as well as the origins of many of the modern concerns of records managers and archivists. Writings specifically concerned with archival administration, as well as the commencement of private and institutional manuscript collecting, suggest a new importance for records.[41] The maintenance of government records emerges as a greater concern during this period, partly because of the growth in government and efforts to govern more effectively, to protect prerogatives, and to satisfy the interest in social statistics.[42] There are also great similarities between Europe with recordkeeping and archives in the early American years, although there has been little research done on the actual relationship of these changes.[43]

Recordkeeping in the nineteenth century became more sophisticated and innovative. Centuries-old techniques were evident, such as "bundling" in which records were folded, wrapped with string, and stored in boxes, chests, barrels, or on shelves. As the quantity of records rapidly increased, a variety of other storage methods became prominent, such as registry systems, specially constructed pigeonholes for filing by a subject classification system,[44] and in 1868 the Woodruff File, a wooden box for standard paper sheets twice or thrice folded.[45] Other innovations like the flat or vertical file, carbon paper, and the increasing reliance on the typewriter and microfilm began to change radically the manner in which records were both created and stored.[46] Among other things, these changes contributed to a rapid transformation in the office. Before the Civil War, offices were small, all-male operations with minor task specialization (copyist, bookkeeper, office boy, and clerk); after the Civil War offices were feminized, much larger, and had greater task specialization.[47] This century also laid the foundation for a modern communications revolution, with profound implications for recordkeeping, with the invention of the telegraph, telephone, the "wireless," and magnetic tape recording.[48] The twentieth-century innovations of radio, television, photocopying, and the computer all had origins in the previous century. What is not clear, however, is the profundity of change on personal recordkeeping during this tumultuous transformation of communications practices. While it is obvious that personal records, like diaries and even account books, remained generally unchanged from those of centuries before, it is uncertain whether this stability was due to the greater societal changes or not.[49]

Changes in information and communications technology are indicative of general societal changes, many spurring an interest in the past and establishing national and local archives. While it is generally the view that the development of national and other archives as "revolutionising" the study of the past in the mid-nineteenth century,[50] preserving the sources of the past was also a new way of coping with societal changes. Looking at the past helped those caught in the rapid progress of the nineteenth century to understand where they had come from and their present role.[51] These various technologies brought fear for the home, family, and the individual; telephones and other electronic communications gadgets were perceived to be a major threat to individual and family privacy.[52] Private autograph collecting, genealogy, and similar interests emerged as individuals coped with such concerns.[53] Not only was this the age of the founding of many private and public archives but also the formulation of basic principles influencing modern archival administration.[54]

By the turn of the twentieth century, other significant factors, besides information technology, were at play in the formation of modern archives and recordkeeping systems. The origins of modern archives lay far afield from the creators of modern communication systems and other information technologies. The modern historical profession had an important continuing role in the sponsoring of archival work, including an emerging archival professionalism.[55] Economic and social challenges, such as the Great Depression and two world wars, also provided opportunities, most notably the Historical Records Survey, for the young archival profession to undertake activities benefiting its work in preserving the documentary heritage.[56] Just as important was the increased quantity of recorded information, in both government and the corporate worlds,[57] and the archival community's own increasing self-consciousness leading to professional associations, self-studies, and major publication programs, a process continuing through the twentieth century.[58]

The mid-twentieth century brings the student to the computer. The records professions struggle with managing and preserving electronic records possessing continuing value, and it should not be surprising that teaching the development of modern electronic information systems poses problems. Students need to be introduced to the basic characteristics of electronic records and their historical context in graduate archival education programs. The problems confounding the teaching of this area are not for a lack of secondary materials for teaching but have more to do with the nature of graduate archival education programs. There are many studies covering the development[59] and social and personal impact of the technology. Students should learn how information technologies have revolutionized records creation and maintenance, leading to new notions of institutions and office work. The development of the microchip, various computers up to the microcomputer, off-the-shelf software, telecommunications, optical fibers, artificial intelligence, and other aspects of the modern information revolution are important topics about which the archival student should possess some basic knowledge. Students should also be introduced to some of the recent writings focusing on the cultural parameters of modern information systems and provide more balanced views than the futurists, who are either excessively pessimistic or optimistic about technology's influence on society.[60]

It is also important for the archival student to be exposed to the international nature of recordkeeping and archival development and the contemporary problems of the archival profession. Electronic records have pushed archivists to reconsider the ways in which they identify, preserve, and manage records with archival value, causing them to re-evaluate their professional structure and basic archival principles. Some, like Richard Kesner, question whether the archivist even has a place in the electronic office, while others have tried to identify more effectively the precise nature of the challenge with new means for dealing with them.[61] Still others have looked at these challenges and attempted to re-formulate basic archival approaches. In one of the most provocative assessments, David Bearman contends that the "shortfall between documented needs and proven methods is greater than one order of magnitude (a factor of ten)." Bearman calls for a "redefinition of the problems, the objectives, the methods or the technologies appropriate to the archival endeavor" rather than merely seeking for "greater resources."[62]

Putting the development of recordkeeping and archival administration into an international perspective is complicated. While there are many excellent essays and monographs discussing archival matters and information systems in specific countries, few are comparative.[63] Students should learn something of ancient, medieval, and early modern recordkeeping and archival development in the Middle East and Europe, receiving some notion of their similarities and differences in the modern era in various nations. The UNESCO RAMP Studies are a excellent source on international comparisons, covering a wide range of archival functions. In general, the archival educator will need to select only aspects to concentrate on in already crowded courses. The educator must convey that the nature of information systems and the challenges faced by archival institutions cuts across national and cultural boundaries.[64]

Studying the history of recordkeeping provides considerable *practical* information about the nature and characteristics of the documents archivists manage. Studying archival development socializes students in understanding why certain archival principles are essential to their work or why they are presently debated. Teaching the history of recordkeeping and archival administration is, then, only possible in *comprehensive* archival education programs. Teaching this topic also introduces students to other disciplines—anthropology, history, records management, sociology, and information and library science—making up the multi-interdisciplinary records professions. These topics are not esoteric exercises but sources of practical value to the working records professional regularly asking difficult questions requiring a comprehensive graduate education. If archivists are to select what recorded information is to be preserved for present and future use, they must not only have an educational background equipping them to apply archival appraisal theory, principles, and practices, they must know how that appraisal methodology has developed, the nature and characteristics of the records they work with, and how new information systems challenge accepted archival appraisal practice.

THOUGHTS ON THE PRESENT EDUCATION OF RECORDS PROFESSIONALS

A new millennium has inspired self-reflective critiques of various disciplines, organizations, and society. In educating records professionals, we could use such reflections. Before 1970 and the issuance of various professional standards, writings on education were efforts to determine the content and nature of training programs. After 1990 writings on education appeared because of the rapid and sometimes confusing changes in information technology, organizations, legal issues and disciplinary boundaries. What one teaches in the classroom needs to be continually transformed, or it risks being out of date. New ideas, technologies, and methods in the academy have not been always welcomed by archivists and records managers, risking increased tensions between educator and professional, researcher and practitioner, theorist and technician.

If being an archivist or records manager is important, then teaching people to become one is quite a responsibility. Why is an archivist or records manager a crucial professional at we turn into a new century promising technological marvels? Records are essential to guarantee accountability, ensure the maintenance of a public memory, and provide evidence for private and public, family, and organizational life. There is a new seriousness about the business of archives and records, extending far beyond their maintenance for scholarly historians and hobbyist genealogists. Archives have become a part of debates about the *mean-*

ing of the past, crucial links in *documenting* the unpleasantness of the recent past, center pieces in *litigating* unethical business corporations, and significant in *accounting* for the performance of public officials.

With the importance of records, the educational preparation of a records professional should be a focal point for standards, evaluation, and effort. It appears that this has happened in the North American archival community, with a substantial growth in the number of schools and regular educators specializing in this area. Twenty years ago, we could count on one hand such educators, while now there are a couple of dozen. While history departments have tended to curtail their interest in public history (their umbrella concept supporting archives and records management), by the early part of the twenty-first century virtually every library and information science program will support archival studies. Unfortunately, education for records managers has remained mired at the undergraduate level, robbing this segment of the records professions of vitality in rigorous educational standards or research.

It is worth reflecting about *why* this recent growth in archival education has occurred. Because of the importance of records, society should be extremely interested in who controls records and what these people know and think about the management of the records. Yet, society and its policymakers have not expressed much interest. There are problems with the societal images of archives and archivists or records and records managers. In a self-help book providing advice on the management of personal records, the following image emerges: "Does the top of your desk look like the national archives? Is it so cluttered with piles of paper that you don't have any space left to do your work?"[65] With such images prevalent, the growth of graduate archival education programs has not developed because of some new, intense demand for archivists or records managers but because of lobbying, negotiating, and positioning by archivists in higher education. History programs have wanted to find jobs for its graduates and library and information science programs have breathed in a new vigor and enthusiasm to its training venues. Archival work seems like a fertile ground for both.

Tension is evident in the past decade of change *within* graduate archival education, primarily between educators and practitioners. Such tensions are endemic in any profession where educators stress *knowledge* and practitioners emphasize *experience*. That this knowledge incorporates experience requires the educator to develop some premium skills. The educator must be able to build students' knowledge to be able to critique practice and to emphasize other skills not always stressed in the field (such as research methods and in-depth knowledge of disciplines with an emphasis on records and recordkeeping).

The report of the Council of State Historical Records Coordinators on historical records repositories suggests archivists are undereducated (in regards to archival education) and only interested in quick training opportunities (workshops and institutes). Vicki Walch, the coordinator of the survey, found 28 percent of the repositories operate only with volunteers and "less than one-third

... have one or more professionals on staff." She must have been using a very broad definition of "professional," for she also finds that "staff with graduate degrees in archival administration are still fairly rare, reported by only 5% of the repositories overall, although 10% of the academic repositories noted them." Although Walch does not comment on the perceived "best methods" for training and education, she found that only 3 to 5 percent of the total repositories saw graduate courses as the best method while up to two-thirds wanted one- to two-day workshops.[66]

A Marxist, stressing that a lack of equal access to resources leads to a culture marked by social conflict, might suggest that the inequality of resources between archival programs leads to conflict. There is conflict between programs, between those able to afford professional staff and those not or those possessing substantial resources and those existing marginally. The conflict is expressed in attitudes rather than revolution or social conflict, such as between archival educator and practitioner. The educator possesses a wealth of ideas, more time to develop them, and a constantly changing array of students bringing fresh ideas. The practitioner brings limited financial resources, pressing daily duties, and constant crises to resolve.

Ironically what fuels such tension is also what provides some of the supreme joys of moving to the academy. Despite serving on committees, engaging in academic politics, and administering academic programs, joining a faculty still provides more time to think and reflect. Daily pressures are far different from what one encounters in other work situations, and the faculty member has more latitude for what he or she decides to focus on. In the academy we ask and explore basic questions about professional work, challenge its assumptions, and engage with bright and inquisitive students about new ideas. After a few years of teaching archives, I had learned more about archives and records management than in sixteen years of professional work. Preparing a single lecture forces reconsidering a topic's historical development, its implications, how it was being treated in the field, the strengths and weaknesses of its literature, whether there was any supporting research, the relevance of new concepts, how other disciplines viewed the topic, and the degree of consensus held by practitioners.

There are perils in being an archival educator, contrasting the academic orientation on knowledge with the vocational emphasis of a profession. Building on the old idea of pursuing a profession as heeding a calling ("to profess"), many entering the records professions do so with a single-minded intent to acquire *current* marketable skills. Show how (*not* why) to prepare an archival finding aid, determine an appraisal decision, construct a records schedule, or assist a researcher. This is the classic tension between long-term education and short-term training, and the archival profession remains intensely committed to the latter. The fact that the U. S. National Archives continues to focus on its on-the-job training of archivists and other records professionals, something it has done for fifty years, is perhaps the most obvious manifestation of this orientation. Individual certification, with its stress on knowledge gained via experience, is another.

These perils emanate from the differences between skills building and education and thinking, reducing, as Terry Eastwood comments, "education to a narrow form of training that merely reinforces the status quo and divorces skill building from the larger conceptual framework within which it operates." Eastwood points to a more basic issue: "Education is about *thinking*, not about skill building directly."[67]

The American archives and records management profession is also plagued by numerous tensions due to critical internal problems. One is the stress caused by the presence of *both* humanists and technocrats with disparate approaches to archives and records management, characterized as a tension between the placement of graduate archival education programs in history departments or library and information science schools.

The debate about history- or library and information science–based education has raged since the 1960s, when this field's graduate education began to expand. This debate is more complex than simply whether archivists are historians or librarians. It is whether archivists and archival educators view their roles as primarily knowing the records' content (for use by researchers) or understanding the technologies of recordkeeping (for designing and implementing records systems). It is also more complex because, in effect, archivists and archival education programs need to be *both* things, a daunting task given the different cultures of the humanities and sciences. As an educator tries to demonstrate to future records professionals why they need to understand both arenas because of the changing technological nature of recordkeeping systems *and* the demands placed on their knowledge by a wide array of researchers, it is easy to be caught in a crossfire between elements within the records community who are still arguing *where* their education should be located. The location should be less important than the substance of what is being taught, but the profession seems unable to move to this level of sophistication in its discussions about education.

When I became an educator, I was told I had "sold out" by accepting an appointment in a library and information science school; unfortunately, the tone of the debates about education have not substantially changed. Other records professionals provide some insights into why such views are myopic. Ira Penn, pleading for establishing records management within the academy, tied it to the management: "Until records management is classified as *management* and included as part of the curricula in schools of management and business administration, until managers and executives can learn the lifecycle theory from 'esteemed professors' who will give it an aura of respectability, then the function will be considered superfluous and the 'professionals' who practice it considered second-class citizens."[68] Unfortunately, archivists have not considered other possibilities for hosting their education, while they have often denigrated even the utility of graduate education. We rarely hear archivists wishing they had "esteemed professors."

The intensity of this debate is also due to another problem within the records professions, its fixation with credentials, drifting in the direction of *no* specific qualifications. This may be little more than tensions caused by the mixed bag of professional credentials for entry to the field—after all, the profession seems intent on accepting *anyone* on *equal* terms. On the other side, many enter into the records management field with minimum educational preparation and weak qualifications other than experience. This is, of course, at odds with an educator who is trying to build a sophisticated and comprehensive curriculum available to anyone who meets certain admission standards. This is not an egalitarian function, and it suggests that certain kinds of educational credentials do matter. Graduate archives and records management education programs are being built on the foundation that archivists and records managers should possess a solid knowledge of archives and records and that this knowledge is squarely based in the classroom where principles, theories, and methods are discussed. Obviously, being an educator and holding to such a view makes one an easy target for many vocal individuals in the field who contend that experience is more important than education and that anyone with desire and dedication can make an acceptable records professional.

Being an archival educator is complicated by the lack of public recognition of the field. Archival educators need to build programs within their own academic departments and the university, and general understanding about the importance of records and archivists makes this easier to accomplish. Despite the daily news stories about records, there persists a lack of comprehension about what records are, what constitutes archives, and what records professionals do. Archivists and records managers, lacking political advocacy, have not become visible in the media or with policymakers. More than a decade ago, a researcher concluded that one of the substantial problems limiting archivists' ability to deal with tangled questions of privacy and access was their *own* lack of political activity and acumen.[69] Such weaknesses continue to plague archives and records management educators as they argue for expanded faculties and curriculum, forcing them to start from scratch, explaining what archives and records represent and what archivists and records managers do. This has tremendous implications for recruiting students. A records management student wrote in the early 1990s that she had to *find* educational programs in records management.[70]

The archival educator is akin to a military scout moving into hostile territory. The enemy territory has been formed by the origins of the archives and records management fields, the bumpy trends in education and training, and the changing technologies of recordkeeping.

The difficulties created by the origins of the modern records professions have most often been characterized as the debate about the disciplinary location of such education—history or library and information science in the case of archives and business, public administration, or library and information science programs in the case of records management. Although this debate has been cast as an *either-or* debate, this is not appropriate. Certainly by the 1980s, archival studies was recognized as being interdisciplinary, making the debate seeking to place such studies either within history or library and information science seem a bit specious.

A greater challenge is the splintering of the records professions. First, there was a gradual splitting of archives from history and the humanities. But there has been the loss of records management from archives, the predominant placement of archival studies within library and information science, and the difficulties of relating the records professions to other information professions. This presents some challenges to socializing students to the records professions because the identity of the profession is so fluid (or for the students, confusing). It has also scattered the literature through many disciplines, making it challenging to orient students to a core knowledge and theory. Archival educators find it difficult since they must position themselves in *one* discipline and then provide a multi-disciplinary view about their field.

Since the profession sees graduate archives and records management education programs as factories for producing practitioners, the array of places employing records professionals poses another difficult challenge. There is a wide range of institutions employing archivists—from traditional historical societies and other cultural organizations to corporations employing the latest information and recordkeeping technologies for entrepreneurial purposes—and this certainly has placed a stress on what archival educators teach and try to have students learn. At our program at Pittsburgh, the two archival educators have approximately 270 classroom contact hours in their six archives and records management courses. While this seems like a considerable number of hours, it is not many with the need to cover *all* the basic archives and records management functions as well as trying to relate how and why these functions fit in cultural, government, private, and public organizations.

This is a daunting task, and it is not one many records professions seem to understand. The professions want each graduate to be an instant expert, a professional capable of relating each records task to each type of organizational setting. This is an impractical assignment. The responsibility of the educator is to support the initial development of a knowledgeable archivist or records manager, not to complete the product. No other graduate programs have such pressure to create instant professionals.

Another part of the hostile territory has been produced by the divergent trends in archives and records management education and training. The long-standing debate about whether prospective archivists should receive degrees in history or library science, which usually ends either with harsh words about the relevance of either education or resigned comments about the most utilitarian of the degrees for employment purposes, has long stifled creative development of graduate archival education. No matter *what* educators teach, they are branded by *where* they teach. The fact that I have students immersed in many different disciplines, including history and the humanities, makes little difference to those who perceive that my interest must be credentials or a technocratic approach because I am a faculty member in a department of library and information science. In reality, my approach to having students become experts in records and recordkeeping systems could fit comfortably in a history department (focusing on these systems' historical development and understanding of sources), law school (stressing the regulatory notion of records and these systems' importance for evidence and accountability), or business school (focusing on the value of records to the creators of records and for purposes such as corporate memory).

Developing trends in education and training make it difficult for contemporary archival educators for other reasons. There is the fascination with apprenticeship, perhaps sustained because so many entered the profession in the 1960s and 1970s with little more than a single introductory course and a heavy dose of learning on the job. Some educators, myself included, have created graduate programs helping new archivists *not* to have to endure this gestation period, creating a wonderful collision course with those who believe that everything worth knowing must be learned about *in* the archives or records center. This may explain why in certain areas, such as electronic records management and appraisal, practice has lagged far behind theory and reality.

There are other challenges. For whatever reason, archival and records management education placed itself within the academy at a relatively late and difficult time to establish new programs. The records community has been too complacent about educational venues including little more than apprenticeship, a few courses, and educators who were full-time working archivists and records managers. Despite calls for national institutes, cooperative multi-disciplinary programs, and separate degrees, archivists and records managers have been content to accept a mishmash of options. Now they are happy to see a school acquire one or two full-time educators, hardly putting the archival or records management profession on a par with other professional programs or providing it the resources deserving for the importance of records.

The most surprising aspect of an educator's hostile territory concerns the purpose of archives and records. Within the archival community, there is no consensus about this. In the 1980s, as part of the Society of American Archivists energetic efforts at profession-wide planning, a mission to identify, preserve, and make available records of enduring value was formulated. But this mission disguises disagreement about what it means, including continuing debates about the particular archival functions represented by this mission—such as those about appraisal's theory and applications. Some are expected, since such debates are part of the continuing development of professional knowledge. What is not expected is the diversity of opinions about archivists' clients—a tiny band of scholars visiting their repositories, the records creators, or a broader public. While the educator is right at home in dissecting basic principles and concepts of archives and records management, it is a different challenge trying to deal with myriad audiences. Concerning the mission, the educator either has to present the conflicting versions of the mission (which is the option I partially follow) or choose one around which they will construct their curriculum (which is the option I heartily endorse). The problem with the latter is not the coherence it provides (it does that very well), but it is the reception prospective employers may have towards the graduates of such a program. Educators are, after all, in business to place their graduates.

The most visible element of the hostile territory graduate archival educators travel in is the changing nature of recordkeeping technologies, considered the primary challenge for archivists and records managers for at least the past decade. Electronic records management generates crucial and controversial issues for all records professionals. Is an archival record best characterized as a collectible artifact? If so, how does an archival record relate to other "artifacts" if it is part of an electronic recordkeeping system? What about the symbolic importance of records to a social group's identity and self-worth, especially re-emerging in this time of culture wars and ethnic tribalism? Given the pervasive nature of electronic *information* systems, should archivists and records managers view electronic records as information sources *or* as evidence? Such considerations have massive implications for whether archivists and records managers view themselves as part of the information professions or as part of history and the social sciences.

Electronic recordkeeping systems brought unprecedented challenges for maintenance, especially the control of privacy and access to records. While archivists have been concerned about such issues for generations, the new electronic systems brought new problems. The ability of these systems to make complicated linkages and speedier access is what businesses and governments find appealing about them in the first place. How can archivists balance access and privacy in these systems? The predominance of electronic records has increased the span between humanists and technocrats in the field, fueling the continuing controversy between those who see themselves as historians and those who see themselves as information scientists. Of course, an educator can try to teach individuals to be archivists and records managers, but this does not always go over well in a profession that seems so divided.

What makes the records professions a contested field is also what makes it a joy to teach. As the culture wars and other academic debates emerged in the late 1980s, a number of scholars called for innovation in teaching conflicts. At the heart of higher education beats the need to present conflicting ideas that stimulate students to *think* and that prepare them for whatever professional endeavor they pursue. There is writing from a multiplicity of perspectives that can engage students to re-think what being an archivist or a records manager means. Consider the kinds of questions needing to be asked and discussed within graduate courses. Does the record have a future? There are many Information Age technocrats who see traditional information purveyors, like books and records, disappearing. Is there still a need for archivists and records managers? Likewise, Information Age pundits are predicting the convergence of many traditional information workers, such as librarians and archivists, into new disciplines.

Some are arguing that the power of the Web is eliminating the need for any form of information gatekeepers. Who do records professionals work for? Some still argue for a purely cultural role, but this seems too limited given the value of records. Is this Information Age more hype than reality? At the least, prospective archivists need to be equipped to identify the relevant issues.

Students need to be exposed to thinking through the major issues they face upon accepting a professional position. It is when future archivists and records managers are students that they need to be exposed to learning how and what to read, how to approach problems and challenges, and what they need to do to situate themselves for continued learning. Students need to become familiar with issues such as privacy versus access, ethical concerns, the priorities of employers versus other researchers, information haves/have-nots, and how to build responsible systems supporting all of society. For an educator, what makes this sometimes difficult is that most of these issues have not been resolved, plunging them into heated debates.

In many professions there has developed hostility between teaching and research. While many academics, including myself, hold to the notion of a symbiotic relationship between research and teaching, new challenges have emerged as universities move to a corporate model for both research and education. This has not been much of a problem in the archives and records management discipline. While recordkeeping is a universal and historical issue of great practical value, the records community has done little research on these issues. What writing and research has been done has not reached the public or made an impact on other disciplines logically interested in records. We are not alone. Donald Norman writes, "I have been increasingly bothered by the lack of reality in academic research. University-based research can be clever, profound, and deep, but surprisingly often it has little or no impact either upon scientific knowledge or upon society at large. . . . Most academic study is designed to answer questions raised by previous academic studies. This natural propensity tends to make the studies ever more specialized, ever more esoteric, thereby removed even further from concerns and issues of the world."[71]

The records community has an intense need for applied research, and discussions about these needs enliven classroom teaching. There is a symbiotic relationship between these two functions. As I research certain topics, I bring the research into the classroom to support certain points I am making and to support why research can be illuminating in its challenging of the profession's most cherished assumptions. Some of my own research has been generated specifically to help students better understand the archives field. As part of my sabbatical, I conducted an analysis of entry-level job advertisements to provide additional information to students who sought vocational advice. That this study is a rarity in the archives and records management fields reflects the poverty of our own basic and applied knowledge about what we do.

There is another benefit in teaching in this discipline. As an educator formulates ways of explaining and orienting students to the various disciplinary concepts, he or she begins to develop ways of explaining crucial matters in a way that can reach a broader audience. As graduate archival education has expanded, it has been linked to a rejuvenation of theory and a growth in applied research. There are other potential benefits. Some of these teaching exercises can be turned into essays targeted at audiences we need to reach. In my own case, I have written essays trying to consider the future of the traditional printed book, the difficulties of conducting archival appraisal in a contentious age framed by multiculturalism and culture wars, and the importance of records as reflected in what carries in one's own wallet or purse.[72] While others will need to determine just how valuable these particular essays have been, I can attest that they are essays that I probably never would have written had I not been teaching.

Why such challenges may exist is that the field has not really settled on the purpose of professional education. Does the profession want educators to immerse someone in the technical dimensions of records and archives systems, the historical developments of records and recordkeeping systems, or the social uses of records and archives? Each has different implications for the organizational placement of archival education programs, demands for resources, and possibilities for success. It is not as easy as wanting to see students transformed into good archivists or records managers, since the definition of a "good" records professional constitutes a range of opinions, not consensus. Rather, each educator must determine what he or she believes is a professional archivist and records manager and be prepared for both praise and criticism.

What I want students to know is the importance of records and why archives and records management is a historic and honorable profession, while understanding that there is a public image of archivists and records managers counter to administering records in a manner that supports their significance. Educators are change agents, not just teaching to reflect only what the profession thinks it needs but teaching to make positive changes so that records are managed properly. This is another source of tension between educators and practitioners. Educators are looking for innovation, dissecting failures, and scrutinizing writings that are provocative and controversial. They are also trying to make students innovators, equipped to evaluate critically and able to recognize new directions for the field. Such challenges are not unique. Other professions struggle with public image, status, collective self-doubt, education, their influence on policy matters—all destined to keep practitioners up at nights. Even engineers worry about attracting people to their discipline who are "smart and well trained," "ambitious and entrepreneurial," "idealistic," "committed to public service," and "leaders." Records professionals also need to work to move their discipline into "everyday discourse."[73]

Educators have a unique and crucial role to play in ensuring that people enter the profession and that the discipline becomes engaged in the public forum. But not everyone in the records community wants the profession to change in this way, nor can everyone agree on what this change should be. Educators are required, however, to make decisions about such matters, as they design courses, select readings, develop assignments, and develop relationships with other academics and working records professionals. While this objective should be for the good of the records professions, it is a good that not all professionals might agree about, making being an educator in this field both exciting and frustrating.

ANOTHER VIEW: THE CONTINUING CHALLENGE OF THE PRACTICUM IN GRADUATE EDUCATION IN THE RECORDS PROFESSIONS

Prior to 1940 there was no formal education or training for records professionals in the United States; in effect, what people learned to become archivists and later records managers was completely experiential. This is not a bad approach if one believes that records work is a craft and apprenticeship the best means to learn. It is also a good entrée to any field only committed to gradual change, since a focus on experience tends to encourage change that is always within the tightly prescribed parameters set by practitioners serving as mentors and organizations providing experience.

During the twenty years after 1940 isolated graduate courses and institutes were created. These educational venues provided a sort of archives or records management *appreciation*, skipping lightly over the facets of archival work. Or these courses and institutes could be seen as self-study groups, where people came to build networks for mutual assistance. The individual seeking a records career was dependent on *working* to gain a base for career development. In one of the few assessments of the practicum's role in archival education, Frederick Stielow focused on a continuing problem with this aspect of archival education—exposing the student to all archival functions within 150 hours.[74] The practicum was, after all, not a solution to graduate archival education but a continuation of the larger problem in nurturing the development of a rigorous education. One of the problems is just how much can be crammed into the existing archives and records management education programs.

The reliance on experience has remained intact. In the 1960s and 1970s, there was a simultaneous growth in academic archives, a proliferation of adjunct faculty, and the emergence of the three-course sequence, with one being the practicum (the other two courses were an introductory one and an advanced topics or issues course). This later development institutionalized the practicum as a crucial part of American graduate archival education. The three-course sequence was formalized in the Society of American Archivists graduate archival guidelines in 1977. Since then, there has been a near revolution in graduate archival education with the emergence of full-fledged master's degrees and multiple, tenure track and tenured faculty. An array of philosophical orientations to archival education has also developed—some focused on records and recordkeeping systems, others on technology, some on cultural sources, and, finally, others on the importance of records for accountability and evidence. For some programs there appears to be no stated philosophical reasons or, at least, any that have real substance. Proponents would argue that archives and records are a public good; but the lack of any specificity in how educational programs support this is a major problem. These developments have been captured in the 1988 and 1994 SAA graduate guidelines and the 1996 guidelines on continuing education.[75] Like the earlier guidelines there is a reliance on experience as an essential aspect of education.

Experience's predominance in archival education is evident in the 1994 graduate SAA archival education guidelines, suggesting that "archival science . . . is divided into theory, methodology, and practice," including the "study of practical implications and implementations of theory and method in actual circumstances (archival practice)." The guidelines provide a separate statement on the practicum emphasizing that "practical experience . . . is an opportunity for students to verify their understanding of archival principles by applying them in real-life situations. The practicum should be viewed as an integral part of the student's program of study." This statement affirms that the practicum is educational, although it does not really address the tension between theory and practice, knowledge and application residing in the practicum. Stielow argues that "students must be recognized for the advanced theoretical knowledge that they can bring to the site. Although relative neophytes on the bench, these are graduate students who have had the leisure to study abstract concepts, which could aid the repository. They should not be exploited as cheap labor . . . , but managed to ensure the development of pleasant and effective future colleagues."[76]

The challenge is even greater. The structure of American graduate archives and records management education programs suggests that experiential training is still the linchpin of preparing individuals to enter the field. Twenty-one of 38 programs (55.3%) listed in a recent Society of American Archivists education directory consist of three courses or less, in addition to the practicum or internship. The chances are extremely good, therefore, that one's formal education for entering the archives segment of the records professions is still an apprenticeship—with as much as 25 to 50 percent of a student's time devoted to work.[77] While the SAA's educational guidelines call for this to be part of an educational process, it is difficult to know whether this is happening.

Since graduate archives education has traditionally been positioned in either history departments or library schools, with a shift toward the latter, it is possible to examine the issue of the archives practicum and graduate education in the context of the continuing concern about the relationship between practical training and theory-based education in library and information science. Since the emergence of the first library school, there has been debate about the relationship between theory and practice. From the late nineteenth century to the 1923 Williamson Report on library education, the practicum, internship, or fieldwork was a major element of the education of librarians. Although in the intervening years the practical training of prospective librarians has slipped in its prominence in graduate library education, most schools continue to offer directed practical training. A continuing appearance of studies on theory versus practice reveals that this issue remains important. There has been a steady parade of surveys of ALA-accredited library schools to determine their attitudes and commitments to the practicum, internships, and fieldwork, along with historical reviews on the topic and studies of employers' and students' perceptions of the respective values of practical training.[78]

Studies on archives education likewise affirm that the practicum is perceived as an integral part of the training of prospective records professionals. Although the vast majority of the literature is essentially arguments for certain educational forms and content, nearly all accept the practicum. A survey of archival educators two decades ago revealed that "practical work ... looms large in the minds of the instructors."[79] Although a survey of educators today might show some shifting of emphasis away from the practicum, every graduate archives education program in the United States includes it as an element. What is fascinating is what has been ignored about *other* requirements for graduate education. The Society's educational guidelines suggest that "archival education is both academic and professional; therefore, it includes both scholarly and experiential elements" (that is, both a thesis and a practicum). Yet, while every program provides the opportunity for the practicum, the opportunity for scholarly research is severely limited.

Practical experience has been a driving force behind graduate archives education. This can be extended to all the records professions, since the records management field accepts an undergraduate degree with practical experience as its primary professional attainment. Practical experience has also been a millstone, impeding educational development and perhaps the field itself. This reliance continues despite many questions about how experience supports or supplements graduate education. What should a student know? If the recent SAA guidelines are any indication, everything identified as part of archives knowledge can be dealt with as part of a heavily structured experience, stating that "no graduate program in any discipline can provide all the scholarly and experiential knowledge needed for its practitioners."

Can a student know *everything* as they start their career? It seems unlikely. Are there limitations between theory (or knowledge) and practice? While theory is often assailed as impractical, even carefully coordinated practice could be immune from similar criticism. That is, can practice provide a full and rich experience, educating future archivists for the broadest range of possible problems and challenges that they might face? Is experience crucial or essential for graduates to get their first position? Experience is heavily featured in all job advertisements, but we do not know whether experience is more important than learning about archives and records management theory and methodology.

Such questions must be answered to sort out the role of the practicum in graduate archives education and the relationship of theory and practice in the records professions. It is surprising that the relationship of internships to practice and education, despite a vast literature in other professions, has not spurred on much in the way of research or deeper reflection. What is the ideal knowledge to be taught to archives graduate students? These individuals need to become records experts, encompassing records and recordkeeping systems and the traditional spectrum of archives and records management functions (appraisal, systems analysis, representation, preservation, reference and access, public outreach and advocacy). Students must be oriented to all dimensions of records and recordkeeping systems (including the legal, political, social, cultural, economic, administrative, and scholarly aspects), information technologies and their application in records, access and privacy concerns, and the various needs and methodologies of researchers. As Terry Eastwood writes, the "first object of archival theory is the nature of archival documents or records."[80] How well can the practicum support this?

How do students learn about such matters? I posit they learn by a deep immersion into the historical, methodological, and theoretical literature, defined to include many disciplines and requiring a framework for knowledge. For example, students need to understand that the growth of writing about ethnic, racial, and gender archives is also the result of the influence of social history, the influx of individuals with training in this area, and that these same trends also contributed to the growth of public history (providing both a boon to and competition for other archival education venues). The student learns to appreciate each professional essay as a historical document reflecting its own era and begins to understand that present trends may shift dramatically in the future.

The practicum also does not support the kind of interdisciplinarity the records professions require. For decades the debate was about *where* graduate archives education should be located. More recently, there has been discussion about educational content as it relates to the traditional structures of the archives, records management, library and information science, and history fields. Either way, the practicum is reasonably static in its ability to reflect the nuances of archives or records management knowledge. Graduate archives and records management education can change more quickly and react to external forces more effectively than what actual archival and records programs do or might do. This is another reason why practicum students should be encouraged to reflect on the differences between the classroom and the real world workplace—balancing theory with practice. However, since educators are mostly motivated to place students in order to change the field in a positive way, there is always going to be some tension.

Students secondarily learn by directed practical exercises drawing them more deeply into various aspects of an ideal knowledge. These practical exercises work because they are embedded in formal evaluation in the classroom of what records professionals know and do. And these practical exercises should be like the more objective process of writing case studies intended to teach principles and to support more critical evaluation skills.[81] How many students in a fieldwork experience obtain such a focus? Many are not mentored, they are *super-*

vised, and this is very different from what is required in an educational process. There is also little room for any two-way knowledge transfer of the kind that occurs in the more formal classroom experience.

It may be because of such concerns that the records professions still rely on basic manuals and why crucial areas like electronic records management have been underdeveloped. How critical is experience in graduate education about electronic records programs when there are so *few* programs dealing effectively with electronic records? Experience giving way to apprenticeship does not generate new ideas. It was for the purposes of needing a stronger knowledge and research base that the development of graduate archives education was initially said to need strengthening.[82] The result is troubling.

Can students learn *everything* they need to know *before* entering into their first professional position? It is amazing to ask such a question when reflecting on earlier graduate archival education programs. Prior to 1980 the quantity and range of formal coursework was remarkably limited, suggesting there was little room for debate about the relationship of theory to practice because education was focused on practice, in-service training, or apprenticeship. Being theoretical meant little more than sitting down and reading, maybe even discussing, the volumes by Jenkinson and Schellenberg, the collected writings of Margaret Cross Norton, and some essays in a limited number of archives and records management journals or assembled readers. Even today, in the more comprehensive education programs, it is unlikely that everything can be taught *or* experienced. When I spend twelve to fifteen class sessions on archival appraisal, for example, I hardly ever think that I have done anything but given students a good foundation for approaching this crucial archival function.

Archivists and records managers, debating theory and practice, often lose sight of the fact that neither is monolithic. It is not wise to speak of *practice* as the anecdote to the unrealistic musing about *theory*. Even in that most besieged discipline, literary studies, there are those who remind us of how careless we can become in typing other viewpoints. Denis Donoghue writes that "it may be prudent to distinguish between Theory as an institution, which comes armed with the coercive force of a capital letter, and theories, which are more modest plays of mind, local notions."[83] Likewise, many of the theories helping archivists are there for forming a perspective to approach huge and often seemingly hopeless tasks—like appraisal.

This becomes more complicated. We have programs educating students with an amazing quantity of academic backgrounds, interests, experiences, and career objectives. This is helpful in discussing the reasons for the importance of records, but it can be maddening when giving class lectures and hosting student discussions supposed to provide some common orientation. Students also bring many career objectives. Some want to go work in local historical societies with personal manuscripts collections and small business holdings, while others desire to work in larger corporate or government organizations. While there are some *common* principles for *all* records, how can you teach them basic administrative approaches when there may be some who will work nearly by themselves and others in a staff of fifty of more? The educator picks an orientation and tries to factor in other scenarios and issues to cover as many bases as possible. A practicum, if well designed, can help, but if it is poorly designed, it detracts from the course work—using valuable course time and more formal orientation to archival principles and practices. The value of the practicum may be neutralized because a student could do fieldwork in one kind of institution and ultimately work in a very different environment—indeed, there is more than a fair chance this will happen. The only surety that this would not occur is if both educators and site supervisors focused on records and recordkeeping systems, a somewhat theoretical approach that seems counter to what the archives practicum has traditionally supported.

A similar problem occurs among the educators themselves. Nearly all of the regular educators bring their *own* interests and experiences to the classroom. Although it is not nearly as bad as thirty years ago when all educators were adjuncts and essentially teaching what they did, there are nevertheless serious limitations if an educator relies too much on his or her own experience. The point is, *everyone's* limitations are substantial—the only solution is to go beyond practice to theory and methodology and, even more preferable, to multiple faculty arrangements for a range of experience, professional practices, and disciplinary orientations. Others have struggled with similar problems. Terrence McDonald, in his introduction to the edited volume of essays reflecting how many disciplines have adopted a historical orientation, laments that historians themselves have provided a "bad example." They "have for the most part refused to put their own practices at risk by much methodological or theoretical writing, preferring instead to know history when they see it and therefore being more proficient at boundary maintenance—identifying what is 'not history'—than at theorized reflection on their own practice."[84] The same problem occurs when graduate archives education is supported by adjuncts or if the practicum becomes the focal point of such education—providing attention to immediate practical problems and concerns, rather than in building frameworks for knowledge, searching for more creative solutions, or solving problems.

These issues should get archives and records management educators thinking about the limitations of practice as education. Each institution can possess different emphases and missions. A for-profit institutional archives will operate with a distinct mission from a government archives or historical records collecting repository. Missions transform how one approaches appraisal, descriptive services, and especially access. Students will only be able to understand such differences if educators prepare them for this. The problem gets murkier. In most archives, arrangement/description and reference/access remain the strongest and most dominant functions. In most records management operations retention scheduling and records center operations are the main responsibilities. It is questionable whether these are the most important archives and records management functions. Appraisal, with implications for every other archives and records management function, is more crucial. However, despite a rich debate about appraisal, this function often seems to be neglected.

The same is true about administration and public programs. Archivists and records managers in for-profit, corporate environments should not emphasize arrangement and description but, instead, target other critical problems with more potential impact. They should be focused on designing and implementing electronic information systems supporting records, ensuring the use of records for accountability and evidence purposes, and contributing to the viability of corporate memory in their organizations. Some of this can be learned on the job. It is more likely that such matters will only be learned in the classroom where students have directed reading of organizational management and related research, participate in discussions critically evaluating traditional archival approaches, and engage in deconstructing key archival and records management concepts and practices.

The limitations of practice are revealed in other ways. A number of programs rely on adjunct educators. How much time can any adjunct put into developing and teaching one or more courses? The tendency is for these individuals to reflect their own professional responsibilities, both to be efficient with their time as well as to build on their own knowledge base (often based on their practice). Many consider this as the strength adjuncts bring to archival education, but the result may be little more than an unwieldy apprenticeship system. The larger problem is that what should make people archivists should be what they *know*, not what they *do*. Adjuncts are often hired for what they do. Many adjuncts have little interaction with the academic departments in which they teach. How can they have any influence in the development of curriculum? Then, there are the students. Can they learn by bad experience (can they recognize bad examples)? Can they relate classroom learning to the experience they hear about or gain in their fieldwork? Can students relate archival and other records-oriented literature to whatever experience they gain as part of their educational programs? This requires more comprehensive courses providing expansive reflection by both students and faculty. For example, an extensive orientation to the history of records, recordkeeping and archives can provide a much-needed context for comprehending current records issues and challenges, but this is not likely to happen if the education programs are concentrated on experience.

Finally, there is the experience that the field requires for hiring. Experience is preferred above all other attributes. This seems so limited. How do you assess the quality of experience? How do you assess whether an individual has been able to make sense of his or her experience? Can they relate their particular experience to what is common or standard in the field? Can they rise above the experience—understanding how to relate it to another work situation and how to define it as a work requirement when they ultimately gain responsibility for recruiting and hiring? Experiential requirements are a hangover from the days when education was thin, as is certification, with its reliance on experience. Preappointment education, at a more rigorous level, is developing.

The practicum can be better integrated into graduate education. Specific experiences for particular student needs could be targeted. Some students have already worked in archives, and do not need to replicate the experience. They may need different experiences to broaden their expertise. This can be done in formal practicum experiences or by having specific coursework assignments with a practical twist. If educators are going to keep the practicum, then they need to formalize it as *real* graduate education, rather than allow it to remain as technical training or a form of remedial education.

Some educators have been careful to distinguish between the more formalized internship and the less structured practicum: A "practicum is used to refer to programs of briefer scope and duration involving less responsibility for theory formation and more emphasis on skill development." An "internship is defined . . . as a full professional experience involving all phases of an assignment from theorization to application."[85] At present, graduate students in archives and records management have the opportunity only to participate in something that seems to fit the practicum, whereas it needs to be evolved into something like more formal internships if it is to have a key role in graduate education. The practicum might be tied to more formal research, leading in turn to publishable research benefiting both students *and* profession.

Experience, of virtually any kind, can be made a positive because it opens up an opportunity for students to be able to relate formal exposure to theory and methodology to what actually happens in an archives or records program. As long as the field emphasizes experience over or as a crucial part of formal education, it is important that students be given some opportunity to acquire it. There is no need that this experience be part of a practicum. Students could be required to work in part-time archives positions, either paid or as volunteers while they attend classes, and educators could relate students' work experiences to class. The important matter is a synergy between the experience and classroom discussion, so that the experience can be critically analyzed and enrich classroom discussions.

Students benefit from fieldwork when they have the opportunity to work with professionals who are well read, engaged by archival knowledge matters, and committed to the advancement of the professional mission. These professionals must also be committed to providing good supervision, rather than only seeing the fieldwork students as cheap labor. These people are not always easy to find. Many students work in organizations where there is an animosity towards archival education and where practice, no matter how mundane, is seen as the way to learn to be an archivist. This could be counterbalanced by having a formal course focused on helping students relate theory to practice, which they attend along with fellow students who are also taking the practicum option. Students would be asked to read seminal works on theory versus practice, the nature of professional practice and professional education, and on other related topics intended to help them understand what they observe in their work experiences.

Graduates must be prepared for a rapid and ever changing world. Their knowledge is only as good as it prepares them to deal with unanticipated circumstances or to look toward future archives and records scenarios. The practicum, sitting loosely within graduate education as it does (as a sort of fossil of earlier educational programs), possesses many limitations for this. The practicum is focused on what is going on in the field at present, generally with little connection to what came before or what might be developing. It must be diverted away from arrangement and description work or administering records centers *unless* this work involves new standards or major evaluative and decision-making processes. Students need to learn how archivists grapple with crucial challenges, relate to their parent organizations, and serve the needs of researchers.

The practicum is a potential liability if educators see their role as change agents in the field. This certainly points out how important the classroom is to education. With daily news stories featuring records and archives, the student must be oriented to their significance in formal discussion. It is difficult to imagine that this would happen in the field. If students can be placed in a practicum where they not only experience records work but are able to develop skills in critically analyzing what happens in the typical archives or records management program, then the practicum has a future. But if the practicum is little more than a means for students to build a resume or to supply inexpensive labor, then I doubt if the practicum is worth much attention or that it possesses much of a future; it is only a historic milestone in the development of education for records professionals.

NOTES

1. James M. O'Toole, "Curriculum Development in Archival Education: A Proposal," *American Archivist* 53 (Summer 1990): 462–463.

2. Angelika Menne-Haritz, "Archival Education: Meeting the Needs of Society in the Twenty-First Century" (Montreal: International Congress on Archives, 1992), pp. 6–11.

3. Ann Pederson, "Writing and Research" (Montreal: International Congress on Archives, 1992), p. 4.

4. The full text of these education guidelines is available at www.archivists.org/education/masguide.htm/.

5. Tom Nesmith, "Hugh Taylor's Contextual Idea for Archives and the Foundation of Graduate Education in Archival Studies," in Barbara L. Craig, ed., *The Archival Imagination: Essays in Honour of Hugh A. Taylor* (Ottawa: Association of Canadian Archivists, 1992), p. 18.

6. "Society of American Archivists Guidelines for Graduate Archival Education Programs," *American Archivist* 51 (Summer 1988): 380–389.

7. The bibliography was the basis for the reading list included in Paul Conway, "Archival Education and the Need for Full-Time Faculty," *American Archivist* 51 (Summer 1988): 262–265.

8. Timothy Ericson, "Professional Associations and Archival Education: A Different

Role, or a Different Theater?'' *American Archivist* 51 (Summer 1988): 298–311 and
'' 'Abolish the Recent': The Progress of Archival Education,'' *Journal of Education for Librarianship and Information Science* 34 (Winter 1993): 25–37.

9. Alan D. Gabehart, ''Qualifications Desired by Employers for Entry-Level Archivists in the United States,'' Ed.D. diss., Texas Tech University, 1991. An article of the same title, from which I have extracted this quotation (p. 439), was published in the Summer 1992 issue of the *American Archivist*.

10. Gabehart, ''Qualifications,'' pp. 435, 437.

11. Frederick J. Stielow, ''The Impact of Information Technology on Archival Theory: A Discourse on an Automation Pedagogy,'' *Journal of Education for Library and Information Science* 34 (Winter 1993): 62.

12. O'Toole, ''Curriculum Development,'' p. 463.

13. Donald L. DeWitt, ''The Impact of the MARC AMC Format on Archival Education and Employment During the 1980s,'' *Midwestern Archivist* 16, no. 2 (1991): 83.

14. Elsie Freeman, ''Soap and Education: Archival Training, Public Service and the Profession—An Essay,'' *Midwestern Archivist* 16, no. 2 (1991): 88.

15. Luciana Duranti, ''The Archival Body of Knowledge: Archival Theory, Method, and Practice, and Graduate and Continuing Education,'' *Journal of Education for Library and Information Science* 34 (Winter 1993): 10.

16. Frank Burke, ''The Future Course of Archival Theory in the United States,'' *American Archivist* 44 (Winter 1981): 40–46.

17. Terry Eastwood, ''Building Standards of Competence,'' *Janus* no. 2 (1992): 213.

18. Unpublished paper presented by Ericson at the Midwest Archives Conference, May 5, 1989.

19. Richard J. Cox, ''American Archival History: Its Development, Needs, and Opportunities,'' *American Archivist* 46 (Winter 1983): 31–41.

20. These guidelines specify that ''an understanding of information and its recorded forms, including historical documentation, is crucial to the work of the archivist and to building a true documentary heritage. Archivists need to understand the development of record keeping techniques over time as well as the dynamics of modern information systems.'' The guidelines also suggest that archival students ''need to gain a firm understanding of the history and present nature of the archival profession, recognizing that the profession is dynamic, changing in response to the challenges of documenting modern society.'' ''Society of American Archivists Guidelines for Graduate Archival Education Programs,'' pp. 382–383.

21. This can be seen in the experimentation that went on in the early days of the National Archives; see Donald R. McCoy, *The National Archives: America's Ministry of Documents 1934–1968* (Chapel Hill: University of North Carolina Press, 1978), ch. 5.

22. Paul Heyer, *Communications and History: Theories of Media, Knowledge, and Civilization*, Contributions to the Study of Mass Media and Communications, no. 10 (Westport, Conn.: Greenwood Press, 1988), p. x.

23. I have described these values in greater detail in my essay, ''On the Value of Archival History in the United States,'' *Libraries and Culture* 23 (Spring 1988): 135–151.

24. James O'Toole's analysis of a basic archival concept such as permanence illustrates the potential value of such work; ''On the Idea of Permanence,'' *American Archivist* 52 (Winter 1989): 10–25.

25. Comparisons of archival appraisal principles and practices to library collection development, preservation selection, artifact selection by museum curators, and the use of documentation by historical researchers need more attention than they have been given. There have been some useful efforts in this regard, such as Jutta Reed-Scott, "Collection Management Strategies for Archivists," *American Archivist* 47 (Winter 1984): 23–29 and Margaret Child, "Further Thoughts on 'Selection for Preservation: A Materialistic Approach,' " *Library Resources and Technical Services* 30 (October/December 1986): 354–362.

26. Comparative analysis of archival development in different cultures would provide insight into the importance of archives and why some programs are more successful than others. The development of comparative history is instructive in this regard. As George M. Fredrickson has written, "The object of comparative history in the strict sense is clearly a dual one: it can be valuable as a way of illuminating the special features or particularities of the individual societies being examined—each may look different in the light of the other or others—and also useful in enlarging our theoretical understanding of the kinds of institutions or processes being compared, thereby making a contribution to the development of social-scientific theories and generalizations." "Comparative History," in Michael Kammen, ed., *The Past Before Us: Contemporary Historical Writing in the United States* (Ithaca, N.Y.: Cornell University Press, 1980), p. 458. A theory of archival repository development, among other things, could emerge from such work.

27. Elizabeth Eisenstein, *The Printing Press as an Agent of Change: Communications and Cultural Transformations in Early-Modern Europe* (Cambridge: Cambridge University Press, 1979), p. 24.

28. See, for example, JoAnne Yates, "Internal Communication Systems in American Business Structures: A Framework to Aid Appraisal," *American Archivist* 48 (Spring 1985): 141–158.

29. Hugh Taylor, " 'My Very Act and Deed': Some Reflections on the Role of Textual Records in the Conduct of Affairs," *American Archivist* 51 (Fall 1988): 457, 466.

30. See Rollo G. Silver, "The Training of Rare Book Librarians," *Library Trends* 9 (April 1961): 446–452; Ann Bowden, "Training for Rare Book Librarianship," *Journal of Education for Librarianship* 12 (Spring 1972): 223–231; Roderick Cave, "Historical Bibliographical Work: Its Role in Library Education," ibid. 21 (Fall 1980): 109–121; and Lawrence J. McCrank, *Education for Rare Book Librarianship: A Reexamination of Trends and Problems*, University of Illinois Graduate School of Library Science Occasional Papers no. 144 (April 1980).

31. For historical writing, for example, see Donald E. Brown, *Hierarchy, History, and Human Nature: The Social Origins of Historical Consciousness* (Tucson: University of Arizona Press, 1988), which contends that whether a society has a highly developed sense of history depends to a large extent on the way that that society is structured. For the French Revolution see the classic essays by Ernst Posner, "Some Aspects of Archival Development Since the French Revolution," *American Archivist* 3 (July 1940): 159–172 and Carl Lokke, "Archives and the French Revolution," ibid. 31 (January 1968): 23–31 and, especially, the more recent Judith M. Panitch, "Liberty, Equality, Posterity? Some Archival Lessons from the Case of the French Revolution," *American Archivist* 59 (Winter 1996): 30–47.

32. J. R. Pole, *Paths to the American Past* (New York: Oxford University Press, 1979), pp. xii–xiii.

33. Taylor, " 'My Very Act and Deed,' " p. 467. See also Hugh Taylor, "Transfor-

mation of the Archives: Technological Adjustment or Paradigm Shift?'' *Archivaria* 25 (Winter 1987–1988): 12–28.

34. Saul Herner, ''Brief History of Information Science,'' *Journal of the American Society for Information Science* 35 (May 1984): 157–163.

35. There are some general studies that suggest some of these issues, such as Heyer, *Communications and History*, pp. 157–169; Norman D. Stevens, ''The History of Information,'' in Wesley Simonton, ed., *Advances in Librarianship*, vol. 14 (Orlando, Fla.: Academic Press, 1986), pp. 1–48; and Ivan Illich and Barry Sanders, *ABC: The Alphabetization of the Popular Mind* (San Francisco: North Point Press, 1988).

36. Jan Vansina, *Oral Tradition as History* (Madison: University of Wisconsin Press, 1985), pp. xi–xii.

37. See, for example, the interesting, provocative writings of Denise Schmandt-Besserat, ''An Archaic Recording System and the Origin of Writing,'' *Syro-Mesopotamian Studies* 1/2 (1977): 1–32; ''The Earliest Precursors of Writing,'' *Scientific American* 238 (1978): 38–47; ''How Writing Came About,'' *Zeitschrift fur Papyrologie and Epigraphik* 47 (1982): 1–5; and ''The Emergence of Recording,'' *American Anthropologist* 84 (1982): 871–878, all now conveniently summarized in her *How Writing Came About* (Austin: University of Texas Press, 1996; abridged ed.). Some of the anthropological analyses of orality and literacy are also valuable for understanding some of the issues involved in the emergence of records; see Jack Goody, *The Logic of Writing and the Organization of Society* (Cambridge: Cambridge University Press, 1986) and Walter J. Ong, *Orality and Literacy: The Technologizing of the Word* (New York: Methuen, 1982). There are also many popular histories of writing, such as Donald Jackson, *The Story of Writing* (New York: Taplinger Publishing Co., 1981), chs. 1 and 2.

38. Posner, *Archives in the Ancient World* (Cambridge, Mass.: Harvard University Press, 1972). There are other useful studies as well on ancient recordkeeping, such as Giovanni Pettinato, *The Archives of Ebla: An Empire Inscribed in Clay* (Garden City, N.Y.: Doubleday, 1981).

39. The recent thousandth anniversary of the Domesday Book produced a number of interesting studies about its creation and use; one of the more interesting of these studies is by Elizabeth M. Hallam, *Domesday Book Through Nine Centuries* (n.p.: Thames and Hudson, 1986). For a broader treatment of the nature of records in early Europe see M. T. Clanchy, *From Memory to Written Record: England, 1066–1307* (Cambridge, Mass.: Harvard University Press, 1979), quotations pp. 214, 231. Other studies of value are C. H. Cheney, *Archives of Medieval Europe* (Cambridge, England, 1956) and Ernst Posner, ''Archives in Medieval Islam,'' *American Archivist* 35 (July/October 1972): 291–315.

40. Goody, *The Logic of Writing and the Organization of Society*, pp. 21–22, 142–143.

41. Lester K. Born, ''Baldassare Bonifaco and His Essay 'De Archivis,' '' *American Archivist* 4 (October 1941): 221–237 and ''The 'de Archivis Commentarius' of Albertino Barisoni (1587–1667),'' *Archivalische Zeitschrift* 50/51 (1955): 13–22; Lester J. Cappon, ''Collectors and Keepers in the England of Elizabeth and James,'' in *Sibley's Heir: A Volume in Memory of Clifford Kenyon Shipton* (Boston: Colonial Society of Massachusetts, 1982), pp. 145–171.

42. There are a number of excellent essays on early English recordkeeping: Maurice F. Bond, ''The Formation of the Archives of Parliament, 1497–1691,'' *Journal of the Society of Archivists* 1 (October 1957): 151–158; Thomas G. Barnes, ''The Archives and

Archival Problems of the Elizabethan and Early Stuart Star Chamber,'' ibid. 2 (October 1963): 345–360; Elizabeth M. Hallam, ''Problems with Record Keeping in Early Eighteenth Century London: Some Pictorial Representations of the State Paper Office, 1705–1706,'' ibid. 6 (October 1979): 219–226; and Charles F. Mullet, ''The 'Better Reception, Preservation, and More Convenient Use' of Public Records in Eighteenth-Century England,'' *American Archivist* 27 (1964): 195–217. For development of the early statistical mind, refer to James H. Cassedy, *Demography in Early America: Beginnings of the Statistical Mind 1600–1800* (Cambridge, Mass.: Harvard University Press, 1969); Patricia Cline Cohen, *A Calculating People: The Spread of Numeracy in Early America* (Chicago: University of Chicago Press, 1982); and Margaret Stieg, ''The Nineteenth-Century Information Revolution,'' *Journal of Library History* 15 (Winter 1980): 22–52.

43. Compare European occurrences and interests with what is happening in one American state as written about by H. G. Jones, *For History's Sake: The Preservation and Publication of North Carolina History 1663–1903* (Chapel Hill: University of North Carolina Press, 1966). A suggestive recent essay on the role and nature of the transmission of letters between England and the American colonies in the early seventeenth century is in the vein of the kind of research that is needed; see David Cressy, *Coming Over: Migration and Communication between England and New England in the Seventeenth Century* (Cambridge: Cambridge University Press, 1987), ch. 9.

44. Stephen H. Helton, *Recordkeeping in the Department of State 1789–1956*, Reference Information Paper no. 74 (Washington, D.C.: National Archives and Records Service, 1975).

45. Victor Gondos, Jr., ''The Era of the Woodruff File,'' *American Archivist* 19 (October 1956): 303–320.

46. Sue Walker, ''How Typewriters Changed Correspondence: An Analysis of Prescription and Practice,'' *Visible Language* 18 (Spring 1984): 102–117.

47. Margery W. Davies, *Woman's Place Is at the Typewriter: Office Work and Office Workers 1870–1930* (Philadelphia: Temple University Press, 1982).

48. Richard B. Du Boff, ''The Rise of Communications Regulation: The Telegraph Industry, 1844–1880,'' *Journal of Communication* 34 (Summer 1984): 52–66; Ithiel de Sola Pool, *Forecasting the Telephone: A Retrospective Technology Assessment of the Telephone* (Norwood, N.J.: Ablex, 1983); James R. Beniger, *The Control Revolution: Technological and Economic Origins of the Information Society* (Cambridge, Mass.: Harvard University Press, 1986).

49. For example, diaries remained a way for the individual to deal with the larger world around him or herself, as recounted in Thomas Mallon, *A Book of One's Own: People and Their Diaries* (New York: Ticknor & Fields, 1984). Diaries kept by women traveling westward in nineteenth-century America were partly consciously written as ''guides'' for others traveling afterwards, much in the same way that correspondents from early colonial America wrote home to family and friends; see Lillian Schlissel, *Women's Diaries of the Westward Journey* (New York: Schocken Books, 1982). Even the ordinary financial records maintained by farmers can be partially read as diaries. Phillip Lott's farm accounts ''are ordinary financial record books, not diaries; they record debits and credits, not detailed reports of thoughts and events. But they do give the names of the people with whom Lott did business, and the nature of that business, and where it was done. And they do tell us how he worked and what he bought and sold''; it would be interesting to try to determine whether Lott himself used these records as

more than just accounts to keep his farm running, but as efforts to chart and anchor his life. See Yasuo Okada, "The Economic World of a Seneca County Farmer, 1830–1880," *New York History* 66 (January 1985): 5.

50. Herbert Butterfield, *The Origins of History*, ed. Adam Watson (New York: Basic Books, 1981), p. 197.

51. Henry D. Shapiro, "Putting the Past Under Glass: Preservation and the Idea of History in the Mid-Nineteenth Century," *Prospects* 10 (1985): 243–278; David D. Van Tassel, *Recording America's Past: An Interpretation of Historical Societies in America 1607–1884* (Chicago: University of Chicago Press, 1960); George H. Callcott, "Antiquarianism and Documents in the Age of Literary History," *American Archivist* 21 (January 1958): 17–29.

52. Carolyn Marvin, *When Old Technologies Were New: Thinking About Electric Communication in the Late Nineteenth Century* (New York: Oxford University Press, 1988), ch. 2.

53. Lester J. Cappon, "Walter R. Benjamin and the Autograph Trade at the Turn of the Century," *Proceedings of the Massachusetts Historical Society* 78 (1966): 20–37; Joseph Edward Fields, "Israel K. Tefft—Pioneer Collector," *Manuscripts* 6 (Spring 1954): 130–135; Francis C. Haber, "Robert Gilmor, Jr.—Pioneer American Autograph Collector," ibid. 7 (Fall 1954): 13–17; William B. Hesseltine, *Pioneer's Mission: The Story of Lyman Copeland Draper* (Madison: State Historical Society of Wisconsin, 1954); Lucile M. Kane, "Manuscript Collecting," in William B. Hesseltine and Donald R. McNeil, eds., *In Support of Clio: Essays in Memory of Herbert A. Kellar* (Madison: State Historical Society of Wisconsin, 1958), pp. 29–48.

54. There are many studies on the development of archival operations in this period. For a suggestion of the nature of these, refer to Lester J. Cappon, "American Historical Editors before Jared Sparks: 'They Will Plant a Forest . . . ,' " *William and Mary Quarterly*, 3rd series, 30 (July 1973): 375–400; Roland M. Baumann, "Samuel Hazard: Editor and Archivist for the Keystone States," *Pennsylvania Magazine of History and Biography* 107 (April 1983): 195–215; Richard J. Cox, "A Century of Frustration: The Movement for a State Archives in Maryland, 1811–1935," *Maryland Historical Magazine* 78 (Summer 1983): 106–117; Cox, "The Origins of American Religious Archives: Ethan Allen, Pioneer Church Historian and Archivist of Maryland," *Journal of the Canadian Church Historical Society* 29 (October 1987): 48–63; Nicholas Falco, "The Empire State's Search in European Archives," *American Archivist* 32 (April 1969): 109–123; Bruce W. Dearsytne, "Archival Politics in New York State, 1892–1915," *New York History* (April 1985): 165–184; Maynard Brichford, "The Origins of Modern European Archival Theory," *Midwestern Archivist* 7, no. 2 (1982): 85–101; and Ernst Posner, "Max Lehman and the Genesis of the Principle of Provenance," *Indian Archives* 4 (July/December 1950): 133–141.

55. Waldo Gifford Leland, "The First Conference of Archivists, December 1909: The Beginnings of a Profession," *American Archivist* 13 (April 1950): 109–120; Victor Hugo Paltsits, "An Historical Resume of the Public Archives Commission from 1899 to 1921," *Annual Report of the American Historical Association for the Year 1922* (Washington, D.C.: Government Printing Office, 1926), I: 152–160; Mattie U. Russell, "The Influence of Historians on the Archival Profession in the United States," *American Archivist* 46 (Summer 1983): 277–285; William F. Birdsall, "The Two Sides of the Desk: The Archivist and the Historian, 1909–1935," ibid. 38 (April 1975): 159–173; Robert R. Simpson, "Leland to Connor: An Early Survey of American State Archives," *American*

Archivist 36 (October 1973): 513–522; and Victor Gondos, Jr., *J. Franklin Jameson and the Birth of the National Archives 1906–1926* (Philadelphia: University of Pennsylvania Press, 1981).

56. Waldo Gifford Leland, "Historians and Archivists in the First World War," *American Archivist* 5 (January 1942): 1–17; Burl Noggle, *Working with History: The Historical Records Survey in Louisiana and the Nation 1936–1942* (Baton Rouge: Louisiana State University Press, 1981); Edward Francis Barrese, "The Historical Records Survey: A Nation Acts to Save Its Memory," Ph.D. diss., George Washington University, 1980; David L. Smiley, "The W.P.A. Historical Records Survey," in *In Support of Clio*, pp. 3–28.

57. James Gregory Bradsher, "A Brief History of the Growth of Federal Government Records, Archives, and Information 1789–1985," *Government Publications Review* 13 (1986): 491–505; Bradsher, "An Administrative History of the Disposal of Federal Records, 1789–1949," *Provenance* 3 (Fall 1985): 1–21 and "1950–1985," ibid. 4 (Fall 1986): 49–73.

58. Posner, *American State Archives*; H. G. Jones, "The Pink Elephant Revisited," *American Archivist* 43 (Fall 1980): 473–483; Jones, *The Records of a Nation: Their Management, Preservation, and Use* (New York: Atheneum, 1969); Jacqueline Goggin, "That We Shall Truly Deserve the Title of 'Profession': The Training and Education of Archivists, 1930–1960," *American Archivist* 47 (Summer 1984): 243–254.

59. Examples of general histories include Michael R. Williams, *A History of Computing Technology* (Englewood Cliffs, N.J.: Prentice-Hall, 1985); Joel Shurkin, *Engines of the Mind: A History of the Computer* (New York: W. W. Norton and Co., 1984; revised 1996); and R. Moreau, *The Computer Comes of Age: The People, the Hardware, and the Software*, trans. J. Howlett (Cambridge, Mass.: MIT Press, 1984).

60. Ian Miles, Howard Rush, Kevin Turner, and John Bessant, *Information Horizons: The Long-Term Social Implications of New Information Technologies* (Hants, England: Edward Elgar Publishing, 1988); Jennifer Daryl Slack and Fred Fejes, eds., *The Ideology of the Information Age* (Norwood, N.J.: Ablex Publishing Corporation, 1987).

61. Richard Kesner, "Automated Information Management: Is There a Role for the Archivist in the Office of the Future?" *Archivaria* 19 (Winter 1984–1985): 162–172; Committee on the Records of Government, *Report* (Washington, D.C.: The Committee, March 1985); National Academy of Public Administration, *The Effects of Electronic Recordkeeping on the Historical Record of the U.S. Government: A Report for the National Archives and Records Administration* (n.p.: NAPA, January 1989).

62. David Bearman, *Archival Methods*, Archives and Museum Informatics Technical Report 3 (Spring 1989): 4–5.

63. For examples of comparative studies, see Thomas Wilsted, "Kiwis, Kangaroos and Bald Eagles: Archival Development in Three Countries," *Midwestern Archivist* 4 no. 1 (1979) and Hugh A. Taylor, "Archives in Great Britain and Canada—Impressions of an Immigrant," *Canadian Archivist* 1 (1969): 22–33.

64. For example, the similarities in national archival development can be effectively examined by comparing the studies of the National Archives in the United States with the development of the similar institution in Canada by using Ian E. Wilson, " 'A Noble Dream': The Origin of the Public Archives of Canada," *Archivaria* 15 (Winter 1982/1983): 16–35 and William G. Ormsby, "The Public Archives of Canada, 1948–1968," ibid. 15 (Winter 1982/1983): 36–46. Differences in archival development and practice caused by differing political philosophies can be seen in Patricia Kennedy Grim-

stead, "Lenin's Archival Decree of 1918: The Bolshevik Legacy for Soviet Archival Theory and Practice," *American Archivist* 45 (Fall 1982): 429–443.

65. Stephanie Culp, *Conquering the Paper Pile-Up* (Cincinnati, Ohio: Writer's Digest Books, 1990), p. 8.

66. Victoria Irons Walch, *Where History Begins: A Report on Historical Records Repositories in the United States* (n.p.: Council of State Historical Records Coordinators, May 1998), pp. 12–13, 31.

67. Terry Eastwood, "Educating Archivists about Information Technology," *American Archivist* 56 (Summer 1993): 458–466 (quotations pp. 463 and 465).

68. Ira Penn, "Records Management: Still Hazy After All These Years," *Records Management Quarterly* 27 (January 1993), p. 20.

69. Alice Robbin, "State Archives and Issues of Personal Privacy: Policies and Practices," *American Archivist* 49 (Spring 1986): 163–176.

70. Eireann Carroll, "In Search of . . . Records Management," *Records Management Quarterly* 25 (October 1991): 32–36.

71. Donald A. Norman, *Things That Make Us Smart: Defending Human Attributes in the Age of the Machine* (Reading, Mass.: Addison-Wesley Publishing Co., 1993), pp. xii–xiii.

72. Such as Richard Cox, "Debating the Future of the Book," *American Libraries* 28 (February 1997): 52–55 and "Archival Anchorites: Building Public Memory in the Era of the Culture Wars," *Multicultural Review* 7 (June 1998): 52–60.

73. Samuel C. Florman, *The Introspective Engineer* (New York: St. Martin's Press, 1996), pp. 4–5.

74. Frederick J. Stielow, "The Practicum and the Changing Face of Archival Education: Observations and Recommendations," *Provenance* 8, no. 1 (Spring 1990): 1–12.

75. The current SAA guidelines for the MAS degree and for continuing education can be found at http://www.archivists.org.

76. Stielow, "The Practicum," p. 11.

77. The education directory is at http://www.archivists.org/education/prog.html.

78. For a recent example, see J. Gordon Coleman, Jr., "The Role of the Practicum in Library Schools," *Journal of Education for Library and Information Science* 30 (Summer 1989): 19–27.

79. Ames Sheldon Bower, "Whence and Whither: A Survey of Archival Education," *Georgia Archive* 5 (Summer 1977): 47.

80. Terry Eastwood, "What Is Archival Theory and Why Is It Important?" *Archivaria* 37 (Spring 1994): 122–130 (quotation p. 125)

81. Richard M. Kesner, "Employing the Case Study Method in the Teaching of Automated Records and Techniques to Archivists," *American Archivist* 56 (Summer 1993): 522–531.

82. See Frank G. Burke, "The Future Course of Archival Theory in the United States," *American Archivist* 44 (Winter 1981): 40–46 and Conway, "Archival Education and the Need for Full-Time Faculty."

83. Denis Donoghue. *The Practice of Reading* (New Haven, Conn.: Yale University Press, 1998), p. 21.

84. Terrence J. McDonald, ed., *The Historic Turn in the Human Sciences* (Ann Arbor: University of Michigan Press, 1996), p. 7.

85. John Hempstead, "Internship and Practical Application in Educating School Library Personnel," *Journal of Education for Librarianship* 12 (Fall 1971): 116–132.

8

Archives, Documentary Editing, and the Quarrel about Preserving Our Documentary Heritage

INTRODUCTION

In the last months of 1996, a conflict erupted among documentary editors, historians, and archivists. In November the National Historical Publications and Records Commission, the granting agency within the National Archives and Records Administration, issued a new strategic plan for using its $5 million in funds.[1] The commission, usually quietly handing out small grants for the preservation and maintenance of America's historical records, suddenly entered into a maelstrom of controversy.

The contested strategic plan suggested changes in the commission's funding priorities, targeting grants for state historical records projects and for research and development projects, especially for support of new approaches for the management of electronic recordkeeping systems. Dropping lower on its list of priorities was the commission's support of documentary editing projects, such as the papers of Thomas Jefferson, George Washington, and the Adams family, some that had been in progress for over half a century. The commission explained that the "previous plan contained seventeen objectives at four levels of priority" that were being reduced to four, with two identified as priority— "grants for improvements in documentary fields (research and development, tools, training, publications), and . . . grants for state collaborative efforts to meet documentary needs (state plans, state regrant programs, and work under collaborative agreements)." The revised plan also had a "simplified mission statement": "The NHPRC exists to carry out its statutory mission to ensure understanding of our nation's past by promoting, nationwide, the identification, preservation, and dissemination of essential historical documentation." New factors to evaluate grant proposals were also suggested: "Usability: the relative

usefulness of the material to be published; Availability: the relative current availability of the records to be published; Ability to Complete: the relative prospects
for completing publication of the records to be published; and Productivity: the
relative rate of progress of a project." Historians and their allies cried foul,
suggesting that the very core of our American heritage was endangered. A joint
statement of the Organization of American Historians and American Historical
Association argued "historical documentary editions provide the American people with a lasting legacy and physical and intellectual access to a broad range
of its fundamental historical documents" and called for reconsidering the "strategic plan, thus giving to constituent groups an opportunity to examine the issues
its adoption raises, and to comment to the Commission on their findings."[2] This
statement raised certain questions about the interpretation of the commission's
original mandate, just how the "American people" are really benefiting from
these editions, and the degree to which "constituent groups" had really been
excluded in the commission's deliberations.

This organizational statement was mild in comparison to statements by individual historians. Constance Schulz, the American Historical Association's
representative on the commission, prepared a statement for the National Council
for Public History, providing a history of the commission that she interpreted
as being "firmly rooted in the belief that preservation of the nation's fundamental documents was important but not sufficient: that 'major publication efforts under existing conditions of scholarship' were also needed to ensure that
the most important source materials for American history, using the term history
in its broadest sense' were also 'readily available to scholars and leaders in all
fields.' " Schulz considered the continuing meager funding of the commission
for all of its projects, noting that this has "forced" the commission "into a long
and often divisive struggle to balance the relative importance of 'records' and
'editions' projects." She also added to the pressing needs the challenges of the
"addition of new technologies—not simply electronic capabilities of the recent
past, but of microphotography and related issues before that." Schulz suggested
that the revised strategic plan resulted from the commission's executive director,
Gerald George, recommending his plan instead of one being prepared by an ad
hoc committee made up of commission members, leaving "no opportunity for
the constituencies who use historical source materials, either in the form of
documentary editions, or as original records in archives and manuscript repositories, to comment on how these changes in funding priorities would affect
their individual interests."[3]

For Schulz, this "constitutes a reversal of what have been the historical primary goals and objectives of the NHPRC—support for scholarly editing and
publication of nationally significant documentary materials since 1934, with
availability of grants in behalf of that goal since 1964, and grant support for
preservation of and creation of intellectual access to significant records in archives and manuscript repositories since 1974." This commentator noted the
importance of recent efforts by the commission to address concerns with elec-

tronic records, suggesting that the "Commission's meager funding can do relatively little to address across-the-board solutions to these problems." Finally, Schulz pleaded for calm among the various constituencies, believing that "we are spending our energies and time fighting each other for a claim on the distribution of these limited appropriations, rather than directing those same energies to demanding more nearly adequate funding for all of these priorities."

Schulz's statement raised interesting points. Was the commission's historic mission compromised by the revised strategic plan? Are electronic records issues simply the most recent challenge facing those concerned for the management of the country's documentary heritage? Was this plan the result of an action by a federal agency not allowing for ample comment? Was the debate an unfortunate misuse of energies by those protecting the documentary heritage?

Another shot fired in the early stages of this new records war came from Raymond Smock, former historian of the U.S. House of Representatives, in an article in the *Chronicle of Higher Education*. The title, "The Nation's Patrimony Should Not Be Sacrificed to Electronic Records," was sensationalist. Smock referred to the documentary editions as "monuments to this nation with more majesty and enduring value than the monuments we build of stone and steel." Smock condescendingly characterized the archival profession, using J. Franklin Jameson's seventy-year-old statement that Smock interprets as "historians should not rely on archivists alone to make decisions about what history to save or to publish." Smock believed that the commission revised its strategic plan due to some insidious influence by archivists. Smock saw a threat to the documentary editions coming from the "National Archives' overriding concern about preserving electronic records." Smock alluded to a statement made by archivist Carlin that "solving electronic records issues was a higher priority for him than the publication of the papers of Thomas Jefferson." Smock believes the "handling of electronic records should be a completely separate issue from support of editions of documents that are an important part of our national patrimony," contending that "much larger government agencies than the National Archives, with much larger budgets and technical staffs, probably will make headway on electronic records long before the National Archives have the resources to do the job properly." Smock defends NHPRC's historic mission, stating that "robbing the grants for documentary editions to carry out research and development on electronic records flies in the face of the very purpose for which the publications and records commission was established." In this we see the same concerns about violations of the commission's original mandate, the importance of the editions to the American people, and the false or poor objective of diverting funding to electronic records.[4]

Some historians complained that this new strategic plan was politically motivated. In the February 1997 issue of the *Newsletter* of the Organization of American Historians, Archivist of the United States John Carlin, who by virtue of his position chairs the meetings of the commission, answered such insinuations directly: "The charge of political motivation is not true, but what if it were? . . . Would it be so terrible if the NHPRC made itself politically appealing enough to reverse seventeen years of inflationary erosion of an appropriation that was inadequate from the start? The bigger question might be, why has the historical profession let that erosion happen?'' Carlin's dismissal of this charge stems from his conviction that the revised strategic plan dealt with the practical limitations of the current ways that the commission doles out its grants. ''The rationale for the revised plan is simple,'' argues Carlin. ''We are giving priority to activities through which our scant funds can have the widest impact. Our investments in R&D will help documentary editors and archivists at all levels, nationwide, learn to deal with electronic technologies for creating, preserving, and providing access to information of historical value.''[5]

The official response by the commission to these resolutions and individual charges was one of deliberation. At its meeting on February 20, the commission withheld approval of the revised plan to provide an opportunity for the plan's critics to make their case at its next meeting in June 1997, with a focus on the ''legislative history of the NHPRC . . . on how the Commission allocates its resources''; the ''statutory objectives of the commission''; ''public benefits'' and the ''changing circumstances in technology, user expectations, and scholarly communications''; the ''appropriate way for the NHPRC to determine, in principle, how its funds should be allocated''; and the ''implications of the new strategic plan for the NHPRC's ability to achieve its statutory objectives''[6] At the mid-June commission meeting, it was decided that the documentary editions for the nation's Founding Fathers would be restored to a top-level funding priority, adopting the recommendations proposed by the commission's Executive Committee a month before. It is difficult to surmise if any of these questions were answered, even though in the June 19 press release issued by the National Archives announcing the commission's decisions archivist Carlin was quoted as saying that ''we've had a good, long debate over priorities, but the Commission is now reunited around goals that deserve the support of all Americans.'' All one can ascertain from this controversy is that Founding Fathers attract media attention, documentary editors and their historical allies are more adept in politics and advocacy than archivists responsible for the preservation and management of hundreds of millions of archival records, and the challenges of a society increasingly utilizing electronic information technology are still not understood by historians, the media, and policymakers.

The facts of this case can be understood *only* by considering three important historical contexts for this debate, *not* by stressing the often emotional and inflamed threats to the publication of the papers of Thomas Jefferson and George Washington. First, it is important to have some understanding of the history of documentary editing and the commission as a supporter of a variety of agendas related to the preservation of the documentary heritage. Second, it is crucial to know about the relationship of historians, documentary editors, and archivists, for this may be the most important element of the debate. And third, we must keep in constant view the evolving nature of the technologies used to create records, one that cries out for new priorities and mandates for bodies like the commission. And we must re-consider the importance of records for society, not just scholarly users of archival records.

HISTORICAL CONTEXT 1: DOCUMENTARY EDITING AND THE NHPRC

Documentary editing has a rich history. Many of the early historical works, dating from the seventeenth century, were often lengthy strings of quotations, varying in accuracy, from key historical documents. John Winthrop, first governor of the Massachusetts Bay Colony, wrote a journal intended for many purposes—helping other early settlers adjust to the New World, capturing his own changing ideas about the colonial venture, and leaving for posterity a record of the initial days of the colony. This kind of history-memoir-archive was typical of much of the early writing in colonial America. Thomas Prince, another New Englander, published in 1736 his *A Chronological History of New England*, with copious quotations from early records. Numerous similar volumes appeared in the first two centuries of American settlement.[7]

The protection of key historical documents was always present for some Americans, partly as a justification for claims in the mounting crisis with England and, later, to create a stronger sense of the history and destiny of a new nation. In 1778, in the midst of the American Revolution, Ebenezer Hazard wrote to the president of Congress, Henry Laurens, and proposed publishing a "Collection of American State Papers." Hazard argued this would "furnish Materials for a good history of the United States." Hazard's work was finally published in the early 1790s. By the mid-nineteenth century documentary publishing, with or without government support, was a major business with projects such as Peter Force's *American Archives*, focused on the American Revolution and published in 1837–1853, and *American State Papers*, covering the years of early nationhood from 1789–1832 and appearing between 1832 and 1861. Hundreds of volumes of documents poured from the presses. Advocates of historical editing can point to a long federal government involvement with the publication of historical records. Between 1817 and 1904, at least fifteen projects were funded or partially supported by the government to publish the records of American foreign relations, the Constitutional Convention, diplomatic correspondence of the American Revolution, early congressional proceedings, and the papers of individual American leaders.[8]

These nineteenth-century documentary editions were part of an intense movement historians have dubbed "documania."[9] Besides these documentary projects, Americans collected autographs, read historical novels laced with descriptions of old records, and bought the works of the Romantic historians who told epic stories using eyewitness accounts. The proliferation of state and local historical societies over the first half of the nineteenth century contributed both to the collecting of important records and the publication of documentary editions.

Before the twentieth century, however, the methods of documentary editors were unsystematic. Jared Sparks modernized documents and even changed the content in order to portray heroes in the right light. The idea of these editions being American monuments was much stronger in the nineteenth century than today. These editors worked quickly, and the success of their ventures was completely dependent on getting their books into the market to recoup their investments. Many of these editions were by necessity incomplete, although this was due to repositories like historical societies being in the earliest stages of their collecting. Americans wanted to experience any old record as providing a visible, tangible link to the past, and they were not always particular in matters such as historical accuracy of the document.

It is the past half-century when documentary editing became systematic and profesionalized. The late nineteenth century "scientific" history, emphasizing the careful use of documentary sources akin to the running of experiments in scientific laboratories, helped develop more rigorous standards for documentary editing. Historian J. Franklin Jameson, the advocate of the development of guides to archival records through his work at the Carnegie Institute in Washington, D.C., as well as the promoter for the formation of both the commission and the National Archives, was a pivotal figure in the development of early modern twentieth-century documentary editing. He was educated in the scientific approach to history taught by Herbert Baxter Adams at Johns Hopkins University in Baltimore. Jameson, while serving a long stint as editor of the *American Historical Review*, pioneered in the publication of large groups of documentary sources with careful annotation and stellar historical introductions. He was one of the designers of the Institute for Historical Research at the Carnegie Institution in Washington and served as the institute's second director from 1905 until 1928. From this vantage, Jameson oversaw the preparation of a number of important guides (twenty-two in all) to sources in Europe and other foreign nations concerning early American history and lobbied for the establishment of institutions that could aid in preserving valuable historical records, including a commission on historical publications.[10]

It was necessary for the formation of the National Historical Publications Commission for a new era in documentary editing to emerge. The NHPC (later the NHPRC) has played an important role in the development of American documentary editing in the past forty years, assisting in securing funding, training editors, nurturing standards, convening conferences of editors, and encouraging the adoption of modern technology in the production of the documentary volumes. With calls for its creation coming as early as 1909, and after its initial dormancy from 1934 to the early 1950s, the NHPRC has emerged as the most visible player in the documentary editing business.[11]

The rebirth of the commission is generally attributed to Julian Boyd, in 1950, presenting President Truman with the first volume of the Thomas Jefferson

Papers. Truman responded by asking the commission, which had no staff or grant funds, to plan for a national program for the publication of papers of other famous Americans. This led to the commission's first staff and its first major report in 1954. *A National Program for the Publication of Historical Documents* is worth attention because it is directly relevant to the recent debate. The report stressed that in a democratic society "it is important that the people understand the history of their country and of its relation to the rest of the world." This sentiment was contrasted with an argument that our knowledge is "incomplete" because so "much of our past remains hidden from us" in inaccessible original sources. The commission proposed a systematic publication of the papers of many significant Americans (a list of 361 appeared in the report), cautioning readers of the report "that is not itself concerned directly with the study and writing of history," but instead for the highest editorial and scholarship standards.

Even with such recommendations the commission viewed itself involved in a "selective" publication of papers and records, with only a portion published in volumes and the remainder reproduced through microphotography. The 1954 report only *recommended* comprehensive editions of the papers of *five* Americans—Thomas Jefferson, Benjamin Franklin, John Adams and John Quincy Adams (the Adams family), James Madison, and Alexander Hamilton. The report also recommended a funding mixed of government and non-government sources, with itself attracting such funding through its responsibility for overall planning of the documentary program. It was not until 1964 that the commission actually had money for grants, relying instead on its mandate to "promote" and to engender "cooperation."

The commission kept current with changing fashions of historical scholarship. After its 1954 report, listing the important Americans whose papers were worthy of publication, the commission expanded this list. In the 1960s, it began supporting projects to publish the papers of important African Americans. In the 1970s it focused on the papers of Native Americans and women. The question emerged, however, whether the letterpress editions are collections of source materials or historical scholarship in their own right, harking back to the refurbished commission as described in the 1954 report.

Out of the commission's work came a variety of efforts supporting documentary editing. The start, in 1972, of the Institute for the Editing of Historical Documents has had a noticeable effect on editing standards. The 1978 formation of an Association for Documentary Editing was a byproduct of a generation of commission work creating an identity for historical editors. The commission has continued to serve as a forum for the ideas and concerns of documentary editors, explaining why the recent revised plan was greeted with so much suspicion and harshness. Its current legislative mandate (Public Law 100–365[44 USC 251]) gives it the authority to "make plans, estimates, and recommendations," "cooperate with" other government and non-government agencies, and "recommend the expenditure of appropriated or donated funds" "in collecting and preserving and, when it considers it desirable, in editing and publishing papers of outstanding citizens of the United States and other documents as may be important for an understanding and appreciation of the history of the United States.''

Lost in the debate were earlier commission concerns about the state of documentary editing. In 1976 the commission issued statements about the lack of selectivity used by many of the projects and the excessive annotation employed by some editors, overdescribing routine documents. Such concerns were prompted by the immense length of time needed to produce particular volumes and the lack of reasonable completion dates for multi-volume projects. Calls for re-thinking and for using available technologies, such as microfilm and then word processing, were sounded two decades ago and were alluded to in the 1954 report. Also lost in the recent debate have been the critical comments made by outsiders about historical editing, notably G. Thomas Tanselle. Tanselle, in the 1978 *Studies in Bibliography*, critiqued the modernization found in most NHPRC-supported editions and started by Julian Boyd in the Jefferson Papers project. Tanselle complained about modernizing texts, not recording the changes, and related issues by stressing that in ''private documents, then, where errors and inconsistencies are an integral part of the text, the argument against modernization is doubly strong.'' Tanselle considered such changes as ''indefensible'' because they bring with them a loss in part of the ''total body of evidence.'' ''Most of the editions . . . are praiseworthy in many respects: most of them reflect through research and exemplary annotation. But their treatment of the actual texts is relatively casual and unsophisticated by comparison.''[12] These issues cause second thoughts about just what these editions represent; are they primary sources, ripe for the plucking by historical scholars, or elaborate interpretations of particular historical personages and eras? Given the claims of the defenders of these documentary editions in the recent flap about the commission's strategic plan, these are questions worth more deliberation.

To earlier complaints, there were responses. Elizabeth Hamer Kegan, in her address as president of the Society of American Archivists, noted that the length of time required to prepare such volumes was often due to the scattered nature of the records and argued that ''one of the chief values of a large documentary publication . . . [is that] an entirely new resource for research is created.'' Concerning the expensive and time-consuming aspect of the letterpress editions, and the prospects of resolving this by using microfilm, Kegan appealed to a sort of antiquarian fondness—''I have yet to hear of anyone who prefers a [microfilm] reel to a volume.''[13] This posed the matter in the wrong fashion. If the question had been asked a researcher of delivering all the known papers of an individual on microfilm in a few to a half-dozen years or waiting fifty to 100 years for a full edition to be published, any sort of reformatting such as microfilm would look better. Constance Schulz's argument in 1988 that the millions of dollars spent on these projects is worth it because it moves the ''province of writing history and reading [of] primary sources out of the exclusive precincts of the scholars who have had access to travel funds" is yet another remarkable stretch at justifying the documentary editions.[14] Where is the evidence that these editions make it "possible for every man and woman to be his or her own historian"?

Through all of this we have an array of positive statements by which to assess the value of documentary editing. In 1986 Mary Giunta, an NHPRC staff member, wrote that "publications continue to meet the needs of the interested scholar and the general reader, and the country's need to document its heritage." Where is the evidence for this? How is the "interested scholar" defined? And are these editions really being used by the "general reader"?[15] A few years later another former editor, Charles T. Cullen, argued that one of the reasons why such editions are important is that "documentary editors sometimes make discoveries that are so unusual that one could argue the discovery would have been missed in any context other than the kind of labor editors put into their task." Cullen acknowledged that "most often, the discoveries are of relatively small importance," but this is counterbalanced by his belief that documentary editing may be the "last bastion of traditional historical research, where the written record is paramount and the documents lead the scholar toward a thesis that unfolds in a well-written narrative."[16] Obviously, this takes us far afield from the argument of documentary editing as a means to preserve and make available our documentary heritage and places it squarely back into historical scholarship.

A remarkable assessment came from another commission-sponsored study to "learn more about the researchers who consult sources made available through projects it funds." Completed by documentary editor Ann Gordon, *Using the Nation's Documentary Heritage* was more about the supposed value of the documentary editing projects with little understanding of the basic work of archivists.[17]

Gordon, like the advocates for editing cited earlier, holds documentary editing in a positive light: "With the start of a new era of documentary editing in the 1950s came the grand promise that any household could have Jefferson and Franklin on its shelves. Inflated as the image may have been, the editions do bring documents of national importance within reach."[18] Within reach by whom? Who is using these editions? What difference have they made in historical research or on larger public understanding of the past? Since there has been little evaluation of the impact or importance of documentary editions (reviews of such volumes do not usually consider the larger issues but most often treat the publications as scholarly histories), these questions are even more crucial to an evaluation of the use of archives.

The Gordon report is prejudiced evidently in favor of documentary editions. This first appears in Gordon's chapter on microfilmed records, when she writes that "documentary editing superseded archival practice as the foundation for microfilmed projects. . . . The microform editions are a compromise; they rarely incorporate the annotation expected in book editions, and though their guides exceed the archival finding aid, they rarely achieve the standard of a book."[19]

The statement seems to be carefully worded to suggest that documentary editions are somehow the best means for bringing documentary records to researchers. Her full chapter on documentary editions is even more revealing. While she suggests that the marketing of these editions has not been as successful as hoped for (there are references to the fact that they have been criticized as not the ideal means by which to present historical records for use), there is little analysis of their use or merit. Gordon suggests that sales figures are not a reliable mechanism by which to evaluate the documentary editions but, then, what is? Furthermore, there is little discussion about what the documentary editions actually represent. At one point Gordon notes that "people who use documentary editions rely on the scholarship of the editors to augment their own work."[20] This raises the question whether these works are documentary sources or scholarly works, and this is an important distinction. Should we think that these editions are *preserving* documentary sources? If they are, it is an infinitesimal portion of the documentary heritage.

There is another source for Gordon's version of the debate between archivists and documentary editors—an essay she published in the Association for Documentary Editing's journal. In this revealing essay Gordon suggests that the inability of researchers to get to the archival and historical manuscripts repositories "suggests new perspectives on a host of issues, including the importance of microfilm and of published documents which the researcher can bring close to home."[21] This leads to a re-statement of her larger study's finding that the NHPRC should "regain its position of leadership in the field of documentary editing."[22] Ann Gordon writes as a documentary editor, lamenting the argument between archivists and documentary editors over a "single, slim pot of federal money" while lambasting "critics within the Commission and their allies outside [who] have tried to redefine editing as an extension of archival management and practice."[23] Gordon believes that editing is a superior approach to making primary source materials available to the researcher. It is clear that the main purpose of the Historical Documents Study was to carve out a role and funding for documentary editing and not to evaluate objectively how researchers use historical records.

This perspective is misapplied when Gordon makes final recommendations to the commission. She candidly suggests the commission has been too wedded to the archival profession: "Because the records program evolved as a partner in extending the professional development of archivists, many of its grants have a remote relationship with researchers and the public at large. They improve skills, support long-range planning, and address technical problems of preservation. When such projects publish results, the works are written for other archivists, not for users of the historical record or the public."[24] So what should the commission do? Gordon suggests, as she did in the ADE journal, that the "Historical Documents Study urges the Commission to reassert leadership not only through support for specific editions but also through national programs."[25] The recent debate can only make one hopeful that the commission now realizes what these documentary editions represent, although the compromise solution suggests that the political, romantic, and emotional aspects represented by the Founding Era documentary editions are still blinding many to the more critical needs represented by modern records.

Such values have long been expressed. Paul Bergeron wrote in 1971 that "after the industrious editor has been immersed in his work for many months, the letters and documents begin to speak to him. The voices of the great and the near great, as well as the obscure, are heard; these persons seem alive again. While reading their comments and observations about business, politics, religion, family, marriage, death, and even the weather, the sensitive editor becomes aware of historical figures as humans."[26] This is historical research. Can the users of these editions have the same experience as the editor, as described by Bergeron? Or are these documentary editions really subsidized federal historical research and the source of the debate really the fear that the livelihood of the editorial staffs will be threatened by a simple change of NHPRC priorities? Even though the commission did not argue for the abandonment of these projects, what must appear to be positions with nearly life-long security (given the decades of work remaining for many of the larger projects) are challenged by the commission's new plan.

The most insightful glimpse into the inner workings of these editorial projects came in a 1997 essay by Jack Hitt. The title of the essay says it all—"In the Franklin Factory: Slow-Motion Scholarship in an Age of Academic Obsolescence." Hitt's article lovingly describes the forty-year old Franklin Papers project at Yale University, focusing on the people editing the volumes and their own self-images as historical editors. Hitt believes that the work of these projects is romantic, noting that "those who sign on no longer view the volumes that slowly emerge as mere books, but rather see in them the kind of enduring work that Aquinas imagined for *Summa theologiae* or Ptolemy for his *Almagest*." The ludicrous notion that these editions will somehow last forever is, thus, once again stressed. More importantly, what emerges from Hitt's essay is the gnawing concern about the status of these editors and the fact that their work is more like a biographical project. Hitt notes that "since many if not most of these editors lack doctorates, . . . the culture of achievement is not measured by the usual perks of tenure or the prestige of an endowed chair but rather by an Old World-style guild system of long, hard work."[27] Coupled with his observation that "what is also revealed by spending time with [the editors of the Franklin Papers] is just how differently they think of Franklin than the rest of us. . . . [T]he editors I interviewed talked about Franklin in the way one might gossip about somebody alive and nearby." This type of assessment ought to make us wonder about these works, especially in the lofty terms by which they are described. These observations suggest a kind of tenure and, as well, more of the way biographers wind up getting closer to their subjects. Neither are serious problems, except in how they relate to the grandiose importance attached to these projects in a democratic society's understanding of its own past.

Hitt also published a brief column in early 1997 in the *New York Times*, entitled "Devolving History," criticizing the commission's revised plan.[28] Hitt described the documentary editing projects as "some of the smallest and most efficient expenditures of taxpayer dollars," although one could ask smaller and more efficient than what? Hitt cried that the documentary projects have been placed behind the "vaguest state programs" such as "regrants" for professional education and planning. He adds that "local archivists" are now getting ready for the "easy money" and the papers of the Washingtons and Jeffersons will be less important than the "memos of ex-governors and the collected receipts of beloved town clerks." What "vague" programs? Educating individuals to work as professional archivists and manuscripts curators an essential activity. And why is it that Hitt believes that money is being diverted to support the preservation of *unimportant* records? Much of these funds will be used to preserve records crucial to understanding the twentieth century, something neither Jefferson or Washington can help us do.

HISTORICAL CONTEXT 2: ARCHIVISTS AND HISTORIANS

It is important to understand another dimension of the debate about documentary editing—how it relates to the broader professional relationships between historians and archivists and how editors identify themselves. While some editors see themselves as representing a distinct profession, more want to be accepted as part of the historical academy when, in fact, they really should be more closely allied with archivists.

The historical profession emerged in the late nineteenth century, marked by the growing number of appointments to teach in the university and the formation of the American Historical Association (AHA) in 1883. While the AHA, in its early days, included with little distinction both professionals (academics) and amateurs (writers and others), by the beginning of the twentieth century the association was a professional organization. Despite this, the association served as an umbrella for historical affiliates. When there began the movement in establishing state government archives in 1901, culminating with the establishment of the National Archives in 1934, a growing number of archivists attended meetings of the AHA. Most of the archivists were history-educated, and in 1909 they formed the Conference of Archivists, continuing to meet as part of the AHA for another quarter of a century.[29]

Archivists began to see the need for a separate professional association, an objective reached in 1936 with the founding of the Society of American Archivists. The relationship between archivists and historians is complicated, and even now many archivists think of themselves as either historians or as supporting historians using their records. Over the past twenty years, however, there has been a widening gulf between archivists and other records professionals and historians.[30] For one, archivists established graduate education guidelines that stress an independent core body of knowledge, even if they recognize that this knowledge is fundamentally interdisciplinary. For some historians, clinging to the notion that all that is needed for someone to be an archivist is to be trained as a historian or that the penultimate role of an archivist is to provide records for historical researchers, this shift in education has been troubling. More problematic, however, has been that most major archival education programs have become established in schools of information science, suggesting more an information discipline than one belonging to the humanities. Given that the majority of those teaching in these schools possess history degrees, it is hardly as serious a concern as some have made it out to be. Yet, the historical profession has become suspicious. It is quite probable that the NHPRC's revised plan, with new priorities to deal with issues like electronic records rather than the traditional documentary editions, is viewed by many historians as part of what they believe to be the influence of archivists who see themselves as technocrats rather than humanists or historians.

Some of the problems between historians and archivists also certainly stem from the changing ideas of historical truth in a post-modern age and the impact of this on the value of archival records. While more reasonable approaches have emerged, such as in Alan Spitzer's *Historical Truth and Lies about the Past*, a series of four case studies demonstrating a common ground of "criteria of veracity and validity" between positivists and postmodernists (usually best seen in debate in the public arena),[31] there is little doubt that the often acrimonious debates of the past two decades about the nature of historical evidence has weakened the academy's interest in archival sources. The fact that scholarly historians represent a meager portion of the researchers visiting archives may be a manifestation of changing historiographical fancies (although there are certainly many historians who shun the latest historiographical fads in favor of reliance on the evidence of archives), but this trend has had a fundamental influence on the thinking of archivists about their mission and the potential uses of their records.[32]

Archivists can take heart about the centrality of their work. Whether it stems from some of the debate about the veracity of historical evidence in a information age or whether it emanates from the declining eyewitness survivors of one of the most horrific events in human history, the Holocaust, an industry of research and writing has emerged on public memory.[33] It appears that the Information Age may leave a legacy of being the era when humanity seemed to create systems with far too much information to control. While the dazzling devices and the industry advertisements promise instant success or gratification, we daily face millions of words. The philosopher Michael Heim writes, "Infomania erodes our capacity for significance. With a mind-set fixed on information, our attention span shortens. We collect fragments. We become mentally poorer in overall meaning. We get into the habit of clinging to knowledge bits and lose our feel for the wisdom behind knowledge. In the information age, some people even believe that literacy or culture is a matter of having the right facts at our fingertips."[34]

Archivists and documentary editors alike need to determine how to harness the power of computers in order to make people aware of the important information found in their records. Part of the frustration many archivists may feel toward the traditional letterpress documentary editions is their stress on a printing and access technology less suited for the changing information access patterns and desires. If today a CD-ROM can hold the equivalent of 500,000 pages of text and can be reproduced for about a dollar, it stands to reason that reproducing the papers of these significant historical figures and the records of organizations need to be re-evaluated (especially if the goal is to make these records more widely available to the general public). A March 1992 letter by Ralph Orth to the editor of *The Chronicle of Higher Education* about the Mark Twain documentary edition describes the problem with the way such projects have been managed. He notes that an eleven-word telegram receives a twenty-seven-line explanation, suggesting that at the rate that the project is proceeding it will "take 100 years to publish the full 60 volumes required to print them all" and about $32 million in federal funding. The Founding Era documentary editions (the Adams Papers, First Federal Congress, Franklin Papers, Jefferson Papers, Madison Papers, Constitution Ratification, First Supreme Court, and the Washington Papers) will continue to the year 2060; the Jefferson Papers project, the documentary edition heralded for its scholarship, will have taken 116 years to complete at the present rate.[35] The average NHPRC support per volume of these editions has been to date over $86,000. While electronic library catalogs may provide better linkages to these volumes, it seems that the evolving ways people access information may leave the use of these volumes behind if they are not provided in full text digital form at considerably less expense. *Both* archivists and documentary editors share a common concern. That all but one of the Founding Era projects is working on or planning for some sort of full electronic access is commendable, but this should make the editors, archivists, historians, and public question the need to extend the letterpress editions into the middle of the next century.

Similar anxieties can be stated about the new interest in public memory. Historians and members of other disciplines are producing a wide-ranging set of studies on how a people perceives its past. From writers like Ian Buruma, who provides startling testimony about how both the Germans and Japanese have distorted and destroyed evidence about their activities in the Second World War, to scholars like Mike Wallace, who documents the Disneyification of the past, we have hundreds of volumes providing insights into how a community or a nation reinvents its own past for its use and convenience.[36] We can add the debates about multiculturalism and political correctness in the academy but have played in the public arena with discussions about such matters as national history standards, textbook writing, museum displays, and even festivals and pageants (as the debate about the Enola Gay exhibition at the Smithsonian reflected). Central to these debates is the evidence and the value of archival or primary sources, although we often see little reference to archives and even less to published documentary sources. While archivists have been developing the means to use the Internet and the World Wide Web to heighten awareness of their sources, they can be easily frustrated by the documentary editors who seem prone to cling to slowly producing volumes in limited runs mostly purchased by university libraries.[37]

The arguments about the centrality of documentary editing to the American public's appreciation of its heritage seem silly in current society's ongoing debates about its identity. The March 3, 1997 *New York Times*, looking at revelations of how the Nazis stockpiled looted gold from European Jews through Swiss bank accounts and how long it took for the facts of such activities to come to light, stated that "few countries deal honestly with their past." What archivists and historians can be cheered about is that these revelations were possible through the use of routine bank accounts and related records. As an article in a news magazine stated, "As with most reconsiderations of history, there is no single reason behind the new urge for total recall. The enormity of the Nazis' crimes makes it impossible ever to truly close this chapter of history. And the passage of time, rather than permitting memories to fade, has opened troves of long hidden or long ignored documents both in America and in Europe."[38] The disparaged "other" priorities of the commission may be far more relevant to the present than most of the ongoing documentary editing projects.

One would think that documentary editors could take heart as well with the renewed stress on public memory as they view their works as "monuments." But this concern or opportunity may be lost in the issue of the status of the documentary editors. Much of the discussion about the nature of these projects focused more on the apparent lack of recognition accorded by the historical profession for the editors or with how the editors relate to archivists, reminiscent of the views in the 1992 Gordon report. Frederika Teute's analysis of the reviews of these works in historical journals, published in 1980, reflect concerns about the editors' status, scholarship, biases, subsequent use by other historians, and overannotation, while acknowledging that many of these concerns had declined by the mid-1970s, perhaps because of the advent of the Bicentennial of the American Revolution. Yet, as Teute points out, these problems had not been resolved by 1980 (or by now). She argued that "in the process of doing justice to our documentary inheritance, ever more money, more time, and more detailed historical exegesis of the texts has been nationalized. It is time to stop . . . and, further, to recognize that these projects are not like the great cathedrals. Not only should they not take centuries to be completed, but also they may not and perhaps should not endure that long." Instead of doting on some great benefit of public democracy of these projects, Teute rightly argued that these works need to be considered "to be like any other work of history, as a project of a particular generation out of whose values they evolved."[39] Robert McCown, summarizing the proceedings of a 1975 conference on documentary editing, captured this attitude perfectly when he wrote that "editorial projects do take a great deal of time and money. Some would object to the great amount of money spent on the preparation of one volume. Yet society spends a great deal of money for things much less permanent than a standard edition. A good editorial project is worthwhile because such a project will really be permanent. This permanence gives the editor his status.''[40] But this sentiment has to be juxtaposed against other worries, such as those of Richard Kohn and George Curtis, who wondered twenty years ago that the NHPRC ''perhaps unwittingly has fostered editing as a separate enterprise and editors as a separate and distinct group within the historical profession.''[41] So much of the worrying about the documentary editions has resulted from such status concerns, rather than the matching of mission to success.

What such views may reflect is a group, the editors, caught between two diverging disciplines, historians and archivists. Providing these editions seems similar to the historical interpretations done by historical scholars and the appraisal, cataloging, and preservation carried out by archivists.

This no-man's-land of documentary editing leads to arguments that are difficult to defend. In 1989 one former editor, Brooks D. Simpson, published a brief article suggesting that the angst of documentary editors ''contributed to the balkanization of the historical profession through launching retaliatory strikes and engaging in self-celebration, congratulation and commiseration rather than demonstrating how the skills and products of documentary editing contributes to ongoing historical research and teaching.''[42] This sense of the permanence of the documentary editions seems illogical. Given the vagaries of historical scholarship, its changing interpretations and constant search for new and improved methodologies, it is difficult to believe that historically trained editors believe that their editions will remain permanent elements of scholarship. The long annotations, historical introductions, and other supplementary devices must, by necessity, reflect both the currency of scholarship (the time they were written) as well as the in-depth analysis of the historical papers being collected and edited. Projects now approaching the half-century mark must reflect the changing scholarly times, making them historical artifacts just as were the pioneering editorial projects of Hazard, Sparks, Force, and Ford. Future users of the volumes will probably spend as much time struggling to interpret the scholarly apparatus of these editions as using the source materials the projects published.

HISTORICAL CONTEXT 3: CHANGING RECORDKEEPING SYSTEMS AND ACCESS

In this debate documentary editing advocates have been aghast that the commission would subjugate their ''monumental'' tasks and responsibilities to the current struggles with electronic records. This attitude misses two fundamental points. First, the role of the archivist is to understand recordkeeping systems, and putting resources into working with these new systems is logical. Second, the current nature of recordkeeping systems threatens, perhaps in an unprecedented fashion, society with the loss of the majority of its documents.

While the concept of the record (the evidence of a transaction) has remained fundamentally unchanged in many centuries, the manner in which records are created and captured has been transformed many times over.[43] The origins of writing have been tied to the need to create a remembrance of a transaction.[44] The development of the clay tablet societies, using moist clay marked with a wedge-shaped stylus and establishing elaborate classification and storage systems led to the first recognizable archives and libraries. The establishment and rapid use of alphabetic writing in ancient Greece, starting about the eighth century B.C.E., led to the uses of writing for marking possessions, memorial inscriptions, making lists of officials and codification of laws, and the preparation of rules and procedures. While writing for recordkeeping was less systematic, formalized, and legalistic than its more modern counterparts, we still see the importance of records. Rosalind Thomas sees "an enthusiasm for writing as a means of memorial, preservation or self-advertisement—enabling memory of the individual self to be perpetuated somewhat more easily."[45] Her argument that the ancient Greeks used memorial inscriptions, carved in stone, to capture the more important records is reminiscent of the argument by the documentary editors that their works are monuments, with one exception—new and improved technologies enabled this practice to be abandoned.

Within a half a millennium, other recording technologies developed to enable more elaborate recordkeeping systems. The use of papyrus, wood bound into a codex (a book form), and parchment allowed for more complex organizations of records. By the late medieval period in Europe there was a record culture. The growth of government, trade, and communications (with a concomitant growth in literacy) led to a desire for records of every transaction to be captured and kept for later use. During this period the meaning of a "record" shifts from that of bearing witness to an activity to the literal written document.[46]

By the time of American colonization, records were an indelible aspect of civilization. Colonists' private libraries included ample numbers of legal manuals with guidelines for preparing both personal and business records, and the county courthouses evolved into recordkeeping as well as social centers. Until well into the nineteenth century, recordkeeping technologies did not dramatically change, allowing for fairly informal means of control of businesses and households. The advent of the telegraph, typewriter, and telephone dramatically changed this. The first half of the twentieth century, with improvements in the typewriter, accompanied by tabulating machines, sorters, copiers, and, finally, the start of the use of computers, changed this even more. Records proliferated and grew more complex. The old uses of technology to create paper records that could be filed in traditional fashion gave way to newer systems that could only be used in machine-readable format.

The late twentieth century, in terms of electronic information systems (including those maintaining records), has been the most remarkable period in the history of creating and handling both information and records. John Green, in a popular book on communications, describes the immense technological changes wrought by the computer. He reviews Moore's law, predicting that the "power, speed, and capacity of microprocessors . . . would double every 18 months and the cost would be halved in the same period." Green reflects on the immense software improvements, the ability now "to digitize all forms of information and media" for speedy transmission, the construction of the "information superhighway" with fiber optic cable and the use of wireless technologies, and the unparalleled impact of the Internet and the World Wide Web.[47] All of these are being used for recordkeeping.

What this summary of recordkeeping technologies suggests is that the archivist must be an expert on the history, purposes, and technology of records systems. It is the only means by which the archivist can carry through with the functions of evaluating, cataloging, preserving, and making available for use the records of continuing value to society. This should not be that contrary to the role of the documentary editor, since the editor should become an expert as well about the recordkeeping technologies and methods used by the creator responsible for the records being edited. However, it is clear that here we also have the source of one of the reasons why archivists and documentary editors do have distinct differences and why the pleas for these professionals to work together— while seeming to take the moral high ground in this debate—are really quite meaningless.

The real reason why electronic records must be a priority over the documentary editions is simple. Most of the records represented by the documentary editions are not immediately threatened. Left alone and provided moderate storage, the papers of the Jeffersons and Washingtons will be here next year, the next decade, and most likely the next century. This is not the case with the records produced in the modern electronic systems, as the computer has become the core of modern living. As Nicholas Negroponte argues, "Computing is not about computers any more. It is about living. . . . Like a force of nature, the digital age cannot be denied or stopped."[48] The computer does not provide, however, the solution to modern recordkeeping. Yet, electronic recordkeeping has taken hold because of what computer technology enables the modern organization to accomplish, the "transcendence of the information-processing capabilities of the individual organism by a much greater technological system."[49] Like it or not, then, we know that organizations will continue to use electronic recordkeeping technologies and that traditional recordkeeping systems will diminish in use and importance.

What does this have to do with the argument about the publication of documentary editions? The designers of these new recordkeeping systems have been computer specialists and not the experts in records and archives. These systems have been designed without a worry about long-term maintenance issues and with an eye on documents that can be manipulated and changed at will, both threatening the records of any modern day politician, civic leader, businessperson, military officer, or leader who may be declared a century or less from now as being his or her generation's Jefferson or Washington. These systems, when they are designed, do not take into account the need to maintain records for more than a brief period of time. Will we lose the papers of today's Jefferson as a result?

The Internet brings out these issues because it is through such networks that an increasing quantity of modern records are being created and transmitted. Nevertheless, the World Wide Web may be the most volatile of all information devices. Clifford Lynch writes that the "Internet—and particularly its collection of multimedia resources known as the World Wide Web—was not designed to support the organized publication and retrieval of information, as libraries [and we could add archives] are."[50] We could also expect that incessant letter writers like Thomas Jefferson or John Adams could be expected to have used the electronic mail technology, the best-known feature of the Internet, to correspond with friends and colleagues.

The greatest irony may be that the protesting American Historical Association and the Organization of American Historians were both co-litigants in the suit known as the PROFS case. When the Iran-Contra scandal moved to the front page in late 1986, principals in this affair begin to purge electronic mail messages related to it. The Tower Commission report in 1987 included many of these messages, saved by other public officials. When the Reagan administration was working on its transition out of office in 1989, it was learned that the National Archives was prepared to allow thousands of e-mail messages to be dumped because they did not constitute "records." The National Security Archive, a public citizen action group using Freedom of Information Act requests to gain access to classified federal records, led an effort to stop this, thus beginning a long court case about the preservation of these records. Another irony about this case may be the role of the National Archives. Tom Blanton, executive director of the National Security Archive, wrote in 1995 that none of the litigation would have been necessary "if the National Archives & Records Administration had simply done its job under the law, holding even the White House accountable. Perhaps that the final lesson of the White House e-mail case: We need a reinvented National Archives, a vigorous information watchdog. Otherwise, NARA will be relegated to the role of the nation's attic; and there, among the cobwebs, will roam the ghost of government accountability."[51] It may be that the National Archives, with Carlin's leadership moving electronic records to the top of its priority items, *is* becoming more vigorous. Now it is time for the documentary editors, and their historical association allies, to understand the *bigger* picture.

THE REAL ISSUE: THE IMPORTANCE OF RECORDS

What this debate lacks is recognition of the values of records, the big picture. The debate suggests records become valuable when they become archival that is, they are determined to have value for documenting or understanding the past. The implication is that archivists work to prepare the fodder for scholarly historians and others needing to do historical research. But records are far more important than this, and an understanding of this puts to rest this tempest in a records box.

Records are maintained for purposes of evidence, accountability, and memory. The evidential value of records is found in their documenting of events, activities, and trends. All records, created whenever a transaction in a business process occurs (sending a directive, endorsing a contract, closing a purchase) provide evidence of the activities of individuals, organizations, and government. Not all evidence is created equal, of course, because the nature of activities it relates to runs from the routine (answering a memo in order to accept a lunch invitation) to the immensely important (signing an international peace treaty). What makes this more difficult is that routine activities can become important in their connection to important events (agreeing to go to lunch in which it is later determined that those who attended this particular lunch were involved in planning a political coup). Adding to this difficulty is the idea of discovery used by lawyers to sweep up all records and even miscellaneous information found in non-records (scribbles on a telephone message pad or notes found in a desk drawer).

Accountability is the value of records ensuring that public officials or the managers of a company or those responsible for any private or civic organization are held responsible for their actions, especially those that have an impact on individual rights or the welfare of society. Kevin Kearns defines accountability as involving "answering to a higher authority in the bureaucratic or interorganizational chain of command."[52] In a democratic society we can also view the government process being held to the scrutiny of that government's citizens. Accountability is best seen through examples. In November 1996 three New York municipal government officials were accused of taking bribes to falsify computerized property records to eradicate due tax payments totaling over $13 million. A month later the Prudential Insurance Company was charged with deliberately destroying 10,000 customer files to impede an investigation into sales fraud; the company was ultimately fined $1 million for revealing a "consistent pattern of failing to prevent unauthorized document destruction." The Clinton-Gore administration has given us countless examples. The ongoing problems of alleged illegal campaign contributions, always followed by high-sounding denials, have produced documents demonstrating the exact opposite of the denials. Shortly after Vice President Gore stated ignorance that a visit to a luncheon at a Buddhist temple was to raise money, a memorandum from the Democratic National Committee was made public. That this document was dated just three days before the luncheon and addressed to Gore'e office indicated that Gore was expected to "extend appreciation for participant support and inspire political and fund-raising efforts." All demonstrate the value of records for holding every person or organization with a public trust responsible to that public as the higher authority.

Corporate memory has become a research cottage industry, partly because the Information Age has become as much characterized by the drowning of organizations and individuals in information as by the growing availability of greater quantities of information on any conceivable topic. Studies of organizational memory have identified every conceivable source for such memory, ranging from the literal memories of people to institutional symbols to warehouses of information including records. Corporate memory is probably the closest to what those engaged in the debate about the publication of documentary sources hold sacred regarding the value of records, although those concerned with corporate memory perceive it as a far broader idea of everything that is of potential use to the functioning of the organization.

The value of records for memory has become more evident in the last decade, as the Cold War has ebbed and records related to it and most of the major events in the twentieth century have come under closer scrutiny because of the opening of millions of previously unavailable records. Early in 1997, for example, a 1946 American intelligence memorandum and the transcript of a 1945 military interrogation of the Nazi official responsible for Germany's gold department during the Second World War became available through declassification by the National Archives. The documents revealed the degree in which the Swiss had been involved in helping Nazi leaders hide gold in Spain and Portugal, gold that most assume was the result of seizures of fortunes of European Jewish families and companies. The subsequent announcement that a guard at one of the Swiss banks had stopped the destruction of records, supposedly a mistake, related to the transfer of this Nazi gold only made these and other records seem that much more significant. Examples such as these appear in the newspaper and through news services every day, each confirming the importance of records to our continued understanding of ourselves and society.

In none of this discussion of the values of records did the concept of historical value appear at the top of the list, although clearly those records with such research value can fit into any of the broader categories of evidence, accountability, and memory. It is in this perspective that the crisis over commission funding and prioritization of documentary editing has to be viewed. It makes little difference what the commission's original mandate required, since it was formed long before the transformation of recordkeeping technologies requiring the commission's priorities to be altered if it intends to be able to assist in the maintenance of post–World War II documentary heritage. The arguments about the value of the documentary editions for the American public's recognition of its past as a nation sound compelling, but regulating the rise of electronic recordkeeping systems has a much greater stake in this. As to the exclusion of constituent groups in the shifting of the commission strategic plan, all constituencies have been long represented and the issue has more to do with the differences between the historical scholarship of the documentary editors and the mission of preserving the documentary heritage held by archivists. Dismissing the potential impact of a small amount of commission funding on the management of electronic records misses the point, since a number of relatively modest investments in this realm by the commission have provided significant positive strides.[53] And, finally, the pleas for not having constituencies fight among themselves over a small pool of funds sounds noble, except that we must ask whether these are really constituencies at all in the larger battle for our documentary heritage.

In a 1791 letter from Thomas Jefferson to pioneer editor Ebenezer Hazard, Jefferson mused on the loss of the records of the American Revolution: "The lost cannot be recovered; but let us save what remains: not by vaults and locks which fence them from the public eye and use, in consigning them to the waste of time, but by such a multiplication of copies, as shall place them beyond the reach of accident." It is difficult to imagine that if Jefferson were alive today he would not be concerned with harnessing the Internet or the World Wide Web to provide this multiplication of copies. It was Jefferson, after all, who tried to perfect a portable version of the "polygraph" in the early nineteenth century to make his correspondence more productive. I can see him now learning to use an electronic mail system, while worrying about whether his papers would be preserved for posterity. I can see him wanting to talk with Bill Gates about this. But would we be able to help him?

NOTES

1. Additional information about the commission and its strategic plan can be found at its homepage, http://gopher.nara.gov/nara/nhprc.

2. This statement is available at http://www.indiana.edu/~oah/nl/nares297.html.

3. Her statement was posted to the Archives and Archivists Listserv on February 26, 1997.

4. Smock was a leading figure in the 1980s arguing that a number of professional associations should band together to create a coalition for raising funds from the private sector and public agencies for a trust fund for supporting a variety of projects, from documentary editions to archival processing work to educational ventures and professional publications. I was on the Society of American Archivists Council when this idea was suggested. The SAA seriously discussed it, but the idea never got off the ground, primarily because it emerged too late in the Bicentennial of the Constitution for the effort to get organized as well as was necessary. There were also too many different agendas present in the proposal, failing to take into account the differences between archival work, the research interests of historians, and the numerous other reasons archival records need to be preserved and managed.

5. His statement, "News from the Archivist of the United States: NHPRC Revises Its Plan," is available at http://www.indiana.edu/~oah/nl/na0297.html.

6. See "NHPRC: NHPRC Plan Revisions February 1997 Action," at http://gopher.nara.gov/nara/nhprc/action.html.

7. A basic orientation to the early history of American documentary editing can be

gained by reading Lester J. Cappon, "American Historical Editors Before Jared Sparks," *William and Mary Quarterly*, third series, 30, no. 3 (1973): 375–400.

8. Bert James Lowenberg, *American History in American Thought: Christopher Columbus to Henry Adams* (New York: Simon and Schuster, 1972) provides ample discussion of these editorial projects.

9. David D. Van Tassel, *Recording America's Past: An Interpretation of the Development of Historical Studies in America 1607–1884* (Chicago: University of Chicago Press, 1960).

10. Victor Gondos, Jr., *J. Franklin Jameson and the Birth of the National Archives 1906–1926* (Philadelphia: University of Pennsylvania Press, 1981).

11. Mary A. Giunta, "The NHPRC: Its Influence on Documentary Editing, 1964–1984," *American Archivist* 49, no. 2 (1986): 134–141.

12. G. Thomas Tanselle, "The Editing of Historical Documents," *Studies in Bibliography* 31 (Charlottesville: Bibliographical Society of the University of Virginia by the University Press of Virginia, 1978) and issued as a separate pamphlet.

13. Elizabeth Hamer Kegan, "A Becoming Regard to Posterity," *American Archivist* 40, no. 1 (1977): 5–15.

14. Constance B. Schulz, "'From Generation Unto Generation: Transitions in Modern Documentary Historical Editing," *Reviews in American History* 16, no. 3 (1988): 337–350.

15. Giunta, "The NHPRC."

16. Charles T. Cullen, "Casual Observer Beware: The Need for Using Scholarly Editions," *Prologue* 21, no. 1 (1989): 68–74.

17. For my full view on this study, see Richard Cox, "Archivists and the Use of Archival Records: Or, A View from the World of Documentary Editing," *Provenance* 9 (1991 [1992]): 89–110. The study is Ann D. Gordon, *Using the Nation's Documentary Heritage: The Report of the Historical Documents Study* (Washington, D.C.: National Historical Publications and Records Commission in cooperation with the American Council of Learned Societies, 1992).

18. Gordon, *Using*, p. 35.

19. Gordon, *Using*, p. 69.

20. Gordon, *Using*, p. 83.

21. Gordon, "A Future for Documentary Editions: The Historical Documents Study," *Documentary Editing* 14 (March 1992): 6.

22. Gordon, "A Future," p. 6.

23. Gordon, "A Future," p. 7.

24. Gordon, *Using*, p. 89.

25. Gordon, *Using*, p. 90.

26. Paul H. Bergeron, "True Valor Seen: Historical Editing," *American Archivist* 34, no. 3 (1971): 259–264.

27. Jack Hitt, "In the Franklin Factory," *Lingua Franca* 7 (February 1997): 30–38.

28. Jack Hitt, "Devolving History," *New York Times*, 27 January 1997, p. A17.

29. The best treatment of the early development of the modern American archival profession remains William F. Birdsall, "The American Archivists' Search for Professional Identity, 1909–1936," Ph.D. diss., University of Wisconsin–Madison, 1973.

30. See Richard Cox, *American Archival Analysis: The Recent Development of the Archival Profession in the United States* (Metuchen, N.J.: Scarecrow Press, 1990).

31. Alan B. Spitzer, *Historical Truth and Lies about the Past: Reflections on Dewey, Dreyfus, de Man, and Reagan* (Chapel Hill: University of North Carolina Press, 1996).

32. See, for example, Edward T. Linenthal and Tom Engelhardt, eds., *History Wars: The Enola Gay and Other Battles for the American Past* (New York: Metropolitan Books, 1996) and Philip Nobile, ed., *Judgment at the Smithsonian* (New York: Marlowe and Co., 1995).

33. Publications on this topic are far too numerous to cite or even to summarize, but the implications of such writings for archival writing have been explored in Richard Cox, "The Concept of Public Memory and Its Impact on Archival Public Programming," *Archivaria* 36 (Autumn 1993): 122–135, included in chapter 6.

34. Michael Heim, *The Metaphysics of Virtual Reality* (New York: Oxford University Press, 1993). See also his *Electric Language: A Philosophical Study of Word Processing* (New Haven, Conn.: Yale University Press, 1987).

35. It is interesting to note that in other contexts we have used the length of time to edit and publish texts as an illustration of the problems of technology and language. Johanna Neuman, in her *Lights, Camera, War: Is Media Technology Driving International Politics?* (New York: St. Martin's Press, 1996), p. 55, noted that evidence for the burden of printing in China, with its 80,000 symbols in its language, is that "it took 23 years to edit and print the 130 volumes of Confucian classics." Such a time frame for one of these editorial projects would be considered extraordinary.

36. Ian Buruma, *The Wages of Guilt: Memories of War in Germany and Japan* (New York: Meridian, 1994) and Mike Wallace, *Mickey Mouse History and Other Essays on American History* (Philadelphia: Temple University Press, 1996).

37. The Society of American Archivists did issue a statement on the NHPRC situation, posted to this association's homepage at http://www.archivists.org. The statement expressed the importance of electronic records as a priority in managing the nation's documentary heritage.

38. Richard Z. Chesnoff, "Fifty Years Too Late, A Reckoning," *U.S. News and World Report* 122 (March 17, 1997): 43.

39. Frederika J. Teute, "Views in Review: A Historiographical Perspective on Historical Editing," *American Archivist* 43, no. 1 (1980): 43–56.

40. Included in Leslie W. Dunlap and Fred Shelley, eds., *The Publication of American Historical Manuscripts* (Iowa City: University of Iowa Libraries, 1976), p. 97–105.

41. Richard H. Kohn and George M. Curtis, III, "The Government, the Historical Profession, and Historical Editing: A Review," *Reviews in American History* 9, no. 2 (1981): 145–155.

42. Brooks D. Simpson, "Editors, Editing, and the Historical Profession," *OAH Newsletter* 17, no. 2 (1989): 8–9.

43. Richard J. Cox, "The Record: Is It Evolving?" *Records & Retrieval Report* 10 (March 1994) and "What's In A Name? Archives As a Multi-Faceted Term in the Information Professions," *Records & Retrieval Report* 11 (March 1995).

44. Denise Schmandt-Besserat, "The Earliest Precursor of Writing," in William S-Y. Wang, ed., *The Emergence of Language: Development and Evolution* (New York: W. H. Freeman and Co., 1991), pp. 31–45.

45. Rosalind Thomas, *Literacy and Orality in Ancient Greece* (Cambridge: Cambridge University Press, 1992).

46. M. T. Clanchy, *From Memory to Written Record: England, 1066–1307* (Cambridge, Mass.: Harvard University Press, 1979; rev. ed. 1993).

47. John O. Green, *The New Age of Communications* (New York: Henry Holt and Co., 1997).

48. Nicholas Negroponte, *Being Digital* (New York: Alfred A. Knopf, 1995).

49. James R. Beniger, *The Control Revolution: Technological and Economic Origins of the Information Society* (Cambridge, Mass.: Harvard University Press, 1986).

50. Clifford Lynch, "Searching the Internet," *Scientific American* 276, no. 3 (1997): 52–56.

51. Tom Blanton, ed., *White House E-Mail* (New York: New Press, 1995).

52. Kevin P. Kearns, *Managing for Accountability: Preserving the Public Trust in Public and Nonprofit Organizations* (San Francisco: Jossey-Bass Publishers, 1996).

53. See http://www.sis.pitt/~nhprc for links to the ways this project has been used.

9

History's Future: American Archivists, Cyberculture, and Stasis

INTRODUCTION: THE CULTURES OF RECORDS PROFESSIONALS IN THE INFORMATION AGE

Culture is a complex concept. A half century ago American anthropologists cataloged 164 definitions of culture, and the list has expanded since then.[1] My aim here is to draw on what constitutes a "culture" in order to explore what is happening to the records professional in a period of rapid societal change and to speculate on the role of educators. For this purpose, I am paraphrasing a straightforward dictionary definition of culture. By the culture of records professionals, I mean the "integrated pattern of human knowledge, belief, and behavior that depends upon [the records professional's] capacity for learning and transmitting knowledge to succeeding generations [of records professionals]," the "customary beliefs, social forms, and material traits of a [professional] group," and the "set of shared attitudes, values, goals, and practices that characterizes a [professional group]."[2] Such a definition should prompt archivists and records managers to re-consider their beliefs and behaviors, social forms, and shared values and practices—all formed *before* the advent of the computer, elaborate communication and social networks such as the World Wide Web, and the preeminence of *virtual* over *reality*. As records professionals, responsible for caring for the documentary heritage *and* documenting society, we need to understand both our societal and professional cultures. Are these cultures compatible, supportive, or competitive?

THE PERSISTENT AND CURRENT ARCHIVAL CULTURE

We can detect the professional culture by considering the intersection of archivists and the World Wide Web. A remarkable number of archives and records programs are creating sites on the Web. There may not be a broad range of reasons *why* these programs are devoting resources to this activity. *Access*, the preeminent explanation for creating archives and records "homepages," can be accomplished or enhanced in this fashion, but there are as many unknown consequences as there are proven, tested, and reliable techniques in such ventures.[3] Part of this relates to a crucial aspect of the American archival culture, the prevailing need to create means to make archival and historical records accessible *without* determining need or gathering data for what these means should be. This can be seen in the *most* recent form of archival descriptive standards, Encoded Archival Description (EAD). As one of the pioneers of EAD, Daniel V. Pitti, remarks, "The chief motivation for developing EAD was to provide a tool to help mitigate the fact that the geographic distribution of collections severely limits the ability of researchers, educators, and others to locate and use primary sources." EAD was tied to "emerging computer hardware and software technology . . . [and] advances in standards and network communications." These latter technical advantages raised up the idea of "universal access" and the "means to make our collections accessible to educators and students at all levels and to the general public."[4] This sounds noble, but it does presuppose a number of not readily obvious matters—the delivery technology itself does *not* bring substantial issues, the *undefined* public desires access to archival and historical records, and the traditional concept of archival finding aids work in the emerging modern cyberculture. In other words, the values of the professional culture, where access is deemed a good and desirable objective, may have been confused with contrasting values of the larger society in which we live and work; privacy, as just one example, may be deemed more important in many situations.[5]

There are other problems. There *is* a *system* to designing Web sites that meet users' needs, and there has been an increasing amount of reflection about this. There is also another challenge in the formulation of systems. Systems analysts and designers are increasingly aware that even *good* systems create new, unanticipated, and major problems, reminding us of the enduring, engrossing, and exhausting search for perfect solutions or "magic bullets" in designing any kind of system, especially those built on technological imperatives. A recent study of systems reveals the degree of different effects of systems, the complexity of relationships between all actors in a system, and the amazing interactivity of the relations in any system.[6] This seems particularly relevant for modern records professionals, especially as they become engaged using EAD standards to harness the power of the World Wide Web without understanding that the use of the Web is, in effect, operating in a very open, always changing system, creating a layering effect of new and maybe more complex issues about access expectations, archival constituencies, and reference archivist and researcher interactions. Yet, judging by the kinds of archives homepages appearing on the Web, the archival culture suggests that records professionals do not appreciate such challenges. A significant portion of the archives do not include clear mission statements (losing the opportunity to use the Web for public advocacy of the importance of archives and historical records), most do not yet provide searchable indexes of their finding aids and other catalogs (certainly minimizing the power of the Web to enhance the location of source materials), a miniscule number provide direct access to electronic records systems or to digitized collections (precisely what most Web browsers and searchers *might* be looking for), and, finally, a surprisingly small group include direct electronic reference capability via electronic mail on their homepage (virtually a contradiction of the purpose of the World Wide Web).[7]

One might dismiss the current problems with archivists' utilization of the Web as the result of a new technology *and* the profession's struggles to use new technologies with limited resources and already heavy responsibilities. There is some validity with such a view, but are the problems the manifestation of the archival culture? It seems as if much of the archival community's Web efforts have built on the foundation of the historian/humanist as the *primary* user of archives, while the continuing public controversies and debates about the evidence of the past (such as the Enola Gay exhibition and repatriations for Holocaust survivors) suggest a broader community consisting of politicians, scholars, veterans, journalists, and school children. Besides, we know that humanists have a long way to go in utilizing the technologies, from their own availability to hardware and economic resources, orientation to print and certain kinds of scholarship, to resolving problems such as selection and copyright.[8] Historians and humanists remain, in the eyes of many archivists the *desired* users of their records, an audience betraying the fact that many archivists continue to come from these disciplines and even see themselves as members of these groups when these disciplines themselves are fractured.

A debate on the Archives and Archivists listserv in July 1998, featuring at least fifty individuals in an intense discussion for over a week, demonstrates this problem. Ostensibly about the history requirements for entry-level hiring by the National Archives, the discussion revealed many clues about the profession, including a lack of consensus about education and mission, a surprisingly poor understanding about history, and the continuing degree of antipathy between historians, archivists, public historians, records managers, and librarians. The question never discussed in this debate was *what* or *whose history*? The debate not only revealed the sterility of the National Archives entry-level job requirements, but the problems of knowledge about history and historical research reflected by the archivists participating in this debate. History is hailed by some as the great mantra of archival knowledge, but historical knowledge itself has come under question. Critical of the efforts to find a new kind of objectivity in a renewed interest in professionalism, David Harlan writes, "Now, as we approach the end of the millennium, some conservative historians have talked themselves into believing that the Reign of Theory is finally over, that the revolution has spent itself, that we can all go back to the archives."[9] Harlan also writes that the value of some of the new literary criticism for helping historians to understand the present value of texts does not get taught in graduate history programs: "Rather than teaching students how to use historical texts to imagine new arrangements of thought and desire, we teach them to search out the 'discursive structures' and 'textual practices' of the culture in which the text was written. . . . [I]nstead of teaching our students to be alert, responsive, and resourceful, we teach them how to analyze documents. The result, of course, is that they read complex texts as if they were bills of lading."[10] So, the *very* history being defended by archivists is a history moving historians away from thinking about some of the fundamental aspects of the nature of records and recordkeeping systems. If one counters by arguing that it is the *subject* knowledge in history courses that is more important, we are left with the ludicrous spectacle of trying to figure out what subject knowledge an archivist would have to master *before* becoming an archivist, and this is virtually an impossible task.

Another persistent aspect of the archival culture with dubious consequences for laboring in modern cyberculture is an orientation to conservative practices with electronic information technology. This is natural, given the archivist's mission to preserve records with continuing value, but it often works against the tendency to experiment with new and emerging systems to preserve the records created in these systems or to build new alliances and partnerships to determine how to maintain electronic records. Much has improved since I wrote my first study on the American archivist's ambiguous relationship with electronic records (we have research agendas, research projects, more graduate courses, better continuing education, and better educated individuals entering the profession),[11] but there are immense inconsistencies continuing to plague archivists and helping to bolster societal stereotypes, hardly making it easier for them to deal with such concerns. Are archivists considering, for example, all the potential issues regarding their use of the World Wide Web? The answer seems to be a definite "no." A recent study considers Web postings as official records, but it discovers that most state government records programs are not dealing with Web sites at all, taking one of three positions—being totally unaware, seeming to be unsure how to apply knowledge, or demonstrating being incapable of doing anything. Fourteen states have some sort of guidelines or policies, but only one state (Texas) specifically addressed Web sites as records. One of the most interesting points raised by this study is that archivists think publications have permanent value, a disturbing revelation because Web sites are, at the least, publications and deserve to be maintained as such.[12] This has been confirmed in an article by a librarian, arguing for the need to create an archive of Web sites, who seems unaware that there are archivists out there working on such problems.[13] Another, more dramatic, example is the continuing litigation involving Presidents Reagan and Bush over efforts to destroy the records in an electronic mail system used by the National Security Council in international and covert operations. While the case has gone through many stages, from debates about the nature of records to technical issues about the maintenance of electronic records to concerns about the reliability of standard records practices like scheduling, the more disturbing element has been the stances of the U.S. National Archives in defending practices seemingly inconsistent with federal records legislation and records management best practices.[14]

These issues point to an archival culture best characterized by the word "stasis." Stasis refers to a "state of static balance or equilibrium: stagnation." It derives from the Greek word meaning the "act or condition of standing, stopping."[15] Archival stasis is probably the result of the inherently conservative nature of the archival community, stemming from its mandate to maintain records of continuing value. It is similar to what Dan Lacy has described about oral cultures: "Because of the almost desperate concern of oral societies to preserve the knowledge they held, change was feared as the bringer of loss, not sought as the path to gain. The idea of 'progress' as the normal flow of history did not exist; indeed, history itself was not seen as a flow but as at best a circling stasis. A deep-rooted conservatism characterized all oral communities."[16] This may seem to be an unfair portrait of the archival community given the increasing number of digitization projects going on and the building and refining of Web sites by archives programs. Yet, beneath it all there seems to be an attitude of business as usual—digitization merely replaces microforms as a means to preserve records, Web sites merely replace entries in print publications, and new descriptive standards such as EAD merely perpetuate traditional notions of finding aids. It is hard to discover rationales for these new endeavors and, more importantly, explanations for how the Web will support the archival mission. How do these efforts fit into the nature of the Web? The electronic highway may, according to one commentator, "soon" "be more like a warehouse filled with fragments of recorded sound, visual images, and printed material that electronically cruising subscribers can combine and recombine to their own tastes and purposes."[17] How do archivists' efforts fit into this warehouse? Is a warehouse the appropriate term for what archivists and records managers want to accomplish? If so, how do they participate in building and managing a new societal information warehouse? If not, how do archivists proceed to demonstrate that they have a very different role, that the mission to preserve and maintain evidence does not fit into the warehouse analogy?

Educators have an important role to play in such professional debates, as seen in the change in computer literacy for practicing archivists. Twenty years ago computer literacy was not an issue and hardly mentioned in job advertisements. Given the increasing use of automated bibliographic systems and the growth in dependence on electronic records systems, computer literacy is now mentioned frequently and as particular applications and skills in most position announcements. Both archivists and educators encourage students to take courses in technology (often taught by instructors with no concept of or sensitivity to records and archives) or to push out traditional emphases in courses in order to squeeze in more technology. Part of the problem has been, obviously, that what has passed for education "programs" has been little more than apprenticeship systems with a couple of courses and a heavy dose of fieldwork in the *real* archives.

The problem is actually much more complicated. An examination of entry-level archives positions (defined as positions requiring *less* than two years experience) from 1976 through 1997 reveals that there has been very little change in these position requirements, other than the growth in computer applications and computer literacy. Educational requirements, knowledge areas, archival functions and position responsibilities, a demand for organizational and communications or interpersonal skills, and the kinds of organizations hiring records professionals *all* remain remarkably *unaffected* through these two decades. Remarkable is the right word given the impact of personal computing, high-speed telecommunications networks, *and* renewed interests in records for accountability, evidence, and societal or corporate memory.[18] Yet, the position advertisements do *not* reflect an orientation to a recovery of the concept of "record" or the renewal of commitment to "recordkeeping" systems as reflected in a variety of professional musings by such a diverse group as Bearman, Duranti, Hedstrom, McKemmish, and myself.[19] In other words, even with the disparity of viewpoints represented by such authors, educational programs, where such diversity can be made of good use and where both new and traditional ideas can be considered, seem *disconnected* from the field or lack an authority of leadership to *change* the field. Again, there is an overwhelming professional stasis affecting both the academy and jobs in the real world.

CYBERCULTURE

What does cyberculture do to a professional culture, such as archivists, that must *directly* contend with all of its implications and ramifications? "Cyberspace" may be the place to start. Cyberspace was coined by novelist William Gibson in *Neuromancer* (1984), referring to an "artificial environment created by computers." The term has been adopted by critics and supporters of the use of computers. As one observer sees it, "At the root of Gibson's notion of computer-simulated worlds and electronically assisted experience is the prospect of a meeting of machine and human at a near-organic level."[20] It is precisely these kinds of ideas that people have become more cognizant both of a *distinct* cyberculture as well as the impact of computers on society and its culture.[21]

There are aspects of cyberculture counter to an archival culture. The use of electronic information technology has led to talk of a "permanent technological revolution." In this view, "anything that really works is already obsolete."[22] Another expert on computer technology believes that there is "no status quo."[23] Some critics argue that this relentless pursuit of speed *and* change can result in a condition that is similar to the slowness or steadiness exhibited by archivists: "Faster and faster can only mean, in the end, stasis. The logical outcome of efficiency is uselessness: solving problems has no point but the ultimate elimination of problem-solving itself. What is the point of being able to read a page every three seconds? To read every book ever written? Then what? Meanwhile, the vehicles of our speed ruin the planet as fast as we move around it."[24] It is this aspect of cyberculture, the speed and change, *even* if such factors twist back on themselves to result in a new kind of technocratic stagnation, that the records professional must learn to cope with. After all, individuals' expectations about access to information in records will be preconditioned by how they access other information. They will probably be less interested in the fact that the information they acquire from archivists derives from *evidence* than in how fast, efficient, and in what form they can receive it. Are prospective records professionals being taught to work in such organizational environments?

This requires educators to focus their students on *understanding* how technology influences traditional and new communications systems. For example, the developing software, networks, and hardware have all worked to bring a *renewed* interest in the value, design, and future of the printed book. The discussion about the book in the modern Information Age is a reminder that technology does have a profound impact on culture and especially on culture associated with information. It is possible to associate the increased use of printed books with the establishment of another technology, electricity: "The role of electricity in reading was to be sure, indirect—extending the environment in which reading took place—but it was no less profound in its empowerment of the written word than it had been with the telegraph in the past and would be with the online network in the future, where electricity would literally carry encodings of printed words."[25] Such views have been countered with more strident notions of the end of reading. Michael Heim glimpses into the differences of networks from books, arguing that "books in the medieval period were far from indifferent receptacles of information. Reading was a *practice* in the strict sense of the term, a discipline and a way of life. Active reading was connected with prayer and the transformation of the spirit." Now, "digital writing turns the private solitude of reflective reading and writing into a public network where the personal symbolic framework needed for original authorship is threatened by linkage with the total textuality of human expressions."[26] It is why some are now arguing for the placement of studies in the history of reading and readership in library and information science schools.[27] It is not hard to imagine that the threat of information technology to the long-term maintenance of books, libraries, and other information sources has been a contributing factor to the increased hiring by such schools of regular faculty with expertise on archives and records.

Part of archivists' responsibility is to place students *not* only in the world of records and recordkeeping systems (itself an improvement over the long-standing tradition of teaching students how to master content and to judge value for those desiring access to the content of records) but within the emerging cyberculture with the culture of the organizations and other entities that create records. Wiegand, arguing for a different focus in library schools, laments that the typical curriculum stresses access, meaning we "treat information primarily as an object" and ignore other scholarship that demonstrates the complexity and dynamism of information.[28] Archival educators, likewise, can and do slip into teaching students to manage records as objects or artifacts, as neutral and discrete blobs of stuff awaiting some scholar or other researcher to come and use it—*and*, in some magical fashion, to give these things *value*. Some advocate that archivists need to understand the cyberculture by placing themselves in it, countering the postmodern view that Internet technology is trying to help people escape from the real body. They see changes, but ones that ''can be addressed as questions of emerging structures of interaction and reorganization of social boundaries that can occur in any medium of communication.'' Such critics adopt the view that ''people are engaged in a constant effort to structure experience together and to establish order in conventions of discourse so that shared meanings are possible.'' They perceive the world as a society: ''Another way to cast the fragmentation that is claimed for Internet activity is to view Internet as a new social domain where boundaries that pertain to the physical world or prior domains of convention not yet have been worked out.''[29] Somewhere in this ''social domain'' or the intersection of this domain with institutions, professional cultures, and the legal and regulatory realms is *where* archival students will take the message about the importance of records and evidence.

RE-EXAMINING ARCHIVAL CULTURE

Should archivists be worrying about the demise of their species in the Brave New World of cyberspace? Carl Sagan describes a ''species'' as a ''group that can produce fertile offspring by crosses within but not outside itself.''[30] This is difficult for archivists to imagine how to accomplish. They have splintered among themselves—records managers from archivists, government records administrators from manuscript curators and other archivists, historically trained and oriented archivists from information science–educated records professionals, and preservation administrators from records managers and archivists. Some of this splintering, especially away from historians and other humanists, has been painful and distracting—a debate still *not* resolved after sixty years.[31] The real debate and worry ought to be discerning what the role of archivists in cybernetic culture should be and where this culture raises archival issues—evidence, reliability, preservation, accountability. In other words, how can a species continue that, on one hand, seems no longer able to breed its own and, on the other, seems predestined to fail if it tries to mate with outside professionals—namely, information resources managers, knowledge experts, information scientists, information policy administrators, and chief information officers? Archivists need to re-imagine their culture by taking some very deliberate actions, and each of these actions has a central role for educators of archivists and other records professionals.

Archivists and records managers must become engaged in ''public'' scholarship. By this I mean we need to see more archivists, especially educators, either on their own or working with others such as journalists and freelance writers, address the importance of records in a manner engaging *public* debate and interest. Archivists are improving in this regard, in that the Society of American Archivists now has an array of position statements on copyright, intellectual property, the mismanagement of Internal Revenue Service records, grand jury records, resources for documentary editing, the scheduling of electronic records, digital preservation, and space for the storage of federal archives.[32] *But* the society still has *no* effective and active lobbying mechanism, has meager resources for getting its positions onto the table for consideration by policymakers, and remains far more reactive than proactive in its public awareness efforts.

Public scholarship raises the level of awareness in other ways and in other venues. If one of the leading information scientists/theorists, Nicholas Negroponte, can write an accessible and popular book about the potential replacing of traditional books and records with electronic systems, creating *both* excitement and dismay (depending on your point of view), why can't someone from the records professions do likewise?[33] If a novelist can lead a public outcry about the discarding of old library catalogs because of online access catalogs, why could not an archivist or records manager bring attention to the challenges posed to society by the eradication of some traditional records systems, if such a case is merited, or at least graphically portray the importance of preservation and the dangers imposed by digitization?[34] Records professionals need to captivate some interest in the many *records* issues being brought to the fore by the reliance on the computer, but it seems that both librarians *and* records professionals are missing opportunities to build a stronger case for their missions in the public arena. In a typical influential journal, *The Atlantic*, we can find over seven recent years (1990–1996) articles on books, computers, deciphering ancient languages, software, library architecture, telecommunications and democracy, the First Amendment, virtual reality, educational uses of computers, secrecy, a speculation about the end of the book, the challenges of saving *too* much in the modern Information Age, and *one* essay about the Thomas Edison archives—but not *one* essay written by an archivist, records manager, or anyone associated with the records professions.[35] Archivists may have no individuals *prominent* enough to be published in such a publishing venue—but these essays were authored by freelance writers, editors, an architecture professor, a sociologist, lawyers, a journalist, a science writer, and a management consultant. Is this the result of a *low*-profile profession (despite the importance of records) or simply a *failure* of collective will?

A substantial part of teaching, if not recruiting individuals to become archivists, needs to be devoted to equipping students to consider writing about crucial concerns for a wider audience. How is this accomplished? One way is to have students read broadly beyond the more narrowly focused, albeit essential, professional literature into areas considering topics with value for understanding both records and archives. The engaging, well-researched, scholarly and popular literature on public memory is an example.[36] It can introduce students to how *others* see and understand records, how individuals address technical issues in a way that engages public interest, and help students to be exposed good writing in general. Such reading might assist students learn about how to prepare convincing arguments to non-records professionals, a task that is more crucial in today's organization and society for any individual working as an archivist or records manager. Students also can be required to do in-depth analyses of public debates featuring records (such as the continuing revelations about the Swiss banking industry, the Nazi regime, and the assets of Holocaust victims),[37] rather than only technical functions well-known to archivists and other records professionals. Since records professionals need to learn how to appraise, describe, preserve, and provide access to the records of these increasingly complex events and trends, there is much more to be gained by such exercises. Educators can request students to prepare writing assignments with very different audiences in mind—government officials and policymakers, the general public, scholars, journalists and the media, and the records creators—all of which can attune them to operating more positively in their complicated environments with diverse aims, languages, and mandates. Finally, *all* archives and records students should read newspapers and news magazines as a means of increasing their sensitivities about impacts on records, their creation, and their continuing use. Our understanding of the *context* of records and recordkeeping systems must be expanded to include not just the *immediate* warrants creating records but the political, economic, social, and cultural dimensions of breaking news. Who would have guessed that half-century-old routine Swiss banking accounts or internal memoranda governing the research activities of American tobacco companies would be daily *front* page news in major newspapers and news magazines.[38]

Given the decided lack of writing in critical public journals and other outlets, an outsider to archives might assume that records professionals are spending their time building a professional and research literature. Such is not the case. The professional journals often struggle for submissions. Not too many years ago, when editing the *American Archivist*, I presented a paper on the opportunities for and need of research in the profession; the paper was an effort *both* to characterize what had been done and to demonstrate that there was sufficient *applied* research needed (and perhaps being done but *not* written up for professional dissemination).[39] After my presentation, in the question and answer section of the session, the first questions expressed a lack of understanding about the need for research. What is the cause of such a problem? Is it a lack of imagination? Is it a response by a profession too far overloaded with responsibilities and other practical problems? Are we attracting the wrong people to the archival and records professions in general? Is it the result of an archival culture more based on clerical responsibilities and attitudes than on a common professional knowledge or a commitment to a professional scholarship?

Whatever attributes are conspiring to work against support for research about records and recordkeeping systems, archives and their selection, preservation, and use, and the management of current records for evidence, information, and knowledge sources, archival education programs have a *very* important role in changing this aspect of our professional culture. Over the past two decades graduate programs of all sizes and shapes have been formed, and they certainly constitute the *primary* means by which individuals entering the profession become aware of what constitutes archival knowledge, how that knowledge relates to practice, and how and why this knowledge is shaped and changed as record-keeping systems, warrants for records, and demands for records and archives continue to evolve. Yet, *most* archival graduate programs have modest, *if any*, requirements for research about archival functions, responsibilities, or images. This is despite the immense gaps in knowledge about virtually *every* aspect of archival work (size of the professional community, resources, job profiles, and cost analysis of our basic work) affecting the ability of each professional records manager to do much more than guess about what decisions they are making within their institutions on a wide array of activities. It is hard to imagine asking *why* research is needed. Perhaps the educators are to blame for this—for having allowed their education programs to grow little beyond rudimentary training, remaining so wedded to *practice* that they cannot see where the role of good professional research and scholarship fits into their societal mission. One of our more articulate archival educators, James M. O'Toole, puts this into theological terms: "Too many believe that everything which can be said about archives has already been said, either in the Old Testament (Jenkinson) or in the New (Schellenberg). . . . Archival educators, however, must be the ones who recognize, as John Henry Newman reminded theologians, that doctrine develops, that each new generation comes progressively to a new understanding of the tasks to be done and why they are important. Thus, educators have a responsibility to explore new approaches to archival truths, both with their students in the classroom and in their research and writing. Teaching and research are intimately connected; that both of these are poorly developed in the archives profession is hardly an accident."[40] That this has not occurred is indicated when O'Toole states that "between 1990 and 1996 . . . the *American Archivist* published 169 substantial research articles and only 17 of them (ten percent) were contributed by full-time archival teachers."[41] This is even worse than it sounds, because it does not mean that seventeen *different* educators contributed such articles; in fact, four of seventeen were written by me.

If research is tied to classrooms, it is here that we may find one of the most important areas requiring serious reformation. In the United States, archival education, for the most part, has remained tied for thirty years to an introductory course, an advanced course of some type, and a fieldwork or practicum experience, with the content or focus of these courses often dictated by whether the "program" is located in a history department or library and information science school. There are programs breaking away from this pattern. At my own school, as part of the master's in library and information science degree, we have *eight* courses in records and information resources management, archives and manuscripts management, archival representation (descriptive standards), library and archives preservation, preservation management, digital preservation, archival appraisal, and archival access and advocacy. This is, however, hardly the norm for American programs. O'Toole reveals that only about a third of archival programs even have *one* advanced seminar in addition to the basic course or have any kind of course concerned with automation or electronic records; he notes that the "apprenticeship model endures."[42]

It is with the content and requirements of the programs that the most serious flaws appear in preparing individuals to function as modern archivists. Again, O'Toole, in his examination of syllabi, finds a scenario that can only be described as potentially disastrous for *both* the new records professionals and for society and its institutions hiring these individuals to manage records and archives. He determines that these programs require little reading and, in general, an "unimpressive" work load. Most programs do not ask students to do much more than read a few basic textbooks, leading O'Toole to conclude that this is an "unfortunate expression of the profession's ambivalence toward its literature" and, "at worst, it is evidence of a deep anti-intellectualism."[43] This commentator limits his assessment to the use of the professional literature. I would go one step beyond this. It is imperative that educators introduce students to see the remarkable diversity of scholarship with implications for understanding records and archives—jurisprudence,[44] history,[45] public history,[46] bibliophiles,[47] information scientists,[48] sociologists,[49] geographers,[50] professional writers,[51] medical researchers,[52] anthropologists,[53] and even philosophers.[54] Delving into such studies can help future records professionals gain a better understanding of records and recordkeeping systems as well as help them communicate with other professionals in their own organizations. Educators must help records professionals develop a intellectual curiosity, assisting them to consider research and to take risks—both activities especially crucial in the emerging modern cyberculture.

Educators in other fields argue it is important to consider teaching more about *understanding* cyberculture, not just what others think cyberculture may or may not be. This assists students to see what interactivity or connectivity does for one's outlook on their society and world, a task that ought to be seen as doubly important for those of us teaching future records professionals.[55] Archivists and records managers, given a mission requiring them to work across organizational units and across a variety of institutions and social groups, must be able to work in both organizational and societal cultures. Interesting and provocative readings can be assembled to help students understand cyberspace as a social space, community, and its impact on personal and social identity—all with implications for how we understand the possible future of records in our organizations, homes, and other entities.[56]

There needs to be a transformation, then, in what passes for the content of our graduate archival education programs. There must be a firm grounding in the core knowledge of archival and records management principles, but these principles need to be related to the new and emerging records and information technologies. In the United States the traditional emphasis of education programs has been archival arrangement, description, and reference—usually related to scholarly users such as historians. There is a need for programs that also stress appraisal, access, preservation, advocacy and outreach while helping students first to understand that their responsibility is to comprehend records and record-keeping systems for purposes of accountability, evidence, and memory. This necessarily requires programs with more courses, a stronger interdisciplinary focus, and a research requirement.

Archival educators must work harder to develop stronger relationships with the field, establishing more rigorous requirements for hiring archivists and other records professionals. Earlier I referred to the remarkable lack of change over two decades of entry-level positions and the disappointing lack of change of the National Archives' hiring practice, itself reflecting little change for *over half a century*. What passed for education programs was too closely tied to everyday practice; these programs unabashedly developed to provide free or inexpensive labor for existing archives and records management operations, a relationship clearly reflected by the continuing *centrality* of fieldwork or practicum as a component of graduate education. Without getting into the myriad of problems posed by offering education that is really little more than *training*, what has also been reflected in the American profession's long-standing love affair with *basic* workshops,[57] archivists must nevertheless understand that the rapid change of recordkeeping in the typical office has not remained matched to what has been offered as course content in many graduate programs. This has been made more complicated by the fact that many graduate programs have been dependent on archives and records programs *not* representing the most current uses of emerging electronic information and recordkeeping technologies, grossly represented by many technological optimists who view "paperwork" as an evil to be eradicated (often not realizing that the new technologies represent as difficult and costly problems as the old paper-based systems).[58] All of this has led to a continuing separation between educators of records professionals, the organizations hiring records professionals, and the records professions themselves.

For years there has been angst at professional conferences and in the professional literature when "theory" and "practice" is discussed. Theory is deemed by many working professionals to be impractical, academic, and useless for real-life situations. Practice is deemed by some educators to be clerical, low-level, technician work—intellectually vacuous by academic or scholarly standards. Some of this tension is typical of that usually found between academics and practitioners in many disciplines, probably exaggerated a bit more in the professional schools situated (sometimes uneasily) in universities. This context has to be kept in mind when practitioners issue calls for archival educators to be sensitive to job requirements and practical knowledge or when educators call on employers to provide input about the kinds of knowledge, skills, and attitudes needed by them of their graduates. While there needs to be increased dialogue between employers and educators, the roles of these two groups are quite disparate. Educators are, by necessity, elitists, in the sense that they are committed to recruiting the *best* students to give them the *best* education in order to equip them for the *best* jobs. Employers are, by necessity, pragmatists, in the sense that they need to balance many legal, organizational, and social requirements and still get the job done effectively, efficiently, and economically. Somewhere in between is a place where employers and educators can work cooperatively to advance entry-level requirements so that the archives and records programs are superbly staffed to meet the new recordkeeping challenges in organizations and society. The United States has been hurt by the loss of leadership by the National Archives in the definition of basic requirements for archivists, a diversity of educational "programs" ranging from single courses to full degrees, and a misplaced egalitarian bent that often results in a "dumbing down" of educational standards. As O'Toole called for a claim to research and publication by archival educators, it is clear that some of this research needs to be done about issues impacting on the education of records professionals, such as employment needs and graduates' placement and success as professionals.

A practical example of the kind of education I am considering here can be seen in how students approach the use of Web sites. Educators can teach students the technical details of building Web sites (although this is probably a short-term objective since more and more of our students will enter programs knowing the technical details) *or* they can work with them in *thinking* about how to use these sites. Having students reflect on purpose and content rather than the technical applications is how I conceive of the differences between education and training. I have already discussed some of the problems with how archivists are using Web sites, so how and what would I have students learn about the World Wide Web? Students can be asked to evaluate existing archives programs' Web sites in how and what they communicate to the public, their success in providing access to records, and their design and general usability. Students will find some surprising things, such as archivists' reliance on a professional jargon that is just as difficult for non-records professionals to wade through as the computer "technobabble" many of them complain about and the absence of reasonable efforts to help the public use their records. The latter is part of a lost opportunity to use the Web to reach the public about the nature, significance, and powerful potential uses of records.[59] Exploring such uses of the Web helps students to understand better both cyberculture and the manner in which records professionals reach or do not reach the public and policymakers with the value of records. This is a much different task than what is being attempted in many archives education programs—going far beyond teaching "tools" to instilling understanding. It cannot be accomplished, however, by assigning only basic archives texts, not pushing students to read widely and deeply, and moving only one level beyond apprentice systems.

CONCLUSIONS: RESURRECTING AN OLD CULTURE

If we understand the role that the early Irish played in the saving of the manuscripts of the ancient world, then we should begin to comprehend what archival educators need to be doing in the opening of the twenty-first century. Thomas Cahill chronicles the impact of the massive copying by medieval Irish monks and scribes, with this witty analysis: "They did not see themselves as drones. Rather, they engaged the text they were working on, tried to comprehend it after their fashion, and, if possible, add to it, even improve on it. In this dazzling new culture, a book was not an isolated document on a dusty shelf; book truly spoke to book, and writer to scribe, and scribe to reader, from one generation to the next. These books were, as we would say in today's jargon, open, interfacing, and intertextual—glorious literary smorgasbords in which the scribe often tried to include a bit of everything, from every era, language, and style known to him."[60] Archivists need to stop thinking of themselves as servants or drones and, instead, they should be striving to be imaginative, resourceful, outspoken, and risk takers. Their Web sites need to reflect this; their digitization projects need to be selected and presented in this way; and their working with electronic records ought to explore new and creative mechanisms to deliver records that instill an appreciation of records. Needless to say, none of this will probably happen unless it starts in the classroom with the educators and the students.

NOTES

1. "The Concept and Components of Culture: The Concept of Culture," *Britannica Online*, http://www.eb.com:180/cgi-bin/g?DocF=macro/5001/61/0.html; assessed September 8, 1998.

2. This definition is adapted from the *Merriam Webster Collegiate Dictionary*, part of *Britannica Online* at http://www.eb.com:180/alpha/lists.htcl?qu . . . ture&aDB =dictionary_alpha&nHits=10&mode=4. That professions are part of societal or corporate cultures and, as well, creators of their own cultures can be seen in the voluminous literature about professions; see, for example, Eliot Friedson, *Professionalism Reborn: Theory, Prophecy and Policy* (Chicago: University of Chicago Press, 1994).

3. See Richard Cox, "Access in the Digital Information Age and the Archival Mission: The United States," *Journal of the Society of Archivists* 19, no. 1 (1998): 25–40.

4. Daniel V. Pitti, "Encoded Archival Description: The Development of an Encoding Standard for Archival Finding Aids," *American Archivist* 60 (Summer 1997): 268–283 (quotations pp. 269 and 283).

5. For example, the poignant work by the daughter of the writer Bernard Malamud brings us this commentary: "Records of our bank account balances, medical prescriptions, and credit card purchases are considered saleable commodities, while we are denied our rightful ownership of this information. Yet society can only decide how to regulate these practices if we can determine what parts of privacy and private experience we wish to protect—and why." Janna Malamud Smith, *Private Matters: In Defense of the Personal Life* (Reading, Mass.: Addison-Wesley Publishing Co., 1997), pp. 11–12. Smith argues for greater personal privacy, as does Timothy Garton Ash, *The File: A Personal History* (New York: Random House, 1997). How are such concerns reconciled with the long-standing idea of universal access espoused by the American archival profession? It is *not* an easy reconciliation.

6. Robert Jervis, *System Effects* (Princeton, N.J.: Princeton University Press, 1998).

Stephen M. Walt, reviewing the Jervis book, concludes that "viewed as a whole, *System Effects* offers a sobering and valuable moral. Because everything is connected to everything else, even our greatest accomplishments will sow the seeds of future problems. Accepting that fact is itself an achievement, however, if it frees us from a fuitless search for 'magic bullets' or an unwarranted faith in the perfectibility of human societies." See Stephen M. Walt, "The Hidden Nature of Systems," *Atlantic Monthly* (September 1998): 130–134 (quotation p. 134).

7. An examination of three types of the preeminent forms of American archives—state government archives, academic archives, and state historical societies—and their respective sites on the World Wide Web seems to confirm such a bleak view. Of the state government archives (n = 43) 58.1% included a mission statement, 30.2% had searchable indexing, 4.6% provided direct access to electronic records, 11.6% included digitized full-text documents, and 32.6% enabled visitors to the site to contact reference staff by e-mail. For academic archives (n = 59), the respective figures are 59.3%, 23.7%, 0%, 11.9%, and 11.9% again. For state historical societies (n = 28), the respective figures are 57.1%, 28.6%, 0%, 10.7%, and 3.6%. An effort was made to find Web sites for all the state government and state historical societies, while the academic archives were selected by prominence of holdings and geographic distribution. My graduate student assistant, J. Christian Savine, conducted this review in the Summer of 1998.

8. Refer to "Computing and the Humanities: Summary of a Roundtable Meeting," American Council on Learned Societies, Occasional Paper No. 41 (1998) at http://www.acls.org/op41-i.htm.

9. David Harlan, *The Degradation of American History* (Chicago: University of Chicago Press, 1997), p. xx.

10. Harlan, *The Degradation of American History*, pp. 191–192.

11. See Richard Cox, *The First Generation of Electronic Records Archivists in the United States: A Study in Professionalization* (New York: Haworth Press, 1994), a study considering the evolution of work with electronic records from 1960 to 1990.

12. Charles R. McClure and J. Timothy Sprehe, *Analysis and Development of Model Quality Guidelines for Electronic Records Management in State and Federal Websites; Final Report January 1998* at http://istweb.syr.edu/~mcclure/nhprc/nhprc%final%20 rpt20in; pc20wp8.htm.

13. Carol Casey, "The Cyberarchive: A Look at the Storage and Preservation of Web Sites," *College & Research Libraries* 59 (July 1998): 304–310. Casey considers the fragility of Web sites and discusses collecting them onto CD-ROMs or creating archives sites on the Internet.

14. The fullest study on this case is David A. Wallace, "The Public's Use of Federal Recordkeeping Statutes to Shape Federal Information Policy: A Study of the Profs Case," Ph.D. diss., University of Pittsburgh, 1997. For a different view, see Tom Blanton, ed., *White House E-Mail: The Top Secret Computer Messages the Reagan/Bush White House Tried to Destroy* (New York: The New Press, 1995); Blanton has been one the leading litigants in the case, seeking to stop the destruction of the electronic mail messages.

15. *Merriam Webster Collegiate Dictionary*, at Britannica Online, http://www.eb.com: 180/alpha/lists.htcl?query=stasis&aDB=dictionary_alpha&nHits=10&mode=4,   retrieved September 9, 1998.

16. Dan Lacy, *From Grunts to Gigabytes: Communications and Society* (Urbana: University of Illinois Press, 1996), p. 6.

17. Paul Goldstein, *Copyright's Highway: From Gutenberg to the Celestial Jukebox* (New York: Hill and Wang, 1994), p. 200.

18. Richard J. Cox, "Employing Records Professionals in the Information Age: A Research Study," *Information Management Journal* 34 (January 2000): 18–33.

19. Listing all the works relevant to this matter would be daunting. David Bearman, *Electronic Evidence: Strategies for Managing Records in Contemporary Organizations* (Pittsburgh: Archives and Museum Informatics, 1994) is a pivotal work in the rediscovery of the record.

20. Robert Everett-Green, "Special Report: Cyberspace," *Britannica Online*, http://www.eb.com:180/cgi-bin/g?DocF=boy/96/J02670.html, accessed September 8, 1998.

21. For the diversity of literature, from the most utopian to the most cynical, refer to Richard Cox, "Drawing Sea Serpents: The Publishing Wars on Personal Computing and the Information Age," *First Monday* (May 1998).

22. Bruce Sterling, *The Hacker Crackdown: Law and Disorder on the Electronic Frontier* (New York: Bantam Books, 1992), p. 193.

23. Don Tapscott, *The Digital Economy: Promise and Peril in the Age of Networked Intelligence* (New York: McGraw-Hill, 1995), p. 11.

24. Mark Kingwell, "Fast Forward: Our High-Speed Chase to Nowhere," *Harper's* 296 (May 1998): 37–39, 42–46, 48 (quotations pp. 46, 48).

25. Paul Levinson, *The Soft Edge: A Natural History and Future of the Information Revolution* (New York: Routledge, 1997), pp. 71–72.

26. Michael Heim, *Electronic Language: A Philosophical Study of Word Processing* (New Haven, Conn.: Yale University Press, 1987), pp. 175, 215.

27. Wayne A. Wiegand, "Out of Sight, Out of Mind: Why Don't We Have Any Schools of Library and Reading Studies?" *Journal of Education for Library and Information Science* 38 (Fall 1997): 314–326.

28. Wiegand, "Out of Sight, Out of Mind," pp. 315–316.

29. Eleanor Wynn and James E. Katz, "Hyperbole over Cyberspace: Self-Presentation and Social Boundaries in Internet Home Pages and Discourse," *The Information Society* 13 (1997): 297–327 (quotations 298, 302, 305).

30. Carl Sagan, *The Dragons of Eden: Speculations on the Evolution of Human Intelligence* (New York: Ballantine Books, 1977), p. 22.

31. The endless debate about history and archives (archives and history) has produced a literature far too lengthy to summarize or describe in this brief chapter. For my own views, see chapter nine in my *American Archival Analysis: The Recent Development of the Archival Profession in the United States* (Metuchen, N.J.: Scarecrow Press, 1990), an essay then examining how archivists related to the public history movement of the 1970s and 1980s.

32. These position papers can be viewed at the society's Web site, http://www.archivists.org.

33. Nicholas Negroponte, *Being Digital* (New York: Alfred A. Knopf, 1995). I tried to respond to many of the issues raised by this author, at least about the book, in my "Debating the Future of the Book," *American Libraries* 28 (February 1997): 52–55.

34. Nicholson Baker's two controversial essays on "discards" and "books as furniture" can be found in his *The Size of Thoughts: Essays and Other Lumber* (New York: Vintage Books, 1997). I tried to respond to some of this in an essay co-authored with two doctoral students, Jane Greenberg and Cynthia Porter, "Access Denied: The Discarding of Library History," *American Libraries* 29 (April 1998): 57–61.

35. Pamela Petro, "Books as Works of Art," *The Atlantic* 266 (October 1990): 130–134; James Fallows, "Computers: IBM Van Winkle," ibid. 266 (November 1990): 153–154, 156; David Roberts, "The Decipherment of Ancient Maya," ibid. 268 (September 1991): 87–88, 90–92, 94–96, 98–100; James Fallows, "Hidden Powers," ibid. 269 (May 1992): 114–117; Witold Rybczynski, "Design: A Good Public Library," ibid. 270 (August 1992): 84–87; Amitai Etzioni, "Washington: Teledemocracy," ibid. 270 (October 1992): 34–35, 38–39; Wendy Kaminer, "Feminists against the First Amendment," ibid. 270 (November 1992): 110–112, 114–116, 118; James Fallows, "Computers: Crash-Worthy Speedster," ibid. 271 (February 1993): 103–108; Jacques Leslie, "Technology: MUDRoom," ibid. 272 (September 1993): 28, 30–32, 34; Sarah Finnie Rockwell, "Computers: Serious Fun," ibid. 272 (April 1994): 115–116, 118–120; James Fallows, "Technology: Open Secrets," ibid. 273 (June 1994): 46, 48–50; James Fallows, "Technology: Networking," ibid. 274 (July 1994): 34–36; Frederick Allen, "Notes & Comment: Unreasonable Facsimile," ibid. 274 (July 1994): 20, 22–23; D. T. Max, "The End of the Book?" ibid. 274 (September 1994): 61–62, 64, 67–68, 70–71; Edward Lazarus, "The Law: Electronic Hash," ibid. 274 (October 1994): 36, 38, 40–41; James Fallows, "Computers: Flat Growth," ibid. 274 (November 1994): 134–139; Peter F. Drucker, "The Age of Social Transformation," ibid. 274 (November 1994): 53–56, 59, 62, 64, 66–68, 71–72, 74–78, 80; James Fallows, "Computers: Not Yet Net," ibid. 275 (May 1995): 108–110, 112; Kathleen McAuliffe, "The Undiscovered World of Thomas Edison," ibid. 276 (December 1995): 80–83, 86, 88, 90, 92–93; James Fallows, "Computers: The Java Theory," ibid. 277 (March 1996): 113–117; Cullen Murphy, "Notes and Comments: Backlogs of History," ibid. 277 (May 1996): 20, 22.

36. The possibilities are nearly endless. An example of the scholarly literature is David Lowenthal, *The Heritage Crusade and the Spoils of History* (Cambridge: Cambridge University Press, 1996). An example of the popular literature is Ian Buruma, *The Wages of Guilt: Memories of War in Germany and Japan* (New York: Meridian, 1994). An example of another popular trade-published volume with direct implications about recordkeeping is Timothy Garton Ash, *The File: A Personal History*.

37. Tom Bower, *Nazi Gold: The Full Story of the Fifty-Year Swiss-Nazi Conspiracy to Steal Billions from Europe's Jews and Holocaust Survivors* (New York: HarperCollins Publishers, 1997); Isabel Vincent, *Hitler's Silent Partners: Swiss Banks, Nazi Gold, and the Pursuit of Justice* (New York: William Morrow and Co., 1997); Jean Ziegler, *The Swiss, the Gold, and the Dead*, trans. John Brownjohn (New York: Harcourt Brace and Co., 1998).

38. For the latter, see the disturbing Stanton A. Glantz, John Slade, Lisa A. Bero, Peter Hanauer, and Deborah E. Barnes, *The Cigarette Papers* (Berkeley: University of California Press, 1996).

39. The paper was subsequently published as "An Analysis of Archival Research, 1970–1992, and the Role and Function of the *American Archivist*," *American Archivist* 57 (Spring 1994): 278–288.

40. James M. O'Toole, "The Archival Curriculum: Where Are We Now?" *Archival Issues* 22, no. 2 (1997): 112–113.

41. O'Toole, "The Archival Curriculum," p. 105.

42. O'Toole, "The Archival Curriculum," pp. 106–107.

43. O'Toole, "The Archival Curriculum," pp. 108–109.

44. Ellen Alderman and Caroline Kennedy, *The Right to Privacy* (New York: Vintage Books, 1997).

45. Margo J. Anderson, *The American Census: A Social History* (New Haven, Conn.: Yale University Press, 1988); Ash, *The File: A Personal History*; M. T. Clanchy, *From Memory to Written Record: England 1066–1307*, 2nd ed. (Cambridge: Blackwell, 1993); Patricia Cline Cohen, *A Calculating People: The Spread of Numeracy in Early America* (Chicago: University of Chicago Press, 1982); David Cressy, *Coming Over: Migration and Communication Between England and New England in the Seventeenth Century* (Cambridge: Cambridge University Press, 1987); Margery W. Davies, *Woman's Place Is at the Typewriter: Office Work and Office Workers 1870–1920* (Philadelphia: Temple University Press, 1982); Patrick J. Geary, *Phantoms of Remembrance: Memory and Oblivion at the End of the First Millennium* (Princeton, N.J.: Princeton University Press, 1994); William V. Harris, *Ancient Literacy* (Cambridge, Mass.: Harvard University Press, 1989).

46. Shelley L. Davis, *Unbridled Power: Inside the Secret Culture of the IRS* (New York: HarperBusiness, 1997).

47. Nicholas A. Basbanes, *A Gentle Madness: Bibliophiles, Bibliomanes, and the Eternal Passion for Books* (New York: Henry Holt and Co., 1995).

48. James R. Beniger, *The Control Revolution: Technological and Economic Origins of the Information Society* (Cambridge, Mass.: Harvard University Press, 1986).

49. T. K. Bikson and E. J. Frinking, *Preserving the Present: Toward Viable Electronic Records* (The Hague: Sdu Publishers, 1993); Martha S. Feldman, *Order Without Design: Information Production and Policy Making* (Stanford, Calif.: Stanford University Press, 1989).

50. Kenneth E. Foote, *Shadowed Ground: America's Landscapes of Violence and Tragedy* (Austin: University of Texas Press, 1997).

51. Ian Frazier, *Family* (New York: HarperPerennial, 1994).

52. Glantz et al., *The Cigarette Papers*.

53. Jack Goody, *The Interface Between the Written and the Oral* (Cambridge: Cambridge University Press, 1987) and *The Logic of Writing and the Organization of Society* (Cambridge: Cambridge University Press, 1986).

54. Heim, *Electronic Language*.

55. See Leonard Williams, "Teaching Cyberian Politics," *First Monday* 3 (June 1998) at http://www.firstmonday.dk/issues/issue3_6/williams/index.html.

56. A good introduction to readings on cyberculture can be seen at the Research Center on Cyberculture Studies at http://otal.umd.edu/~rccs/biblio.html. This research center also provides links to undergraduate and graduate courses around the world on cyberculture, all of which include additional readings.

57. This was a recurrent theme in James M. O'Toole's "Curriculum Development in Archival Education: A Proposal," *American Archivist* 53 (Summer 1990): 460–466.

58. The classic comments on this would be Arno Penzias, *Digital Harmony: Business, Technology and Life After Paperwork* (New York: HarperBusiness, 1995)—whose title reflects his view about records and paperwork—and Thomas K. Landauer, *The Trouble with Computers: Usefulness, Usability, and Productivity* (Cambridge, Mass.: MIT Press, 1995)—who includes many references to complications caused by computers in orderly paperwork and recordkeeping.

59. Some of this utopian-like musing can be seen in the popular and oft-cited Howard Rheingold, *The Virtual Community: Homesteading on the Electronic Frontier* (New York: HarperPerennial, 1993).

60. Thomas Cahill, *How the Irish Saved Civilization: The Untold Story of Ireland's Heroic Role from the Fall of Rome to the Rise of Medieval Europe* (New York: Doubleday, 1995), p. 163.

Index

Access and privacy, 11–12, 178
Accountability: and appraisal, 103, 111–112; and documentary editing, 215, 216; and the education of archivists, 187, 235; and electronic records management, 55–56, 151; and media image of archives and records management, 5, 172, 216–217; and national system of records and archives administration, 72; and office automation, 48. *See also* Holocaust survivors' assets
Account books, 169
Adams, Herbert Baxter, 202
Adams, John, 215
Adams, John Quincy, 116
Adams family, 197, 203, 210
Adoption records, 12
Advocacy, 67, 225
African Americans, 107, 203
Afro-centrism, 108, 112
Alabama, 130
Alldredge, Everett, 53
Alphabet, 24, 25
American Archivist, 8
American Historical Association, 79, 198, 208, 215
American Historical Review, 202

American Institute of Physics Center for the History of Physics, 103
American-Irish Historical Society, 130
American Jewish Historical Society, 110
American Revolution, 35, 129, 130, 218
American Revolution Bicentennial, 211
American Telephone and Telegraph Company, 131
Ancient archives, 9, 23–26
Annapolis, 116
Appraisal: and the education of archivists, 171, 186–187, 191 n.25; and a national system of records and archives administration, 69–71; and preservation, 96–97; and records management disposition and scheduling, 3, 97–104. *See also* Functional analysis; Macro-appraisal; Re-appraisal
Apprenticeship, 177, 233–234
Architectural records, 143–144
Archival History Round Table, Society of American Archivists, 164
Archival theory and principles: debates, 41 n.33, 74, 100; and education, 160, 173–181, 183–184, 185–186, 235–236; origins, 37–38
Archivaria, 8

Archives and Archivists listserv, 225
Archivists: and education, 159–189, 230–
   236; and national system of records
   and archives administration, 65–84;
   and records managers, 2–3, 50, 230;
   and research, 232
*Armstrong v. Executive Office of the
   President* (PROFS case), 53, 55, 77,
   93, 215, 226–227
Artifacts, 137, 230
Association for Documentary Editing,
   203, 206
Association of Canadian Archivists, 101–
   102, 159
Athens, 24
Atlantic, 231
Atlas, James, 118–119
Authenticity, 141
Autograph collecting, 12, 78, 94, 169,
   201
Automation of records, 45–48. *See also*
   Electronic records management
Automobile, 142, 150

Bailey, Catherine, 103, 104
Balch Institute for Ethnic Studies, 110
Baltimore, Maryland, 46
Bancroft, George, 78
Barlow, John Perry, 120–121
Barrow, William, 95–96
Barzun, Jacques, 139
Baseball, 105
Bauer, G. Philip, 99
Bearman, David, 53, 57, 170, 228
Belknap, Jeremy, 78
Beniger, James, 46, 52
Bergeron, Paul, 207
Berry, Wendell, 109
Bill of Rights, 107, 117
Birkerts, Sven, 139, 145
Blanton, Tom, 55, 215
Bodnar, John, 116, 129–130
Body of Liberties of 1641, 32–33
Boles, Frank, 101
Bolotenko, George, 2
Books, 12, 229. *See also* Rare books and
   special collections
Boorstin, Daniel, 115

Bowyer, Robert, 31
Boyd, Julian, 202–203, 204
Brichford, Maynard, 38, 82
Briet, Suzanne, 51
British Empire, 12
Brooks, Philip C., 2, 3, 99
Brown, John Seely, 150
Brown, Richard, 8, 30
Buckland, Michael, 51, 53
Bureaucracy, 48–50
Burke, Frank, 163
Burns, Ken, 105
Burton, Thomas, 30
Burton Library, 133
Buruma, Ian, 210
Bush, George, 226
Business records, 70–71, 87 n.35, 103

Cahill, Thomas, 237
Calcott, George, 132
Calculators, 47
Calvert, Benedict Leonard, 34
Canada, 2, 103
Cannon, Walter, 48
Carbon paper, 45–46, 169
Carlin, John, 199–200, 215
Carnegie Institute, 202
Carp, E. Wayne, 12
Cartularies, 29
Cassedy, James, 30, 32
CD-ROM, 210
Census, 37
Certificates, 29
Certification, of archivists, 162, 187
Chancery records, 24, 26
Chandler, Alfred, 38, 46
Charters, 27, 29
Chartier, Roger, 118
Chirographs, 29
Church records, 28, 30
Cistercian abbey of Meaux, 30
Civil War, 105, 129, 130, 169
Clanchy, M. T., 9, 27, 168
Clapp, Verner, 117
Clay tablets, 25, 213
Clinton-Gore administration, 216
Codex, 24, 144, 213
Cold War, 105, 217

Collectors and collecting, 31–32, 92–93.
  See also Autograph collecting
College and university records, 103, 130
Commission of Federal Paperwork Report, 4
Computer, 11–12, 169, 170, 213–214.
  See also Electronic records management
Conference of Archivists, 82, 208
Congressional records, 71
Connecticut, 33
Conservation treatment of records, 96.
  See also Preservation
Constitution, 37, 107, 117, 121, 218 n.4
Constitution Ratification documentary edition, 210
Continuing education, 160, 162, 172–173, 235. *See also* Education
Control Revolution, 52
Cook, Terry, 100, 101, 102, 113, 134
Cooperation, 102
Copiers, 47, 213
Copybooks, 39
Copying records, 94
Copyright, 77, 81, 231. *See also* Intellectual property
Corporate records. *See* Business records
Council for Basic Education, 107
Council of State Historical Records Coordinators, 172
Courthouses, 34, 36–37, 213
Court of Wards records, 31
Cressy, David, 9
Crown records, 31
Cullen, Charles T., 205
Curtis, George, 212
Cyberculture, 12, 135–151, 223–237
Cyberspace, 142–146, 223–237

Data warehouses, 54
Declaration of Independence, 79, 114–121, 130
Democratic National Committee, 216
Department of State, 79
Detroit, Michigan, 133
DeWitt, Donald L., 163
Diary writing, 12, 105, 169, 193 n.49
Digitization of records, 94–95, 223–237.

See also Electronic records management
Diplomatics: and archival history, 3, 5, 8, 9, 13; and modern archival theory, 41 n.33; and origins of medieval recordkeeping, 29, 30
Documentalists, 51, 56
Documentary editing, 33, 78, 80, 88 n.42, 93, 94, 197–218. *See also* Association for Documentary Editing; Institute for the Editing of Historical Documents
Documentary filmmaking, 149
Documentation strategy, 102–103, 112–114. *See also* Appraisal
Documents, 150
Doheny-Farina, Stephen, 143
Domesday Book, 27, 28, 168
Donoghue, Denis, 185
Double-entry bookkeeping, 28, 38
Draper, Lyman, 78
Drucker, Peter, 135
Duguid, Paul, 150
Duranti, Luciana, 5, 57, 101, 102, 163, 228

Eastwood, Terry, 57, 163, 174, 184
Ebla, 24
Ecole des Chartes, 37
Education of archivists: and current issues, 171–181; and development of recordkeeping, 37; and electronic records management, 178, 185, 227–228; and historical study of archives, 8; history of, 159–163; and placement of education programs, 174–177, 184, 208–209; and the practicum, 181–189; and records and recordkeeping systems, 163–171; and research, 179, 183, 188
Egypt, 24
Eisenstein, Elizabeth, 165
Electronic mail, 51. *See also Armstrong v. the Office of the President*
Electronic records management: and appraisal and scheduling, 98–99; and archival culture, 223–237; and the debate about national funding, 197–218; and preservation, 93–94; re-defining, 53–59; and shifting notions of records, 50–53

Encoded Archival Description (EAD), 224–225, 227
England, 27, 28, 29, 31, 32, 34, 168
Ericson, Timothy, 134, 162, 163
Erlandsson, Alf, 51
Europe, 26–30, 31, 170–171
Evans, Frank, 2
Evidence, 72, 151, 216, 229, 235. *See also* Records and recordkeeping systems

Fabre, Genevieve, 110
Faxes, 51, 140
Federal government, 1–6, 201. *See also* National Archives
Federal Paperwork Commission, 81
Federal Records Act of 1950, 3, 55, 77, 98
Federal Reports Act of 1942, 1
Federalism, 73
Field branches. *See* National Archives
File cabinet, 46
Financial records, 29, 31, 39
Finding aids. *See* Encoded Archival Description
First Federal Congress documentary edition, 210. *See also* Documentary editing
First Supreme Court documentary edition, 210. *See also* Documentary editing
First World War, 131
Fleckner, John, 76
Force, Peter, 201, 212
Ford, Worthington, 212
Forgery, 12
France, 37
Franklin, Benjamin, 203, 205, 207, 210
Frederick II, Emperor, 27
Freedom of Information Act, 215
Freedom Train, 132, 133
Freeman, Elsie, 128, 163
French Revolution, 166
Functional analysis, 102–104
Functions of records and recordkeeping systems, 26. *See also* Records and recordkeeping systems
Funding, 72, 75–76. *See also* Documentary editing

Gabehart, Alan D., 162
Gans, Herbert, 5
Gates, Bill, 218
Gay, Lesbian, Bisexual, and Transgendered Library/Archives, Philadelphia, 110
Geary, Patrick, 9
General Disposal Act of 1939, 98
George, Gerald, 198
Georgia, 35, 36, 38
Gestetner, David, 45
Gibson, William, 228
Gillis, John, 134
Gitlin, Todd, 55, 109
Giunta, Mary, 205
Glassberg, David, 130–132
Glazer, Nathan, 108, 109
Gondos, Victor, 79
Goody, Jack, 168
Gordon, Ann, 205–207
Gordon, Mary, 147
Gore, Al, 49, 216
Government records and recordkeeping: American colonies, 32–37; England, 27, 28, 31–32; Europe, 27; Greece and Rome, 24–26; and national system of archives and records management, 65–84; Sumeria, 23–24
Gracy, David, 129
Grafton, Anthony, 12
Graham, Peter S., 137
Grant, Michael, 24–25
Graphic interface, 144–145
Greece, 9, 24–26, 138, 213
Green, John, 214
Greene, Mark, 101
Gutenberg, Johann, 138, 144

Hackman, Larry, 67, 81, 83
Halbwachs, Maurice, 4
Haley, Alex, 133
Hall, Hubert, 59
Halman, Talat S., 150
Hamilton, Alexander, 203
Hamilton, Paula, 147
Hammer, Michael, and James Champy, *Reengineering the Corporation*, 49
Hancock, John, 116

Handwriting, 12, 39
Harlan, David, 225–226
Harris, William, 26
Harvard Medical School, 48
Haworth, Kent, 134
Hazard, Ebenezer, 33, 78, 201, 212, 218
Hedstrom, Margaret, 57, 228
Heim, Michael, 209, 229
Herodotus, 26
Hieroglyphics, 24
Historians and archivists, 208–212. *See also* Education
Historic preservation, 136
Historical Documents Study, 205–207
Historical literature on archives: and archival education, 163–171; and documentary editing, 201–208; and the failure of the records professions to use it, 7–8; on the origins of archives and records management, 4–5; outside disciplines and research, 9–13; promising trends, 8–9
Historical Manuscripts Commission, 79, 94
Historical pageants, 129–132
Historical Records Survey, 79, 131, 169
Historical research, 31–32, 127–134, 225–226
Historical societies, 78, 79, 92, 104, 105, 110, 111, 129–132
Hitt, Jack, 207–208
Hollerith, Herman, 37, 46
Holocaust survivors' assets and accountability of records, 10, 109, 209, 211, 217, 225, 232
Hoover Commission on the Organization of the Executive Branch of the Government, 2, 3
Hyper Text Markup Language (HTML), 118

Illinois, 99
Incas, 29
Information policy, 65–84
Information resources management, 3–4, 50, 70–71, 77, 178–179
Information science, 167

Institute for the Editing of Historical Documents, 203
Institute of Library and Museum Services, 72, 76
Intellectual property, 231. *See also* Copyright
Internal Revenue Service, 231
International archives, 170–171, 191 n.26
International Council on Archives, 51
Internet. *See* World Wide Web
Intrinsic value, 101
Ireland, 237–238
Italy, 30, 38

Jameson, J. Franklin, 79, 199, 202
Jefferson, Thomas, 39, 78, 107, 114, 115, 121; and documentary editing, 197, 199, 200, 202–203, 204, 205, 208, 210, 214, 215, 218
Jenkinson, Hilary, 5, 100, 101
Jet Propulsion Laboratory, 117
Johns Hopkins University, 202
Jones, H. G., 2

Kammen, Michael, 132–134
Kasson, John, 47
Katz, Jon, 141
Kearns, Kevin, 49, 216
Kegan, Elizabeth Hamer, 204
Kennedy, John F., 10, 127
Kesner, Richard, 170
Knowledge Age, 119
Kohn, Richard, 212
Kornegay, Van, 148
Kremer, Alvin W., 117

Lacy, Dan, 227
Lamination of records, 95–96
Landauer, Thomas, 11
Landscape, 142, 146–147
Latin America, 12, 48
Laurens, Henry, 201
Lechford, Thomas, 32
Leffingwell, William Henry, 47
Lefkowitz, Mary, 108
Legal records, 29, 32–33
Leland, Waldo, 82

Letter writing: and modern technology, 215; and the origins of ancient record-keeping, 24; and the origins of medieval recordkeeping, 28; and public memory, 105; Thomas Jefferson, 39, 215, 218
Levine, Lawrence W., 112–113
Levine, Robert, 140
Libraries, 75, 79, 142, 150, 229
Library education, 166, 182–183. *See also* Education
Library of Congress, 75, 76, 98, 117
Library Services and Construction Act, 72
Life cycle management, 3, 54, 92, 100
List making, 24
Literacy, 9, 25–26, 213
Local government records, 68–69, 85 n.14
Localities, 103, 129–132
Logan, Robert K., 25, 28
Lycurgus, 24
Lynch, Clifford, 215

Mabillon, Jean, 29
McCallum, Daniel, 46
McClure, Charles, 138
McCown, Robert, 211–212
McDonald, Terrence, 186
Mckeever, Robert, 82
McKemmish, Sue, 228
Macro-appraisal, 103–104, 113. *See also* Appraisal
Madison, James, 203, 210
Magnetic tape recording, 169
Maier, Pauline, 118
Martin, Henri-Jean, 23, 28, 31
Maryland, 30, 33, 34, 35, 130
Massachusetts Bay Colony, 32, 33, 201
Massachusetts General Hospital, 48
Massachusetts Historical Society, 92, 132
Matsuda, Matt, 147
Maya, 32
Media images of records management, 5, 129, 216–217, 230–232
Medical records, 48, 103
Medieval archives, 8, 9, 26–30
Memory-aid devices, 25, 29–30
Menkus, Belden, 53–59
Mercantilism, 36

Mesoamerica, 9
Mesopotamia, 23–24
Metroon, 24
Meyrowitz, Joshua, 120
Microfilming records, 94–95, 169, 198, 204, 205, 206
Middle East, 170
Mississippi Territory, 37
Mitchell, William J., 146
Momigliano, Arnaldo, 25
Monuments, 147
Moore's law, 214
Mullett, Charles F., 31
Multiculturalism, 11, 104–114, 210–211
Museums, 75, 79, 142

National Academy of Sciences, 116, 117
National Archives: and appraisal and scheduling, 98–100; and the Declaration of Independence, 114–121; and education, 173–174, 225–226; and electronic records management, 54, 114, 118; and employment, 235, 236; field branches, 3, 67–68; histories of, 7, 8; and national system of records administration, 65–84; new building, 93; and origins, 130, 131, 133, 202, 208; and the PROFS case, 55–56, 93, 215, 226–227; and records management, 2–3; and regional records centers, 3
National Archives of Canada, 76, 103
National Association of Government Archives and Records Administrators, 69
National Center for History in the Schools, 107
National Council for Public History, 198
National Endowment for the Humanities, 72, 97, 107
National Historical Publications and Records Commission, 72, 75, 76, 80–81, 197–218
National Park Service, 129, 130
National Security Archive, 215
National Security Council, 226
Native Americans, 107, 203
Negroponte, Nicholas, 53, 214, 231
Nesmith, Tom, 160
Netherlands, 37

New England, 32, 36, 103
New Social History, 110, 112
New York, 5–6, 97, 216
New York Public Library, 133
Nixon, Richard M., 10, 81
Nora, Pierre, 113
Norman, Donald, 39, 179
North Carolina, 33, 35
Norton, Margaret Cross, 100, 101
Norwegian-American records, 130
Nostalgia, 148

Objectivity, 111
Office of Management and Budget
    (OMB), 4
Office technology, 30–39, 45–48, 169.
    See also Calculators; Carbon paper; CD-
    ROM; Computer; Copiers; Data ware-
    houses; Electronic mail; Faxes; File
    cabinet; Magnetic tape recording;
    Paperless office; Photocopying; Pigeon-
    hole desk; Tabulating machines; Tele-
    graph; Telephone; Typewriter; Vertical
    filing; Woodruff file
O'Meally, Robert, 110
Orality, 27, 167, 227
Organizational memory, 58, 72, 92, 103,
    111, 216–217
Organization of American Historians,
    198, 215
Orth, Ralph, 210
Orthography, 29
Osborne, David, and Ted Gaebler, Rein-
    venting Government, 49
Otlet, Paul, 51
O'Toole, James, 129, 160, 163, 233, 234,
    236

Paleography, 32
Paperless office, 53
Papermaking, 24, 27–28
Paper records, 48–50
Paperwork Reduction Act of 1980, 3–4
Papyrus, 24, 213
Parchment, 24, 27, 28, 213
Parliamentary recordkeeping, 31
Patent Office Building, 116
Pederson, Ann, 102

Penn, Ira, 174
Penn, William, 35
Pere, King, 27
Permanence, 91
Persia, 25
Personal papers, 11, 71, 112, 169
Petroski, Henry, 13, 150
Pew Charitable Trusts, 117
Philadelphia, 116
Photocopying, 169
Photography, 12, 104, 148
Pigeonhole desk, 39
Pitti, Daniel V., 224
Place, 136, 142–146
Poeppel, Edna B., 99
Pole, J. R., 166–167
Pope Boniface VIII, 28
Pope Innocent III, 28
Popular culture, 149
Portugal, 217
Position descriptions, 227–228. See also
    National Archives
Posner, Ernst, 99, 167
Postman, Neil, 52, 109, 140, 145
Postmodernism, 147, 148, 149, 209, 230
Presidential Libraries, 68
Presidential Records Act, 10, 68, 77, 81,
    127–128
Press copying, 37, 45, 46
Prince, Thomas, 201
Princeton, 116
Printing, 115, 145
Privacy, 77, 81, 169, 224. See also Ac-
    cess and privacy
Professionalism, 108, 169
PROFS case. See Armstrong v. Executive
    Office of the President
Provenance, 37–38, 102
Prudential Insurance Company, 216
Prussia, 37–38
Public Archives Commission, 79, 94
Public history, 172
Public memory: and appraisal, 104–114;
    and archival education, 235; and docu-
    mentary editing, 209, 210–211; and the
    historical study of archives, 9–11; and
    impact on archives and records manage-
    ment, 127–151; and preservation, 92

Public programs, 127–135, 163, 175
Public Record Office, 34
Public welfare records, 72
Punch cards, 46–47
Puritans, 34

Quakers, 34
Quipus, 29

Radio, 169
Rama, Angel, 48
Rare books and special collections, 137.
    See also Books
Reading, 229
Reagan, Ronald, 215, 226
Re-appraisal, 96, 97. *See also* Appraisal
Records and recordkeeping systems: in
    American colonies, 29–30, 168, 213;
    and ancient recordkeeping, 25, 167,
    213; changing perceptions in the Infor-
    mation Age, 50–53, 135–151; conflicts
    concerning, 32–33; and documentary
    editing, 215–218; as a key to under-
    standing archival history, 13–14; in
    medieval period, 26–30; and national
    policy, 65–84; as physical artifacts, 57–
    58; warrant for, 55, 138, 144, 232. *See
    also* Account books; Adoption records;
    Architectural records; Business records;
    Cartularies; Certificates; Chancery re-
    cords; Charters; Chirographs; Church
    records; Clay tablets; Codex; College
    and university records; Congressional
    records; Copybooks; Diary writing;
    Double-entry bookkeeping; Financial
    records; Hierogyphics; Legal records;
    Letter writing; Local government re-
    cords; Memory-aid devices; Paper re-
    cords; Papyrus; Parchment; Personal
    papers; Public welfare records; Punch
    cards; Quipus; Registers; Registry
    systems; Religious records; Rolls;
    Science and technology records; Sphra-
    gistics; Stone memorials; Tokens;
    Wills and probate records; Women's
    records; Writs
Records centralization, 31–32, 34–35, 38,
    93

Records custody, 57
Records Disposal Act, 2, 98
Records maintenance and preservation, 91–
    97
Records management, 4, 50
Records retention schedules and schedul-
    ing, 3, 4, 54, 58, 97–104. *See also* Ap-
    praisal
Records standardization, 29–30
Records values, 100, 106. *See also* Evi-
    dence
Reformatting records, 94. *See also* Micro-
    filming
Registers, 29
Registry systems, 168
Reliability, 141. *See also* Authenticity
Religious records, 103
Renaissance, 149, 167
*Report of the Committee on the Records
    of Government*, 81
Rheingold, Howard, 53
Rhoads, James B., 68
Ritchie, Donald, 51
Ritzenthaler, Mary Lynn, 97
Rolls, 24
Rome, 9, 24–26
Roszak, Theodore, 119
Rothenberg, Jeff, 51

Sagan, Carl, 230
Said, Edward, 108
Sale, Kirkpatrick, 141
Schellenberg, T. R., 5, 100, 101
Schlesinger, Arthur, Jr., 109
Schlesinger Library at Radcliffe College,
    110
Schmandt-Besserat, Denise, 23
Schomburg Center for Research in Black
    Culture at the New York Public Li-
    brary, 110
Schudson, Michael, 127–128
Schulz, Constance, 198–199, 204–205
Schwartz, Lynne Sharon, 151
Science and technology records, 103
Scribes, 26
Second Hoover Commission, 3
Second World War, 111, 131–132, 210,
    217

Secrecy, 11–12
Secretary of State, 116
Shenk, David, 145–146
Shils, Edward, 134
Simpson, Brooks D., 212
Smithsonian Institution, 75, 111, 113, 210, 225
Smock, Raymond, 199, 218 n.4
Society of American Archivists: and advocacy, 231; and appraisal, 99; and documentary editing, 204; and education, 159–164, 181–183; and origins of the archives profession, 66, 74, 208; and planning, 177–178
Sophia Smith Collection at Smith College, 110
South Carolina, 33, 34, 35
Southern state archives, 106, 132
Soviet Union, 105
Spain, 29, 32, 217
Sparks, Jared, 78, 202, 212
Sphragistics, 32
Spitzer, Alan, 209
Sprehe, J. Timothy, 138
State government: and national system of archives and records management, 68–69; and origins of archival programs, 48, 133; and preservation, 93; and records management, 5–6; and Web sites, 138, 226
State Historical Society of Wisconsin, 130
State, War, and Navy Building, 117
Statistics, 32, 36
Stencil copying, 45
Stenographers and typists, 38
Stephens, David, 99
Sterling, Bruce, 50
Stielow, Frederick J., 162–163, 181, 182
Stille, Alexander, 114
Stix, Gary, 136
Stock, Brian, 26, 29
Stoll, Clifford, 141, 145
Stone memorials, 25–26
Sumeria, 24
Symbolism of archives and records, 105, 114–121

Tabulating machines, 213
Taft, William Howard, 98
Tanselle, G. Thomas, 294
Taylor, Hugh, 165, 167
Taylorism, 47
Telecommunications Reform Act, 120–121
Telegraph, 52, 140, 169, 213
Telephone, 6, 11, 47, 51, 140, 142, 150, 169, 213
Television, 138, 150, 169
Tenner, Edward, 49–50
Teute, Frederika, 211
Texas, 226
Thelen, David, 119
Third Reich, 105
Thomas, Rosalind, 5, 137, 213
Thornton, Tamara Plakins, 12
Time and records, 137–138, 140–142
Tokens, 23
Tower Commission Report, 215
Tower of London, 31
Treasury Department, 98
Trenton, 116
Truman, Harry S, 202–203
Turkle, Sherry, 135, 143
Twain, Mark, 210
Typewriters, 39, 45, 169, 213

UNESCO, 170
United Nations, 52
United States House of Representatives, 199
United States Senate Historical Office, 75
University of British Columbia, 55, 57
University of Minnesota Immigration History Research Center, 110
University of Pittsburgh, 55
University of South Carolina, 148
Using the Nation's Documentary Heritage, 205–206
US MARC Archives and Manuscripts Control format, 75, 163

Vansina, Jan, 167
Van Tassel, David, 132
Vertical filing, 39, 45, 169
Video and computer games, 143

Virginia, 30, 32, 33, 34, 35, 36, 116
Virginia State Library, 95

Walch, Vicki, 172–173
Wallace, Mike, 104, 109, 210
Walsh, Kevin, 136
Warner, Robert, 8
Warrant, for records and recordkeeping,
    138, 144
Washington, George, 107, 197, 200, 208,
    210, 214, 215
Washington, D.C., 116
Watergate, and presidential records, 68,
    127–128, 133
Watson, John Fanning, 132
Watt, James, 37, 45
Webster, Daniel, 116
Wedgwood, Ralph, 45
Weissman, Ronald, 53
Wiegand, Wayne, 229
Williamson Report on library education,
    182

Wills and probate records, 27, 29
Winthrop, John, 33, 201
Women's records, 110, 203
Woodruff file, 169
World Wide Web: and the Declaration of
    Independence, 114–121; and documen-
    tary editing, 211, 214, 215, 218; and
    history of recordkeeping, 12; and im-
    plications for archives and records
    management, 135–151, 223–237
Wright, Louis B., 33–34
Writing: and the education of archivists,
    167–168; and historical development of
    recordkeeping, 9, 23–26, 28; and relig-
    ion, 28; and the World Wide Web, 138;
    and writing masters, 31, 39
Writs, 29
Wroth, Lawrence, 115

Yates, JoAnne, 46

Zelizer, Barbie, 127
Zuboff, Shoshana, 47

About the Author

RICHARD J. COX is Associate Professor at the University of Pittsburgh's School of Information Science.

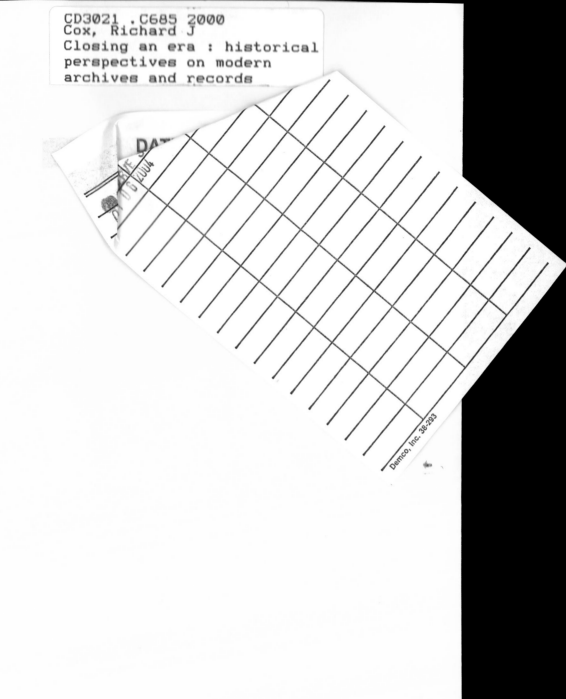

Demco, Inc. 38-293